SECOND EDITION

Family Life
EDUCATION

SECOND EDITION

Family Life EDUCATION

Principles and Practices for Effective Outreach

Stephen F. Duncan
Brigham Young University

H. Wallace Goddard
University of Arkansas Cooperative Extension Service

Los Angeles | London | New Delhi
Singapore | Washington DC

For information:

SAGE Publications, Inc.
2455 Teller Road
Thousand Oaks,
California 91320
E-mail: order@sagepub.com

SAGE Publications India Pvt. Ltd.
B 1/I 1 Mohan Cooperative Industrial Area
Mathura Road, New Delhi 110 044
India

SAGE Publications Ltd.
1 Oliver's Yard
55 City Road
London, EC1Y 1SP
United Kingdom

SAGE Publications Asia-Pacific Pte. Ltd.
33 Pekin Street #02-01
Far East Square
Singapore 048763

Printed in the United States of America

Library of Congress Cataloging-in-Publication Data

Duncan, Stephen F.
Family life education : principles and practices for effective outreach /
Stephen F. Duncan, H. Wallace Goddard. — 2nd ed.
        p. cm.
    Includes bibliographical references and index.
    ISBN 978-1-4129-7908-5 (pbk.)

    1.   Family life education. I. Goddard, H. Wallace. II. Title.
HQ10.D853 2011
306.850973—dc22   2010033454

This book is printed on acid-free paper.

11   12   13   14   10   9   8   7   6   5   4   3   2

Acquisitions Editor:	Kassie Graves
Production Editor:	Astrid Virding
Copy Editor:	Gillian Dickens
Permissions Editor:	Adele Hutchinson
Typesetter:	Hurix
Proofreader:	Ellen Brink
Indexer:	Gloria Tierney
Cover Designer:	Gail Buschman

CONTENTS

PREFACE

F amily life educators are found in many settings. Much important family life education (FLE) is done in school and university classrooms. This book is designed as a practical yet scholarly how-to volume for a different set of family life educators: those who work outside a traditional classroom setting. The broad goal of this book is to help upper division and graduate students who are preparing to be family life educators as well as FLE professionals who serve on the front lines. This book is intended to develop and enhance the knowledge and skills needed to take family life education principles to citizens where they live and work. To this end, we have tried to incorporate some of the leading scholarship with years of our own professional experiences, to provide a scholarly yet practical guide for the family life education professional and professional-to-be.

This book is based on the assumption that there are specialized skills and knowledge a family life educator needs to succeed with the general public, those persons who are not likely to return to college to learn about family life. The needs and motivations of this audience usually differ from the traditional family science college or high school students. For example, it is known that adult education audiences are more likely to be motivated by a personal or family need (e.g., see Knowles, 1998). In addition, venues for family life education outside the traditional classroom vary greatly, from radio broadcasts and newsletters to home visits and workplace training. Thus, for family life educators to succeed in the business of educating the public requires a somewhat different skill set than teaching students in traditional classroom settings. This book is intended to arm students and professionals with practical, educational experiences in their college curriculum and continuing education to become more effective ambassadors of family science scholarship to citizens of the world.

Various works have been published on family life education prior to the current volume. The comprehensive *Handbook of Family Life Education, Vols. 1 and 2,* published in 1993 and edited by Margaret Arcus, Jay Schvaneveldt, and Joel Moss, provided solid coverage of the scholarship and practice of family life education to that date. These volumes clarified many issues and raised questions that have spawned research and theory in family life education. These volumes provide a strong academic treatment of family life education with leanings toward college-level family life education. They are more oriented toward basic scholarship than practical application.

A more recent work, titled *Family Life Education: An Introduction,* published in 2001 (with a second edition published in 2007) and written by Lane Powell and Dawn Cassidy, updates several of the content areas of the *Handbook* volumes and provides many useful ideas as a solid primer for the practice of family life education.

Family Life Education: Principles and Practices for Effective Outreach is the first book on family life education to combine both the scholarly foundation and the practical how-tos for successfully carrying out family life education outside a traditional classroom setting. We have tried to improve upon and extend this focus in this second edition.

A comprehensive, scholarly, yet practical how-to text has been needed in the field for a long time, both to train upper division and graduate-level students how to do family life education as well as to strengthen professionals already in the field. Thus far, many have been consigned to learn the principles and practices of effective family life education through limited university training or the crucible of experience alone.

Family Life Education: Principles and Practices for Effective Outreach had its genesis when we generated a topical outline collected from our professional experiences as Cooperative Extension specialists in four states. We also drew on the experience of colleagues across the country. We have continued to draw on this experience as we updated and crafted additional materials for this edition.

The book is organized into five parts and 18 chapters, including 5 new chapters, followed by appendices. The first part, Foundations of Family Life Education, lays the foundation for effective outreach work by discussing the historical and philosophical underpinnings of current outreach family life education, guiding readers to develop their own FLE philosophy and role as an FLE. The second part, Development of Family Life Education Programs, includes chapters that present an integrated framework for developing comprehensive prevention programs and approaches for evaluating such programs. The third part, Implementing Family Life Education Programs, includes several chapters to help readers learn principles and methods for teaching the lay audience, including designing effective instruction, engaging an audience, teaching skills and tools, and working with diverse audiences. The fourth part, Content and Contexts for Family Life Education, includes four new content chapters on education for personal well-being, marriage and relationship education, parenting education, and sexuality education. It also adds three additional contexts chapters detailing how to do family life education in settings other than traditional workshop teaching, such as using Internet technology, traditional and social networking media, and writing for the lay audience. The final part, Promoting, Marketing, and Sustaining FLE Programs, contains chapters to assist the reader to learn principles and practices for forming effective collaborations and marketing family life principles, practices, and programs. The book concludes with a new "Narratives of Family Life Educators" chapter, providing a window into family life education through the experiences of several currently practicing FLEs, and an improving practice in family life education chapter, designed to highlight the needs of future research and practice in family life education. Each chapter includes an "Explorations" section at the end, designed as a real-life application of the chapter material.

We appreciate and acknowledge contributing authors Susan Calahan, author of Chapter 11 on sexuality education; Steven Dennis and Aaron Ebata, authors of Chapter 12 on technology; and Tonya Fischio, author of Chapter 13 on media. We also express appreciation to Heidi Stolz, author of Chapter 10 on parenting, and Alan Hawkins for his contribution to Chapter 9 on marriage and relationship education. We are indebted to these colleagues for generously sharing their expertise.

We acknowledge also the individuals who provided critical reviews of the first edition. These individuals provided many helpful insights that led to important additions that made this second edition a better product for our intended audiences. We express gratitude to Kassie Graves of Sage for her support throughout the development of this book. Her encouragement has helped us keep on track. We also thank the following reviewers:

Cassandra Chaney, Louisiana State University
Jennifer M. Crosswhite, University of Nebraska at Kearney
Wm. Michael Fleming, University of Northern Iowa
Charles B. Hennon, Miami University
Sally M. McCombie, Indiana University of PA
Maresa J. Murray, Indiana University
Cheryl M. Robinson, The University of Tennessee at Chattanooga
Carolyn S. Wilken, University of Florida

We thank you, the reader, who is committed to helping families in your sphere of influence to live more satisfying and loving family lives. We wish you every success in your family life education pursuits.

Finally, we express appreciation to loving and supportive family members, particularly our wives, Barbara and Nancy, whose constant encouragement is always a major factor in any of our worthy accomplishments.

—Steve Duncan and Wally Goddard

PART I

FOUNDATIONS OF FAMILY LIFE EDUCATION

CHAPTER 1

HISTORICAL AND PHILOSOPHICAL PERSPECTIVES

Family life education (FLE) that takes place in communities is a unique type of education. The business of outreach FLE involves taking family science principles and practices to the general public—individuals, couples, parents, whole families—in varied educational settings outside the traditional classroom. Some outreach family life educators are employed as field agents or as university campus-based specialists within the Cooperative Extension System. Others may work in social work or other human service agency contexts or as media representatives. Those with an entrepreneurial spirit may develop their own FLE business and market their programs nationally. Still others may hold traditional university positions that include some outreach expectations.

To succeed in educating the public about family life requires a somewhat different skill set than teaching students in traditional classroom settings. With these skills, family life educators become more effective ambassadors of family science scholarship to citizens of the world.

This text endeavors to provide a comprehensive response to the following need: There is knowledge and skills that family life educators need to be most helpful and effective in work with their clientele. To arrive at the response, we first generated a content outline that represented our collective experiences totaling nearly three decades as family life Extension Service specialists at several universities. We sent the content outline to other specialists and colleagues and incorporated their ideas. Since this first edition was published in 2005, many FLE scholars, practitioners, and students have used the book in their work and studies and have provided us with ideas to improve upon what we first developed. We have incorporated their ideas into this second edition. The result is what we hope is a practical, how-to reference volume on effective outreach FLE that you will use for years to come.

This first chapter provides a foundational and philosophical discussion of FLE in outreach settings. We begin with a brief discussion of the definition and history of outreach FLE, as well as the role universities and communities have played in the movement. We next turn to a discussion of contemporary developments also making FLE history, including evolution in how knowledge about families is disseminated and the various roles family life educators can play in communities. Finally, we discuss elements pertinent to the development of a working philosophy of outreach FLE. At the end of the chapter, you'll have the opportunity to create a personal philosophy of FLE in outreach settings, integrating the various perspectives presented in the chapter.

● DEFINING FAMILY LIFE EDUCATION

Much effort has been expended to define FLE, with definitions dating back over 40 years (Arcus, Schvaneveldt, & Moss, 1993b). Overall there has been little consensus reached on a specific definition and greater consensus reached on aims or principles underlying FLE (Arcus et al., 1993b). Moreover, no attempt has been made to distinguish FLE taking place in high school and college settings from FLE taking place outside these environments.

We define *outreach* FLE as any educational activity occurring outside a traditional school classroom setting, usually involving adults, that is designed to strengthen relationships in the home and foster positive individual, couple, and family development. Such education comprises many topics—from marriage education to parenting skills, from stress and anger management to strategies for adapting following divorce—and occurs in many venues. For example, an outreach FLE might hold a 6-week marriage education program in the town's community center for interested couples and place important follow-up readings on the program's website. This kind of FLE is any form of education that has as its goal to "strengthen and enrich individual and family well-being" (Arcus et al., 1993b, p. 21) and falls within any of the 10 content areas of FLE set forth by the National Council on Family Relations (Bredehoft & Cassidy, 1995), save that it assumes a lay audience that may not turn to a traditional classroom for FLE. Such education follows the operational principles set forth by Arcus et al. (1993b, pp. 15–20), which we have adopted and adapted for community settings. Specifically, these principles state that FLE (a) is to be relevant to individuals, couples, and families across the life span; (b) is based on the felt needs of individuals, couples, families, and communities; (c) draws on material from many fields and is multiprofessional in its practice; (d) is offered in many venues, including community workshops, video and print media, publications, the Internet, and many other settings; (e) is educational rather than therapeutic; (f) is respectful of diverse values; and (g) requires qualified family life educators to realize its goals.

By now it should be clear that this is a book about how to do FLE in outreach versus traditional classroom settings. The guiding principles for each are identical, but the practices vary widely. However, we don't want to continue repeating "outreach FLE" or "FLE in outreach settings" every time we speak of FLE. Therefore, anytime we use the term *family life education* (or FLE) from here on out, we are speaking specifically about *outreach* FLE as we have defined it above.

A BRIEF HISTORY OF OUTREACH FAMILY LIFE EDUCATION ●

Many disciplines have contributed to the history of FLE: traditional home economics, family sociology, social work, marriage and family therapy, social psychology, education, and parenting education (Lewis-Rowley, Brasher, Moss, Duncan, & Stiles, 1993), which in turn draws upon child development and medicine. Truly, FLE is multidisciplinary in focus and multiprofessional in practice.

Early Roots

The earliest FLE efforts in the United States can be traced to a collaboration between church and state to ensure that children were raised according to biblical standards. Self-help books emerged around 1800, how-to books became visible in the 1850s, and child and mother study groups developed, a precursor of what has come to be known as the Parent Teacher Association (PTA) in the public school system (Lewis-Rowley et al., 1993).

Informal discussions among support groups were perhaps among the first community venues of FLE. For example, as early as 1815, groups of parents met in Portland, Maine, to discuss child-rearing practices (Bridgeman, 1930, cited in Lewis-Rowley et al., 1993). Also, mother study groups, termed *material associations*, were organized in the 1820s to discuss child-rearing approaches (Sunley, 1955, cited in Lewis-Rowley et al., 1993) followed by mother periodicals titled *Mothers Assistant* and *The Mother* magazine believed to be the first known parenting periodicals.

Around the turn of the 20th century, FLE as a field of endeavor emerged in response to what was perceived as the negative impacts of social conditions such as industrialization, urbanization, and changing roles of women. Changing conditions in society were seen as problems or creating problems with the decrease in socialized behavior taught to children. This was theorized to be the cause of the increasing rate of juvenile delinquency, a greater divorce rate, and other current societal ills during that time period. FLE programs were created on the theory that they could help families deal with these new changes in a "complex and changing society," hopefully decreasing or making family-related social problems disappear (Arcus, 1995, p. 336).

The American Land Grant University System

A more formal FLE movement was also taking place in universities and colleges throughout the United States and some of its territories. The land grant university system was created by the Morrill Act, signed into federal law by President Abraham Lincoln on July 2, 1862. This act provided 1.7 million acres of land to the states so that each might have at least one college that promoted "the liberal and practical education of the industrial classes in the several pursuits and professions of life." Some of the "practical education" was to be taken out among the people where they lived and worked. The signing of the Morrill Act became the catalyst for the establishment of academic programs in home economics throughout the United States. Within this context, home economics/human ecology emerged as a dominant theoretical paradigm at the turn of the 20th century (Lerner, 1995). From a human ecological perspective, put forth first by Ellen Swallow Richards, the family was seen as affecting the well-being of the larger society. Thus, as the home environment could be enhanced, so too could the community at large. Leaders in the home and family movement during this time saw scientific knowledge about the family, disseminated to the masses, as an important way of correcting or preventing social ills so pronounced in the family (Lewis-Rowley et al., 1993). The "home oekology"

(Buboltz & Sontag, 1993) perspective brought many disciplines to bear on the problems pronounced in families.

Cooperative Extension

The Morrill Act also set the stage for an educational delivery system that would transmit knowledge about families to the masses, which came to be known as the Cooperative Extension System. This system, created by Congress through the passage of the Smith-Lever Act in 1914, provided a major federal thrust in the furtherance of FLE in community settings. So enthused was President Woodrow Wilson about the new system that he called it "one of the most significant and far-reaching measures for the education of adults ever adopted by the government." Its purpose was "to aid in diffusing among the people of the U.S. useful and practical information on subjects related to agriculture and home economics, and to encourage the application of the same." Extension work was to consist of "giving practical demonstrations in . . . home economics to persons not attending or resident in said colleges in the several communities, and imparting to such persons information on said subjects through field demonstrations, publications and otherwise." The underlying philosophy was to "help people help themselves" by "taking the university to the people" (Rasmussen, 1989, p. vii).

Thus, land grant institutions became known as universities *for* the people of the state: The teaching, research, and outreach done there was primarily to benefit the masses in the state (Lerner, 1995). The land grant idea was committed to applying the best science possible to the practical problems of families. Extension home economics agents, later known as family and consumer science agents, were hired to be the conduits through which information about family life could be communicated to the local communities, through the carrying out of community-based FLE programs. Some states hired family living agents, in addition to family and consumer science agents, whose specific charge was to carry out FLE programs. Today there is a county agent in most of the over 3,000 counties of the United States who have at least a partial charge to promote strong family living through extension programs. These agents often carry out their responsibilities in this area in collaboration with other like-minded professionals. FLE programming is carried out through a specific curriculum designed for target audiences, fact sheets, bulletins, pamphlets, videos, newspaper series, online learning modules, and other various means. During the late 1980s, Cooperative Extension in the family area was zero funded by the Reagan administration, later to be restored due to a public outcry of support.

Areas of family life emphasis within Cooperative Extension have evolved over the years to meet the needs of the constituency. Beginning in the 1980s, programs became more focused on interdisciplinary national initiatives than disciplinary programs (Rasmussen, 1989). For example, families underwent radical changes over two decades that culminated in the 1980s, which brought about increased stresses and risks for family disruption and dislocation. Complex issues such as these demanded a comprehensive, interdisciplinary response. During this time, family and economic well-being received increased emphasis among local family life educators affiliated with Extension.

Concern for limited-resource families, defined as families at risk for not meeting basic needs, received increased programmatic emphasis in the early 1990s and continues today. This increased emphasis has led to adopting teaching strategies and practices that are best suited to meet the complex needs of limited-resource families, such as peer support, professional/ paraprofessional teaching efforts, one-on-one home visits, and working in small groups (Cooperative Extension System, 1991).

Other recent emphases in the Extension System have included a focus on children, youth, and families who possess greater risks for not meeting basic life needs. The Children, Youth, and Families at Risk (CYFAR) initiative has received federal funding since 1991. Since that time, CYFAR has supported programs in more than 600 communities in all states and territories. Other major family life efforts have been made in the area of parenting education. In 1994, the National Extension Parent Education Model (Smith, Cudaback, Goddard, & Myers-Walls, 1994) was developed. This model made an important contribution to guiding the development of community-based parenting education programs. Web-based FLE to both professionals as well as clientele has also rapidly advanced with the advent of the Children, Youth, and Families Education and Research Network (CYFERNet), making research-based FLE resources available at the click of a mouse. While traditionally, marriage education programs in communities have been offered through the church, more programs are being offered though community adult education and extension programs and other nonreligious settings (Stahmann & Salts, 1993).

Other University-Based Outreach Efforts

In addition to organized efforts within the land grant university system, other outreach activities have been established at universities of recent date that have also contributed to what FLE is today. Perhaps most prominent in this movement has been the explosion of service learning and internship opportunities that, while helping the student, richly benefit the communities that receive the associated services. Service-learning pedagogies, of which internships are a type, enhance traditional modes of learning and actively engage students in their own education through experiential learning in course-relevant contexts. But they also foster lifelong connections between students, their communities, and the world outside the classroom (Crews, 2002). These experiences enable students to contribute to the well-being of families within the context of their service-learning assignments. For example, students in the School of Family Life at Brigham Young University can select from more than 300 family- and youth-serving agencies in surrounding communities and in other parts of the United States and the world. Some examples of these agencies include writing for FLE websites, designing and marketing FLE curricula, and visiting families one-on-one to offer direct services.

Community Movements

In addition to developments within the land grant university system, outreach FLE was also fostered by the contemporary expansion of parenting education volunteer groups and community organizations. Certainly one of the earliest aspects of FLE is actually the growth of parenting education (Brock, Oertwein, & Coufal, 1993). For example, the National Congress of Mothers was founded in 1897, renamed the National Congress of Mothers and Parent-Teacher Associations in 1908, was dedicated to promoting the notions of mother love and mother thought (Bridgeman, 1930, cited in Lewis-Rowley et al., 1993). In addition, the Society for the Study of Child Nature had also grown to several chapters and by 1908 was consolidated into the Federation for Child Study. Among other things, this organization performed FLE functions such as distributing information on children, promoting lectures and conferences, and cooperating with other like-minded groups (Bridgeman, 1930, cited in Lewis-Rowley et al., 1993). The federal government began to realize the value of these efforts when, in 1909, the first White House Conference on Child Welfare took place, becoming the first of many for continued governmental support and funding of family parenting programs (Tilsen, 2007).

Expansion of FLE continued into the 1920s with the growth of parenting education. In 1924, the Child Study Association held a conference that invited the participation of 13 smaller organizations. The outgrowth of this conference was the National Council of Parent Education, which had as one of its goals to suggest guidelines and qualifications for the training of parents. By 1924, 75 major organizations were conducting parenting education programs (Brim, 1959, cited in Lewis-Rowley et al., 1993). Parenting education grew with the support of the Spelman Fund, and the Child Study Association of America was born, with the primary purpose of development and supervision of the use of parenting education materials. By 1930, there were some 6,000 members of this association acting as parenting educators (Bridgeman, 1930, cited in Lewis-Rowley et al., 1993). Parenting education declined somewhat during the 1930s as attention was turned to financial survival. We also saw the end of the Spelman Fund and some organizations focused on parenting. Growth picked up again in during the 1940s as a preventive intervention but with largely a mental health perspective (Lewis-Rowley et al., 1993).

Parenting education has come to be both preventive and remedial (Brock et al., 1993). Even some specific parenting programs are more preventive or remedial, depending on the needs of the clientele. In recent decades, parents, churches, courts, and community mental health professionals are turning to parenting education as a remedy. Divorcing couples are being assigned to divorce education to minimize stressful and destructive aspects of divorce on children. Abusive parents are being court-ordered to parenting education classes. More programs are becoming available for teenage parents.

The medical community—namely, physicians—has also been an active contributor to the FLE movement, often offering child development–related advice to scores of patients. Professionals trained as medical doctors with a specialty in pediatrics have written very popular parenting advice books (e.g., Brazelton, 1992). The American Academy of Pediatrics, a highly respected professional group, periodically issues news releases containing recommendations for parents on such things as limiting the amount of television watched by children under age 2 (see http://www.aap.org).

Linked with the movement of FLE, especially that of early childhood intervention through parenting education, is the family support movement, developing essentially since the mid-1970s (Weissbourd, 1994). During the 1970s, a call for more preventive services, rather than customary, crisis mode interventions, led to more family service agencies taking a more active part in FLE. Influenced by a human ecological perspective (Bronfenbrenner, 1979), family support focuses on a strengths-based approach to strengthening and empowering families and communities so that they can foster the optimal development of children, youth, and adult family members (Family Support America, 2003). The family support movement was founded on the following guiding principles (Weissbourd, 1994) that cut across disciplines:

- The most effective approach to families emanates from a perspective of health and well-being.
- The capacity of parents to raise their children effectively is influenced by their own development.
- Child-rearing techniques and values are influenced by cultural and community values and mores.
- Social support networks are essential to family well-being.
- Information about child development enhances parents' capacity to respond appropriately to their children.
- Families that receive support become empowered to advocate on their own behalf.

Family support initiatives strongly rely on the use of collaborations to carry out programs. A number of family support program offerings have emerged throughout the United States. Resource centers for parents in schools and family-strengthening services offered through nonprofit agencies have become part of the family life educational landscape. FLE programs in communities following a family-support model often use home visits and peer educators as major methods of teaching principles and skills.

Reaching Diverse Audiences

For years, observers have acknowledged that FLE receives "underwhelming participation" from the masses (Bowman & Kieren, 1985). But even more alarming is the finding that FLE is not reaching audiences at greatest need (e.g., Sullivan & Bradbury, 1997). There is a movement afoot to help change that. For example, the CYFAR initiative of the Cooperative Extension System mentioned earlier is an example of taking FLE beyond the traditional audience to meet the needs of groups at greatest risk, who are often socioeconomically and racially diverse. Government agencies are also increasing their efforts in this regard. For example, the Administration for Children and Families (ACF), an agency of the U.S. federal government, has contracted with family scholars, family life educators, and professional organizations to develop, implement, and evaluate programs for strengthening marriage among audiences that historically have been underserved, such as disadvantaged families (Dion, Devaney, & Hershey, 2003), who are disproportionately Black and

Hispanic. Practical approaches for working with diverse audiences will be discussed in detail in Chapter 8.

Professional Associations and Professionalization of Family Life Education

In 1938, the National Council on Family Relations (NCFR) was established as a "multi-disciplinary non-partisan professional organization focused solely on family research, practice and education." One of its key missions is to promote the field of family life education. Thus in 1984, NCFR created guidelines, standards, and criteria for the certification of family life educators. NCFR now administers an internationally recognized credential—the Certified Family Life Educator (CFLE). Approximately 100 college and university Family Science degree programs in the United States and Canada use the NCFR Family Life Education curriculum standards as guidelines for their undergraduate and graduate students.

Professionals holding certification are expected to be able to demonstrate competence in 10 substance areas, including the following: Families and Individuals in Societal Contexts; Internal Dynamics of Families; Human Growth and Development Across the Life Span; Human Sexuality; Interpersonal Relationships; Family Resource Management; Parenting Education and Guidance; Family Law and Public Policy; Professional Ethics and Practice; and Family Life Education Methodology (see Appendix B for more details about these 10 content areas and guidelines for practice).

Ordinarily, those desiring CFLE status first complete coursework at one of the approved schools. At completion of coursework in the 10 content areas, graduating students may apply for *Provisional Certification*. After an additional equivalent of 2 years of full-time work experience related to family life education (which can be accumulated over 5 years), professionals may apply for *Full Certification*. In 2007, NCFR did a practice analysis survey and created another avenue to receive CFLE status: the CFLE exam. The CFLE exam can be completed in lieu of completing coursework at an approved university. For details on CFLE and the application process, see www.ncfr.org under "CFLE Certification." The first Certified Family Life Educators were approved in 1985, and currently there are 1,425 practicing Certified Family Life Educators (Bredehoft & Walcheski, 2009, p. 14).

In 1996, NCFR created the Academic Program Review to recognize university and college degree programs that offer coursework necessary to complete the certification courses. In 2002, 235 incomplete family programs in the United States and Canada offered undergraduate, master's, and doctoral programs. As of 2008, there are 83 approved schools with 101 complete undergraduate and graduate programs in the United States (Bredehoft & Walcheski, 2009, p. 15).

Web-Based Family Life Education

An overview of the history of FLE is not complete without some discussion of the role of evolving technology in FLE. For example, individuals are increasingly turning to the Internet for all kinds of information, including matters of personal and family well-being. Because the Internet is a powerful medium that has much to offer family life educators (Elliott, 1999; Hughes, 1999; S. N. Morris, Dollahite, & Hawkins, 1999), over the past few years, many family life educators have developed websites (Elliott, 1999). In fact, currently hundreds of FLE websites are available (Elliott, 1999). Some argue that this medium of FLE has revolutionized the manner in which FLE is disseminated to the masses (Smith, 1999). Limited evaluation data suggest that web-based FLE can positively benefit its audiences (Steimle & Duncan, 2004), even rivaling more traditional means of educational delivery in marriage education (Duncan, Steed, & Needham, 2009). But whether it is an adequate substitute for face-to-face FLE is still largely unknown and an important area of needed research.

With the advent of social networking sites such as Facebook, MySpace, YouTube, and Twitter and recent data suggesting Internet populations are spending an increasing amount of their browsing time at these sites, we expect the role of the Internet in FLE to increase. Much has yet to be learned about reaching the next generation of FLE participants, who are marvelously literate in technology, which, according to some observers, is "literally changing the dynamics of informal social relations, the exchange of information and support within social networks and affecting learners' skills, expectations and development" (Walker & Greenhow, 2008, p. 3).

Using technology in FLE will be discussed in detail in Chapter 12.

EVOLUTION IN THE DISSEMINATION OF SCIENTIFIC ● KNOWLEDGE ABOUT FAMILIES

The field of family sciences emerged during the 1920s largely with the belief that problems plaguing the family could be addressed through systematic research. The ideal envisioned the university as the institution that could, through research, address the real-life problems and concerns pertaining to children, youth, and families. Doherty (2001) explains, "[Family science] embraced a vision of making the world better through the work of University-trained professional experts who would generate new knowledge and pass it on to families in the community" (p. 319). What evolved, according to Doherty, was a "trickle-down model of research and practice" (p. 319). According to this model, scientific knowledge for families is generated by university researchers, who then transmit this knowledge to practitioners (e.g., family life educators), who then, in turn, disseminate the information to the masses. The strength of this model, according to Doherty, lies in its ability to address problems scientifically when experiential knowledge about a topic is relatively lacking or when the issue is so hotly debated as to prevent a more objective view of an issue. The weakness of this model is that it ignores the collective wisdom of families and communities garnered through experience, although it is from families that much of what we call research data is generated. In addition, instead of being seen as partners in knowledge generation, this perspective relegates families to the "role of consumers of academic knowledge" (p. 321).

There are other dangers inherent in the traditional model of research generation and dissemination. Historically, researchers have failed to engage and partner with communities in the research process, neglecting to study the issues of greatest interest to them (Lerner, 1995). Without community/family collaboration in the research process, research that becomes available to pass on to communities can become increasingly irrelevant to the needs of real families, causing the vision of scientific information benefiting families to go unrealized. In fact, Richard Lerner (1995) argues that much of the research generated by universities is of little value to communities. Furthermore, this top-down model of knowledge dissemination has been criticized as being inadequate at best, evidenced by the fact that the problems targeted still continue to plague children, youth, families, and communities (Lerner, 1995), even many of the same problems that experts were trying to fix when they first had a vision of a better world, made better with their discoveries.

A new model of taking family scholarship is emerging, critical to effective FLE in community settings. Scholars are now arguing that effective FLE will integrate the best scientific information with the knowledge, lived experience, culture, and expertise of community clientele (Doherty, 2000; Lerner, 1995; Myers-Walls, 2000). To accomplish this requires a community-collaborative approach where there is extensive interface of the worlds of families in communities and institutions where scientific knowledge about these families is generated (Lerner, 1995). Families and professionals become partners in identifying strengths and needs and mobilizing to address identified problem. FLE professionals bring their expertise not to dominate or give pat or complete answers but as "a potential part of a confederation of community members, a partnership that brings to the 'collaborative table' knowledge-based assets" (Lerner, 1995, p. 114). Hence, such FLE professionals would seek to be "on tap" but not "on top" (Doherty, 2001, p. 322), viewing themselves as one of the many sources of knowledge in a community, but being careful not to "stifle families' own wisdom and initiative" (p. 322). The next section expands the discussion of the many roles family life educators in community settings can take in their professional role, including those most consistent with the perspectives above.

VARIED APPROACHES OR "ROLES" IN FAMILY ● LIFE EDUCATION

There are many educational approaches one can take or "roles" one can play as a family life educator. These approaches, reflecting various teaching philosophies and paradigms, are based on one's sense of responsibility for program content and methods, as well as the assumptions one has about education, the educator, the learner, and the content. It is important for family life educators to be knowledgeable about each of these various approaches, their strengths and limitations, and when a certain approach might be recommended over another. While by no means exhaustive, these approaches comprise several prominent options: an expert approach, a facilitator approach, a critical inquirer approach, a collaborator approach, an interventionist approach, and an eclectic approach.

The Expert Approach

An expert approach fits a liberal educational philosophy, which is the oldest and most enduring educational philosophy, with roots tracing back to classical Greek philosophy (Price, 2000). A liberal education philosophy emphasizes the development of intellectual powers through the mastery of a disciplinary area of study. According to Elias and Merriam (1995), "Liberal education produced a person who is literate in the broadest sense—intellectually, morally, spiritually, and aesthetically" (p. 26).

Family life educators operating from an expert approach view themselves as "subject matter authorit[ies] whose function it is to transmit a fixed body of knowledge to the learner" (Price, 2000, p. 3). Family life educators are seen as possessors of important knowledge and skills that others do not have and who rely on them to transmit them. Those who follow an expert approach believe that answers lie with informed experts and that the lives of participants will be improved if they learn the materials and skills, according to their instructions (Myers-Walls, 2000). Thus, materials tend to be highly structured with predetermined curricula and agenda, leading to the acquisition of predetermined knowledge and skills. Most packaged educational programs ostensibly follow this assumption, especially those that are particularly concerned that programs be delivered as written. A family life educator teaching parenting using the expert approach to teaching would follow carefully a designated curriculum and insist on content mastery before moving on to other concepts.

An expert approach makes certain assumptions about learners as well. One tacit assumption is that the audience is relatively uninformed as to the content or that the experiential knowledge they have regarding a topic is of less importance than the specialized knowledge the expert is bringing to them. Lecture is often a common mode of delivery; the learner's task is to soak up, reflect upon, and analyze the information. This traditional form of education is often referred to as the "banking" model of education, where students are viewed as empty cash receptacles needing to be filled with the instructor's exclusively possessed knowledge. The transfer of knowledge often occurs in a static exchange with little discussion. This FLE perspective also fits with Doherty's (2000) notion of trickle-down research and practice discussed earlier.

The Facilitator Approach

Facilitator-oriented family life educators often have no specific agenda. Instead of facilitators deciding how programs are to proceed, participants decide what is important to them and then set the learning agenda. Facilitators acknowledge that participants are already fairly well informed about a topic. The facilitator, while often possessing specialized knowledge, doesn't seek to share that information except as a coequal and as it fits the flow of the group. Instead, the facilitator seeks to help participants gain access to the knowledge they already have within them. Thus, a facilitator approach may best be used when the audience members posses a substantial amount of knowledge and are highly motivated learners. This approach fits the personalistic paradigm (Czaplewski & Jorgensen, 1993) and humanist educational philosophy (Price, 2000), with its emphasis on maximizing the growth of the total person. Humanist adult educational philosophy is based on the assumption that human nature is essentially positive and that each person possesses unlimited potential; therefore, humanist educational goals are bent toward the holistic development of persons toward their fullest potentials. Learning is essentially a personal, self-directed endeavor, and while disciplinary knowledge is important, it is bent toward the ultimate goal of self-actualizing individuals (Elias & Merriam, 1995). Learners know best what their learning needs are. Collaborative learning, experimentation, and discovery are all a part of learning methods used. The learner's background and individual experiences are taken into account. Educators with a humanist philosophy act more as facilitators of individualized learning than as disseminators of fixed knowledge. In fact, the educator is "a colearner in the educational process, and assumes an egalitarian relationship with learners" (Price, 2000, p. 4). A standardized curriculum might not even exist, making evaluation of outcomes more difficult. After welcoming participants to a parenting workshop, family life educators working from this approach would have parents generate the list of topics to explore what would be most beneficial to them.

A related philosophical orientation that fits with a facilitator approach is the progressive philosophy, perhaps the most influential educational philosophy in adult education (Price, 2000). This educational philosophy stresses holistic, lifelong, and life-wide education and an experiential, problem-solving approach to learning as opposed to didactic, passive learning. The experiences of the learner become paramount in determining areas to be learned and problems to be solved. The educator is primarily a facilitator of the learning processes through guiding, organizing, and evaluating learning experiences within which she or he may also be actively involved. Thus, learning is collaborative between the learners and instructors (Price, 2000). Family life educators following this philosophy in a class for married couples might present problem scenarios, then have participants identify possible solutions to the problems or have them try out solutions they generate for a time and report back to the group.

The Critical Inquirer Approach

Educators using a critical inquirer approach use questions to help participants think critically about the issues that are presented. This perspective acknowledges that participants have a responsibility to contribute meaningfully to their society and thus need to critically assess issues about them (Czaplewski & Jorgensen, 1993). This approach is tied to a critical/humanist philosophical orientation, which, like traditional humanistic approaches, promotes self-actualization of the learner. Yet for a critical/humanist, personal fulfillment is achieved through "becoming an autonomous, critical, and socially responsible thinker through an emphasis on rationality" (Tisdell & Taylor, 2000, p. 8). Family life educators might use a critical inquirer approach to help participants evaluate proposed or existing public policies designed to strengthen families.

The Collaborator Approach

Falling somewhere in between expert and facilitator approaches, in terms of responsibility for content and methods (Myers-Walls, 2000), is the collaborator approach. This approach recognizes that both family life educators and participants bring specialized knowledge to the learning experience. The educator brings research-based principles to the learning environment, and the participants bring their own lived experience regarding these principles. The collaborative educator brings a prepared agenda and curriculum, but these materials are fitted around the needs of participants. Participants are encouraged to contribute ideas for the agenda, but the educator maintains some control over the schedule and content of the discussion. After presenting the agenda for a Principles of Parenting program, collaborative family life educators might ask, "Are there any additions you'd like to make to the program, any topics you'd like to see covered that aren't listed?"

The Interventionist Approach

Interventionist-oriented family life educators are change agents; they seek cognitive, attitudinal, and behavior change, even transformation of participants through education. They believe that education for family life goes beyond simply learning for knowing but extends to learning for living (Mace, 1981). Such professionals are not mere knowledge transmitters or discussion facilitators (Guerney & Guerney, 1981). Interventionist approaches can be traced to both behaviorist and radical educational philosophies. For example, a behaviorist philosophy centers on changing behavior though the shaping of the environment to promote the desired behavior. As noted by Elias and Merriam (1995), a behaviorist-oriented educator is a "behavioral engineer who plans in detail the conditions necessary to bring about desired behavior" (p. 88). Such educators extensively use behavioral or learning objectives, model desired behavior, provide behavioral reinforcement for achieving the desired behavior, and use systematic instructional design. Learners are engaged in step-by-step learning of desired behaviors, receiving instructor support and evaluation through the processes. Family life educators working from this perspective with couples might teach and demonstrate Five Steps to Handing Conflict, then have couples practice the skills with the aid of a personal coach, who provides both reinforcement and corrective feedback.

Radical educational philosophies form the basis of educational strategies aimed at bringing about social change and combating social, political, and economic oppression of society. Developers of this approach (Freire, 1971; Mezirow, 1995) saw the traditional liberal forms of education as limiting and paternalistic, because it treats knowledge as a gift of the learned to those who are not. One such approach deduced from the radical philosophical traditions is transformative learning, which promotes increased self-awareness and freedom from constraints, necessary to help create social equity for the oppressed and for real learning to occur (Christopher, Dunnagan, Duncan, & Paul, 2001). In this context, educators are liberators, not facilitators, who help learners become social activists. This kind of learning occurs in three steps (E. Taylor, 1997): (1) Learners engage in critical self-reflection about assumptions and present approaches, (2) learners transform or revise their perspective, and (3) learners actually adopt new ways of behaving, consistent with their renewed perspective. Family life educators working from this philosophy with a group of parents might ask their participants to reflect on the approaches they use to parent their children and reflect on what is effective and ineffective. The family life educators might then discuss a variety of helpful approaches with the group and have parents create parenting plans to try in the coming week.

The Eclectic Approach

Educators coming from an eclectic approach would use elements of all the approaches, depending on the situation. For example, family life educators might wisely use an expert approach to teach others about a topic where little or no experiential knowledge exists or about a topic that is more controversial and needs an expert voice to set the record straight with empirical data (Doherty, 2000). An interventionist approach may be the best approach when working with oppressed and marginalized families who need to realize they have a voice, great opportunities, and unlimited potential.

Which of these approaches do you most readily identify with? Some research shows most family life educators organize and deliver their curricula based a collaborative approach (Myers-Walls, 2000). While thematically, family life educators may use one approach over another, the approach they use may depend somewhat upon the context. For example, the expert approach may be the approach of choice when it becomes necessary to share information about which the audience has limited knowledge or experience or when expert opinion is important to help solve a controversy. However, it would not be a recommended approach for use in a group of experienced, highly motivated parents—a facilitator or collaborator approach would be more successful. A critical enquirer approach is best when you want the audience to think deeply about an issue, even if it is about the quality of their own parenting; a facilitator approach likely would lack the structure and impetus to help accomplish this. When the learning of skills is part of the plan, interventionist approaches are likely the best. All in all, having all these approaches at one's disposal may be the most ideal situation of all, pointing to an eclectic approach. Thus, family life educators need to be sensitive to the best times to use a particular approach.

● DEVELOPING A WORKING PHILOSOPHY FOR OUTREACH FAMILY LIFE EDUCATION

Having a sense of our role as a family life educator and its philosophical underpinnings provides a basis for creating a working philosophy of outreach FLE. It is important for family life educators to take time and ponder their philosophical basis for teaching (Dail, 1984). They need to actively reflect on and contemplate *why* they do what they do (White & Brockett, 1987). Given the practical focus of FLE, some educators may question the relevance of philosophical rumination (White & Brockett, 1987), perhaps even seeing it as primarily an academic exercise they simply don't have time for. However, when we fail to tie FLE practice to philosophical underpinnings, our efforts may take on a mindless, ungrounded quality.

Everyone has some kind of working philosophy that is tied to his or her personal values, experiences, and lifestyles and reveals itself in our professional actions (White & Brockett, 1987). It's wise from time to time to clarify and write down our ideas so that they are subject to our understanding and critical reflection, at the same time realizing that a personal FLE philosophy is ever changing, always subject to modification through experiences and reflection.

Dail (1984) suggested several additional reasons for developing a personal philosophy: It provides a sense of direction and purpose, helps the educator get in touch with his or her own beliefs and their influence, helps the educator assess educational problems (e.g., provide a foundation for deciding what to teach about effective parenting), helps the educator relate FLE to the needs of the larger society, and provides impetus for the scholarly study of families. "In its essence," says Dail, "a philosophy of family life education provides a deeper meaning to the educator's life" (p. 147).

Dail (1984) provides a framework for the development of a personal philosophy of FLE, which we have adopted and adapted below.

Beliefs About the Family and the Nature and Quality of Family Life

Family life educators need to answer for themselves tough questions that even the savviest of politicians would prefer to avoid. For example, what is family? A single father and two children? Grandmother, mother, and daughter? Mom, Dad, and three children? Coparents with each bringing a child to the relationship? The definition of what a family is and/or should be will have profound effects on how an educator relates to clientele, especially those who may be excluded by their definition. Another consideration is the nature of family life. What assumptions do you make about the nature of family life? Are families a mere social arrangement, or do they have greater significance? How important is "family"? Whether family is seen as *the* fundamental unit of society or as one of the major entities among a cast of many players will affect educational practices with families. A third consideration is the quality of family life. For example, what characteristics comprise an ideal family, contrasted with a low-functioning family? Because of our beliefs about how parents ought to treat their children, we could never support coercive parenting as a functional ideal in a family. Your beliefs about the way families should be may lead you to draw the line on some family behaviors.

We think a working philosophy of FLE must also consider the answer to questions at the heart of the human experience. For instance, what does it mean to be human? Since humans have common existence and relationships in families, is membership in a family a key part of what it means to be human? What assumptions underlie our beliefs about human nature?

Beliefs About the Purpose of Family Life Education

Family life educators must be clear about what they want to accomplish and why (L. H. Powell & Cassidy, 2007), so that appropriate goals and objectives can be created. Preceding goals and objectives are a sense of vision and mission. For example, what value does education about family life have in society? David Mace (1981) envisioned FLE as something that originates from a cloudburst of information that becomes part of the knowledge base of a learner, which then produces personalized insight that leads the learner to experiment with new behaviors in family relationships. When family members coparticipate and mutually reinforce such action, the result is shared growth of members. Thus, does FLE in communities exist to be a catalyst for such a process? Guerney and Guerney (1981) reflected on whether family life educators could be considered "interventionists." That is, do family life educators take some "clearly defined" action "designed to induce some change" (p. 591)? The Guerneys argue that if family life educators believe that their purpose goes beyond mere knowledge transmission to "changing attitudes/values and behavior," they should "class themselves . . . as interventionists and be willing to stand up and be counted as such" (p. 592). This kind of "intervention" is distinguished from the focused, brief intervention strategies and family therapy that constitute the domain of the clinical professional and is outside the scope of FLE (Doherty, 1995). Thus, an important question at the heart of the purpose of FLE for outreach professionals is, "How 'interventionist' should FLE be?"

Beliefs About the Content of Family Life Education

There is no shortage of family-strengthening ideas to teach others. For example, there are literally hundreds of parenting books designed to impart advice to eager readers who want to do the best by their children. Some works are based on sound scholarship, others on clinical impressions, and still others on the simple convictions of the authors. What should be taught in FLE settings? How do you decide what to teach? Of what value is university-based theory and research? Even the best research has limitations in its application to individual/family needs. Much research has been completed with a disproportionate amount of White, middle-class participants. Thus, the data may have systematic bias. Participants in FLE programs also bring with them a rich array of personal experiences. How can the rich learning that is the lived experiences of individuals, families, and communities become part of the content of FLE?

Our personal values may also lead us to choose certain materials to teach certain ideas while ignoring or giving limited exposure to others. For example, if your personal values dictate that teens should avoid having sex outside of marriage and you are called upon to give a 45-minute talk at a high school assembly, your selected material may likely be quite different than it would be if you valued the full, unlimited, but responsible sexual activity of teens.

Beliefs About the Process of Learning for Families and Individuals Within Families

There are many ways to share information about family life in community settings. We can teach in small or large groups; through media channels such as radio, newspapers, magazines, television programs, and videos; through newsletters, publications, the Internet, and leaflets; and through one-on-one meetings in homes or an office. How do individuals and families learn most effectively? From a family systems approach, it can be argued that the best learning for family strengthening will occur as a full family group. New knowledge can be co-learned and reinforced at home. However, when any member of the family is missing, newly learned attitudes and behaviors are at risk of being sabotaged by the missing member. Still, one person behaving positively can influence the others. In addition, individuals and families differ in terms of their primary learning styles and sensory modalities (Powell & Cassidy, 2007), which effective education must account for. What learning processes invoke positive change in knowledge, attitudes, skills, and behaviors? How important are learning goals and evaluation in these processes? What assumptions do you hold about learners? Are they lights to be lit or cups to be filled?

CONCLUSION ●

Family life education in outreach settings has a long history. It is evolving from an expert top-down approach to addressing family problems to a collaborative, strength-based, community-strengthening model that integrates scientific knowledge from family sciences with the values and experiences of families in communities. It is expanding its reach into increasingly diverse audiences using a wider range of technology and refining its professional core. There are many philosophical bases from which we can craft FLE and varied approaches associated with these philosophies. Generally, the best strategies are community-collaborative in nature, but each approach discussed may have a role depending on the circumstances. Crafting a philosophy of FLE has the potential to purposefully guide and direct our efforts. Following are exercises to help guide you in writing your personal philosophy and approach in FLE.

● EXPLORATIONS

1. Follow the guidelines below and design your own working philosophy of family life education. Address the questions in your discussion.

- What are my beliefs about the family and the nature and quality of family life and the human experience?
  - What is a "family"? How important are families? What values do I hold regarding families and the human experience? What does it mean to be human?
- What are my beliefs about the purpose of FLE?
  - What is the nature of FLE? What value does FLE have in communities? Is it to provide insight, skills, and knowledge? Is it to change behavior? How "interventionist" should FLE be?
- What are my beliefs about the content of FLE?
  - Of what value is university-based theory and research to families? Of what value is the lived experience of individuals, families, and communities, and how can it become part of the content of FLE? How do my personal values regarding families and the human experience influence the content I select?
- What are my beliefs about the process of learning for families in outreach settings?
  - How do individuals and families learn most effectively? What teaching strategies have the greatest impact? How important are learning goals and evaluation in these processes? What assumptions do I hold about learners?

2. Describe what you are like as an FLE. Different FLE settings may necessitate different approaches, but most of us will find a place where we are most comfortable and effective. Review the various approaches discussed in the chapter. Which approach best describes you and why?

PART II

DEVELOPMENT OF FAMILY LIFE EDUCATION PROGRAMS

CHAPTER 2

DESIGNING COMPREHENSIVE FAMILY LIFE EDUCATION PREVENTION PROGRAMS

Beyond philosophically grounding our work as family life educators, it is important that family life educators place their programmatic efforts in a scientifically supported, organizing framework. This chapter presents a prevention perspective and an integrative step-by-step framework for designing, creating, and implementing family life education (FLE) programs, which includes the following broad stages: problem analysis, program design, pilot testing, advance testing, and dissemination. Found within each stage are many subprocesses. For example, during the problem analysis stage, FLE professionals would be engaged in defining the problem or goal, identifying risk and protective factors, assessing accessibility of the target group, and forming a coalition of stakeholders who work together to address the problem.

● THE SCIENCE AND PROFESSION OF PREVENTION

As a guiding principle, family life educators focus on preventive education rather than therapeutic remediation (Arcus & Thomas, 1993). The modern prevention movement as related to family strengthening is about 25 to 30 years old (Small & Memmo, 2004). L'Abate (1983) was among the first to articulate the concept of prevention in the family field. L'Abate describes three levels of prevention: primary, secondary, and tertiary. Primary prevention-oriented family life educators help families develop the knowledge and skills they need to build strong relationships before any problems or issues present themselves, preventing problems before they occur. For example, most FLE websites are primary preventive in focus, as they are geared to transmit information and skills to the audience. Secondary prevention involves working with audiences who have some signs of risk, where inter-vention would prevent more serious problems from occurring (Small & Memmo, 2004). For example, a program developed to help parents over-come unbridled anger tendencies learned in their families of origin would be operating at this level. Tertiary prevention programs are designed for FLE audiences already experiencing a good deal of distress and for whom educational programs alone would not be adequate. Participants at this level require therapy, and such interventions normally are carried out by clinical professionals or family life educators who also have such training. FLE professionals typically operate at the primary and secondary preven-tion levels and leave tertiary prevention to family therapy (Doherty, 1995).

The concept of prevention has likewise been found in the fields of public health and the psychological and social sciences. In fact, a new dis-cipline has emerged, termed *prevention science*, whose goal is "to prevent or moderate major human dysfunctions," including those associated with marriage, family, and individual development (Coie et al., 1993, p. 1013).

Prevention science integrates the independent risk-focused paradigm (J. D. Hawkins, Catalano, & Miller, 1992) and protective or resiliency fac-tors paradigm (e.g., Werner, 1990). Prevention science when applied to FLE focuses on the understanding of both risk factors and protective factors as a precursor to the development and implementation of FLE programs. Risk factors are variables that increase the vulnerability of individuals, couples, and families to a variety of negative outcomes; protective factors are safe-guarding variables that increase an individual's, couple's, or family's resis-tance to normative, developmental, or unplanned stressors (Bogenschneider, 1996; Rutter, 1987). The presence of risk factors or protective factors is not enough to ensure that a negative or positive outcome will occur but simply makes such outcomes more likely when present. Risk factors increase the odds that negative outcomes will occur; protective factors increase the likelihood that negative states will be thwarted. Protective factors are activated only in the presence of risk factors (Small & Memmo, 2004).

Family science has progressed far enough in its knowledge about marriage and family relationships to be able to detail risk factors and protective factors for the prevention of marital distress, poor child development outcomes, and various psychological disorders. A science of prevention today pertains to marriage and familial disorders as much as it does to the prevention of heart disease and cancer. The most effective FLE programs are those that simultaneously and proactively work to reduce risks while increasing protection.

PREVENTION EDUCATION MODELS IN FLE ●

Since the emergence of prevention science, several models for developing prevention programs have appeared in the FLE scholarly literature. Each model helps us take family life educational program design beyond a "service mission" to a "scientific enterprise" (Dumka, Roosa, Michaels, & Suh, 1995, p. 78). Among the earliest developed was by Hughes (1994). He noted that FLE materials are of varying quality, not always following high development standards. He set about to articulate a straightforward four-step framework for the development of family life education programs that quality programs will incorporate. While some of the elements have a more direct application to program curricula, we agree with Hughes (1994) that most of the items can be applied to any FLE resource. These elements include content, instructional process, implementation process, and evaluation. In the content step, program developers consult appropriate theory and research and make sure that the research fits the audience (context sensitive) and that the ideas reflect best practices. The instructional process focuses on creation of sound teaching plans and presentation of materials in such a way that it is accessible to the audience. The implementation process includes meeting the needs of the target audience and having a marketing plan to reach participants. The evaluation process includes some provision for determining whether an FLE program benefits others, and program materials include evaluation tools that are closely tied to program goals and objectives.

Dumka et al. (1995) constructed a five-stage process for developing prevention programs, consisting of problem analysis, program design, pilot testing, advance testing, and dissemination. Found within each stage are many other subprocesses. For example, during the problem analysis stage (Stage 1), FLE professionals would be engaged in defining the problem or goal, identifying risk and protective factors, and assessing accessibility of the target group. The first two stages address the formulation of an intervention theory, Stages 3 and 4 (implementation) become a test of the theory, and the final stages assess whether the program works and should be widely disseminated (Dumka et al., 1995).

Bogenschneider (1996) began with the epidemiological models of risk and protection from prevention science and placed them within the context of ecological systems theory (Bronfenbrenner, 1979, 1986) and developmental contextualism (Lerner, 1991, 1995). The result was an Ecological Risk/Protective Theoretical Model for the design and implementation of youth development programs. At least four premises derive from this perspective: (1) Outcomes are multiply determined, (2) proximal environments have the strongest and most direct influence on outcomes, (3) risk and protective factors occur at different levels of the human ecology (e.g., individual-family-community), and (4) these factors move and change through developmental time. From this basis, Bogenschneider proposes 12 principles for building prevention programs: (1) identify the real issues or problems facing youth; (2) establish well-defined goals that target the risk and protective processes associated with the identified youth issue or problem; (3) be comprehensive in addressing both risk and protective processes in several levels of the human ecology; (4) collaborate with stakeholders in the community or neighborhood; (5) educate coalition members on current theory and research on adolescent development, prevention programming, and community process; (6) tailor the plan to the community, reducing risks that exist locally and building protective processes that do not exist; (7) involve the target audience in program design, planning, and implementation; (8) be sensitive to cultural, ethnic, and other forms of diversity in the neighborhood or community; (9) intervene early and continuously; (10) select developmentally appropriate intervention strategies; (11) anticipate how changes in one part of the system may affect changes in the system or other settings; and (12) evaluate effectiveness by monitoring changes in risk and protective processes.

Small, Cooney, and O'Connor (2009), in their examination of evidence-based programs (EBP), particularly those designed especially for children, youth, and their parents, identified 11 principles of effective prevention programs. They organized these principles into four categories: program design and content, program relevance, program implementation, and program assessment and quality assurance. The program design and content category comprises four principles: Effective programs are (1) theory driven, (2) of sufficient dosage and intensity, (3) comprehensive, and (4) actively engaging. The program relevance category features the next three principles: Effective programs are (5) developmentally appropriate, (6) appropriately timed, and (7) socioculturally relevant. The program implementation stage emphasizes the next two principles: Effective programs are (8) delivered by well-qualified, trained, and supportive staff and (9) focused on fostering good relationships. The program assessment and quality assurance category emphasizes the final two principles: Effective programs (10) are well documented and (11) are committed to evaluation and refinement.

These models have several similarities but also bring some unique perspectives and emphases important in the development of effective prevention programs. All can be used as guiding principles for developing programs but also for assessing the quality of current programs and improving existing programs. Below we integrate these models to form a how-to framework for the design of comprehensive, high-quality FLE programs. Many of these key elements are discussed in greater detail in chapters that follow. This framework has application to a wide variety of FLE resources: workshop series, websites, DVDs, or other educational approaches. We introduce this framework and provide relevant examples of its use.

A COMPREHENSIVE MODEL FOR THE ● DESIGN OF FAMILY LIFE PREVENTION PROGRAMS

Stage 1: Problem Analysis

Identify Problem and Establish Overall Program Goal(s)

It is important to clearly articulate the problem or need one seeks to address through an FLE program. One way to do this is to formulate a brief research-informed problem statement. The statement also provides a built-in rationale for doing the program in the first place. Students in an undergraduate FLE class crafted the following problem statement for their transition to parenthood program. It is titled Making Room for Two When Baby Makes Three:

> Current research shows that nearly half of all divorces occur within the first seven years of marriage. It has also been shown that the arrival of the first baby to a couple tends to increase the likelihood that either

the husband, wife, or both partners will experience a decline in marital satisfaction. Therefore, it is essential that couples become aware of this problem and make their marriage a priority during the transition to parenthood.

Identification of problems certainly comes from investigating extant scholarship. But as both Bogenschneider (1996) and Small et al. (2009) point out, such problems must be relevant and tied to real issues facing a community. Therefore, concomitant with problem analysis from a research and theory perspective is an analysis of the problem within the specific population we seek to serve, thereby avoiding the potential disconnect noted in Chapter 1. From a human ecological perspective, it is possible that problems identified more broadly may be unique to local community cultures; thus, family life educators will wisely survey individual targeted communities to learn of their specific problems and needs to ensure the sociocultural relevance of their program. Findings from local populations that demonstrate a problem or need may be more likely to motivate community buy-in than more remote research conducted in distant places. Local data collection also is often a more reliable way to determine needs and forestall wasteful spending of prevention dollars. For example, while serving as extension specialists in Alabama, we had the opportunity of conducting a Teen Assessment Project (TAP) survey, modeled after the Wisconsin Teen Assessment Project (Small & Hug, 1991), in various middle and high school locations throughout the state. In one location, school administrators were convinced that they faced a serious drug problem and were preparing to spend lots of district dollars on prevention programs. They invited us to administer the survey. Surprisingly to them, the survey data suggested that there were other risk behaviors going on that were far more serious, even deadly, leading the district to spend dollars on programs to address this higher priority concern.

With a problem defined, an overall program goal statement can be developed that points to the general direction a program will take to address the problem. This statement should also make reference to the target audience. For example, the goal of the aforementioned program was stated as follows: "The goal of Making Room for Two When Baby Makes Three is to enhance marital satisfaction among *expectant and new parents* as they face the birth of their first child." Another example: "The ABC program is designed to help *single parents* identify and build upon their parenting strengths, enhancing their sense of competence as a parent."

Identify Theories, Risk, and Protective Factors and Extract "Teachable" Ideas

The next step is to mine the current scholarly literature for the relevant research and theory addressing the problem and goal. In any outreach setting, from traditional workshops to websites, family life educators must address the following question: What scientific information do people need to know about this topic? In the area of family life, there is an explosion of information, some credible and some incredible, even implausible. Many persons are willing to be called a family "expert" through bringing forth armchair theories and ideas of their own design. In contrast, FLE programs must be grounded in the best current scholarship if they are to enjoy credibility. A strong scholarly base forms the foundation of the content, goals, objectives, and learning activities of FLE materials.

Knowing risk and protective factors associated with the identified problem enables family life educators to target and limit specific processes that lead to negative outcomes and target and increase specific processes leading to positive outcomes. For example, risk and prediction research has identified various negative interaction patterns that place couples at heightened risk for marital disruption, such as criticism, contempt, defensiveness, escalation, stonewalling, and negative interpretations (Gottman, 1994; H. J. Markman, Stanley, & Blumberg, 2001). Research has also identified processes that enhance the well-being of marriage, such as nurturing friendship and commitment. Both risk and protective factors will range from those more or less modifiable within the context of an FLE program. For instance, parental divorce is a risk factor in marriage that is not modifiable. However, how a parental divorce plays out in a current marriage is possible to change. To be effective, FLE programs will need to focus on modifiable factors and increasing protection from the influence of negative processes that may have been produced by the factors.

Extract the "teachable" ideas and principles from theories and research, those ideas that can be summarized from a wide array of well-conducted studies that are practical, useful, and theoretically and empirically sound. Some examples include the following: "The more authoritative a parent is, the better off their children will be as they grow." "The more married couples accurately read one another's love language, the better the marriage." "Risks for divorce are reduced when couples learn to handle conflict and disagreements effectively."

Teachable ideas such as these are usually embedded within or supportive of broader ideas deduced from theories related to or applied to the family, such as family systems theory, family stress theory, communications theory, exchange theory, family development theory, human ecology theory, or social learning theory. For example, in consulting the scholarly literature for a basis for the transition to parenthood program Making Room for Two When Baby Makes Three, program creators discovered that much of the research was informed by family development theory (e.g., developmental transitions) and family stress theory (e.g., transitions, even pleasant ones, can be experienced as stressful).

Some theoretical perspectives naturally lend themselves characteristics of effective FLE, as noted by Small et al. (2009). For example, a program developed with a human ecology lens is likely to be more comprehensive and socioculturally relevant. A family development theory perspective will naturally attune a family life educator to create programs that are developmentally appropriate and appropriately timed. A program for strengthening single parents might in part be based on targeted ecologically sensitive research that identifies the characteristics of effective single parents.

As an example of using theory and research to build an FLE program, some years ago I (Duncan) developed a Making Families Stronger program. It was based on ecological systems theory, which asserts that families have the first and foremost influence on human development (Bronfenbrenner, 1979, 1986). Therefore, of all the human systems deserving attention, the family microsystem deserves prime time. The program also drew on family empowerment theory (Cochran & Woolever, 1983), which holds that families have inherent strengths that can be mobilized to help them have the kind of family they want. These ideas provided a theoretical justification for teaching families about how to be stronger. Finally, the program was based on 30 years of family research conducted all over the world concerning what characteristics make families strong and healthy, or protective factors known as family strengths (Krysan, Moore, & Zill, 1990). Some families focus only on problems (their risk factors). Instead, this literature helps families identify strengths and how families could identify and build them.

Family life educators are wise to have a working knowledge of several major theoretical frameworks and how to use them to build their programs. While we won't attempt to provide a theories course in this text, we do think it is important to show several of the theories, key principles behind the theories, and their application in family life education. See Table 2.1 for a listing of common family theories, general principles of the theories, and their application to family life education. We encourage family life educators to consult good family theory books for more in-depth background on theoretical perspectives (for example, see Chibucos & Leite, 2005, for an excellent orientation to key concepts and research examples that show the features of the theory).

TABLE 2.1	Using Family Theories for the Design of Family Life Education Programs	
Theory	*Key Principles*	*Application to FLE*
Family systems theory	Family members interact with one another in an interdependent, coherently characteristic way. Family systems have a powerful effect on individual family member behavior. Family systems reflect input received by family members synergistically interacting together. Inputs (such as educational information) have predictable outputs (such as relationship outcomes). A system may embrace change (morphogenesis) or resist it (morphostasis). Family systems are nested within and are influenced by larger social systems (community, culture).	Try to teach all members of a target audience system (couples rather than one partner, both parents rather than one parent, parents and children rather than just parents, and children and parents rather than parents alone) because a change in one member may be sabotaged by other family members. One family member can trigger change in a relationship system. Positive change potential is enhanced at timely transitions (during developmental change).
Social exchange theory	Relationship stability and quality predicted by rewards minus costs in interaction.	Programs attempt to build relationship assets (e.g., enhance positivity in marriage) and reduce relationship liabilities (e.g., reduce negativity in marriage).
Family development theory	Families grow and change over developmental time.	Programs targeted in different ways to persons dependent on their family developmental course (Becoming a Couple; Parenting Teens and Handling Your Midlife Challenges; Getting Ready for Retirement).
Human ecology theory	Development occurs through the interaction of a mosaic of factors; family microsystems influence and are influenced by transactions with other systems (e.g., neighborhood, peer group, school, workplace).	"Silver bullet" programs addressing only one aspect of the ecological system typically are insufficient; must address several areas of the social ecology simultaneously. A balancing work and family program teaching parents balance skills should also teach businesses how to establish family-friendly policies.
Symbolic interaction	Families make meaning and interpret events based on norms, values, expectations, patterns of behavior, and interaction.	Allow opportunities for families to construct their own meanings of events and ideas. Ask questions such as, "What meaning does this have for you?"

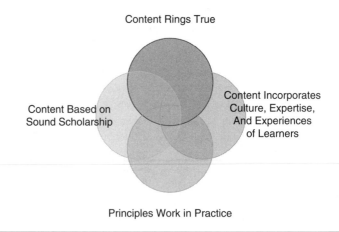

Content Rings True

Content Based on
Sound Scholarship

Content Incorporates
Culture, Expertise,
And Experiences
of Learners

Principles Work in Practice

Figure 2.1   Selecting Content for Outreach Family Life Education

In all of this process, it is important to remember that adult audiences usually have already formed their opinions about many topics we address and in many cases have real-life experiences to support them. For instance, parents have experiences being parents, and family life educators who do not take that into account, regardless of how powerful their science-based ideas are, will risk alienating their audiences. We believe family life educators should seek out and find the principles that their clientele need to know the most. While many factors influence our content selection decisions, we believe that the most useful and valid FLE information is found at the intersection of the following four elements: (1) ideas are grounded in sound scholarship; (2) ideas ring true or fit with our values and instincts; (3) ideas fit with and incorporate the knowledge, culture, expertise, and lived experience of the learners; and (4) ideas work in practice (see Figure 2.1).

Do the ideas ring true? As family life educators, we often strive to empower parents to trust their own values and instincts as they parent their children and are challenged to design learning experiences where they can find parenting solutions within the context of their values (DeBord et al., 2002). The same recommendation seems to apply to us as we endeavor to select the best and most useful information to share with our outreach audiences. Family life educators can critically inquire, "Does the information or research recommendation fit with my own values and instincts? Do the ideas ring true?"

Do the ideas fit with and incorporate the knowledge, culture, expertise, and lived experience of the learners? In Chapter 1, we emphasized that most effective family life educators incorporate the best scientific information with the knowledge, lived experience, culture, and expertise of families in communities (Doherty, 2000; Lerner, 1995; Myers-Walls, 2000). In selecting from scholarly materials, family life educators will seek to choose materials as free from bias as possible and general enough in principle that they can be applied in a variety of settings and cultures. Part of this involves care in reviews of literature to ensure that the basis of our material is as representative as possible of the audiences we seek to serve, realizing that all scholarship will have its limitations. However, beyond this, when family life educators are in teaching settings, they will need to find ways to incorporate what participants bring with them into the educational setting.

Do the ideas work in practice? Experiences with principles may have taken us only so far, and there are ideas our FLE audiences may hear from us or from one another that they haven't tried out. We can encourage them to experiment with the ideas they hear. Part of assessing the validity of an idea is to test it out in our own lives. It may be based on many studies, it may ring true, and it may be reinforced by the experiences of many, but will it work for me? Of course, no one strategy works for everyone under all circumstances. But if a tool proves useful in some instances, it can be kept handy to use when needed. We test the idea out in the laboratory of our own experience so we know whether or not it works for us.

Form a Coalition of Stakeholders Who Work Together to Address the Problem

As will be discussed in greater detail in Chapter 16, most family concerns are too complex and need solutions too comprehensive for any single entity to address alone. Wise family life educators will seek to join forces with other like-minded persons in addressing family concerns. As was discussed in the previous chapter, communities bring with them their own special expertise, with family life educators comprising one player at the collaborative table. "Involving local citizens in planning helps ensure that prevention programs fit the community, promotes local ownership, and engenders commitment to seeing that the program is implemented and maintained" (Bogenschneider, 1996, p. 132). Once a coalition is formed, family life educators can use their expertise to educate coalition members on current theory and research addressing the problem. After a coalition to address youth concerns was formed in a small Montana town, an FLE professional shared with them the risk factors and protective factors associated with youth development and worked with them to design and implement a survey that assessed these factors in several high schools in the area. Findings from the survey provided an empirical basis for targeted youth development programs within the participating schools.

Stage 2: Program Design

Consult the Target Group

As a prelude to or concomitant with other aspects of program design is the task of assessing target audience needs. Many FLE programs fail because they do not spend time thoroughly investigating the needs of target audiences (more about this will be discussed in Chapter 17 in the context of marketing FLE programs). Consulting the target audience is a way of checking out the fit of the research literature with the actual audience for whom an educational product is intended. There are at least three kinds of needs to assess (Arcus et al., 1993b). *Felt* needs are those sought from audiences in response to direct questioning through questionnaires, interviews, and focus groups. It is what they say they need. For example, the question, "What concerns do you have about parenting teenagers nowadays?" asked of parents of teens would be a question designed to elicit felt need responses, as well as, "If a program were designed to help you be a better parent for your teenagers, what would it contain?" *Ascribed* needs are those family life educators may observe because of their specialized knowledge. These are the needs family life educators may attribute to the group as a result of a review of the literature. To continue with the example of parents of teens, a large representative study of teens may reveal that they are much less likely to participate in risky sexual behavior when their parents appropriately monitor their activities. From these data, family life educators might decide that parents of teens need to learn how to monitor their teens, such as using the who-what-where-when approach (who are you going to be with, what will you be doing, where will you be going, and when will you be home?). *Future* needs involve the skills and abilities required to accomplish future tasks and perform future roles. The idea of anticipatory socialization suggests that transitions to new roles are easier when we learn as much as we can about a role before we perform that role. Future needs can be tapped by asking such questions as, "What do couples preparing for marriage need to know prior to marriage?"

There are numerous ways to consult the target audience, from conducting interviews, sending mail questionnaires, and using existing data about the audience. To aid in the design of their parenting program for high-risk families, after reviewing the literature, Dumka et al. (1995) conducted focus group interviews with various subgroups of their targeted population. A total of 53 parents divided into six groups participated and were asked open-ended questions that probed their needs as parents, their children's needs, and the resources in the community currently available to meet those needs. Parents requested a program that would provide information regarding drug and alcohol abuse to parents and children and teach parenting skills such as improved communication and disciplining children. There was some variation in reported felt needs among the groups, and these variations were considered accordingly in program design.

The involvement of the target audience is critical not only in program design but also in the planning, implementation, and evaluation of the program. Wise family life educators will include members of the target audience on their coalition and will seek their input at every stage of the program. When deciding on how best to evaluate the effectiveness of our program to help families on public assistance gain self-sufficiency, a group of family life educators (Duncan, Dunnagan, Christopher, & Paul, 2003) first field tested their evaluation protocol with several low-income, limited-literacy participants and made some adjustments based on their feedback.

Select Change Objectives

Change objectives, also called learning objectives, refer to the knowledge level, attitudes, values, behaviors, skills, and aspirations targeted for change by the program. Fulfillment of these objectives lead to the positive outcomes predicted by the theories and research and desired by the target audience.

Family life educators may be tempted to make a simple list of topics from their literature review of teachable ideas as a means of guiding their instruction. A learner-centered approach changes this focus and invites the educator to specifically identify what learners should get out of the learning experience (Fink, 2003). Thus, change objectives (also called learning objectives) are stated in specific, measurable, learner-centered (e.g., what *participants* will learn, do, feel, not the instructor), action-oriented terms (e.g., what will occur as a result of the program) that include active verbs (e.g., learn, understand, apply, practice, identify, compare and contrast, critique, do).

Thus, as you formulate learning objectives, there are certain questions that are important to ask (adapted from Fink, 2003):

Knowledge. What do you want your learning audience to know (or think about, reflect upon)? For example, what key information (facts, terms, concepts) is important for the learners to understand and remember? What key ideas or perspectives are important for learners to comprehend? One educator wanted his workshop audience to understand the difference between a problem-focused perspective and a family strengths perspective to building a strong family, and he formulated the following specific learning objective: Participants will be able to distinguish between a problem-focused approach and a family strengths perspective to strengthening their family.

Caring. What changes would you like to see in what your learners care about, as expressed in their attitudes, values, and feelings? What attitudes and values do you want them to develop or reconsider? What affective experiences do you want them to have with the material?

One educator wanted to change her audience's attitudes toward housework from one of "mere drudgery" to "an opportunity for family connection." Thus, a primary learning objective became "Participants will view housework as a potential setting for family members to strengthen their relationships with each other."

Application. What behaviors would you like them to change? What important skills do you want them to learn?

Interventionist-oriented family life educators often will be interested in structuring instruction in ways that evoke change in behaviors and development of skills. Family life educators leading parenting workshops may want their parents to learn authoritative approaches to parenting. A learning objective appropriate for this area might be the following: Participants will learn and practice three skills pertinent to authoritative parenting: establishing connection, regulating children's behavior, and promoting autonomy. Perhaps in the same program, family life educators are interested in promoting the use of positive approaches to discipline, including reducing the use of corporal punishment as a strategy. A possible learning objective would be the following: Parents will learn and practice numerous options for dealing with a difficult child behavior that they have faced at home.

Select Outcome Evaluation Instruments

The purpose of evaluation is to assess whether a program is showing progress in meeting change objectives. The instruments selected must allow us to evaluate changes in the risk and protective factors that can be attributed to the program and must be directly tied to program objectives. Some tools that have demonstrated reliability and validity can be selected, provided they fit change objectives. Otherwise, they must be created and pilot tested to ensure their usefulness.

In the Making Families Stronger program, I (Duncan) had the goal of increasing the levels of self-reported family life satisfaction through the processes of identifying and building one's family strengths. The change objective was to "increase family life satisfaction levels among participating families." I selected David Olson's Family Life Satisfaction scale (Olson, Stewart, & Wilson, 1990) as my outcome evaluation tool, which is a reliable and valid measure of family life satisfaction directly tied to the change objective that also incorporated a family strengths approach in the development of the items. Thus, it was the "perfect" tool for my purposes.

Quality FLE programs will include provisions for conducting evaluations, including evaluation instruments tied to program goals and objectives. See Chapter 3 for a full discussion of evaluation.

Select Change Methods and Learning Activities

Change methods will be wisely tied to change objectives. An important question to ask is, "What method would be most effective to accomplish this objective?" For example, a skills-related objective calls for a skill-teaching methodology. Steps include the following: (a) describe the skill, (b) model the skill, (c) practice the skill in a nonstressful setting and situation, (d) receive reinforcement and corrective feedback, and (e) use the skill in a real-life setting, that is, at home (also see Chapter 6). Other types of objectives would draw from other methods. In quality FLE programs, a variety of teaching methods effective with adult learners are used, including buzz groups, role-playing, visuals, video clips, and various forms of discussion (see Chapter 6). These methods would be sensitive to a diversity of learning styles, sensory modalities, developmental needs, and abilities (see Chapter 8). Quality FLE programs are actively engaging, using active learning strategies (Small et al., 2009) that incorporate the knowledge, culture, expertise, and lived experience of the learners (Doherty, 2001). Directions on how to facilitate the learning process would be included, including the amount of time to be spent on each teaching activity. Chapters 4 to 6 provide detailed information on how to design effective instruction leading to meaningful learning experiences for our audiences.

In deciding on the best methods, wise family life educators will also examine existing programs for methods that work with their population, often called "best practices." The process of learning about other programs, methods used, and their effectiveness is critical to identifying these practices. It can also save program development time and energy. Ask yourself, "What can I learn from these programs without having to reinvent the wheel, at the same time incorporating my own imagination/creative energy?"

Decide Program Extensiveness

Dumka et al. (1995) identify three dimensions of program extensiveness. The first of these is the selectiveness of the program. A *universal program* is designed for everyone. A parenting program following a Parent-Teacher Association (PTA) meeting billed "for all parents" would be such a program. Such a program avoids the risk of inviting only certain parents, and thus parents avoid a labeling stigma. However, it may be too general to make a significant difference among persons needing a targeted program. A *selective* program would be targeted to particular subgroups of participants (e.g., single parents, seniors) or subgroups exhibiting risk factors a program seeks to address (e.g., families receiving public assistance). An *indicated* program would be developed for an audience exhibiting negative outcomes, such as parents court-ordered to participate in parenting programs as an adjunct to counseling. Such audiences may include participants whose needs cannot be effectively met with preventative FLE alone (Dumka et al., 1995). A second aspect of program extensiveness is *breadth*, or the number and range of change objectives. Following an ecological systems (Bronfenbrenner, 1979, 1986) orientation in relation to prevention programs, Bogenschneider (1996) recommends that change objectives range across several levels of the human ecology. For example, a program designed to help employed parents harmonize work and family would also help employers craft family-friendly workplace policies and promote work-family harmony through media channels. A program focused on only one level will likely be limited in impact, as other systems in the social ecology may act to sabotage newfound insights and strategies. For example, the excitement of learning to harmonize family and work in a community workshop may be drained when the workplace refuses to grant flextime.

A third dimension of program extensiveness is *length*, what Small et al. (2009) refer to as intensity or dosage. While shorter programs may be the desire of a target audience and more appealing from a marketing perspective, longer programs are more effective in producing reliable, longer lasting changes. For example, in marriage education, where the audiences tend to be of lower risk for marital disruption (Carroll & Doherty, 2003), longer programs involving more than 12 contact hours produce somewhat better outcomes than shorter programs (Guerney & Maxson, 1990). Where audiences are of greater risk, the ideal length of contact may be much longer. For programs to have a significant impact on families at risk of child abuse, some argue that programs should be at least 6 to 18 months in length. It has been found that parents who participate for a longer duration (~ 2 years) and who used all services offered (at least 3–5 programs) had better outcomes than those receiving less intense and shorter-term services (Whipple & Wilson, 1996). The National Research Council (1993) reviewed several child abuse prevention programs and found that programs that were short term and low in intensity did not change long-term relationships between parents and children. In an era of social media, dosage and intensity will likely take on different forms than it has in the past (see more discussion on the role of social media in Chapter 12).

Design Recruitment/Retention Strategy

One of the greatest challenges family life educators face is recruitment and retention of audiences. As part of needs assessments surveys, wise family life educators will consult the target audience about the best ways to recruit and retain an audience. Recruitment and marketing, including the creation of a marketing plan, is a focus of Chapter 17. Dumka et al. (1995) followed this strategy during their focus groups and were given several suggestions: (a) include both parents and children in the program so they could talk about what they were learning, (b) help parents develop a support group so they could help each other during and after the program, (c) provide child care and refreshments, and (d) offer the program close to home with no more than one meeting a week.

Tailor Program Content and Delivery

Programs designed after a "one-size-fits-all" model are doomed to failure. Program content and delivery must be tailored to the needs of the audience and the community or made socioculturally relevant (Small et al., 2009). For example, the content and approach should be sensitive to cultural, ethnic, and other forms of diversity (see Chapter 8). This effort is especially critical since much of social science research that undergirds FLE materials is biased toward White, middle-class families. To maximize participation, implementation strategies should be based on target audience felt needs and preferences. For example, a standard curriculum was not acceptable in one community until after the inclusion of recruitment meetings (drummed up by current participants where recruits were invited by current participants), teachers from the same culture, and home visits for those participants facing transportation barriers. In one program for limited-resource families (Duncan et al., 2003), educators kept the material simple and to the point because of the vast differences in participant educational levels. Materials were adjusted to relate to very basic levels of life skills. Written materials were written at a low reading level or were simple enough that they could be easily adapted or interpreted. Family life educators developing curricula to help lower-income families make transitions from welfare dependency to self-support would make sure that the theory, research, and interventions are based on an understanding of the complex needs of limited resource (limited in terms of education and perception of personal resources as well as income) at different levels of their social ecology (at the individual, family, and community levels) (Christopher et al., 2001).

Stage 3: Pilot Testing

Once programs have been developed, they are ready for testing in the field. The goal of pilot testing is to "implement the prototype program with participants and in contexts as similar to the targeted participants and contexts as possible" (Dumka et al., 1995, p. 84). Dumka et al. (1995) recommend doing three kinds of evaluation at this stage: recruitment and retention, process, and formative evaluation.

Recruitment and Retention Evaluation

This is the process of assessing whether your recruitment strategy designed during Stage 2 is working. Since FLE in community settings often suffers from underwhelming participation, and participation is vital for the existence of the program, this piece of evaluation is vital. If the recruitment strategy you used for a parenting program included circulating a flyer to all parents of fourth graders and only 3 of an eligible 100 parents showed up for the program, it would be clear that recruitment strategies need changing. The Dumka et al. (1995) strategy noted above resulted in more than 53% of parents participating in five or more sessions—quite successful for a program such as this.

Process Evaluation

This kind of evaluation provides information about the overall management of the program to assess if the program is functioning as designed. It would include an adjudicated assessment of instruction (e.g., is quality information being taught?), logistics (evaluation of the meeting place, food, and transportation), how evaluation processes are perceived by participants (e.g., do participants find evaluation questions too personal or complex?), level of community support (e.g., media pieces supporting the program), support from stakeholders (e.g., county commissioners giving the program attention), and a host of other elements. Feedback on processes from both staff and clientele is important. We call this kind of evaluation "project quality control."

Formative Evaluation

Quality FLE resources include some provision for determining if the materials benefit others. Formative evaluation assesses participants' direct experience with program material and exposes what modifications may be necessary to improve their learning experience. At a pilot testing stage, it is appropriate for family life educators to administer a brief questionnaire at the end of each session and ask whether the participants learned something new, what were the strengths in the program, and how the program might be improved. Evaluation tools are clearly tied to program goals and objectives. Both process and formative evaluation are part of the "program clarification" tier of evaluation (Jacobs, 1988), which will be fully discussed in Chapter 3.

Program Revision

Process and formative evaluation will likely point to needed changes. Family life educators need to identify and decide what they are going to do differently based on the pilot feedback they receive. Data may suggest needed content, implementation, or evaluation changes. For example, formative evaluation of a website led to changes in the format of the articles and the adding of some user-friendly features (such as the ability to e-mail an article to a friend or family member). In another program, process evaluation revealed that many participants complained about being expected to complete pre- and posttests that were long and tedious. The evaluators decided to provide a nominal financial incentive of $10 per completed questionnaire.

Stage 4: Advanced Testing

Those whose focus is to develop and refine programs toward broad dissemination will want to take advanced steps to establish effectiveness. After integrating changes suggested during pilot testing, a program is ready for more advanced assessment. The goal of advanced testing is to evaluate the ability of a program to make significant changes in targeted risk factors and protective factors. In other words, it asks, "Does the program truly accomplish the stated change objectives?" This is often called summative or outcome evaluation. For a parenting program, this may mean the enhancement of not only reported parenting skills but also translation to better outcomes long term among participating parents' children. To answer these kinds of questions requires assessment sophistication greater than pilot testing.

Advance testing includes the processes of choosing an experimental design, implementing the revised program, analyzing the data, and continuing to refine the program. While some programs collect data that masquerade as impact data (Small, 1990), advance testing of program impact requires an experimental research design. This is because experimental designs most effectively control competing explanations for what may be positive outcomes. Perhaps the most common experimental research design is the pretest, posttest, control group design. If a program is important enough to collect experimental design data, the data deserve more sophisticated treatment as well, to help answer more definitively important questions. For instance, a common FLE question, beyond one of general program impact, is, "For whom is the program most effective?" Analyses such as multivariate analysis of variance (MANOVA) can help answer that question.

Stage 5: Dissemination

Imagine this: You have developed a program for families with widespread community support. You have field tested it with the families for whom it was intended and have made some adjustments in the program and how you carry it out, as a result of the candid input from program participants and staff. You have taken the revised program, continued to make refinements, and have subjected it to an ultimate test: an evaluation using an experimental design. Findings from your evaluation suggest that the program successfully meets change objectives and is significantly reducing some risk factors among parents (e.g., harsh discipline strategies, lack of social support) and significantly increasing protective factors (e.g., use of affirming, loving messages with youngsters, more shared parenting). Your program is a success, and you feel justifiably proud of the effort you and your coalition have made with families in your community. You are now ready to take your program forward to the masses, to export it and what you have learned to other communities, so that your efforts might strengthen families in those communities as well.

The goal of the dissemination stage is the widespread adoption of the program. Programs beginning in one area expand to other communities and often become institutionalized and part of community culture. Dissemination involves identifying potential users of the program, promoting the program (through publications and other targeted venues; more about promotion and marketing will be discussed in Chapter 17), publishing results of evaluation studies in scholarly journals, and providing technical assistance to those interested in adopting the program.

Table 2.2 summarizes the steps we have discussed.

TABLE 2.2   A Comprehensive Framework for Designing Family Life Prevention Programs

Stage 1: Problem Analysis

Identify Problem/Establish Overall Program Goal

Program goal should clarify the audience (e.g., The ABC program is designed to help *single parents* identify and build upon their parenting strengths, enhancing their sense of competence as a parent.)

Consult the Scholarly Literature

Identify current theories/research addressing the problem/goal

Risk factors/protective factors, predictors of positive outcomes, etc.

Extract the "teachable" ideas/principles from theories/research, those that are practical/useful in addressing the problem. Examples:

"The more authoritative a parent is, the better off their children will be as they grow."

"The more married couples accurately read one another's love language, the better the marriage."

"Risks for divorce are reduced when couples learn to handle conflict and disagreements effectively."

Form a Coalition of Stakeholders Who Work Together to Address the Problem

Educate coalition members on current theory and research addressing the problem

Stage 2: Program Design

Consult Target Group—Assess Their Needs

Assess needs using focus groups, interviews, questionnaires, existing data, etc.

Felt, ascribed (those you discern because of your specialized knowledge), and future needs (e.g., what do couples preparing for marriage need to know?)

Involve the target audience in program design, planning, and implementation
Seek their input at every stage

Select Change Objectives

Knowledge, attitudes, behaviors/skills, and aspirations targeted for change
Tied to promoting the positive outcomes predicted by the theories and research and desired by the target audience

(Continued)

Stated in specific, action-oriented terms (e.g., what will participants be able to do as a result of the program?)

Select Evaluation Tools

Formative and summative

Instruments directly tied to program objectives

Select Change Methods

Tied to objectives—a skills objective needs a skill development method

Review existing programs to find "best practices"

Use adult learner methods focused on active learning—buzz groups, role-playing, discussion groups, skill practice, etc.

Give attention to learning styles, sensory modalities, and developmental needs/abilities

Decide Program Extensiveness

Selectiveness: Universal (y'all come), selective (audience exhibiting risk factors), or indicated (audience exhibiting negative outcomes)

Breadth: Range of change objectives (e.g., comprehensive, in terms of level of human ecology, or more focused on one or two levels)

Length: Shorter or longer? Dosage and intensity

Design Recruitment/Retention Strategy

Ask the target audience what is best way to recruit and retain an audience

Marketing plan

Tailor Program Content and Delivery

Tailored to needs of audience/community; appropriately timed; developmentally appropriate

Sensitive to cultural, ethnic, and other forms of diversity; sociocultural relevance

Implementation strategies, based on target audience needs and focus group findings, to maximize participation

Recruitment meetings

Teachers of same culture

Home visits

Stage 3: Pilot Testing

Implement Program

Recruitment and Retention Evaluation

Is it working? Are people coming and staying or returning?

Process Evaluation

Project quality control

Formative Evaluation

Program Revision

Stage 4: Advanced Testing

Select Experimental Design

Implement Program

Summative Evaluation

Analyze Data

Refine Program

Stage 5: Dissemination

Widespread Adoption of Program

SOURCE: Adapted from Dumka, Roosa, Michaels, and Suh (1995); Bogenschneider (1996); Hughes (1994); and Small, Cooney, and O'Connor (2009).

ASSESSING ELEMENTS OF PROGRAM QUALITY ● IN EXISTING PROGRAMS

The integrated framework shows us step by step how to develop a comprehensive FLE program. It also tells us what to look for in quality FLE programs and suggests a framework to assess ways an FLE resource could be improved. On the basis of his parsimonious four-step program development model, Hughes (1994) created an assessment tool to use as a means of evaluating the extent to which elements of effectiveness occur in existing programs. While not all of the elements above are evaluated by this tool, many are. You may want to use it to evaluate existing resources and identify areas needing improvement. See Appendix C for the Family Life Education Program Resource Review Form.

CHARACTERISTICS OF STRONG, SUSTAINABLE ● FAMILY LIFE EDUCATION PROGRAMS

As important as it is to have strong program curricula consisting of a strong theory and research base, clear goals and objectives, methods consistent with objectives, attention to diverse audiences, a guide for implementation, and evaluation tools tied to the objectives, program curricula are only part of successful, sustainable FLE programs. Many elements of quality comprehensive programs transcend specific curricula. Drawing on the published literature and experiences of leading community-based programs, Lee, Mancini, Miles, and Marek (1996) identified eight characteristics of quality community-based programs. These characteristics are important to keep in mind as you seek to build a comprehensive FLE program in a community that will stand the test of time. Some of these characteristics are also reiterations and extensions of important elements found in quality community-based FLE curricula.

1. Successful community programs are community based and carried out in collaboration with many community partners.

Successful programs emerge from the needs of the community rather than from the desires of outsiders. Instead of "one size fits all," these programs are flexibly implemented and adapt to community needs. They embed themselves in the local community, becoming part of a network of supportive services carried out by collaborative professionals and volunteers (Lee et al., 1996). This collaborative approach minimizes turf issues, brings more resources to bear on a community issue, maximizes effectiveness in program planning and implementation, and increases the likelihood a program will stand the test of time (Duncan et al., 2003).

2. Successful community programs are comprehensive in scope, based on an ecological or systems view of individuals, families, and communities.

The best programs operate at many levels (e.g., individual, family, and community) and incorporate not only specific family-based programs but efforts to strengthen the community context as well (Lee et al., 1996). Clientele are viewed as individuals within families within communities, and programs are designed accordingly. Successful, long-lasting prevention results are most often the result of consistent, multilevel, multifaceted efforts. For instance, in addition to parenting skills, a comprehensive "Parenting Teens" program might also provide "peer mentoring" to encourage prosocial teen activity, newsletters for parents and other caring adults who work with teens, and media messages promoting positive parent-teen relationships. Successful efforts at adolescent drug abuse prevention would seek to minimize or eliminate risk factors occurring at the individual level (e.g., low self-efficacy), the family level (e.g., uninvolved parenting), and the peer group level (e.g., peers who use drugs) as well as enhance protective factors at the same levels (individual: religious commitment; family: involved parenting; peer: peers who are non-drug users). Likewise, during program design stages, program developers would include persons in their task forces representing different levels of the social ecology, including parents, youth, school personnel, and other adults who have an interest in the development of youth. Many researchers report that such an approach is critical to the success of prevention programs (Lee et al., 1996).

3. Successful community programs are inclusive of program participants in program planning, delivery, and evaluation.

Successful programs involve participants at every level of program development, from predesign stages to implementation and evaluation. Even if programs are employed in different areas, clientele from those specific communities are involved so that the program is responsive to local needs. In addition, there is what Lee et al. (1996) refer to as an "integrative approach" to program planning. Local leaders are identified and trained, and local participants are fully involved in the planning and decision making regarding a program or its policies, philosophy, or procedures.

4. Successful community programs are preventive in nature through successfully interfacing service and education, as well as recognizing and building on participants' strengths to enhance skills.

Successful programs designed to foster resiliency and limit risks among children, youth, and families accomplish their goals through preventive, empowering means rather than through remediation. Thus, these programs aim to stop problem behaviors before they get started, often as early intervention (Lee et al., 1996). In addition, some of these programs focus on helping clientele identify and build upon strengths they already have.

5. Successful community programs are developmentally appropriate and based on current research.

Successful programs are based on best practice models of effective programming noted in the scholarly literature and on the specific needs of their communities. The research comprises community needs assessments, the existing scholarly literature, and the best strategies for reaching a target audience. Needs assessments may include existing data already available (e.g., state child abuse data) as well as new data collected from the target audience to refine an understanding of the issue for a specific community population, as well as how to best reach them.

Such programs often follow a community-university partnership model, where the community presents the issue in a unified context and university-based researchers provide the expertise of the scientific literature to address the community need.

6. Successful community programs are accessible to participants with a mix of program deliveries based on participant needs.

To be effective, FLE programs must be accessible to their intended audience (Lee et al., 1996). Clientele may face significant barriers that prevent them from attending programs located at community centers or other venues. Increasing accessibility may mean that the program is held in small groups or one-on-one in the homes of clientele. For many clientele, location may be a critical factor as well as its perceived safety, ease of access via public transportation, and free parking nearby.

Other aspects of accessibility are also important. Successful programs consider language needs, literacy rate, and educational level of the participants and then gear the material accordingly (Lee et al., 1996). For example, instructional classes might be offered in small groups or one-on-one, as needed, allowing for more individualized attention and for materials to be more effectively adapted to individual participant needs. Other strategies include keeping material simple and to the point, using a variety of hands-on activities, and conducting support groups in and out of a learning setting. Successful programs also use existing services as a means to achieve their ends, such as community forums, newsletters, conferences, and workshops.

7. Successful community programs are accountable to stakeholders and are able to demonstrate positive outcomes in participants and community environments.

To be sustained, comprehensive community-based programs need to demonstrate some defensible measure of effectiveness. They need to be able to show stakeholders that the results achieved have been worth the investment in time and money. Such programs incorporate an ongoing evaluation of what works, what does not work, and what changes need to be made to improve services to clientele and the community. These data are often both quantitative (e.g., statistics showing improvement in parenting competence attributed to a parenting course) and qualitative in nature (success stories of family budgeting principles in practice) and report data not only from program participants but also from staff, partners/collaborators, and stakeholders.

8. Successful community programs have leaders with vision.

This final characteristic of strong, sustainable programs has more to do with leadership than with program substance. Leaders of these programs are, according to Lee et al. (1996),

> able to think through an organization's mission and establish it clearly and visibly. They serve as models, symbolizing a group's unity and identity. They view themselves as ultimately responsible and therefore surround themselves with strong associates and subordinates who function ably and independently and whose development they encourage. They function in a team relationship. Importantly they demonstrate long range vision, showing an ability to think beyond the day's crises, beyond the quarter. They are able to reach and influence constituents beyond their jurisdictions. They think in terms of renewal, seeking the revisions of process and structure by an ever-changing reality. (pp. 13–14)

These leaders offer strong and committed leadership, keeping the program's vision in front of decision makers over years, being consistent with service at various sites, facilitating partnerships and ongoing community collaboration, bringing key partners together to renew and articulate program visions and strategies, and developing consensus. These eight principles are summarized in Table 2.3.

Table 2.3   Elements of Strong, Sustainable, Comprehensive Programs

Successful community programs are community based and carried out in collaboration with many community partners.

Successful community programs are comprehensive in scope, based on an ecological or systems view of individuals, families, and communities.

Successful community programs are inclusive of program participants in program planning, delivery, and evaluation.

Successful community programs are preventive in nature through successfully interfacing service and education, as well as recognizing and building on participants' strengths to enhance skills.

Successful community programs are developmentally appropriate and based on current research.

Successful community programs are accessible to participants with a mix of program deliveries based on participant needs.

Successful community programs are accountable to stakeholders and are able to demonstrate positive outcomes in participants and community environments.

Successful community programs have leaders with vision.

SOURCE: Lee, Mancini, Miles, and Marek (1996).

● CONCLUSION

It is important for prevention-oriented family life educators to ground their work in a scientific framework of program design. This chapter has presented a practical how-to framework for the design of comprehensive FLE programs. Family life educators can use these guidelines to help them develop their own resources and assess or improve the quality of existing resources. FLE programs constructed with careful and appropriate attention to these elements of quality design, implementation, and evaluation are likely to serve FLE audiences better than those that do not and certainly improve FLE practice. In addition, when family life educators seek to establish comprehensive community-based programs that transcend curricula, they are wise to model programs that use the eight characteristics of sustainable programs discussed in this chapter.

The following activities can help you translate these ideas into your own program development efforts.

● EXPLORATIONS

1. Identify a problem topic and create a rough outline of your program strategy in Stage 1 and Stage 2 of the framework. Try it out with topics of widespread importance in communities, such as strengthening single parents, preventing adolescent drug use, preparing for remarriage, and managing stress and crisis in families.

2. Do an inventory of existing family life programs. Identify the levels of prevention at which they operate (primary, secondary, and tertiary) and how extensive they are (universal, selective, or indicated).

3. The authors recommend analyzing the problem through exploring related research and theory prior to consulting the target group to assess their needs. What are some advantages and disadvantages of doing this? How can the disadvantages be addressed?

4. Identify an FLE resource (curricula, website, etc.) and, using the review form provided in Appendix C, do a "quality elements" assessment. On the basis of this evaluation, discuss whether you would use the resource and how you would improve it. Use the review form as a checklist for ensuring the quality of your own resources.

5. Locate and investigate comprehensive FLE programs in your community. Evaluate these programs against the eight characteristics of strong, sustainable programs discussed in this chapter. Find out how long the programs have existed. Do the longer lasting ones have more of the characteristics?

CHAPTER 3

PRINCIPLES OF PROGRAM EVALUATION

EVALUATION AS FRIEND AND FOE: ●
STEREOTYPES AND OPPORTUNITIES

Family life educators who enjoy program evaluation are rare birds. Evaluation is generally viewed as a necessary evil. It requires time, provides sobering and often disappointing feedback, is difficult to design, and may seem impossible to analyze. Evaluation arouses deep dread in most family life educators. But it is required by most funders.

There is another way of thinking about evaluation. It can be seen as a process for gathering information to make your program stronger. It can provide vital data about what parts of the program are working well and which need tweaking. It can provide data that justify further funding. It can provide priceless information about how to match program options to program clients. According to this view, evaluation is our friend.

Evaluation is a systematic gathering of information that can be used to inform good decisions. It is much more than pretests and posttests, numbers and charts. In this chapter, you will be introduced to many different ways of getting and using information to strengthen your programs.

● ESTABLISHING THE TARGET: VISION AND GOALS

A respected parenting program funded by the Alabama Children's Trust Fund took part in the field test of a new evaluation instrument. The instrument was designed to measure a broad array of outcomes that are common in parenting programs. It was used with program participants both before the program began and again at the conclusion of the program. The instruments were sent for analyses, and a report was returned to the program site.

When the program director received the report, she called the instrument developers in a panic. "Your report shows that program participants only had significant improvement on 49% of the variables. That is failure by any standard! Are we really that bad?"

There is no simple answer to that question. The fact is that it depends. If the 49% of the variables on which there were significant changes are the variables that are important to the program leaders, then they are a remarkable success. If, in contrast, most of the variables of interest for the program are a part of the 51% in which there was no significant change, then the program leaders have cause for serious reflection. There simply is no way to interpret any outcome without having goals and objectives as a standard.

Even goals and objectives should be embedded in a larger picture of the desired outcome. That larger picture might be called a vision. One of the characteristics of effective program leaders is that they can articulate the big picture of their program efforts (Lee et al., 1996).

● DEVELOPING A VISION

Vision statements are shared expressions of a program staff. The vision describes what they want the program to accomplish by focusing on the end result. A shared vision is essentially the answer to the question, "What do we want to create?"

Vision statements generally have the qualities of being lofty, big picture, and ambitious. They are also dynamic, needing revisiting and renewal periodically. When people share a vision, they are connected by a common aspiration. It can focus the energy and guide the decisions of the organization.

The meaningful vision statements are created by persons who have a stake in the program, such as program staff, partners, and recipients of services. Vision statements focus and express the shared hopes and dreams for the program.

Imagine gathering all the people together who are involved in delivering a program, inviting them to spend a morning around a conference table sharing how they would like the community to be different as a result of their program over time. Do you think the group would quickly converge on a common vision?

Experience suggests otherwise. When people united in a common cause begin to share their vision with each other, there are often a lot of surprises. Each person has a very different vision. While this person may think that the group is doing what they are doing "in order to help people in our community break the cycle of poverty," a colleague involved in the same program may see the central purpose as "arming citizens with a clear sense of purpose." Another person may see the core cause as "strengthening family bonds in our community."

Those visions are not necessarily incompatible. Each person in a work group may be driven by a personal vision that is different from that of anyone else in the group. Such diversity can enrich both collegiality and the quality of work.

The differences in vision can also lead to meaningful discussions about the core purposes that unite the work group. In the course of the discussions, each person is likely to enlarge and enrich his or her vision. As the group converges on core purposes, members will be better able to work in unified support of those purposes. Those core purposes can inform program activity and guide evaluation efforts.

Just a note of caution: Any attempt to come up with a single statement of vision for which all members of the group will express complete support will often be difficult. The discussion may be more important than a totally unified statement. The reasonable goal for this vision discussion is to better understand each other and to identify some common purposes.

One Montana family program for promoting self-sufficiency gathered together the program staff, state and local collaborators, and Extension administrators for a "visioning and strategic planning" meeting. Each invitee was encouraged to develop his or her own vision statement prior to attending the meeting. At the meeting, each person shared his or her statement in small groups and recorded their shared elements. In the large group, elements of the visions were shared. The group worked together to form a statement that represented the shared vision. It read, "Supportive Montana communities that empower families to develop skills, knowledge, and competencies necessary for managing family resources and progressing toward a self-supporting lifestyle."

Another vision statement might say, "Our vision of our community is a place where parents show love and care for their children." Elements of the

Administration for Children and Families (ACF) vision statement (which ACF calls a mission statement) include the following: "Families and individuals empowered to increase their own economic independence and productivity; strong, healthy, supportive communities that have a positive impact on the quality of life and the development of children" (Administration for Children and Families, n.d.).

● GETTING SPECIFIC: PROGRAM GOALS AND OBJECTIVES

With some common vision in hand, the process can move to the next stage of specificity: program goals and objectives. We first discussed program goals and objectives generally in Chapter 2. We extend that discussion here and in the context of creating an evaluation plan.

Goals are one step more specific than vision. They express general purposes for specific programs. For example, a community program may have as its vision a community where parents are closer to their children. A goal in that program might be to teach the concept and use of languages of love to program participants. An objective is the most specific level of intent. For a program such as the one described, the objective might be that every parent who takes part in the program will be able to name three languages of love and identify the one or combination that best helps him or her connect with each child in the family.

Objectives are the place where our thinking must get most clear and specific. It is an unusual person who finds the writing of objectives to be fun. The creation of objectives requires very careful thinking yet allows us to design and assess more effective programs.

Maybe the process is made more unpleasant when we require that objectives fit some preestablished pattern. The objectives only exist to make program delivery and evaluation more in alignment with the program goals and ultimate program vision.

A good objective is clearly tied to the goal, should be specific enough to be measured, and usually describes some action or knowledge that a participant would gain by participation in the program. Some objectives specify an exact level of performance: "Participants will report involvement in daily renewal rituals (yoga, exercise, or meditation) for at least 15 minutes per day at least 4 days per week." Such exactness is important for programs that have both well-developed programs and well-developed measures.

Another dimension to objectives is the time span of effects. The more immediate effects of programs are called outcomes. The long-term effects are called impacts. For example, an outcome objective might be that couples involved in a program commit to set aside time every week for enjoyable activities together. The impact might be that participants report feeling closer to their partners 1 year after the completion of the program.

AN EXAMPLE OF AN EVALUATION FRAMEWORK • IN PARENTING EDUCATION

One example of the development of program goals and objectives is in the area of parenting. The Cooperative Extension System has been interested in supporting parenting education for many years. In 1994, four Extension specialists (Smith et al., 1994) worked together to create the National Extension Parent Education Model (NEPEM), which defined six categories of vital parenting behavior. The document also included sample objectives. But there was still a substantial distance between coming up with objectives and having an effective evaluation system.

It was not until 2002 that a group of Extension leaders attempted to develop more detail as part of the Evaluation and Accountability Systems for Extension (EASE). A group of specialists took the six categories from NEPEM and developed both objectives and measures. While a comprehensive evaluation system would provide many objectives related to each critical parenting practice and each objective could have many different evaluation questions, the evaluation questions in this example are suggestive of an evaluation framework in three areas of the national parenting model.

Table 3.1 shows some representative impacts, objectives, and evaluation items. There are dozens of meaningful objectives that might be written in each vital area of parenting. For each objective, many different items could be written to evaluate the accomplishment of the objectives.

Matching the Parts

Some of these objectives and some of the evaluations items will not be suitable for some audiences. That is a vital point. The objectives must match the program mission. The evaluation items must match the objectives. And the objectives must be suitable for the specific audience in reading level and appropriateness of the target behavior.

Of course there is another vital match: The program with all its instructional activities should match the objectives and the evaluation. If a program sets its objectives to build stress techniques but instead teaches car repair and, for evaluation, measures height and weight of participants, the

TABLE 3.1   Examples of Parenting Impacts, Goals, Objectives, and Evaluation Items

Impact: Parents will provide appropriate nurturance and guidance to their children and youth, resulting in positive development and achievement.

Impact A (NEPEM *Care for Self* dimension): Parents will become more effective in caring for self.

Goal A: Parents report they are managing personal and family stress (more) effectively.

Objective A1. Parents will increase their awareness of exercise as a means of dealing with stress.

Sample measurement item:		*Never*			*Always*	
I exercise to lower stress.		1	2	3	4	5

Objective A2. Parents will develop awareness of their need to take time out and to get control of their own feelings.

Sample measurement item:		*Never*			*Always*	
When I get upset with my child, I take a minute to calm down before I deal with him or her.		1	2	3	4	5

Objective A3. Parents will know some stress reduction techniques (i.e., getting organized, changing attitudes or expectations, changing environments or people who you associate with, limiting the number of things on your to-do list, setting priorities, physical exercise, humor).

Sample measurement item:		*Never*			*Always*	
I have some things I do to help me calm down when I feel myself getting angry like going for a walk, listening to music, or calling a friend.		1	2	3	4	5

Objective A4. Parents will know techniques to support themselves and to cope effectively in times of personal difficulty (e.g., calling a friend and letting off steam, positive self-talk, hot bath, take or plan a vacation, call crisis center).

Sample measurement item:		*Never*			*Always*	
I know what to do or whom to call when I feel like I can't take it anymore.		1	2	3	4	5

Impact B (NEPEM *Guide* dimension): Parents use appropriate positive discipline techniques.

Goal B1: Parents apply their knowledge of child development to support their child's developmental progress—framing choices, setting limits, and monitoring their child's activities appropriately.

Objective B1. Parents will increase the use of positive strategies for learning self-control such as allowing their child to make decisions and avoiding force.

Sample measurement item:	*Never*			*Always*	
I let my child make his or her own choices whenever possible.	1	2	3	4	5

Objective B2. Parents will learn characteristics of effective discipline, including being positive, teaching, and giving choices.

Sample measurement item:	*Never*			*Always*	
Even though I must sometimes correct my child's behavior, I show lots of love to him or her.	1	2	3	4	5

Objective B3. Parents will increase their use of praise, encouragement, and other supportive language.

Sample measurement item:	*Strongly Disagree*			*Strongly Agree*	
I try to notice and encourage the good things my child does.	1	2	3	4	5

Objective B4. Parents will decrease scolding, punishment, and harsh, punitive, and controlling parenting behaviors.

Sample measurement item:	*Strongly Disagree*			*Strongly Agree*	
I say far more positive than negative things to my child now than before this class.	1	2	3	4	5

Objective B5. Parents will increase their knowledge of different ways to help their child develop responsibility and use these techniques, such as allowing their child to make decisions, not being overly intrusive, allowing their child to experience the world as a lawful place, and allowing their child to suffer the consequences for his or her actions in order to help the child understand the relationship between actions and consequences.

Sample measurement item:	*Strongly Disagree*			*Strongly Agree*	
I believe that letting my child make many little decisions on his or her own is a good way to teach responsibility and self-control.	1	2	3	4	5

(Continued)

TABLE 3.1 (Continued)

Impact C (NEPEM *Nurture* dimension): Parents show affection and nurturance to their child.

Goal C1: Parents listen and attend to their child's feelings and ideas.

Objective C1.1. Parents will know that talking with a child is very important to help the child feel significant as well as to help the child develop language, intellectual, and social skills.

Sample measurement item:	Strongly Disagree			Strongly Agree	
My child learns a lot from something as simple as talking to me.	1	2	3	4	5

Objective C1.2. Parents will know that talking with a child is very important to help the child feel significant as well as to help the child develop language, intellectual, and social skills.

Sample measurement item:	Never			Always	
I take time to just talk pleasantly with my child.	1	2	3	4	5

Objective C1.3. Parents will increase their knowledge and use of the varying techniques for providing encouragement/nurturance through both verbal and nonverbal means.

Sample measurement item:	Strongly Disagree			Strongly Agree	
I have learned new ways to encourage and praise my child in the last few weeks.	1	2	3	4	5

Goal C2: Parents show love and caring for their child.

Objective C2.1. Parents will know that praise should be sincere.

Sample measurement item:	Never			Always	
I tell my child about the good things I see in him or her.	1	2	3	4	5

Objective C2.2. Parents will learn to be sensitive to the ways their child gets the message of parental love, including taking time to do things that their child loves and taking time to understand their child's feelings.

Sample measurement item:	Never			Always	
I try to show love to my child in the way that works best for him or her.	1	2	3	4	5

resulting data will be hard to interpret. They will tell us almost nothing about the effectiveness of the program—unless we decide that weight loss is our real program objective. (The theoretical connection between car repair and weight loss will still require attention.)

The matches might be illustrated as follows:

Vision——Goals——Objectives——Instructional activities——Evaluation measures

When all of these program elements are in alignment, greater gains and more meaningful data are more likely.

DEFINING THE KIND OF INFORMATION NEEDED: ● THE EVALUATION QUESTIONS

There are many reasons to gather evaluation data, including assessment of participant progress, guiding program decisions, refining program processes, specifying effective program elements, establishing the merit of specific viewpoints, or maximizing program effects (see J. L. Herman, Morris, & Fitz-Gibbon, 1987, for more details on each of these purposes). When we merely do evaluation because it is expected or because it is considered good form, it is not likely to have the benefits that may accrue when we carefully preconsider what data we need and how we expect it to be used.

Common questions that can guide evaluation include the following:

1. What are the ways in which participants are prepared to function better in their family life as a result of our program? (attitudes, knowledge, skills)

2. In what ways do the participants actually function better as a result of our program? (behavior)

3. What elements or combination of elements have the greatest impact?

4. What needs related to program objectives remain unaddressed despite program efforts?

5. What evidence do we have that our program satisfies the objectives of our funders?

These questions can lead to the creation of evaluation objectives. Some scholars (Dunnagan, Duncan, & Paul, 2000) recommend simply changing the phrasing of program objectives to make them evaluation objectives. For example, if your program goal is to "help enhance couple satisfaction with marriage," one objective might be the following: *Significantly increase levels of marital satisfaction as a result of the program.* One way to write it as an evaluation objective would be, *"Determine whether participation in the program significantly increases reported couple satisfaction."*

● THE FIVE-TIERED APPROACH TO PROGRAM EVALUATION

Meaningful answers to evaluation questions are not found readily. In fact, Francine Jacobs (1988) has argued that many discouraging outcomes in evaluation are not necessarily evidence of inadequate programs; the outcomes may be evidence that we have asked the wrong questions at the wrong time. When we apply comprehensive outcome measures to still-developing programs, we should not be surprised that we have disappointing results. Jacobs suggests that evaluation should grow with the program. In fact, she describes five tiers of evaluation. This model incorporates needs assessment, formative evaluation, and summative evaluation.

In the first level of evaluation, called the preimplementation tier, a community needs assessment is conducted to first establish fit between a community need and a proposed program. While often not thought of as a part of evaluation, it puts all program efforts in the larger context.

There are many sources of data for such a needs assessment. Sociodemographic data may indicate community problems and risks in the program area. Local press coverage can provide an indication of community awareness and concern. Interviews with community leaders (social service agencies, faith communities, business managers, etc.) can provide vital information on both the problems and previous efforts to address them. In some cases, it may be helpful to conduct a community survey. For example, some communities have surveyed both youth and parents about youth challenges (Olson, Goddard, Solheim, & Sandt, 2004) to better target youth-serving interventions.

The second level of evaluation, the accountability tier, involves "the systematic collection of client-specific and service-utilization data" (Jacobs, 1988, p. 54), answering the question, "Who is getting what services?" Data include not only the number of people served but their characteristics. As a result, it may be possible to determine the extent to which the program's target audience is being served with the intended intervention. This level may not seem like serious evaluation in the traditional sense. Yet such data are essential for understanding the progress of the organization toward its goals. For a beginning program, this may be some of the most helpful feedback that can be obtained.

A vital part of all evaluation is the gathering of "use" information from program personnel. Effective evaluation includes asking instructors and participants about the pattern of service delivery and client participation. It is possible, for example, that program objectives are not being met simply because the program is offered at the wrong time of day or in the wrong location. This is not information that will readily emerge from a paper-and-pencil test given to those who do attend the program.

Some (Thomas, Schvaneveldt, & Young, 1993) have argued that Jacobs (1988) may emphasize the ways that programs affect participants and neglect the ways in which program participants affect the program. Programs are certainly affected by the participants, including in ways that may have an enduring impact on programs and delivery. It can be useful to gather data about the ways that the program has adjusted to accommodate participants.

On the third level, the program clarification tier, program staff and participants provide feedback on how to improve program content and delivery. This level includes close scrutiny of program goals and objectives. The essential question is, "How can we do a better job serving our clients?" (Jacobs, 1988, p. 57). Both staff and participant feedback are essential to answering this question.

Client satisfaction data are valuable on this level. It is often helpful to gather data not only from active program participants but also from those who registered but dropped out of active participation. Such interviews may yield important clues for greater effectiveness. For example, sensitive inquiry may determine that the current, middle-class, college-educated teacher is not the right person to deliver this program for limited-resource, young, Hispanic mothers. There may be language and cultural barriers that need to be addressed.

Evaluation at Levels 2 and 3 is formative in nature. We want to see who is participating in a program and how they are experiencing it. Formative evaluation data are very important to help guide your efforts toward better service to clientele. As pointed out by Small (1990), "Good formative evaluation can provide the type of information that will lead to program improvement and ultimately greater program impact if and when an outcome evaluation is conducted" (p. 133).

At Level 4, the progress-toward-objectives tier, more mature programs (ostensibly that have had favorable formative reviews) give careful attention to outcomes, including the questions, "Which participants achieved which of these proximate objectives? Are there differential program effects based on participants' ages, races, or opinions?" (Jacobs, 1988, p. 59). Thus,

Level 4 represents a distinct shift from formative evaluation to summative evaluation. This intensity of evaluation is suitable for programs that "are longer lived, more experienced, and relatively secure financially" (Jacobs, 1988, p. 59). While these are the activities that most people think of as standard evaluation activities, such intensive evaluation requires greater program maturity than most programs have.

Level 4 evaluations will often require the help of professional evaluators or others with specialized knowledge of evaluation. Measures may include items such as those listed above in the discussion of EASE. Careful measurement and statistical analysis can provide evidence that program clients are making progress toward stated program objectives.

Jacobs (1988) makes the point that, while standard measures may be an important part of the evaluation, customized measures that tap the unique character of the program are essential.

The final level, the program impact tier, is the most rigorous. It often entails random assignment of participants to treatment and delayed treatment groups, longitudinal data collection, and complex analyses. In evaluation-intensive funded projects, as much as 30% to 40% of the total budget may be allocated to evaluation activities. Such investment of resources can support careful, exacting analyses with persuasive conclusions. Table 3.2 summarizes the Jacobs (1988) model.

TABLE 3.2   Summary of Jacobs's (1988) Five-Tiered Model of Evaluation

Tier/Level	Purpose	Tasks
Tier 1 Preimplementation	Establish fit between community need and program	1. Conduct a community needs assessment 2. Revise program plans and focus based on needs assessment data
Tier 2 Accountability	Determine who is getting the program and if it is reaching the intended audience	1. Accurately determine the number and characteristics of people served, such as through examining sociodemographic data from program surveys
Tier 3 Program Clarification	Gather feedback from program staff and participants on how to improve program content and delivery	1. Collect client satisfaction data 2. Collect staff data on program fidelity, fit of processes with goals and objectives, needed adjustments

Tier 4 Progress Toward Objectives	Document program effectiveness and short-term outcomes	1. Collect outcome data using reliable measures tied to goals and objectives
		2. Do data analysis that shows the extent to which outcomes are being achieved, at the short term
Tier 5 Program Impact	Document program effectiveness and long-term outcomes Recommend model programs for widespread dissemination	1. Collect sophisticated data analysis to show effectiveness that uses random assignment, longitudinal data collection, and complex analyses

It is clear that this is not the right level of evaluation for a young, still developing program. It is no more reasonable to ask a toddler to wear adult shoes than it is to ask a developing program to do effective, comprehensive outcome evaluation. McCall and Green (2004) argue that, in our rush for such rigorous testing, we may have undervalued other methods of evaluating programs.

One of the commonest problems in the evaluation of family life education (FLE) may be placing evaluation burdens on programs that are not prepared to support them. Evaluation should be matched to the program. It is also wise to educate funders and other stakeholders to expect the kind of evaluation that is appropriate for the maturity of the program.

Most programs fail to get enough information from program staff. Careful scrutiny of the delivery process may include not only staff discussions but also observations of teaching or service delivery by fellow staff members.

THE LOGIC MODEL APPROACH TO EVALUATION ●

Jacobs's (1988) five-tiered model of evaluation sensitizes program developers to the need to match evaluation efforts to the maturity of the program. It encourages program evaluators to gather and use different kinds of data. It also provides a philosophical context for the enterprise of evaluation. It does not provide a step-by-step process for evaluation.

One popular method for conceptualizing program and evaluation efforts is the development of a logic model. Logic models were first developed by Edward Suchman (1968) and have become increasingly popular.

Logic models commonly begin with a description of the situation and priorities. The situation can result from an effective needs assessment. Priorities are related to the vision of the program. This section of the logic model may also include a list of stakeholders and a summary of research or best practices related to the identified problem.

The next step in the model is to specify inputs. What are the human, financial, material, and knowledge resources that can be applied to the problem?

Next are outputs that are divided into activities and participants. What are the processes that will be used to effect change? Will the program use newsletters, group meetings, conferences, home visitation, or some other process? Related to participants, who will take part, what agencies will be involved, who are the customers of services?

Next are the outcomes or impacts divided into short term, medium term, and long term. Clearly, the short-term results are easiest to measure. What are the changes in knowledge, attitudes, skills, and aspirations (Rockwell & Bennett, 2004)? Medium-term results such as changes in behavior or social policy are generally more difficult to measure. Long-term impacts include changes in communities such as lowered divorce rates or teen pregnancy. They are clearly the most difficult to impact and to measure. Since there are many factors outside those affected by the program, it is especially difficult to establish that a specific program had a societal impact. Such forces are labeled external factors in some logic models.

Undergirding the other elements of the logic model are assumptions. Many programs struggle under a load of unchecked assumptions. For example, the assumption that raising self-esteem will remedy a wide range of social problems has wide appeal and popular support. Unfortunately, it has not been supported by research (Kohn, 1994; Mecca, Smelser, & Vasconcellos, 1989).

Logic models are one way of organizing the various elements of a program. They provide a framework for organizing thinking and planning evaluation. See Table 3.3 as an example of how one project used a logic model to map out its evaluation process for one objective. For an effective and more detailed introduction to logic models, consult the University of Wisconsin website at http://www.uwex.edu/ces/lmcourse/#.

TABLE 3.3   Logic Model for ACP/Centro Hispano Capacity Building Project

Community Outreach Infrastructure Plan

Input	Activities	Output	Short-Term Outcome (Learning)	Medium-Term Outcome (Action)	Long-Term Outcome (Capacity)
Contract a facilitator and planning team made up of representatives from key collaborative partners to research, design and put into practice an outreach infrastructure plan to mobilize community resources	Transform ad hoc steering committee to permanent planning team	Sustained committee membership who oversee project	Planning team understands its responsibilities	Team meets regularly to carry out its mobilization agenda	Strong leadership and consistent movement toward goals; project has public visibility
	Hold a series of team meetings to hammer out infrastructure for community outreach	Sustainable infrastructure model and organizational chart created	Collaborative partners clearly understand their roles, responsibilities, and relationship to the initiative and to one another	Collaborative partners carry out their roles and responsibilities	Sustainable infrastructure that supports healthy marriage is in place in the Hispanic community
	Review action plan for healthy marriage with the permanent planning team	Action plan for the healthy marriage initiative reviewed, revised, and refocused	Action plan is used to track progress of the initiative at planning team meetings	Achievement of yearly action plan goals	Achievement of multiyear action plan goals and objectives

Objective: To create an outreach infrastructure that will increase the capacity of our collaborative network to promote stable and healthy marriages and families in the local Hispanic community.

INNOVATIONS IN EVALUATION ●

Transformative Learning

Sometimes we think of professional evaluation as paper-and-pencil tests used to get quantitative measures of progress. But there are many other ways to get very useful information. One way is to invite program participants to meet with an interviewer (someone besides the educator or program delivery person) sometime after the completion of the program. Details of how this evaluation might be done are given in an article by Joy First and Wendy Way (1995). The interviewer can sit with those individuals who are willing to visit and ask questions such as the following:

- About how many times last week did you talk about the class, or anything you had discussed at the class, with friends or relatives?
- Do you talk to friends or relatives about any changes in your parenting as a result of the class? Can you tell me a story about those changes like you might tell a friend or relative?
- What are the most important things you feel you learned by going to the class? Can you remember any feelings you had when you were at the class?
- Has attending the class made parenting any easier? Has it made it more difficult? How?
- Can you tell me about any experiences that show how the class has affected your life—either parenting or in other ways?
- What is your best experience from the class? What is your worst experience?

(For First & Way's [1995] full list of interview questions, see p. 109 of their article.)

Such information gathered by a sensitive interviewer can provide very valuable information about the strengths of the program and ways to improve it. Themes can be tallied and presented in reports to stakeholders. Such information should also be reviewed by program staff in order to get fuller feedback than just quantitative data.

Results Mapping

Success stories have the ability to add flesh to evaluation bones. But success stories have been suspect for many reasons. They are not systematic and may capture more about the author's enthusiasm than the program's effects.

Barry Kibel (1999, n.d.) has developed a process of results mapping as a creative blend of quantitative and qualitative methods of evaluation. Results mapping is not held hostage to the limiting assumption of quantitative methods that a standard treatment has a significant effect on all recipients. This process allows portraits of different kinds of benefits from similar or customized services of an agency.

In results mapping, the storyteller explains "how the program first got involved with the client, what actions it subsequently initiated to promote client health and growth, and how the client responded to these actions" (Kibel, n.d., p. 12). The coding system even provides a results ladder with seven levels, from providing general information to attaining mastery level.

The following is an example of a story used in results mapping:

> Frances is a 78-year-old [who, after surgery] received warm lunches through the meals-on-wheels program operated by our senior center. This was her first contact in Cincinnati with adults her own age. The volunteer who delivered the meals encouraged her to visit the center after she got well. She arrived one day, stayed a few hours, then left. A week later she was back, and remained most of the day. She has been a regular ever since. For the past two months, she has been volunteering in the kitchen helping to prepare the meals we deliver. (Kibel, n.d., p. 9)

Posttest First Methods

The gold standard of evaluation has traditionally included a pretest and posttest. There are times when a posttest without a pretest may be the preferred way to evaluate. For example, parents under the supervision of a social service agency or mandated by a judge to participate in classes may not be willing to complete a pretest with candor. They may be suspicious of program personnel and the objectives of data collection.

There may also be problems with participants' interpretation of pretest items. Consider the case of a parenting class where improved empathic listening is a major objective. If we ask parents how well they are doing at empathic listening before they start the program, they may think they are doing very well. But as the program progresses and the parents learn more about what empathic listening involves, they may realize that they have much more to learn. They may give themselves a lower score on the posttest than the pretest even though they may actually be doing better. The lower score represents not diminished skill but heightened expectation. Participants' definition of empathic listening was changed by the program.

This phenomenon, called response shift bias, has been the subject of concern for many scholars (Cronbach & Furby, 1970; Doueck & Bondanza, 1990; Golembiewski, Billingsley, & Yeager, 1976; Howard & Daily, 1979; Howard, Ralph, et al., 1979; Howard, Schmeck, & Bray, 1979; E. A. R. Robinson, 1994;

Sprangers, 1989; Terborg, Howard, & Maxwell, 1980). While the most advanced evaluation requires sophisticated designs, the present point is that there are good reasons that a person may choose some design besides the traditional pretest and posttest.

Response shift bias should be less of a problem when parents are merely asked to describe their behavior. For example, if we ask how much time a parent spent with a child in a play activity requested by the child, the answer should be less vulnerable to definition bias than questions that ask the participants to evaluate their subjective performance. When the program participants' definition of a behavior is changed by the program, it may be wise to ask participants after the program how well they are doing at that behavior. After each such question, the participants could be asked how well they were doing on the same behavior at the beginning of the program. Alternatively, they could be asked to tell whether they are now doing worse, about the same, or better on that behavior. You can see how this approach avoids the problems associated with a changing definition of the behavior.

The following is a simple example of posttest and a retrospective pretest:

How well do you accept influence from your partner?

_____ Very poorly
_____ Poorly
_____ Well
_____ Very well

Before you began this program, how well did you accept influence from your partner?

_____ Very poorly
_____ Poorly
_____ Well
_____ Very well

The following is a simple example of posttest and change:
How good are you at listening to your child's feelings?

_____ Very poor
_____ Poor
_____ Good
_____ Very good

Compared to when you started this program, how good are you at listening to your child's feelings?

_____ Much worse

_____ Worse

_____ About the same

_____ Better

_____ Much better

USING EVALUATION DATA ●

Not only should evaluation be designed with its end use in mind, but also careful attention should be exercised to the amount, depth, and style of presentation based on its purpose. A presentation to a lunch meeting of the general membership of a civic club that has helped fund a program will probably be quite different from the written report submitted to a governmental agency. In the former case, the appropriate presentation may include a slide show describing the objectives and activities of the program, providing a success story or two, and a very few statistics, together with an invitation for continued support. In the latter case, a complete tabulation of data may be appropriate. Even though gains may not have been shown in some areas, the narrative may justify the finding with the statement that those were secondary or even incidental objectives. The case could be made for continued or expanded funding to better address those objectives.

If you or someone in your office has a reasonable sophistication in statistics, your report might be prepared by your staff. If the organization does not have such expertise in house, you might supplement the expertise you do have with consultants who have successful experience or with print resources (see L. L. Morris, Fitz-Gibbon, & Freeman, 1987).

CONCLUSION ●

There are many ways to evaluate. Complex and ambitious evaluations may not be the best method for gathering the information you need. As you apply your good sense and your knowledge of your program and the participants, you can design the evaluation program that meets your information needs and will be effective at communicating with important stakeholders.

● EXPLORATIONS

1. Visit a community program that delivers FLE. Ask about program objectives. Examine evaluation instruments that are used. Examine any reports on the program. Decide which tier of evaluation (Jacobs, 1988) is appropriate for the program's development and the level on which the program is trying to operate. Consider what information should be collected to facilitate the program objectives.

2. Create a flowchart of evaluation processes or logic model you would recommend to guide a community FLE program you would like to initiate.

3. On your own or with partners, design an evaluation plan for your program. Include the following:

Program vision (e.g., A marriage program might have as a vision the following: *Couples who love and care for each other*)

Program goal (e.g., A parenting program might have as a goal the following: *Enhance parent effectiveness with their children*)

Program objectives (e.g., A marriage program might have as an objective the following: *Significantly increase levels of marital satisfaction as a result of the program*)

Program objectives framed as evaluation questions or evaluation objectives (A parenting program evaluator may wish to know, "What is the effect of this program on parenting confidence?" Or, stated as an evaluation objective, "*Determine whether participation in the program significantly increases reported parenting confidence.*")

Sample evaluation items/measures (e.g., If you are measuring changes in marital satisfaction as a result of the program, what kind of tool would you need? If you are assessing client satisfaction with a parenting program, what would you ask?)

Discussion of the program design (e.g., Will you do a pretest-posttest or posttest-then-pretest? At what level or tier of evaluation will you operate that is appropriate for the age and stage of your program?)

Discussion of what data you will collect and how you will collect them (e.g., Will you collect quantitative and qualitative data? Will you collect formative or summative evaluation data? Will you collect them by survey or interview? In person or otherwise? Who will collect it?)

Include the formative and summative evaluation tools you plan to use, or samples of items from the tools. *Make sure the tools are directly tied to program goals and objectives.*

4. Conduct an evaluation of an FLE program using a formative evaluation tool with quantitative (like the items in Table 3.1) and qualitative items (open-ended items like the First and Way [1995] examples). Summarize the data and practice sharing the findings in different audience formats—more popularized to more scholarly.

PART III

IMPLEMENTING FAMILY LIFE EDUCATION PROGRAMS

CHAPTER 4

DESIGNING EFFECTIVE INSTRUCTION

If you were assigned to provide training or to prepare a publication on the subject of nurturing the developing child, how would you organize or structure your presentation? Are there rules or guides for making it effective?

Many of us would begin with a definition of *nurture*. We might then summarize what is known on the subject of nurturing children, including effective nurturing practices. If we are effective teachers, we will probably include stories to make our instruction more interesting and pertinent. And we will invite listeners or readers to apply the principles to their own situations. But is there something more than intuition and raw experience to guide this process?

The answer is yes. There is a substantial and growing science of instructional design. In fact, there is far more science behind instructional design than average family life educators need to know. So while family life educators do not need to become entirely focused on instructional design, they can be far more effective if they are familiar with many of the core principles.

This chapter is dedicated to discussing and applying two bodies of work by M. David Merrill, professor of instructional technology at Utah State University. His theory or framework is the centerpiece of this chapter because it is widely used in the instructional design industry, has been substantiated by research, and provides practical recommendations to those who are preparing instruction.

● COMPONENT DISPLAY THEORY

David Merrill (1983, 1994) has developed a system of instructional design that is called component display theory (CDT). There are parts of CDT that are beyond the purview of this chapter and most family life educators. However, Merrill's discussion of primary presentation forms can provide a very useful guide in the development of short presentations, extended training, and publications—any form of family life education (FLE).

If you are a person who understands tables readily, Table 4.1 will summarize the key elements of CDT in a simple form. If you do not readily comprehend the table, the text below should make the ideas clear without the table.

Let's use Merrill's (1983, 1994) CDT theory to guide the development of a lesson or publication on the topic named above: nurturing the developing child. A common way to begin would be to share a principle with the learners. Merrill calls this an expository generality (EG), which simply means that the teacher tells (called "expository" mode) some general idea, principle, concept, truth, or process (a generality). So the generality might be "Children are most likely to grow into compassionate, productive adults when they are cared for by people who are sensitive to their needs, are committed to them, and build close relationships with them."

TABLE 4.1	The Component Display Theory		
		Kind of Content	
The Primary Presentation Forms of Component Display Theory		Generality (G), rule, definition, principle, or procedure	Instance (eg), a specific example of an event, process, or principle
Mode of Delivery or Presentation	Expository (E): present, tell, or show	1. EG: Tell a rule or principle	2. Eeg: Give an example or story that supports the principle
	Inquisitory (I): question, ask, or learner practice	3. IG: Invite learners to express the rule in their own way	4. Ieg: Ask learners to think of their own experiences that illustrate the principle

SOURCE: Adapted from Merrill (1994, p. 121).

This simple statement undergirds the most important process in parenting (Peterson & Hann, 1999). Nothing matters as much as nurturing. A clear, direct, simple expression of this principle (EG) is a good way to start the teaching—though not the only way.

For those who are familiar with scholarship on the subject, the clear statement of principle is rich with meaning. For the typical learners, the meaning of the statement and its applications to their lives may not be clear. The typical learner will need far more instruction than a mere statement of principle.

Using Stories That Teach the Principle

To help learners understand just what the principle means, the teacher may next choose to provide examples (Eeg or expository instances) that illustrate the major points. If, for instance, we wanted to illustrate the importance of sensitive caregiving in the development of children, we might tell a story about a caregiver who responds to infant distress with support, soothing, and patience and the beneficial effects of such care. For the sake of clarity, we might also tell a contrasting story of care that is brittle, angry, and impatient and the negative consequences of such care.

To provide parents with an application of the principle, we might tell about a little boy named Riley who had colic. His parents didn't have much experience with babies or with colic. At first they wondered if they had a bad child. They wondered if they should just ignore the boy's crying in order to break the habit. But they had been told that infants sometimes get colic and need soothing. So Mom and Dad took turns rocking, singing, and patting Riley when he had colic. They helped and supported each other. When they were both worn out, they might lay Riley down in his crib for a few minutes. But even in this stressful situation, both parents made real efforts to be sensitive to Riley. Within a few weeks, the colic began to fade. While it had been a difficult time for the family, Riley had developed a sense that his parents would respond sensitively to his distress. What a great foundation for trust!

Teaching is made more interesting and effective by the use of appropriate stories. They can help learners see how an abstract principle applies to real life. They can also help learners remember the general principle. We learn through stories.

The colic story is especially appropriate for parents of infants who are likely to have children with similar problems. Multiple stories with diverse situations might be helpful. For example, Ellyn Satter has written a book

(1999) and developed a video (1995/1997) that illustrate sensitive feeding of children. In the video, she shows a parent whose sole objective appears to be to get the bottle of baby food inside the baby as quickly as possible. The parent does not talk with the child or wait for the child's signs of interest in food. The parent just shovels the food into the child. In fact, it seemed clear that the child ran out of interest in the food long before the food ran out. The parent continued to shovel the food into an increasingly unhappy child. That is a good example of nonsensitivity.

In contrast, Satter (1995/1997) also shows parents who are sensitive to the child. They engage the child in playful conversation. They offer the food so the child can see it. They allow the child time to process the food. They notice when the child loses interest in the food. Her principle related to sensitive feeding is that "nutrition has a way of falling into place when people are the priority rather than the rules that govern them." In a workshop teaching situation, Satter's video might be used or stories from her book might be shared. If you are preparing a publication on this subject, you might tell your own stories (or the stories of parents you know) or seek permission to reprint Satter's stories.

If your audience includes parents of school-age children, the stories would naturally revolve around the challenges and opportunities they will face with their children. For example, they might involve sensitivity to the children's challenges at school, their disappointments, rivalries, or difficulties in getting chores done. Even in such situations, the same general principle presides: When parents are sensitive to their children and their needs, the children are more likely to grow into socially competent people.

Each of the subparts of a principle can be taught in the same way. The principle as stated above has at least three major subparts dealing with the importance of sensitivity, commitment, and close relationship. Stories can be shared to illustrate each part of the general principle. As you can imagine, there might also be additional subprinciples taught along the way. For example, in teaching about the importance of close relationships, the teacher may teach about the characteristics of effective listening or about taking time with children. Each lesson may have one central principle and a network of supporting principles.

As you select stories to illustrate principles, it makes sense that you would use stories that your clientele can relate to. You are not likely to share stories of parents dealing with teens' careless driving if you are teaching parents of young children. In some cases, you may have a very diverse audience, including parents of a broad age range of children and very diverse life situations. It makes sense to offer a range of stories, but it also leads to another mode of learning, the mode that Merrill (1983, 1994) calls the inquisitory mode, suggesting that the teacher is inviting participation by the learners.

Helping Learners Take the Principles Home

Let's start with inquisitory generalities (IG). This step could involve asking participants to recall or repeat the rule or principle about nurturing young children. It should go beyond parroting back the original statement and invite learners to express the principle in their own words and way. Answers may be very diverse. One participant may express the principle as "Ya gotta love 'em." Is that expression of the principle acceptable? The answer is, "It depends." We might ask the participant, "Will those words help you remember to act in the ways we have talked about?" If the answer is affirmative, then that expression of the principle is satisfactory. If not, the participant might suggest how to modify his or her statement to capture the full meaning of the original principle.

The objective is not to push participants toward our words but toward actions congruent with the principle. That is why we ask, "Will those words help you remember to act in the ways we have talked about?"

Each person may have a different way of expressing the principle. "I gotta notice my kid." "I must stop being in a hurry." "I need to take time for my children." While those words may each express something very different from the original principle, each may capture that part of the principle that the participant is ready to live. The object of all instructional activity is to move participants toward actions congruent with principles.

Once the participants have their own handle on expressing the principle, effective application can be advanced by encouraging them to think of situations from their own experience where they can see the principle at work. Since we are asking the learners for their stories, Merrill (1983, 1994) calls this inquisitory instances (Ieg). Participants may tell their own stories related to the principle. An able teacher will help learners see the principle (EG) at work in their stories.

Some of the participants' stories may not seem to illustrate the principle very well. We can invite them to make the connection clear: "Do you see the principle of nurturing young children in that story?" Or if the story simply does not illustrate the principle at hand very well, a sensitive teacher might respond, "That story beautifully illustrates another principle of parenting that we will discuss later in this series. Do you have any stories that illustrate the power of love to help children grow and develop?"

Finding Instructional Balance

One way of thinking about Merrill's (1983, 1994) CDT is as a reminder to balance. Related to mode of delivery, the theory reminds us to balance the leader talk with participant talk. Certainly each participant has something valuable to contribute. The leader should bring expert knowledge as well as facilitation skills. The learners bring their own discoveries, creativity, expertise, and wealth of experience. When they work well together, great discoveries can be made.

Balance between leader and participant does not necessarily mean equal time. Instead, it suggests that each be involved in ways that advance learning. In the early stages of a class, the leader may need to take more initiative. As participants become more comfortable, they may contribute more and more to the class.

Related to the kind of content, Merrill's (1983, 1994) theory reminds us to balance generalities with instances. We have all been bored by lectures that described laws and principles but never touched down in human experience. Perhaps we have also heard presentations that were filled with stories but failed to clearly identify any general principles. When there is a healthy balance of the two, learning is facilitated.

Instruction Outside a Classroom

Much of the foregoing discussion presumes that the instruction will be delivered in face-to-face instruction. It is also useful to use CDT in organizing print materials. While a print teaching process does not allow for full-fledged interaction, many effective parenting publications provide questions that invite participant thought and reaction. Many such publications provide a place for participants to write their reactions. They may also invite participants to discuss the ideas with other family members, respected peers, or potential mentors.

When learning is done in an electronic mode, responses can be programmed into the computer software. Or, in the case of online learning, there may be interaction between the students and between students and teaching assistants.

In Chapter 5, we will explore additional ways to support and encourage learner participation. The focus of this chapter is designing instruction that is likely to help learners understand and apply principles for better family life.

Mixing the Elements of Instruction

The foregoing discussion may seem to suggest a lockstep march through a process. The reality of effective teaching is much more random and exciting. A teacher may choose to mix the instructional elements to fit the learners and the subject. For example, a teacher may choose to begin with one or more stories (Eegs) before making a statement of the principle (EG). Beginning with interesting stories may be an effective way of engaging learners' interest.

A lesson may also begin with an inquisitory generality. For example, you might invite learners to respond to the question, "What do you think is the most important thing parents can do to help their children turn out well?" If the teacher or leader dismisses answers that are not the one he or she has in mind, participants are likely to be turned off. However, a skillful teacher can respond to every answer positively: "What an important principle!" "You have probably seen that make a real difference!" Each can be written on the board or flipchart.

In the course of the discussion, someone is likely to nominate the principle that is the subject of the session, to which the teacher can respond, "That is very important. And it happens to be the one that I would like us to talk about today." An inquisitory generality may be a good way to begin if you want to get participants thinking about the general lessons they have learned.

A lesson might also begin with an inquisitory instance. We might ask, "Would you tell me stories from your parenting experience that taught you important lessons of parenting?" After listening to several stories, the leader might comment, "Thank you for sharing your stories. One of the themes I see in many of them is the importance of nurturing children." Beginning with their stories may allow the learners to see from the beginning that the general principle (EG) is tied to their lives.

Each approach has advantages and disadvantages. It requires a skillful teacher to begin in the inquisitory mode. It may also require more time to get to the central point. Yet this approach may be useful for some audiences and some subjects.

FIRST PRINCIPLES OF INSTRUCTION ●

On the basis of decades of experience in instructional design, David Merrill (2001) has created his own nominations for the first principles of instruction. He has compared his recommendations with those that come from prominent instructional models and found the common themes across most of the models. In the balance of this chapter, we will consider how these principles might be applied to the challenges faced by family life educators.

Instruction Addresses Real Problems

Merrill's (2001) first principle states that "learning is facilitated when the learner is engaged in solving a real-world problem" (p. 461). In this arena, school learning is disadvantaged. Most problems that are presented in school classrooms are artificial. (Think of those story problems in algebra or analyses of poems done in literature classes.) Family life educators have a big advantage in this arena. Family life is filled with real-world problems. Family problems tend to be real and personal. In fact, it is characteristic of family life that our relationships are close and continuing—just the right combination to present real-world problems.

Consider ways of applying this first principle to FLE. Imagine that you are teaching a class about the importance of commitment in couple relationships. You might set the stage by sharing a story from your own life or from a print source that illustrates the challenges of commitment.

For example, you might share a story from John Glenn's (1999) autobiography. He tells that his wife was bashful in part because of a problem with stuttering. He was often in the public eye. There were times when he had to choose to be involved in his profession the way people expected him to be or to be sensitive to his wife's preferences. He chose to honor his commitment to his wife.

You can invite participants to consider times when they were discouraged with their partner relationship, when they felt like giving up. Rather than have them share stories that could be painful for their partners, you could invite them to list some of the difficulties couples face that could challenge their commitment to each other. Such a discussion is likely to make the issue very real for all participants; it would be the rare participant who would not think of his or her own challenges with commitment.

Each person could be invited to identify a specific situation in which he or she found it difficult to show commitment—and make either a mental or written note. Then class members could be invited to share ideas for sustaining commitment. As the group suggests ideas, each person is invited to make note of those ideas that could be useful in his or her relationship.

Of course, group discussion is not the only path to learning. The work of Lev Vgotsky (see Rogoff, 1990) underscores the importance of learning from experts. In many arenas of activity, skill is learned through apprenticeships. Family life educators can invite people to interview those who have succeeded at the processes under study. A young couple might interview a seasoned couple, asking them about ways they have shown commitment to each other. Younger couples can also be invited to be quiet observers of couples who have learned to work well together.

Family life educators may also be involved with problem solving in after-class discussions or in home visits. For example, on a periodic home visit, a parent may ask the visitor what to do about a lazy daughter. The wise educator will not spout some canned wisdom but will model problem solving with her carefully chosen questions. "Tell me more about what your daughter is like." "In what situations is she lazy?" "Are there situations where she is not lazy?" "What have you tried to help her do better?" "Have any of those efforts paid off?" "Can you see any special reasons why she might not do well in the areas where she has seemed lazy?"

All of these questions are intended to help the parent move beyond frustrated judgment of a child to productive problem solving. They set the stage for the most important question: "Can you think of anything you can do to help your daughter function better [i.e., be less lazy]?" The parent might not have ready answers. A helpful educator might suggest some possibilities: "Do you think she fails to do certain chores because she hates those particular tasks? Or because she doesn't like to be rushed? Or because she doesn't know how?" Effective family life educators facilitate their participants' real-world problem solving.

Of course, it is generally unwise to start education with the most emotion-invoking and long-lasting problems. Merrill (2000) recommends that learners deal with "a progression of carefully sequenced problems" (p. 5). That is one reason that it is advantageous to start family life education preventively. When a parenting or partner relationship has been toxic for years, it is difficult to turn the tide.

Activating Existing Knowledge

Merrill's (2001) second principle is that learning is facilitated when existing knowledge is activated as a foundation for new knowledge. For example, if we were interested in teaching a group of parents to tune in to their children's languages of love, we might begin by inviting them to think about times in their childhoods when their family members tried to show them love. We would encourage them to think about efforts that were more or less effective. While all of the efforts to communicate love might be sincere, some were probably effective and others may have been counterproductive. We might discuss what made the difference.

Participants would probably recognize that some efforts were well tuned to our preferences and some were not. If a family member who knows I am on a diet still buys me a candy bar as a gift, I might not be appreciative. By recognizing the importance of attunement to the other person—awareness of that person's needs or preferences—we can become more effective at showing love.

To take this idea one step closer to the parents' task of showing love to their children, we might ask the parents to think about efforts they had made to show love to their children that had been more or less effective. By analyzing their efforts to show love to their children, they might determine their children's preferences or languages of love.

While the discussion of previous experience does not create new knowledge, it does bring existing knowledge to a more conscious level and organizes it into a form that can guide intentional action.

In some cases, it may be useful to create a new experience for learners as a foundation for the new learning. For example, family members in a weekly class might be asked to wear some special mental glasses that allowed them to notice only the good things that their partner or children do. Imagine that the glasses entirely block out annoyances and disappointments. Notice the good, record it, and return to the next session to discuss what they noticed and experienced.

It is possible that such an assignment would set the stage for teaching class members about the processes by which humans judge the motives of others and about the power of the mind to interpret and filter experience. It could provide personal experience relevant to the lesson to be taught.

The Power of Demonstration

Merrill's (2001) third principle states that learning is facilitated when new knowledge is demonstrated to the learner. It is not uncommon for people in classes to be taught a new principle, presented with a dilemma, and asked to tell how to respond. The task may seem easy to those who are familiar with the principle and have tried to apply it for years. But the jump from current experience to new performance can be daunting for many learners.

For example, it is common in both parenting and couple relationship trainings to teach people about empathic responding. We teach people to attend to the emotional experience of their child or partner and try to express in words what that person may be feeling. It may seem easy enough—but decades of experience can work against ready application of the principle.

Imagine that we have taught parents about empathic listening in parenting. To give them a chance to practice, we ask them to imagine that one of their children has come home from school with slumped shoulders and confessed to getting in trouble at school. In fact, the teacher yelled at your child and called him names. At this point, you invite parents in your class to tell what they would say if they were responding empathically to the upset child. We suspect that the natural parental tendency to play like a cross-examining investigator will swamp the valuable lessons parents may have learned in a parenting class. Habit regularly trumps new learning.

Especially as participants learn new and difficult skills, it might be useful to invite them to tell what they would normally say under such circumstances. "Under normal circumstances, what might a parent say in response to a child who has come home and reported trouble at school?" Parents can report their automatic response. For example, one parent might respond, "I would find out what my son did to get into trouble!" Your response as an educator can open the way for the new learning: "That is a very normal reaction. Let's think about how it would work. How do you think your son would feel if you quizzed him about what he did to get himself in trouble? Would it effectively convey your compassion and understanding? Would it prepare him to try better behavior?" The answer should be obvious to any parent who is not defensive.

As the ineffectiveness of our automatic reactions becomes clear, the way is open for the educator to invite new thinking: "What might a parent do that would show more compassion?" In response to any answer, you can direct the person to the effect on the child. This process demonstrates just how difficult new skills can be while pointing the parents to the ultimate test of their actions: How do the actions affect the child?

As a family life educator, you can also suggest parent responses while inviting the parents to test them by the same standard. "How would your child feel if you said, 'Oh, son! You must have felt humiliated to be chewed out in front of your classmates!'" Truly empathic listening is so contrary to humans' automatic and egocentric responses that it takes lots of practice. But "learning is facilitated when new knowledge is demonstrated to the learner" (Merrill, 2000, p. 2). Many demonstrations over many sessions may be necessary for effective learning.

Applying New Knowledge

Merrill's (2001) fourth principle states that "learning is facilitated when the learner is required to use his or her new knowledge to solve problems" (p. 463). There are no written tests that qualify a person as a good family member. The application of knowledge is the end goal of FLE.

Between sessions of FLE, it is common to make assignments to participants. For example, after teaching about the importance of thinking positively about one's partner, each participant might be encouraged to think of a quality or behavior that is most appreciated in the partner. Once the quality is identified, each participant can be encouraged to think of a way to prompt remembering that quality in the hours and days ahead. Some might choose to tie a string around a finger or carry a keepsake in a shirt pocket. Participants are encouraged to use the prompt to remember the quality regularly, especially in times of stress. Each is asked to make a mental or written note of successes and struggles that might be shared with the class in the next meeting of the group (whether face to face or online).

Merrill (2001) observes that "appropriate practice is the single most neglected aspect of effective instruction" (p. 464). The new behavior needs to be practiced. Gottman (1994) refers to extensive practice as overlearning. He recommends that partners overlearn their new skills so that they have a fighting chance when they face a challenge and are tempted by habit to fall into unproductive if overritualized patterns.

Practice can happen in both instructional and real-world settings. Family life educators can facilitate such field learning by providing learners a standard by which to judge their performance. For example, an educator might teach participants in a parenting class to judge any responses to parenting problems by a two-part test: (1) Is the solution likely to improve the behavior? (2) Does the solution show respect for the child? When the parents have a standard for judging their new solutions, they are more likely to turn to new behavior than fall back on old habits.

Turning again to Merrill (2000): "Most learners learn from the errors they make, especially when they are shown how to recognize the error, how to recover from the error, and how to avoid the error in the future" (p. 8). Many of us have spent decades trying to get better at practicing what we preach. We can provide relevant practice to help our participants apply knowledge to their lives across time.

New Knowledge Integrated Into the Learner's World

Merrill's (2000) fifth and final point is that "learning is facilitated when new knowledge is integrated into the learner's world" (p. 2). Learners may benefit from making specific and practical plans for integrating their new knowledge into their family lives. They can engage in periodic discussions with co-learners or support groups. They can keep a journal of their performance.

They may also benefit from teaching their newfound knowledge to others. There is nothing quite like teaching to force us to understand a principle and how it works. Your participants might be invited to give a mini-lesson to the class, to teach a group at work or in their faith community.

Merrill (2000) observes that there is no satisfaction quite like moving from student to teacher or mentor. "The real motivation for learners is learning. When learners are able to demonstrate improvement in skill, they are motivated to perform even better" (p. 8). The combination of integrating the skills into everyday life and sharing them with others cements the lessons.

CONCLUSION ●

When instruction—whether oral or written—is designed according to established principles of instructional design, the message is more likely to be effective. In addition, the instruction is more likely to be enjoyable for both the educator and the participant.

EXPLORATIONS ●

1. Review the lesson that you created using the component display theory above for its consonance with Merrill's first principles of instruction. Enlarge or refine your lesson as necessary. Identify the way you will facilitate learning in each of the ways described in Merrill's five principles by placing a numeral 1 through 5 next to the part of your lesson plan that facilitates learning in that way.

2. Now that you are familiar with all four elements of Merrill's CDT, take a speech, lesson plan, or outline—any deliberate instruction—and identify the four elements: EG, Eeg, IG, and Ieg. Evaluate whether adding more of one or another of the elements would have made the presentation more effective for the purpose it was delivered.

3. Develop a lesson plan or pamphlet to teach a principle with which you are familiar. In fact, it would be useful to select a subject that you have taught before or are likely to teach in the future. Create the instruction using (and labeling) all four elements of Merrill's CDT. Describe your audience and justify your combination of elements based on the needs of your target audience and your instructional objectives. Share your work with a class-mate for feedback. If you have created a lesson plan, seek an opportunity to use the plan to teach a group and invite a classmate or colleague to give you feedback.

CHAPTER 5

ENGAGING AN AUDIENCE

There is much that could be written about processes for engaging an audience; it is as much art as science. There will be four broad themes in this chapter. The first deals with the art of teaching—and special considerations with the adult learner. Next is a short section about personality theories; if we hope to change people with our teaching, we can benefit from insights into human nature. The third section of this chapter reviews some of what is known about "joining" or relationship building as a precondition to effective helping. In addition, Ginott's method of applying these principles is reviewed. Finally, the chapter concludes with some practical applications of the principles to teaching and print efforts.

THE ART OF TEACHING ●

Reflect on your best learning experiences—classes, workshops, or lectures. Do you learn best when a teacher relentlessly pounds facts into you? Have you gained the most when you felt cowed and intimidated by a dismissive teacher? Do you prefer to be a silent, unengaged observer?

One of my (Goddard's) favorite teachers in high school was Ray Gilbert. He taught trigonometry—not a subject that is automatically riveting. He was a tall, gangly man who typically began each class period by sitting on his desk and chatting with us. He might talk about a ball game or a snowstorm or some world happening that affected us all. He seemed to genuinely enjoy us, which was a rare experience for high school students.

Mr. Gilbert was excited about trigonometry. He described the ways we could use trig to track the path of, for example, a potato shot from a potato gun. He talked and laughed easily. The experience I remember most clearly from his class was a day when several of us had written problems from our homework assignment on the board. Each of us in turn discussed the steps in our solution. When it was my turn, I began to trace through the steps but was only midway through the problem when I realized that I had mis-understood the problem and done it all wrong. A blush began at the top of my head and was rapidly working its way through my soul as I stammered my way to the end of the problem. I felt humiliated.

Mr. Gilbert stood up at the back of the classroom, took a deep breath, and said, "Wow. In all my years of teaching, I have never seen that problem done that way." I felt relieved. I might not get credit for accurate trig, but I had gotten credit for creativity.

A Formula for Engaging an Audience

A person can scan the leading guides for family life educators and par-enting educators (e.g., Arcus et al., 1993b; Bornstein, 2002; Fine, 1980, 1989; Fine & Lee, 2000) and fail to find any practical formula for teaching. There are skills approaches (Campbell & Palm, 2004) but no guiding principles.

If this author were to provide a simple formula for effective teach-ing, it would include three elements: relevance, respect, and participation. Mr. Gilbert certainly honored that formula. He got us involved in solving problems, he respected us—even when we made mistakes—and he tried to make trig relevant.

Family life education (FLE) may likewise benefit from considerations of relevance, respect, and participation. FLE enjoys the inherent advantage of being relevant for everyone; everyone is tied to a family in some way.

Respect is also a vital element. It would be painfully ironic to try to teach respect in families using methods employing scorn and contempt. We must model the respect that we invite participants to take to their family relationships.

Participation is fundamental to FLE. Family life is more than book learn-ing; it is a personally engaging enterprise that is best learned in participa-tory ways.

This formulation for engaging lay audiences can take many forms. Some years ago, I (Goddard) was invited to talk to a group of parents about teens and sexuality. I showed up at the appointed time and place with facts, figures, and discussion questions. As I entered the classroom, I found that there were about 20 teens and no adults. I asked the program organizers about the sudden change of audience. "We had these teens from a residential facility show up and thought that they would benefit from a presentation by you about the role of sexuality."

I felt a great urge to panic. Nothing I had prepared for the parents fitted this new audience. My mind raced while I unloaded my books and papers. When I could delay no longer, I introduced myself and went to the board and drew one horizontal line from one end of the board to the opposite end—about 12 feet long. I told the teens that I wanted their opinions about the meaning of sexual behavior. At one end of the continuum I put the word *Never.* "Some people believe that sex is never good. It is best to avoid it your whole lifetime."

I walked to the opposite end of the board and wrote the word *Always.* "Some people believe that sex is always good with another consenting person. Anytime you can get it, take it."

Putting a mark near the middle of the line, I said, "Some people believe that sex is good in some kinds of committed relationships. In other words, sex is good if you are in love or married."

I invited the teens to tell what they thought was the ideal role for sex. Was it always bad? Was it always good? Was it good only under certain circumstances? Of course, I did not encourage them to describe their own sexual behavior, only their beliefs about the appropriate role of sex.

A lively discussion ensued. Students challenged and questioned each other. Many were clearly reflecting on their own position for the first time. In the course of the discussion, one boy who had endorsed an almost predatory view moved to a more conservative and considerate position. Others developed greater clarity about their beliefs.

Of course, I do not believe that we settled all issues in that 1-hour discussion. And such a discussion should not be held without appropriate safeguards such as careful guidance by an experienced teacher. However, the effectiveness of the session at clarifying student views was the result of the teens' lively participation. A lecture probably could not have elicited the reflection and insight that came from the hour-long discussion.

Engaging the Adult Learner With Family Life Education

FLE can happen in settings as diverse as an eighth-grade health class, a church-sponsored marriage retreat, a community fathering class, or a prison mothering class. Traditionally, much of FLE has been done with adults. Hopefully, many more young people will be involved in FLE in the future.

Since the people who are married or parenting are most likely to be adults, and since those who have traditionally enrolled for FLE have often been adults, it is important to be aware of unique considerations for adult learners.

Knowles (1998) summarizes some of the classic observations about adult learners. "In conventional education the student is required to adjust himself [or herself] to an established curriculum; in adult education the curriculum is built around the student's needs and interests. The resource of highest value in adult education is the learner's experience. Experience is the adult learner's living textbook" (p. 39). Knowles also observes that "adults have a deep need to be self-directing" (p. 40). "Adult learners are precisely those whose intellectual aspirations are least likely to be aroused by the rigid, uncompromising requirements of authoritative, conventional-ized institutions of learning" (p. 38).

Some might be tempted to suggest that participants in FLE merely gather and share ideas—an open sharefest. There are times when that may be effec-tive. Yet active participation does not preclude leadership. While a group leader or educator may have more knowledge of research than any of the class members, participants "as a group have more solutions than we do" (Curran, 1989, p. 20). The ideal learning environment will bring the knowl-edge and facilitation skills of the educator together with the experience and problem-solving capacity of the participants. A specific method that provides such a learning environment will be described later in this chapter.

● WHAT CHANGES PEOPLE? CHALLENGING IDEAS FROM PERSONALITY THEORIES

There are no simple answers to the question of what changes people. The complexity is due to both the complexity of people themselves and the diversity of views on the subject. Different psychological schools of thought would offer very different recommendations for changing human behavior on the basis of their assumptions about human nature and motivation.

For the purposes of this discussion, the work of Salvatore Maddi is helpful. He has divided the many theories of personality into three broad categories. The first group of theories is called conflict theories. One of the most prominent conflict theorists was Sigmund Freud, for whom the core tendency in humans is "to maximize instinctual gratification while mini-mizing punishment and guilt" (Maddi, 1989, p. 627). This puts humans in conflict with society, which must manage individuals' drives if the common good is to be maintained.

While there are many other versions of conflict theories in addition to Freud's, an educator who subscribed to a conflict model of human behavior would frame the task in terms of the inherent conflict between family members' interests or between an individual family member and the family as a whole. Complicating the educator's job, many conflict theorists believe that psychological defenses would make it impossible for participants and family members to access their true feelings and motivations.

The task of family life educators who subscribed to conflict models of human behavior would be to teach family members to gratify their own needs while respecting the needs of others. "The best that [families] can do is aim for cooperation and order so as to maximize gratifications for all" (Maddi, 1989, p. 51). The way to engage learners in a class would be to offer ways of reducing tension while minimizing their guilt and punishment.

In contrast to conflict models, consistency models posit that all humans want to reduce the tension or difference between expectation and reality. The best-known conflict model is probably the cognitive dissonance model, which asserts that humans want to minimize the large discrepancies between expectation and occurrence while maximizing small discrepancies between them. Said differently, people like small surprises, but they do not like to be shocked. The activation version of consistency theories suggests that humans seek to maintain a level of activation to which they are accustomed. When people are underactivated, they seek more stimulation. When they are overactivated, they seek to reduce stimulation.

Consistency models might be applied to FLE in a couple of ways. Interest can be stimulated by presenting situations that challenge their traditional ways of thinking. For example, parents in a parenting class might be provided with information that challenges their familiar thinking: "If it is true that children generally do what seems right to them, how do we explain the way children sometimes hurt their siblings?" By presenting two "truths" that are at odds with each other, we can often stimulate our participants to think in more complex ways.

Consistency models can also consider the level of stimulation that is optimal for each learner in a class. While the optimal level will vary from learner to learner, important clues can be gained by observing the class. Are they understimulated or overstimulated? During the course of a session, having a variety of activities is probably optimal. Consistency models sensitize us to the fact that learners will learn best when they are neither bored nor overstimulated. The old adage may be true that it is the educator's job to comfort the afflicted and afflict the comforted.

Maddi's (1989) third way of understanding human behavior is the fulfillment model. Rather than seeing the world as two great forces at odds with each other, fulfillment models focus on one great force, the realization of one's abilities or the striving toward ideals. Carl Rogers and Abraham Maslow are prominent names associated with this view.

Fulfillment models have implications for engaging and teaching family life audiences. Maslow suggested that we do not move to higher levels of functioning when lower needs are gnawing at us. Assuring class members of safety, belongingness, and our esteem for them might make it easier for them to participate. In those cases where they carry burdens and worries from home to class, it may be useful to help them process them. "It looks like you're worried about things at home."

The other practical application of the fulfillment model to engaging the audience is to paint a picture of personal possibilities for participants. What Maddi (1989) has said about therapy might also be applied to FLE:

> In [FLE], it is very helpful—for [participant] and [educator] alike—to believe in a view of the [person] as unlimited in what it can become. It is helpful because you are already dealing with a [participant] who [may be discouraged] and has lost conviction about becoming anyone worthwhile. In such a situation, it is necessary to hold out a view of life that is extreme enough in its opposition to the client's view to be able to serve as the needed corrective. (p. 102)

Comparing the Personality Theories

We are tempted to ask which of the personality theories best describes human reality. Maddi (1989) finds "considerable empirical support for both versions of the fulfillment model and the activation version of the consistency model" (p. 532). Yet savvy family life educators know that there are valuable lessons to be learned from each of the views.

For example, the conflict models remind us that there is often a conflict within families and within classes. We can help participants meet their needs while respecting the needs of the group. The consistency models encourage us to be mindful of the activation levels of class members. The fulfillment models offer an optimistic portrait of personal development that can give us and our participants renewed hope.

All family life educators will form a unique combination of models to form a personal philosophy. Many family life educators subscribe to fulfillment models because of their positive portrayal of humans as having inherent strengths and unlimited potential for growth. Such educators are likely to see themselves as collaborators or facilitators, as described in Chapter 1.

Participants in FLE settings likewise may resonate with this philosophy that credits them with much that is good. So, as Myers-Walls (2000) has suggested, there is merit in assessing learners' models of human functioning and matching them to the curriculum and teaching style that best fits them.

RELATIONSHIPS AS THE BASIS FOR HELPING ●

Prelude to Effective Education

In FLE, it is common to focus on the content to the neglect of process. The relationship between the educator and the learner may be more important than the content of the lesson. As DeBord et al. (2002) observed, "Instructors will be more likely to provide appropriate content and learning experiences if they have developed a relationship with participants, can identify their strengths and challenges, and can modify the program to fit the specific needs of the audience" (p. 32).

This should not be surprising. In family relationships, nothing matters as much as the quality of the relationship. As Smith, Perou, and Lesesne (2002) observe about parent-child relationships, "What is essential for a child's well-being [is] stable loving relationships with parents who provide nurturing, reciprocal interactions" (p. 406).

It is also the quality of the relationship that seems to be the biggest factor in helping relationships, whether educational or therapeutic. FLE is clearly distinct from therapy but employs some of the methods that are successful in therapy. In a study of solution-focused therapies, Miller, Duncan, and Hubble (1997) found that relationship matters more than technique:

> While therapists tended to attribute therapeutic success to the use of solution-focused techniques (e.g., specialized interviewing techniques, miracle questions), the clients consistently reported a strong therapeutic relationship as the critical factor in treatment outcome (e.g., therapist acceptance, non-possessive warmth, positive regard, affirmation, and self-disclosure). (p. 85)

Brammer and MacDonald (1999) report that "all authorities in the helping process agree that the quality of the relationship is important to effective helping" (p. 49). In the absence of a positive, affirming relationship, growth is less likely. In therapy, this relationship is established through the process of joining. Minuchin and Fishman (1981) observed that joining a family is more an attitude than a technique, and it is the umbrella under which all therapeutic transactions occur. Joining is letting the family know that the therapist understands them and is working with and for them. Only under this protection can the family have the security to explore alternatives, try the unusual, and change. Joining is the glue that holds the therapeutic system together. (pp. 31–32)

Hanna and Brown (2004) suggest that "the personal rapport or empathy that therapists develop with those they are trying to help remains the single most proven variable determining the effectiveness of psychotherapy" (p. 89). Jacobson and Christensen (1996) similarly make the case for viewing clients compassionately in integrated couple therapy (ICT):

The skilled ICT therapist has to develop the ability to find compassion and sympathy in each person's story, no matter how unsympathetic and contemptible one partner may appear. Our position is that the vast majority of people act badly in relationships because they are suffering. (p. 99)

To the extent that participants in FLE settings examine personal feelings and assumptions as part of a change and growth process, the same principles can be expected to apply. In fact, a vital process for connecting may be identifying and appreciating family strengths.

Below are Hanna and Brown's (2004, p. 95) six processes for joining together with commentary on their application to FLE.

1. "Emphasize positive statements reported by family members."

   We are all encouraged and energized when people notice and appreciate the good in us and our families: "I am impressed with your resilience."

2. "Encourage family members to share their story about themselves."

   It may be especially useful to notice ways that the family has adapted or coped with problems: "It seems that your family has great determination when difficulties arise."

3. "Note family interactions that reflect strength and competency."

   Each story tells something about the difficulties families face but also about the resources they use to meet them: "I like the way you involve your family in solving problems."

4. "Emphasize those times that family members enjoy together."

   Explore the positive experiences that family members describe; help them put a frame about the best in their family life: "It sounds as if your family enjoys laughter together."

5. "Reframe problems or negative statements in a more positive way."

   Help family members find a positive interpretation for their experiences: "Your worry was a sign that you really care about your children."

6. "Emphasize what families do well."

   Invite them to talk about their successes: "Please tell us more about how you overcame that challenge."

The Boundary Between Therapy and Family Life Education

While FLE may draw on some of the techniques and findings of therapy, it is not the same as therapy. In fact, ethical issues require educators to carefully establish a boundary between their educational efforts and the methods of therapy. Bill Doherty (1995) has described the dilemma in this way:

> In order to accomplish its purpose, parent and family education must have more personal depth than other forms of education, but too much depth or intensity risks harming participants, or at least scaring them away. Participants must be able to tell their stories, express their feelings and values, and be encouraged to try out new behaviors. However, if they recount in detail their most traumatic memories, ventilate their most painful and unresolved feelings, or take major behavioral risks, the experience can be damaging. (p. 353)

Doherty (1995) describes five levels of his family involvement model, from least involvement to greatest:

Level 1: Minimal emphasis on family might include a parent-teacher conference in which the school conveyed policies or information.

Level 2: Information and advice is the level at which the educator undertakes training of the recipients.

Level 3: Feelings and support add to the information of Level 2, the processing of feelings. This is not the intense processing of personal and painful experience. This is the level on which much FLE takes place.

Level 4: Brief, focused intervention "represents the upper boundary of parent and family education practiced by a minority of professionals who choose to work with special populations of parents and seek special training in family assessment and basic family interventions" (p. 355).

Level 5: Family therapy is beyond the scope of FLE.

While warning family life educators against moving into Level 5 interventions, he observes that "a strictly content oriented training program [for family life educators] cannot adequately prepare professionals for affective work with families" (p. 356). Family life educators need to know how to facilitate the processing of personal family experience with their participants.

A Specific Method for Capitalizing on Emotion in Family Life Education

Haim Ginott, famous for his classic book *Between Parent and Child* (1965), spent years working with children in play therapy and with their parents in therapy. Over the years, he came to the conclusion that most parents need education rather than therapy; they are not mentally ill—they are merely uninformed (Goddard & Ginott, 2002).

Ginott conducted parenting groups in New York City for many years and developed a process for working with parents that combines the principles of trust building with emotional education. While Ginott's work focused on parenting education, the same principles apply in delivering couples' education or other kinds of FLE. Ginott's approach helps parenting educators model the behaviors they are encouraging parents to practice with their children.

Ginott's method, described by his student and colleague Arthur Orgel (1980), suggested that there are four steps in the process of supporting parents. Ginott's method has particular merit because it is based on his top-rated (Norcross et al., 2003) parenting books (Ginott, 1965, 1969; Ginott, Ginott, & Goddard, 2003) and because of his experience as a family life educator (Goddard, 1999).

1. *Recitation is the first stage of FLE.* In this stage, parents (partners or other participants) are encouraged to talk about their challenging

experiences as parents. This allows parents to discover that all parents have problems. It also allows the parenting educator to model attention, understanding, and acceptance. Many parents have never had someone sensitively listen to them before. It is important for parents to feel heard and understood.

Such sensitive listening may not be easy for the parenting educator. The educator must listen carefully, resist the temptation to correct or preach, and be skillful in remaining supportive and encouraging: "Wow. That must have been very difficult." "You probably wondered what to do." "Yes. Parenting can be very challenging!"

The objective at this stage of a discussion is not to teach new skills to the parents but to allow them to talk about their challenges while feeling understood, accepted, and valued. This skill is especially important when parents have many challenges or are mandated to participate in a parenting education program. When a parenting educator is supportive and encouraging, parents can embrace their unique strengths and feel safe enough to explore strategies to address their challenges.

Sometimes class members lack confidence in their parenting skills and worry that they make many mistakes. The effective parenting educator recognizes, values, and encourages parents' desires, even as their skills are still emerging. Effective family life educators help family members discover their strengths and build on them.

In fact, insightful psychologist Martin Seligman (2002) suggested that our growth may be more tied to effectively using our strengths than to remedying our weaknesses. In fact, our strengths may define our weaknesses. We may not be able to surgically remove our weaknesses without damaging our strengths.

The central task of the first step in FLE is to give participants the experience of being authentic and still be valued. This is the foundation upon which better parenting and better partnering can be built.

2. *Sensitization is the second phase of Ginott's method.* This second stage of parent (partner or family) education can begin after participants begin to feel accepted, valued, and safe—which may take 30 minutes, a whole session, or many weeks or months. In this second stage, the educator turns the attention of the parents to understanding their children's feelings. "How do you think your daughter felt in that situation?" "Why might that have been especially difficult for your son?"

The parenting educator may help the parents understand their children's feelings by asking them how they might have felt in similar situations.

"How might you feel if you worked all day to get the house clean and your husband (or a friend) only noticed a dirty window?" Parents may come to better understand their children's feelings when they relate them to their own experiences in an environment where they feel understood.

Everyone has struggles and disappointments. One of the challenges of parenting is to apply our own human struggles to understanding how our children and partners feel. While we will never completely understand how an experience feels for others, we can appreciate how real the pain (or joy or confusion) is.

Family life is often made more difficult when family members react to each others' behavior without taking time to understand. Under such circumstances, the person is likely to become angry and resistant. In contrast, when the person feels understood, family members can work together more effectively.

In the first stage, a family member feels understood and valued. In the second stage, that family member learns to understand and value others in the family.

3. *Learning of concepts comes next.* Parents can learn principles that will help them be more effective. For example, "Nurturing strengthens relationships" is a principle that can help family members relate to each other more effectively. Family life educators may have a series of principles to suggest. (A list of principles related to human development and family life is provided in Chapter 14.) They can involve the group by asking them to apply the principles to situations in their homes. The educator may even invite participants to customize the principles and apply them to their family realities.

4. *The teaching and practice of better skills is the final stage of Ginott's process.* Participants learn how to use their new skills and get practice in applying the principles. They may get practice by responding to situations presented by the educator and other parents. They may also get practice by developing ways to deal with situations with their own children.

A wise educator will not try to be the source of all answers but will ask participants for their ideas. For every situation, there are many ways of responding. It is good for class members to hear many different ideas for dealing with a specific problem. If skills are thought of as tools in a tool box, then it is important for participants to have many different tools and to know how to use them well. Each of us has different tools and different skills in using them. We can learn from each other.

It is also important for participants to learn how to evaluate their various options. For any idea that is suggested, you might invite participants to consider two critical questions: "Would that work for me and my family? Does it show respect for all of us?"

The main objective of Ginott's four-step process in parenting education was to provide parents with the personal experience of a warm, caring environment in which they can learn effective, respectful strategies. Then they will be prepared to go home and create a warm, caring environment in which their children can learn more strong and humane ways of acting. In a way, the parenting educator is a parent to the parents. In that role, the parenting educator can be a model of a good parent.

Sometimes there will be parents in a class who are very angry or hostile (just as there will be children in a family who sometimes are very angry or hostile). An angry parent provides a parenting educator a great opportunity to model effective ways to deal with anger. "I can see that you feel very strongly about this." "This must be very upsetting for you."

There are extreme cases when parents feel so angry or stressed that they are not able to participate effectively with others in the classroom. These participants may benefit from individual therapy. Rather than acting as an individual therapist in this setting, educators are encouraged to provide appropriate referrals to trained professionals.

PRACTICAL APPLICATIONS ●

Our objective is to foster growth and learning. Transformative learning theory suggests that this is most likely to happen with "(a) teachers who are empathetic, caring, authentic, and sincere and who demonstrate a high degree of integrity; (b) learning conditions that promote a sense of safety, openness, and trust; and (c) instructional methods that support a learner-centered approach that promotes student autonomy, participation, reflection, and collaboration" (Christopher et al., 2001, p. 135). There are practical ways to make this happen.

Drawing the Best Out of Your Participants: Some Practical Tips

It is common to see educators as the source of solutions and participants as the source of problems. In this view, participants bring their ignorance and their problems to educators, who bring their knowledge, answers, and suggestions to the participants. You can see problems with this approach:

- Participants know far more about their own lives, challenges, and resources than the educator does.
- Any solutions imposed by the educator without the conviction and commitment of the participants will not be effective.

Some of the most important answers in any training will come from participants. The most important answers are those that represent the participants' best thinking and commitments to growth.

Sometimes participants do not volunteer answers to questions because they are not sure how they will be treated. Will they be embarrassed by the educator? Will they be corrected or condemned? If they can't express themselves clearly, will they be humiliated by an insensitive educator?

Educators earn trust with all participants by the way they treat each participant. It is natural for participants to be reluctant to comment until they feel safe with an educator. A skilled educator will set participants up for success by asking questions that allow for many different answers. They ask questions such as the following:

- "What do you think will work?"
- "What have you seen people do in this situation?"
- "Do you have an idea of how to apply this principle?"

After asking a good question, an educator looks at the participants. Sometimes it is clear that one or more of them have ideas but are reluctant to volunteer. We can gently encourage them: "Reba, it looks like you have an idea."

During this first silence, if the educator jumps in with answers, participants learn that the educator doesn't really want to hear from them. They are less likely to answer in the future. If an educator genuinely welcomes input from participants, they quickly warm up. When participants make a comment, the educator encourages effort by honoring every comment.

The best way of thinking about teaching is as an opportunity for people to gather to solve problems. An educator should bring important research-based knowledge. But, equally important, an educator should bring an ability to draw the best answers and enthusiasm for growth out of the participants. When teaching is understood in this way, there are several things educators should do to bring out the best from the participants:

1. Educators should feel and show a great respect for the efforts, skills, experiences, and challenges that participants bring. This respect can be shown by listening carefully and humbly to participants' comments. It can be shown also with words such as

- "You face so many difficulties!"
- "I admire your courage to keep trying."
- "You have tried many things to make your life better."
- "I don't know if I could survive what you face."
- "You have a lot of good ideas."

2. Educators honor participants (and bring out their best) by inviting them to be creative problem solvers. While educators teach true principles, they always invite the participants to find good ways of applying those principles to their lives.
   - "What do you think would work with your family?"
   - "How would you apply that principle to make your family better?"
   - "What have you learned from your experience?"
   - "Can you think of other things you would like to try?"

The best educators help the participants find ideas within themselves.

3. There are times when a participant will make a statement that the educator disagrees with. This is the place where master educators shine. It is also the place where all educators work to be better. A great educator will honor that part of the statement that is true or will honor the participant's efforts while inviting the participant to other possibilities. For example, if a parent in class suggests that "What kids these days need is a good whooping!" there are many things a master educator might say:
   - "I agree that children need to know limits. What do you think is the best way to get children to respect those limits?"
   - "Letting children know that you are serious about limits is important. In my experience, children are more likely to follow the rules when they understand them and believe that they are important. How can we help children with this?"
   - "Respecting rules is important. Can you think of the experiences you have had that helped you want to follow the rules?"
   - "You really want your children to respect the boundaries. What do you do that works best for that?"

Application to Print

While much of this chapter presupposes a face-to-face teaching context for FLE, the same principles apply to print materials that can radiate accusation and austerity or warmth and encouragement. For example, in the

Introduction to his classic parenting book, Haim Ginott (1965) offers warm compassion to his reader:

> No parent wakes up in the morning planning to make a child's life miserable. No mother or father says, "Today I'll yell, nag, and humiliate my child whenever possible." On the contrary, in the morning many parents resolve, "This is going to be a peaceful day. No yelling, no arguing, and no fighting." Yet, in spite of good intentions, the unwanted war breaks out again. Once more we find ourselves saying things we do not mean, in a tone we do not like. (p. xiii)

● CONCLUSION

When educators combine compassion for the participants with a passion for the subject, participants are likely to leave the experience wanting to be better, wanting to grow, and wanting to return for more help to improve their family lives. When educators have both an understanding of human development and skill at conveying, they are likely to be effective at encouraging growth in their participants.

● EXPLORATIONS

1. Think about your greatest learning experiences—whether classes, informal sharing, or solo discoveries. When you have several experiences in mind, consider what they have in common. Visit with others in your group about their experiences. See if you can extract some common elements of great teaching.

2. Based on your experiences, what would you add to this chapter's formulations for effective FLE?

3. Explore your personal strengths by completing the VIA Signature Strengths Survey either in Seligman's book *Authentic Happiness* (2002) or on his website (www.authentichappiness.org).

4. Consider your strengths as a family life educator. For example, do you have an energetic personality? Deep sincerity? Broad knowledge? Wide experience? Creativity? Skill at writing? Compassion? Emotional intelligence? Describe the way you could use your strengths to be an effective family life educator. Get feedback from those who know you and have observed your efforts to share family life principles.

5. As you read this chapter, which ideas or principles would you like to apply to your practice of FLE? How could you try out those ideas in your personal and professional activity? Whom could you take as a mentor?

6. Recall a time when someone shared with you a challenge in family life. Consider how you could employ the six recommendations from Hanna and Brown (2004) on pages 100-101 to help the person identify and appreciate family strengths. Write out specific statements and discuss with classmates or colleagues.

CHAPTER 6

TEACHING SKILLS AND TOOLS IN FAMILY LIFE EDUCATION

I n previous chapters, we've spoken of the nuts and bolts of family life education (FLE) program creation, including creating a problem statement and goal, reviewing leading-edge scholarly content and extracting the teachable ideas learners most need to know, creating change objectives, and evaluating whether your efforts have made a difference. We have also discussed principles for effective instruction and the importance of creating a context of caring in FLE.

With an overall goal, content selected, learning objectives established, and an overall instructional design and procedure of engagement set, we are ready to select delivery methods or learning activities. Thus, in this chapter, we turn our attention to the teaching skills and tools of outreach FLE. Specifically, we discuss a selection of numerous methods that are especially suitable for outreach FLE and provide examples of their use.

● SELECT METHODS FOR FAMILY LIFE EDUCATION

While numerous methods of teaching family relationships have been generated over the years (e.g., Klemer & Smith, 1975), a recent and thorough anthology of methods in FLE does not exist. This chapter reviews several methods we and others have found especially useful and applicable in FLE settings. We have attempted to select a wide variety of methods that would suit a wide variety of learning styles and cultures. Many of the following methods are limited to use in more traditional outreach settings, such as community workshops. (We are indebted to Brynn Steimle for her collection of many of the following methods.)

Leading Group Discussions

Discussion invites active involvement in the learning process (McKeachie, 1999). It allows learners to clarify their thinking through making comments and through listening to the comments of others (Klemer & Smith, 1975). One way to initiate a planned discussion is by presenting a thought-provoking problem statement or question (Harris, 2002; Hobbs, 1972, p. 112; McKeachie, 1999, p. 50). Such questions may begin with words such as *give evidence, explain, interpret, compare, analyze, evaluate, who, what where, how,* and *why* (Hobbs, 1972, p. 112).

During the course of a discussion, appropriate and respectful responses by the educator to student comments will encourage future response (Powell & Cassidy, 2007). Important group discussion skills (Alabama Cooperative Extension Service, 1996) include the following:

Structuring

Make clear the purpose and goals of the discussion, to keep discussion within boundaries. You need to be continually aware of what is happening and judge whether it is appropriate to a group's purpose. You need to limit and redirect discussion when participants wander too far astray.

Linking

Linking identifies the common elements in the group's questions and comments. Listen for themes that are similar and help members see that they share feelings and beliefs. Linking also promotes interaction between participants.

Summarizing

Summarizing, like repetition, promotes learning. Emphasize the most important ideas dealt with during the session. A summary may reveal points to group members they missed earlier. Also, ask participants to summarize what they have learned; this allows the leader to assess their understanding and clarify misconceptions.

Answering Questions

You can be an effective group discussion leader without answering every question directed to you. In fact, when you are occupying a collaborator or facilitator role, it's good to try and get the group to answer the questions. Turn the question back to the group by saying, for instance, "Does anyone have any ideas on that?"

Learn lots of methods for asking questions when leading discussions. Quality questions motivate thinking, participation, and learning. Other questioning techniques include comparing (how is ___ different from/similar to ___), elaborating (what ideas/details can you add to ___; give an example of ___), predicting (what might happen if ___), and describing (describe how you arrived at your answer to ___).

Fish Bowl

A fish bowl is a special adaptation of group discussion and provides the opportunity to learn empathy and understanding of another's point of view. First, the group is split into two groups, often with opposing views about a topic. Two circles of chairs are formed, one inside the other. One group takes a seat in the inner circle, while the other sits on the outside. Participants in the center circle (the fish) are observed by those in the outer circle. If the nature of the room makes this arrangement of chairs inconvenient, the fish may simply go to the front of the room while the observers stay in their seats. Once in place, the educator facilitates a discussion with the fish while the rest of the group observes, taking note of what is being discussed and how it is being done (McKeachie, 1999, p. 211). Members of the inner group talk to one another about some topic suggested by the facilitator while the outer circle group is asked to listen to the discussion without interrupting. After about 10 to 15 minutes, the discussion should be halted and the members of the inner circle asked to be silent while the others discuss what they have heard and understood about the point of view of the inner group, or what new ideas or information they have learned that was previously unknown. Then the groups switch places and repeat the process. After each group has had the opportunity to share their views and to be heard by those in the outer circle, the entire group is brought back together to discuss what was learned from the experience.

I (Duncan) used this technique during a parenting workshop with parents and their preteen children. I first asked the parents and youth to imagine they were asked to write books respectively titled *What Kids Expect of Parents* and *What Parents Expect of Their Kids*. What would be the major points of the books? The kids were in the inner circle first and responded to the question, "If you were to write a book titled *What Kids Expect of Parents*, what would the Table of Contents read?" Parents often bit their tongues as they listened to their children's frank comments, and some started to interrupt on occasion. I jumped in and reminded the parents of the "no interruptions" ground rule. After about 10 to 15 minutes, I then asked the parents what they heard their youth say, which led to increased understanding of their children. Then it was the parents' turn to speak and the preteens to listen and paraphrase their understanding. Parents and teens experienced an increased level of mutual understanding, resulting from truly listening to one another.

Buzz Groups

Buzz groups are another variation on traditional discussion. Buzz groups, or several small groups within a larger group, allow participants to discuss an issue among themselves (Hobbs, 1972; McKeachie, 1999). Buzz groups usually last for 5 minutes or less (McKeachie, 1999). An educator may request that each individual contribute one idea to the group, and then a group spokesperson can summarize the group's discussion for the rest of the participants (McKeachie, 1999).

Also, dilemmas can be used to allow students to solve a problem using skills they have learned in the session (DeBord, 1989). For instance, in a parenting workshop, you could present a scenario and have a group work to a solution such as the following:

Your 13-year-old daughter seems to have been distancing herself from the family lately. One day you get a call from the mother of your daughter's male friend saying she has just discovered they are sexually involved. You have taught your daughter the importance of abstinence. What are possible ways you might handle this situation?

This sort of scenario could also be used in a role-play (see below).

After each group reports, the educator summarizes the discussion as a whole (Hobbs, 1972). To help groups stay on focus, the educator may want to place the problem scenario on an overhead or computer projector. Also, it's helpful for the educator to walk around the room, observing each of the groups during the buzz session (Hobbs, 1972; McKeachie, 1999).

In a balancing work and family program, an educator divided participants into groups of five and assigned them different scenarios. For example, one scenario read,

> Your job takes you away from home several times a month, and your spouse and child have begun to complain about your regular absences. You are feeling stressed each time they raise the issue.

Groups worked together to identify the work-family stressor (e.g., not enough time for family) and then ran it through an ABC model of stress by asking questions such as "How can I ALTER the source of stress? Do I need to ACCEPT the stressor as inevitable? Do I need to BUILD resources? CHANGE perceptions?" Groups selected a spokesperson to share their scenario, the stressor identified, and how they collectively decided to meet the challenges. If the same scenario was used across groups, the educator had the first group report, and successive groups reported only those ideas that were unique to them.

Personal Narrative: Stories of Life

Personal narrative, or stories from one's own life and from the lives of others, grounds abstract principles in reality. Stories have an emotional quality that reaches the heart of participants more quickly than didactic teaching can. Some evidence suggests that stories are effective family life educational tools and motivate good parenting (Grant, Hawkins, & Dollahite, 2001). Personal narratives might reveal family life educators' own struggles with an issue or problem (e.g., "I struggle to be the kind of parent I want to be") and how they have gone about dealing with challenges or solving problems (e.g., "When I was too harsh with a child, I've gone to them and sought their forgiveness"). Sometimes the stories have a "moral" to them—an essential punch line (Thomas & Arcus, 1992). Stories with moral content also build the moral intelligence of adults and children alike (Coles, 1997). The oral tradition of storytelling is found in numerous cultures and is useful for teaching many family life ideas. Some cultures use elders to tell these stories. Thus, family life educators might act as a catalyst for family members to begin telling and sharing their own personal and family narrative.

Here's one of our favorite stories (from author Wally Goddard's life), illustrating the importance of loving children in ways they want to be loved:

> Wally, a high school math teacher, was approached by a young fellow after class. The young man asked Wally to come with him on Saturday at 6 A.M. to the reservoir, crawl through the mud and cattails to the

water's edge, and watch the ducks take off. Now Wally thought of other things he'd rather be doing ("sawing logs," for instance), but since he liked to take pictures, he agreed to go. It was a good experience. Wally took lots of great photos. About 2 weeks later, this same young man told Wally that his dad was taking him to hunt big game. Wally responded, "Wow, you must be pretty excited!" The young man thought a moment and said, "Not really. I'd really like my dad to come with me to the reservoir some mornings and watch the ducks take off."

In a workshop, parents could then be asked to share their impressions about the story and what major messages or principles could be derived from the story. Then a discussion about how to learn and respond accurately to a child's love language could ensue.

Here is a personal narrative of the benefits of marriage preparation, from author Steve Duncan's life. In this case, the marriage preparation was unintentional:

During my master's program, I took an Introduction to Marriage and Family Therapy course. One assignment was to attend five "enrichment" sessions with a partner. The partner could be anyone, but immediately I thought of several women I knew. I decided to ask Barbara.

Barbara and I had been friends for over a year and just recently felt attracted to one another. I assured Barbara that the enrichment experience was just for a class, for "science," I joked. She agreed to participate.

During the first session, we explored our families. We mapped out our families on the chalkboard and described the relationships we had with each member. Our first assignment was to go out and get to know each other. We talked for hours about our families and backgrounds.

We spent the next day together too, having dinner with her grandparents and father, who just happened to be in town. The sessions helped us get to know each other from the inside out. We also benefited from the hour-long ride to and from the university, when we talked about many important matters.

Through this assignment I gained something far more important and valuable than an A on the paper. Barbara and I became engaged and married a few months afterward. This unintentional premarital counseling experience set the stage for understanding, kindness, consideration, friendship, and sharing that continues to be an important part of our very satisfying marriage.

Family life educators could use a story like the foregoing as a real-life illustration of the benefits of marriage preparation, after citing research that predicts a 30% increase in outcome success among those who participate in focused preparation for marriage (Carroll & Doherty, 2003). Such stories make the statistical data meaningful.

Stories are everywhere to be found. Look for them in magazines and books. Seek them in the lives of others, but also in your own life as a family member, from grandparents, and other family "historians." Then share them. As family life educators are open with their own imperfections as parents, spouses, and family members, they encourage an accepting "we're all in this together" climate that increases participants' sense of safety.

Skill Training

Family life educators often have the opportunity to help participants gain skills they need for successful marriage and family life. Here is a common approach based on social learning methods (Dumka et al., 1995):

- Describe the skill

  Example: Listening to children with the head and heart is an important skill for a parent to have. Elements of the skill include giving full attention, acknowledging feelings, inviting more discussion, and showing understanding by paraphrasing.

- Model the skill

  Example: As a parent, I'm going to demonstrate this skill in a role-play with one of you as my child, who has had a particularly awful day at school and wants to talk with a parent about it.

- Practice the skill in a nonstressful setting and situation

  Example: Let's break up into parent-child pairs and practice this skill, using a scenario you come up with.

- Receive reinforcement and corrective feedback

  Example: I'll come around and visit you, to see how you're coming along.

- Use the skill in a real setting

  Example: For homework this week, practice head and heart listening with your children. Come prepared next time to report how it went.

Family Councils/Meetings

Long recommended by family experts, family councils provide a choice opportunity for clarifying family responsibilities and expectations. Family councils can be used to set goals, distribute household work, resolve family problems, and celebrate one another's successes. When councils are conducted properly, they allow each person to voice his or her opinions and feelings and be involved in solving problems and making decisions.

You can use an FLE program to model and practice a family council for use at home, and/or you can use it as a teaching method. For example, one Building Family Strengths seminar held on one Sunday evening drew an overflow crowd of whole families at the local elementary school in a rural area. The family life educator began the evening by asking family members, "What makes families strong?" Answers varied among children and adults. Then the educator shared nine characteristics of strong families, many of which coincided with strengths identified by the participants, and illustrated the characteristics using personal stories and examples shared by participants. Refreshment time arrived, to be held in the school lunchroom. Here is where the second part of the program began. Families sat together as the educator asked, "If you wanted to build strengths in your family, what would you do first? Identify your strengths!" Families worked together family council style to identify where they were strong and where they needed improvement. Then they decided together on one or two areas of strength that needed work and set goals for doing activities that build the strength.

As a take-home assignment, you might ask participants to begin holding regular family councils. Here are some guidelines for holding them:

- Schedule a regular time for family councils, say every other Sunday or once a month.
- Councils shouldn't always be used to air concerns and solve problems. Try to talk about fun things, too—like planning family activities.
- Set and follow an agenda. Rotate conducting responsibilities between parents and older children.
- Prior to the council, encourage family members to write down things they want on the agenda for discussion. You might post a large piece of paper on the refrigerator or a bulletin board for this.
- Set ground rules for the council such as (a) everyone is free to express his or her opinions and feelings without fear of being

blamed or insulted for what they say, and (b) everyone is expected to listen to what is being said. Interruptions are not allowed.

- Limit the council to an hour, and end on a cheerful note—with a joke or refreshments.

Role-Playing

Role-playing is a technique to use when family life educators want participants to see how people would act in a given situation. They learn generalizations about behavior and begin to understand feelings. It includes both prepared or scripted role-plays and spontaneous role-plays. Role-playing also allows participants to practice using a principle that has been learned (Vance, 1989), so that when they encounter a real situation requiring its use, they will be better equipped to respond (Klemer & Smith, 1975). While many feel uncomfortable with using or participating in role-plays, they are effective in rehearsing effective strategies, and one can visualize and anticipate the effects of behavior on others.

The classic manner of role-playing is to select a vignette or problem and explain the situation to the group, explain to the actors their role, explain the audience's role, have the role players start the role-play, end the role-play, and then facilitate a discussion of the role-play. For example, if the role-play involved a parent-child scene, it would be good to discuss how the child felt and how the parent felt. Role-plays are useful to contrast a negative example (e.g., ineffective parenting) against a positive example (e.g., effective parenting).

Seven guidelines for all role-playing, whether it be classic or some variation of the classic type, follow (Institute for Mental Health Initiatives, 1991; Klemer & Smith, 1975; Vance, 1989):

1. There must be a reason for using role-playing other than entertaining the group, such as teaching a principle of behavior and/or helping participants gain insight into their own beliefs.

2. The situation must be emotional; that is, participants must feel an emotional investment in the outcome.

3. Be careful when selecting actors. Use role players (through selecting or volunteering) who will not feel threatened by playing the role.

4. Give the role players a little time to get into the role. They will need to think about the age, the personality, the pressures of the moment on that role, and the reaction that the person might make.

5. Part of good management of role-playing is the selection of the stopping place. The point of role-playing is to dramatize some behaviors and not to fill up time. When the players have shown several reactions in an attempt to solve the problems stated, stop the role-playing before it drags.

6. Facilitate discussion of the role-play. For example:
   a. What was the conflict/problem?
   b. What was going on with each person? Ask the group how they think persons would feel in this situation. Ask the role players to describe their feelings as they enacted their roles.
   c. Was the situation handled effectively or ineffectively? Why or why not? What could be improved? Discuss the practices that would improve the situation.
   d. Role-play the situation again and incorporate the principles and practices discussed.

7. If the roles played were very emotional and out of character for the players, they must be "de-roled." That is, either call each one by name or ask each of them to say to themselves, "I am [my name]." This process may sound unusual, but a peculiar feeling remains with some people if they are not brought back into their own roles.

Movie and Television Clips

Many years ago, pioneer family life educators Richard Klemer and Rebecca Smith (1975) argued that using movies "is a way of studying family relationships . . . including interaction of specific people in specific situations. . . . Students can identify or empathize more easily with the people in [movies] than they can with abstract concepts" (p. 25). Family life educators can use short clips from popular movies to illustrate important points regarding marriage and family relationships. For instance, during a marriage preparation program, a clip from *My Big Fat Greek Wedding* could be used to initiate a discussion on the importance of similar backgrounds between a man and woman considering marriage. In this movie, the man and woman considering marriage and later marrying come from arguably incompatible backgrounds. The movie does a great job of illustrating the differing backgrounds but fails to point out that this will create a lot of complications and difficulties throughout their married life. Family life educators could engage the group in a discussion of some of these potential complications that result from lack of similarity.

It's important to introduce the clip well, so that participants understand what the clip is about and how it fits in the process. Family life educators might also encourage participants to look for certain things in the clips. After a clip has been shown and discussed, it's useful to reiterate the point the clip illustrated before moving on to another instruction.

Television clips can be used in the same way. For example, I (Duncan) use a hilarious skit from *Saturday Night Live* called "Don't Buy Stuff You Can't Afford" featuring Steve Martin and Amy Poehler to introduce debt issues in marriage. I use a *Bob Newhart* segment titled "Stop It!" as a springboard to discuss cultural attitudes regarding mental illness, which may facilitate or inhibit attention given to serious mental challenges. These and many other clips can be found online by simply typing a name or topic in a search engine like Google.

A wise family life educator will generate a broad collection of movie and television clips geared to provide meaningful learning activities in pursuit of program objectives. In Appendix D, we list some of our favorite movie clips, topics they address, and how the clips could be used. You can think of many others!

Educational Videos

Many FLE curricula have companion videos or a strong video component. Not all videos are of equal quality and content, but many excellent educational videos are available for stand-alone instruction or enhancements of a program. Videos should be carefully chosen as aids to accomplish specific objectives, not merely to fill instructional time.

There are various educational videos available to family life educators. One source for accessing such videos is *Audiovisual Resources for Family Programming* (Jordan & Stackpole, 1995). Another refereed source of educational videos is the journal *Family Relations*. Each January issue through January 2005, this journal published a listing of award-winning educational videos that had been reviewed and rated by a committee of family life educators. Many DVDs and videos created for university or commercially developed programs can be used to present educational concepts. Often these entities, as do producers of motion pictures, grant permission to use limited clips for educational purposes under fair-use provisions.

Music and Pictures

The psychological and therapeutic benefits of music are well known. Music can have a calming, mood-altering influence. From a family life educational perspective, music can also be used to help individuals come to understand themselves and others (Klemer & Smith, 1975). Playing songs can help learners explore issues or ideas. For instance, through listening to a medley of various songs, an educator could help a class see the various kinds of love that are discussed (motherly love, deep-rooted love), as well as other things often called love (i.e., sexual attraction).

Music clips can also be used to explore various philosophies of life (Klemer & Smith, 1975) and to generate discussion of the impact that holding these philosophies has on marriage and family life. For example, I (Duncan) use a song series as part of my marriage education programs to illustrate approaches to marital commitment. I enjoy singing and interacting with the audience while I accompany myself on the piano. After posing the question, "How can and does modern Western culture influence our approach to keeping marital commitments?" and allowing some discussion, I sing excerpts from songs that illustrate lax commitment in relationships. These are songs from my era; you will likely find many songs that fit the concepts emphasized:

"Love on the Rocks" (Neil Diamond)

Excerpt:
You need what you need
You can say what you want
Not much you can do when the feeling is gone

Analysis: Shows a lax commitment to marriage by suggesting that there's little that can be done to restore absent love feelings.

"Why Don't We Live Together" (Barry Manilow)

Excerpt:
Why don't we live together
Only the two of us, we'll learn to trust
Don't have to say forever
'Cause we know the rain could start and break our hearts
But we'll never find the future if we hesitate
We'll spend our lives waiting

Analysis: Shows a lax commitment in relationships by suggesting the relationship doesn't have to be permanent.

"Then You Can Tell Me Goodbye" (Neal McCoy)

Excerpt:

> But if you must go I won't tell you no
> Just so that we can say we tried
> Tell me you love me for a million years
> Then if it don't work out
> If it don't work out
> Then you can tell me good-bye

Analysis: Shows a lax commitment in relationships by suggesting promises are kept so long as things work out.

I also provide a song critical of this lax approach:

"What's Forever For?" (Michael Martin Murphy)

Excerpt:

> But I see love-hungry people
> Trying their best to survive
> While in their hands is a dying romance
> And they're not even trying to keep it alive
> So what's the glory in living
> Doesn't anybody ever stay together anymore
> And if love never lasts forever
> Tell me what's forever for

Analysis: A commentary on the state of affairs in relationships: Commitment in relationships is so lax that people aren't really trying to keep love alive.

After this final number, I then lead participants in a discussion of nurturing commitment and protecting marriage from the widespread consumer culture that threatens it.

Many popular songs have family themes that could be incorporated into FLE. Some include "Butterfly Kisses" by Bob Carlisle (fatherhood, parenthood), "Cats in the Cradle" by Harry Chapin (father influence), "Do You Love Me?" from *Fiddler on the Roof* (marriage), and "Through the Years" by Kenny Rogers (marriage).

Pictures can also be used to enhance in FLE. For example, they can be used as a storytelling aid. One family life educator told a story of a family that lost all their worldly goods due to a natural disaster, yet still had each other, while showing photographs of the destruction such disasters leave in their wake. The story was used as a springboard into a discussion of the importance of commitment to family (Krysan et al., 1990), especially during the toughest times. Another use of pictures is to teach generalizations about family relationships (Klemer & Smith, 1975). For example, another educator showed photographs of family members from around the world, where fathers and sons, mothers and daughters, siblings, and entire family groups were posing or engaged in activities, and then asked participants to identify the commonalities among the pictures. In this photo illustration, some commonalities emerged: Family members were touching, there was a theme of togetherness, and all appeared happy together. The overall principle taught was that family bonding is a universal desire and can be nurtured through meaningful time together.

Books, Plays, and Short Stories

A variety of books, plays, and short stories depict themes that would be fruitful for outreach FLE. Some examples are *A Doll's House,* by Henrik Ibsen (good illustration of onset of marital decline, Helmer and Nora's relationship); *I Never Sang for My Father,* by Robert Anderson (teaching how adult children and their aging parents relate); and *A Piece of Strong,* by Guy de Maupassant (illustration of the costs of being unforgiving). Check book reviews to identify other sources.

Comic Strips and Cartoons

Comic strips and cartoons often grab the attention of learners and are useful discussion starters. We can invite participants to comment about the cartoon, such as to what degree they agree or disagree with the sentiment. Also, because of their humorous nature, cartoons can help reduce tension among participants (Warnock, 1988). Many cartoons serve as commentaries on family life. For instance, by exaggerating reality, *Calvin and Hobbes* helps illustrate many issues pertaining to parenting. *For Better or Worse* has very realistic portrayals of grief after losing a life-long spouse, older adult courtship, and marriage adjustments related to the birth of the first child. *Family Circus, Peanuts, Dennis the Menace, Sunshine Club, Family Tree, Cathy, Zits, Baby Blues,* and *Stone Soup* are other useful cartoons.

Editorial cartoons also provide useful illustrations of themes and occasionally present interesting ironies. For example, one cartoon (in Larson, 2000, p. 179) shows a picture of a small car alongside a gigantic flying machine labeled "marriage." The caption reads, "Which one doesn't require a special course of instruction to operate at age 16?" Discussion can ensue on the benefits of preparing for marriage at least as thoroughly as most states prepare young people to drive.

Games

Games can be used as ice breakers (DeBord, 1989), to interest students in a topic (Grieshop, 1987; O'Neill, 2003), or to facilitate active learning (McKeachie, 1999). Games can be presented following a format similar to television game shows (DeBord, 1989). When this is done, the familiarity of the game may encourage greater participation (DeBord, 1989).

Miner and Barnhill (2001) describe one game, *Dollars for Answers,* developed by county agents at Utah State University. In this game, the educator asks for a volunteer to come to the front of the classroom, then proceeds to ask the volunteer multiple-choice questions relating to the workshop topic. When a question is answered correctly, the volunteer receives a $1 prize. Giving this small prize makes the game more interesting and reduces the formality. After the question is answered correctly, the educator can take whatever time he or she wants to elaborate on the answer. If the volunteer answers incorrectly, the educator explains the correct answer and again has the opportunity to teach the class. The volunteer can be given the chance to answer more than one question before another volunteer is chosen. An alternative is to ask the entire class to vote on what they think is the correct answer, rather than putting one individual on the spot.

Another extension specialist (O'Neill, 2003) provides extensive instructions for creating an interactive *Jeopardy*-like PowerPoint quiz game at http://www.joe.org/joe/2003april/tt2.php

Object Lessons

Object lessons engage participants in the learning process. For example, one FLE, when teaching about work and family balance, introduces the session through the use of an object lesson. He asks for a volunteer to participate. He then proceeds to place books on the volunteer, wherever he can hold them—a few in each hand, one on his or her head, one on an uplifted knee, and so on. Through a dialogue with the volunteer, he then establishes how easy it is to become overwhelmed when multiple tasks are placed upon you from all directions. He ties this into demands from home, work, one's faith community, civic obligations, and so on.

Object lessons can also cause participants to reflect on and question assumptions in ways that have the potential to promote action. I (Duncan) use a driver's license to illustrate the need to prepare for marriage. I contrast the requirements for a driver's license with the requirements for a marriage license. It takes far more time, effort, and (usually) money to obtain a license to drive than to obtain legal permission to marry. As participants wrestle with the issue, they may become more motivated than ever before to consciously prepare for marriage.

Homework Assignments and Learning Contracts

Wise family life educators give participants something to work on between sessions or, if one session is all you have, an assignment or challenge to complete at home. Use the beginning of the next session to review how the homework assignment went. For example, following a session for parents on becoming aware of children's emotions, a step in Emotion Coaching (Gottman, 1997), one educator assigned participants to keep a journal of the emotions either they perceived or their children reported experiencing each day of the following week, noting also the events or other circumstances that may have triggered the emotion. Prior to moving on to another skill, each parent was given the opportunity to report on his or her experiences and receive feedback from the educator.

Some participants are reluctant to complete homework assignments. Family life educators who use a homework approach are wise at the beginning of the sessions to explain to participants that homework assignments provide a vital opportunity for them to practice the skills they learn in the program at home and that they will get the most benefit from a program if they complete homework assignments during the week after each session. Alternatively, commitment to homework completion can flow naturally from the use of learning contracts (Knowles, 1998). Learning contracts comprise the following eight steps:

1. Diagnose learning needs ("Where am I today as a parent and where would I like to be, in terms of knowledge and abilities?")

2. Specify learning objectives ("What do I want to be able to *do* as a result of this program?")

3. Specify learning resources and strategies ("What activities in and out of class would help me accomplish my objectives?")

4. Specify evidence of accomplishment ("What can I use to show I have gained the knowledge and skills I sought?")

5. Specify how the evidence will be validated ("Who will verify I have the knowledge and skill?")

6. Review the contract with a consultant (Show the educator the five steps)

7. Carry out the contract

8. Evaluate your learning

As participants create their own learning objectives and then consider what they need to do to accomplish them, they may be more self-motivated to engage in the learning strategy of practice at home (Step 3) and demonstrate their learning in the following session, receiving facilitator feedback (Steps 4 and 5).

Idea Reinforcers

Take-home session reminders are helpful in reinforcing key ideas from a session or presentation. One approach is to type the main ideas and memorable subpoints on a bordered half sheet of paper or on the same size cardstock and include a visual on it that would add to their recollection. For example, a presentation on "Timeless Principles of Parenting" might read like the one in Box 6.1.

Myth Versus Reality

FLE programs offer the opportunity to correct mistaken perceptions about family issues. For example, family life educators can help deconstruct many myths that have arisen regarding marriage that a young adult marriage preparation audience may embrace. Some of these myths might include "there is a one-and-only" or some other myth (Larson, 1988). Belief in myths can lead to expectations built upon false ideas and can become a risk factor in marriage (Larson, 2000). Some older persons carry myths

---

Box 6.1

Timeless Principles of Parenting

1

Learn and Speak Your Child's Love Language
Watch them, as them, don't mind-read!

2

Correct With Love
How you say it matters

3

Use Consequences
Natural, logical, individualized

---

about aging (e.g., all older people become senile if they live long enough) that, if embraced, may limit their ability to have a maximum quality of life.

I (Duncan) developed a program called "Myths of Aging" that was built around this method. The program first began with a quiz, which participants were to answer on paper "True" or "False." In checking the answers, we learned not only the answers but an explanation of the answers using research.

CONCLUSION ●

The tools and skills detailed in this chapter become the delivery vehicle for excellent content carefully linked to goals and objectives. Wise selection of methods and learning activities increases the chances of a significant learning experience participants will not want to miss. Be a collector of learning activities to enrich educational interest and your own creativity. This chapter has provided a starting point to build on. Try out some of the explorations that follow.

● EXPLORATIONS

1. Create a sample instructional outline appropriate for a workshop setting. Write the overall goal, followed by two or three learning objectives following the pattern from Chapter 2. Make sure the objectives are measurable and contain active verbs—what you actually want participants to *do*. Then, for each learning objective you list, select a different instructional method and practice teaching with your class and colleagues.

2. Go on a methods treasure hunt for a few weeks and create a chest of "Family Life Education Methods." Many excellent books developed for adult learners contain ideas that can be adapted to FLE settings. One favorite is Mel Silberman's (1996) *Active Learning: 101 Strategies to Teach Any Subject.*

3. Develop a habit, like radar, of checking for story illustrations when reading magazines, books, newspapers, and other literature, as well as checking comics (in newspapers and at online sources), watching movies and videos, and, when on the Internet, checking for clips that have educational value. Friends and family may think you obsessive, but family life educators often can't help looking for teaching elements in all these materials!

CHAPTER 7

WORKING WITH DIVERSE AUDIENCES

Diversity is an essential part of being human. In one way or many ways, we are all different from each other. When we speak of diversity, we often think of ethnic diversity. Mindel, Habenstein, and Wright (1998) define an ethnic group as "those who share a unique social and cultural heritage that is passed on from generation to generation. . . . In America, the core categories of ethnic identity from which individuals are able to form a sense of peoplehood are race, religion, national origin, or some combination of these categories" (p. 6).

Yet ethnic diversity is not the only kind of diversity. It may not even be the most important kind of diversity for the work of family life educators. Diversity of family experience plays a central role in people's experience of family and life (Hart & Risley, 1995; Peterson & Hann, 1999). Factors that could substantially affect one's experience of family as well as one's approach to family creation include experience of abuse, parental incompetence or mental illness, family mobility, parental conflict, poverty, stress, family size, spacing of children, proximity of extended family, social support, belief systems—the possibilities are innumerable. Of course, there is no tidy formula that connects difficult early family experience to dysfunctional adult family functioning. Werner and Smith (1977, 1982, 1992, 2001) found that many of the stressed children they studied later flourished. Their resilience apparently resulted from various combinations of dispositional and environmental resources. Wide diversity of experience combines with great diversity of disposition and resources to make for very different outcomes.

In addition to accounting for ethnic diversity and family experience, Silver, Strong, and Perini (2000) recommend that effective educators should factor in multiple intelligences and learning styles. In their framework, they use Howard Gardner's eight multiple intelligences and four Jungian learning styles akin to Myers-Briggs personality classifications. The challenge of dealing with diversity can be overwhelming if it is seen as somehow calculating and accommodating differences in ethnicity, family experience, gender, learning styles, and multiple intelligences. There simply is no formula for processing this myriad of factors to create educational recommendations. This is one of the reasons that we must invite learners to take substantial responsibility for their learning.

● SENSITIZING TO DIFFERENCES

It is useful to be familiar with cultural proclivities. For example, Native American families (especially traditional ones) are more likely than many American families to include extended family, a communal family economy, low educational attainment, reverence of nature and ancestors, strong interdependence, and strong loyalty to family (John, 1998).

African American families are more likely than many American families to operate without marriage, have woman-headed households, be based on consanguineal relationships, suffer poverty and poor-paying employment, and have limited education (McAdoo, 1998).

Hispanic families in America are more likely than many American families to have strong religious beliefs; value cooperation, interdependence, and loyalty to family; and have strong extended family relationships (see Mindel et al., 1998). However, the astute reader will recognize the limits of these generalizations. Consider the differences between, for example, Mexican Americans (many of whom live along the southern border of the United States), Puerto Ricans (who are more likely to live in New York City), and Cuban Americans (who are likely to live in Florida). Even with the Cuban American group, there are substantial differences between the backgrounds of those who came in the first wave as Castro took power in Cuba (more likely to be wealthy and educated) and those who came later (Suarez, 1998).

A similar point can be made about Native Americans. "Native Americans represent a large number of tribes with different linguistic and cultural heritages. There is no one kind of Indian, no one tribe, no one Indian nation" (Hildreth & Sugawara, 1993, p. 165).

DIVERSITY OF LEARNING STYLES ●

In the effort to help family life educators work more effectively with various ethnic groups, there have been efforts to describe distinct ethnic learning styles (see Guion et al., 2003). For example, African Americans are said to learn through movement, humor, emotion, imagery, and holistic and oral approaches. In contrast, Asian American learning styles are described as high motivation to achieve, use of intuition, self-discipline, concentration, showing respect or conformity, and use of problem solving. Hispanic/ Latino learning preferences include cooperative learning, interdependence, affection, intuition, and being based in tradition. Native American learning preferences include cooperation, holistic orientation, harmony seeking, visualization and symbolism, and storytelling.

The great danger of generalizations is that they may mask the great individual variation within a group. Social scientists are fond of observing that the variation within groups exceeds that between groups. For example, while there may be some difference in spatial aptitude between men and women (the issue is still debated), the differences among men and among women are so great that knowing the sex of the person tells you almost nothing about the likely spatial aptitude of a given person.

There is an old saying that "All Indians walk single file. At least the one I saw did." Humans tend to be naive psychologists who use their limited experience to form general laws (Heider, 1958). While it may be useful and necessary to see patterns in experience, human history is littered with the wreckage of us-them thinking. Any attempt to reduce a group of people to a few descriptors is certain to leave us unprepared to appreciate the rich diversity within the group. When attempts to describe a group of people cause us to be categorical and prejudiced, they are counterproductive. When attempts to describe a group of people cause us to be humble and appreciative, they prepare us for mutual learning.

ETHNICITY AND VALUES ●

It is useful to be aware that each person we meet brings a unique set of experiences and sensitivities to any interchange. Family life education (FLE) deals with inherently personal and value-laden subjects.

We should be prepared to understand the worldview and logic of those we serve.

McDermott (2001) has described several values pertinent to family life that show considerable variation:

- Individual as the primary unit in society
- Competition
- Communication standards
- Action orientation
- Time orientation
- Work ethic
- Family structure

The Individual

The dominant North American culture places a high value on the individual as the primary unit of society. Many other cultures are more sociocentric, valuing a couple, a family, or a community as the basic unit of society. A related value is competition. While much of American culture values winning, many people within our culture and in other cultures value cooperation and teamwork more highly. Effective family life educators will be aware that many participants within a class may be very sensitive to the well-being of all participants. Not only will they not want to see others humiliated, but they may not want to compete with each other. Common American teaching techniques that emphasize competition such as a quiz bowl may raise anxiety and discomfort with such audiences.

Communication Standards

Related to communication standards, some participants may be reluctant to participate because their English is limited. Some may be uncomfortable with self-disclosure. Some may see strong statements and direct questioning as harsh. Sensitive family life educators will observe carefully the patterns that participants use and will strive to communicate in a way that honors participants' preferences.

Action Orientation

The dominant culture values an action orientation. We tightly program ourselves to avoid wasting precious time. Some cultures are more reflective. They may value being over doing.

Culturally observant family life educators will consider the action orientation of potential audiences in the selection of program content and methods. Once I (Duncan) was invited to do a seminar on time management on the Crow Indian Reservation in Montana by a county Extension agent who was also a member of the Crow tribe. She wanted me to help her audience use their time better. As I prepared, I felt that in-vogue practices of effective time management developed by upper middle-class Whites with a business orientation would have limited applicability among poor single parents on the reservation. While teaching them, I found that instead of being time oriented, participants were event oriented. They organized their lives around events of the day (e.g., mealtimes, beginnings, and endings) instead of by hours and minutes. So instead of framing the discussion around the management of time, we talked about getting things done. Such an approach helped them learn new things about accomplishing more with their lives within the context of their cultural values.

Time Orientation

Time orientation is also an important value. Some cultures are very focused on honoring the past. History and ancestors are highly honored. The dominant American ethos tends to look to the future. Optimism and foresight are valued. Since we are likely to have persons in groups comprising all of these perspectives, wise family life educators can honor each through the wise selection of stories and examples illustrating the virtue of each viewpoint.

Work Ethic

The dominant culture has a strong work ethic. Those who work hard are respected. The great danger is the assumption that hard work translates into success. There are many who work hard (or want to work hard) but are seriously disadvantaged. Poverty is not a sure sign of laziness. Success is not sure evidence of industry.

Family Structure

Family structure is another value that can lead to misunderstanding. Americans tend to value autonomous households. Many cultures value the rich interdependence of extended family households. We should resist the temptation to impose our meaning on living configurations that may be different from our own.

An awareness of these values can sensitize us to preferences and values of those we serve. There is no paper-and-pencil assessment that allows us to pigeonhole them. Given the diversity that can be expected within a seemingly homogeneous group, there is no single method that will be effective with a specific group. There are, however, processes that help us discover and honor the diversity we will find among those we serve.

● SKILLED DIALOGUE

Barrera and Corso (2003) have developed a process that they call skilled dialogue. While their process was developed for use in early childhood education and special education, the principles clearly apply to FLE.

Skilled dialogue challenges the notion that cultural competence is primarily the result of extensive knowledge about cultures. "The belief that one must have information about others before one can be culturally competent is itself a cultural artifact" (p. 42). Beyond cultural education, Barrera and Corso recommend dialogue that includes respect, reciprocity, and responsiveness. "Respect is expressed as a willingness to acknowledge a variety of perspectives as equally valid to achieving a particular goal" (p. 67). Reciprocity "requires entering into interactions ready to learn as well as to teach, ready to receive as well as to give" (p. 69). Responsiveness focuses on communicating both respect and understanding of the others' perspectives.

Sometimes our subject matter expertise works against us. The more we are socialized to the scholarly ways of thinking, the more we may be ready to prescribe solutions before we fully understand those we serve. We may develop hardening of the categories.

Barrera and Corso (2003) give examples that are pertinent for family life educators. One example that is especially pertinent for home visitors involves Betsy, who visited Karen, a single mother from Puerto Rico, weekly. Betsy laments, "When I ask her to tell me what she'd like for her child Maya or when I ask her to work with Maya, she says that I am the expert and that I should tell her what needs to be done. Sometimes she'll even leave me alone with Maya. I know that Karen cares about Maya and is just expressing her respect for me, but how can I get Karen more involved in Maya's activities while I am visiting?" (p. 43).

The instinctive response to Karen might be to explain the importance of her participation and request (or insist) that she remain and participate while Betsy works with Maya. Since the objective of Betsy's visits is not only to help Maya directly but also to train Karen to work more effectively with her, the request seems entirely reasonable. But there is a wonderful opportunity for skilled dialogue here.

The first quality of skilled dialogue is respect. Respect entails believing that people do what they do for reasons that make sense to them. We may not understand the reasons—we may not even know the reasons—that Karen keeps her distance. But if we respect Karen, we believe that her reluctance to take part in Maya's treatment is not a sign of indifference. Karen might not take part because she feels very inadequate in the presence of an expert. (Have you ever felt inadequate in the presence of an expert?) Or she might use Betsy's visits as a chance to get a welcome break. There are many reasons Karen does not take part. We do not have to agree with those reasons. We can identify tension points without making any judgments about the character of the other person.

Reciprocity, the second quality of skilled dialogue, acknowledges that every person has experience and perceptions of value. We don't have to prove that we are right and they are wrong. If we are skilled at listening and understanding, there is much we can learn from Karen. We can observe the ways in which she does interact effectively with Maya. We can ask questions to help us understand. "How would you feel about hanging around while I work with Maya? I would like you to tell me what things I am doing that you think might be helpful to her." Such a request acknowledges that Karen knows more about Maya than we do. It invites her to be a partner in the process of helping Maya.

Responsiveness requires humility, or what Barrera and Corso (2003) describe as being open to mystery. We listen. We observe. We ask questions. We know that we need knowledge that the mother has as much as she needs the knowledge that we bring. We know that we don't have all the answers. We seek to understand and to communicate that understanding by asking such questions that may begin with "What do you think . . . ? Do you think it would help if . . . ?"

Such skilled dialogue can lead to "anchored understanding of diversity"—not the generalizations about cultures but a specific knowledge and appreciation of someone who is different from us. "Simply knowing about something tends to leave one detached, standing outside with a relatively general and perhaps even stereotypical picture" (Barrera & Corso, 2003, p. 54). Such anchored understanding does not come from a textbook; it can only come through personal relationships.

With an anchored understanding of diversity, we are prepared to enter what Barrera and Corso (2003) call "3rd Space." Rather than dragging the parent to our view or abdicating to the parent's view, we look for the new place that incorporates the best of both of our experiences. Third Space invites us "to make a fundamental shift from dualistic, exclusive perceptions of reality and to adopt a mindset that integrates the complementary aspects of diverse values, behaviors, and beliefs into a new whole" (pp. 75–76). Betsy may need to set aside any agenda for Karen until she understands her world. She may offer to help her prepare dinner or wash dishes while they chat.

● GROUP FLE EXAMPLES

I (Goddard) was invited to teach a series of parenting classes to a group of parents whose teens were in trouble with the law. The parents did not come to the class gladly. They were mad at their teens and mad at the judge who required their attendance at parenting classes.

With respect to the issue of diversity, the organizer of the classes had serious reservations about whether a college professor with a happy family would be able to speak the language of angry, working parents who were experiencing hell at home. It was reasonable for him to worry. If I had given university lectures on socialization processes, I would have alienated the parents.

We began the first session with introductions and a question: "Is parenting hard or easy?" The question energized the parents. All agreed that parenting is tough duty. Some of them volunteered their stories. Over the course of several sessions, most of them shared their struggles.

One of the fathers—a tough, crusty, and outspoken man—told that every night he propped a chair against his bedroom door and kept a weapon under his pillow because he was afraid that his daughter might break into his room in the night and stab him.

There are many ways to react to such a statement. One natural reaction might be, "If you weren't such a brute, you wouldn't have to worry about your well-being!" On some level, we might be "right." But such an approach is only helpful in silly movies. If we apply Barrera and Corso's (2003) quality of respect (above) together with Ginott's (1965, 1969) process of sensitization (as described in Chapter 5), our reaction would be very different. I tried to imagine what that man might be feeling. Based on my effort at empathy, I could reply from the heart: "Ouch! It must be very painful to have such an awful relationship with your daughter when you want so badly to be a good dad."

Actually, there was nothing in his statement that spoke to his aspirations as a father. But I speculated that the reason he told that story—and the reason it was so painful for him—is that he would like to have a caring relationship with his daughter. I know how painful it would have been for me if I had been in his shoes. Over the course of the series of classes, that father moved from resentment toward hope.

I am convinced that our effectiveness in FLE has less to do with the match of our education and experience to that of our participants than it has to do with our willingness and ability to be genuinely compassionate. While each of the participants in that class had a different story to tell, each of their stories was about hopes, struggles, and disappointments. Those are stories that should draw compassion out of all of us.

I (Duncan) was invited to one of Montana's Indian reservations to teach a half-day workshop on personal development. I find Abraham Maslow's conceptualization of the self to be very powerful and helpful and was in the process of presenting some of his ideas in a way I thought understandable to my group. At one point, I chose the metaphor of an apple to lead participants into an exercise where they would identify characteristics of their true or "core" selves. I said, "I am like an apple, and at my core you will find. . . ." I then invited participants to complete the phrase by listing their core personal characteristics, which Maslow maintains are always positive and "uncreated." Instead of beginning to write, several smiled awkwardly and some even chuckled softly. So I asked them what they found funny. They were comfortable enough around me to tell me directly what was on their mind. Apples are red on the outside (at least many varieties) and white on the inside. So my asking them to imagine they were an apple was like asking them to pretend they were American Indian only on the outside but actually White on the inside. We dialogued about what metaphors for the self would be more meaningful to them and found that metaphors representing human connection to the earth and other living things held significance. Although some things we will learn only by experience, this one taught me the importance of checking out assumptions with others from the target audience.

PROGRAMMING FOR DIVERSITY •

The primary challenges for programming for diversity are twofold: (1) Create FLE materials and use approaches that are inclusive of heterogeneous groups audiences or (2) be on target with materials developed or adapted for homogeneous groups. In addition to the perspective and strategies we have already discussed, here are several specific guidelines for diversity programming in FLE (Myers-Walls, 2000).

Know Your Audience

There are literally dozens of dimensions on which FLE audiences may vary. Some typical ones include age, income, and marital or parental status. From an ecological systems perspective (Bronfenbrenner, 1979), true understanding of FLE audiences moves well beyond knowing their simple social address. Effective FLE programming involves understanding audiences in the context of their surroundings (Schorr, 1988, 1997). It also includes being sensitive to the unique construction of meaning for each participant. Understanding diversity moves to an awareness of the multiple and intersecting ways in which audiences and individuals within audiences may vary.

All of us have membership in a variety of different groups based on our gender, race, religious beliefs, income, and educational levels. To these group variations can be added the additional diversity noted earlier in the chapter, such as learning styles and communication standards. Other cultural context variations include population-environmental context (What is the age and maturity of the community?), views of children (Are children viewed more as a blessing or a burden?), and interpersonal relationships (Whose needs predominate? Children, adults, or the group?) (Myers-Walls, 2000).

Perhaps the best time to begin learning about audience diversity is during the needs assessment process, where attitudes, values, meanings, and expectations can be explored. Data collection during needs assessment should be representative of the diversity of persons for whom that program is being designed. Wise family life educators will also include members of the intended audience on the assessment team to ensure sensitivity to the kinds of questions that should be asked members of particular subgroups. However, needs assessments alone are insufficient to meet diversity needs. To be effective, family life educators must remain flexible during teaching situations and continually assess the fit of the principles they share with the life experience and meanings of participants.

Know Yourself

Myers-Walls (2000) suggests learning who we are, what we know, and how we feel pertaining to diversity matters. Learning who we are involves identifying our personal characteristics and the various sociocultural groups to which we belong. We can identify the various ways we intersect and overlap with audiences as well as how we differ from them, as well as the implications for FLE. A self-evaluation of what we know and do not know about the various audiences we seek to reach is another important step. When the knowledge gap is too great, then we work to reduce that knowledge gap through greater study of the audience. Some of this beginning knowledge gap may be closed though learning about various cultural perspectives such as those shared at the beginning of the chapter. Assessing how we feel is about asking ourselves questions regarding our attitudes and values, such as we explored in Chapter 1. According to Myers-Walls (2000), "A central question with which to begin a self-assessment is whether one views diversity as a problem to be solved or an opportunity to be realized" (p. 371).

Explore Your Limits

Family life educators may be flexible and comfortable with a certain level of diversity but uncomfortable when diversity exceeds certain personal, ethical, and empirical boundaries. Knowing who we are as family life educators involves knowing where these specific boundaries lie for ourselves. For example, we might never recommend that parents spank their children for any reason because we personally consider spanking disrespectful of children. Professionally, we may consider it unethical to recommend a strategy that potentially could do harm, despite some empirical data showing spanking can be a useful behavior control strategy for a certain age group of children. We may believe there are certain values, attitudes, and behaviors in families that are better and healthier than others, and we are not willing to recommend less effective strategies. For that reason, we might tell participants, "Spanking is probably never the best solution." It is probably not productive to argue against a group's cultural values, but it may be useful to invite group members to consider even better techniques that are consistent with their group and individual values.

Evaluate Program Material for Diversity

There are at least three important questions to ask when evaluating FLE program material for diversity (Myers-Walls, 2000):

Are the goals and objectives of the program appropriate for the individuals and groups in the audience? Family life educators need to assess whether the material shared will benefit all groups equally or whether it will tend to favor specific groups. Goals and objectives should be written to incorporate the various groups' (or targeted groups') values and aspirations.

Are the content of the program and sources of information or knowledge base applicable to the audience? How inclusive and applicable is it to a heterogeneous group? How might it be adapted to meet the needs of a different homogeneous or targeted audience? The ideas on which FLE programs are based are only as good as their scholarly foundations. Many ideas commonly accepted as truth in family science are based mostly on research of the White middle class. Family life educators should examine source materials for their breadth and inclusiveness (e.g., did the summary of studies underlying a parenting idea include data from a diversity of respondents?). For targeted audiences (e.g., single parents with young children), family life educators should examine whether the foundational material applies to the targeted population.

I (Duncan) was working as an Extension specialist in Montana and had been asked to deliver a series of Making Families Stronger workshops at several elementary schools and a middle school in my hometown. The workshop series was based on well-known family strengths literature, prominently based on findings from mostly two-parent, first-marriage, White families. The workshop series was well publicized in anticipation of the events. One afternoon I received a phone call from an interested person who asked whether the workshop would be relevant only to traditional families with a mother and a father and if the examples would feature only that family form. She mentioned that she was interested in attending with her female partner. I told her that while the research underlying the program originated primarily from two-parent, heterosexual parent-headed families, it also included some stepfamilies and single-parent families. Beyond those families, it was unknown precisely how the family strengths ideas would apply to other family forms. However, I hastened to add my professional position that the strengths were about family processes, not family structures, and that the ideas were relevant for any close human relationship. I was pleased to see her and her partner attend my middle school workshop and seem to enjoy the discussion.

Are the teaching methods and styles respectful of and effective with the audience? If an audience had limited educational background, methods might be chosen because of their effectiveness with visual and auditory learners, rather than relying on written materials. For example, wise family life educators might include a variety of visual media such as videotaping and movie clips, telling stories that relate to participant experiences, hands-on activities, group activities, group games, and role-playing to present ideas.

Educators would keep the material simple and to the point because of the vast differences in participant educational levels. Written material would be written at a low reading level or be simple enough that they can be easily adapted/interpreted.

Be Flexible

Effective family life educators will need to respond flexibly to a variety of educational needs. Avoid the one-size-fits-all approach to programming. An individualized approach based on family need rather than a uniform approach across families should be used, especially when working with limited resource families (Schorr, 1988, 1997). Some ideas may go untaught in workshop settings, but human needs will be met. To accomplish this, sessions might be offered in small groups or have built-in one-on-one time, as needed, allowing for more individualized attention and for materials to be more effectively adapted to individual participant needs.

CONCLUSION ●

All of us share something in common: We are alike and different in many ways. To effectively meet the needs of an increasingly diverse FLE audience, family life professionals need to become sensitive to diversity on many fronts, including cultural differences, learning styles, cultural contexts, and values. Important skills that family life educators need to program for diversity include using skilled dialogue, knowing the audience, knowing themselves, knowing their limits, and how to evaluate program materials for diversity. Characteristics important for working with diverse audiences include empathy, compassion, and flexibility. The following applications will help you strengthen your abilities to work with diverse FLE audiences.

EXPLORATIONS ●

1. Think of a group with which you have worked or with which you expect to work. What are some of the unhelpful judgments you have been tempted to make of those you served? How can those judgments be framed differently as you try to apply the qualities of anchored understanding?

2. In leading a training, one mother told of difficulties when her strong-willed child had a tantrum at the grocery store. The educator asked what tactics she had tried and what effect they had had. She told him. He suggested additional possibilities. She insisted that nothing would work. He recommended some alternatives—and did it with greater certainty. She became more resistant. What might the educator have done to be more effective, based on the ideas you have gained from this chapter?

3. As you anticipate the difficult situations you will face in your professional activities, what challenges are you likely to face in connecting with the people you serve? How can you prepare yourself to respond helpfully and sensitively? Discuss with your colleagues and classmates what challenges they have faced and how they have dealt with them. Develop your own plan for growing and maintaining an anchored understanding of diversity.

4. Imagine you have been asked by your family coalition to provide parenting education in your community. In your search for an optimal program, you come across a program called Principles for Parenting Success. As you review it, you notice some good general principles, but they need adapting to fit your community, which is racially, culturally, educationally, and economically diverse. Describe how you would modify this program for diversity based on the social ecology of your community. First, discuss how you would modify the program to make it more inclusive, then discuss how you would alter it for a specific target audience within the community. Describe how you would modify goals and objectives, content, teaching methods, and evaluation approaches.

5. What are some of the signs when you are teaching a workshop that the content or presentation is not reaching the audience? What can a workshop leader do to adjust to the audience?

PART IV

CONTENT AND
CONTEXTS FOR FAMILY
LIFE EDUCATION

CHAPTER 8

EDUCATION FOR PERSONAL WELL-BEING

Flourishing People Make Better Family Members

S ome people might wonder whether a chapter on personal well-being
has a place in a book on family life education. The individual is not
normally considered a family.

Yet our personal functioning has great impact on our ability to be good
family members. The research is clear that a depressed parent is a less
effective one (Oyserman, Mowbray, Meares, & Firminger, 2003). It is likewise obvious that a partner who is unhappy or stressed will have a harder
time contributing to a couple relationship (Bodenmann, Pihet, & Kayser,
2006). A parent or child who is hostile will affect the family negatively as
well (Belsky, Lerner, & Spanier, 1984).

This idea is acknowledged as fundamental in two of the most prominent formulations of family relationships. In the National Extension Parent
Education Model (Smith et al., 1994), the first dimension of parenting is the
parent's *Care for Self.*

In *The National Extension Relationship and Marriage Education Model*
(Adler-Baeder et al., 2010), care for self, defined as "maintaining physical,
psychological, and sexual health and wellness as an individual," is one of

seven core dimensions. Vibrant individuals are better able to be contributing members of families.

None of this is surprising since the happiest people devote more time to family and friends, express more gratitude, offer more help to others, practice optimism, get more exercise, have lifelong goals, and cope better with stress (Lyubomirsky, 2008).

How do we help family life education (FLE) audiences care for themselves, thereby maximizing their well-being and contributing to the quality of family life? What concepts and principles are most useful in the design of such learning experiences? This chapter contrasts two models of well-being and emphasizes the emerging positive psychology model as a theoretical perspective around which to build ideas for personal wellness. It then reviews several concepts and principles that could be incorporated into educational experiences in this area. Finally, it suggests an educational framework for implementation.

● MODELS OF WELL-BEING

The Self-Esteem Era

For decades, *self-esteem* has been nearly synonymous with *well-being* in Western cultures. It was commonly assumed that we cannot have happy, productive lives unless we love ourselves (see J. Powell, 1974). Self-esteem was assumed to be essential to productivity as well as happiness.

Over time, these assumptions about self-esteem have been called into question. As early as 1983, Susan Harter reviewed the research and found two major problems with common self-esteem assumptions. First, self-esteem is not unitary (i.e., self-appreciation is not an all-or-nothing proposition). Most of us feel good about ourselves in some areas and less good about ourselves in others. Second, self-esteem is not predictive. Rather than trying to raise self-esteem to improve performance (as we have often tried to do in families and public schools), the more promising path is to improve performance in order to facilitate self-acceptance.

The news for self-esteem advocates got more dismal after a large California study. When the effects of self-esteem were measured in many settings, the advocates discovered something unexpected: "The news most consistently reported, however, is that the associations between self-esteem and its expected consequences are mixed, insignificant or absent" (Mecca et al., 1989, p. 15). High self-esteem was as likely to predict bad behavior as good behavior. It clearly was not the vital inoculation for personal and social well-being that some had supposed.

More recently, Roy Baumeister, a leading social psychologist, has observed (1992) that the growing emphasis on the individual at the expense of social and family ties has left a culture of narcissism in which people are left with little meaning or solid bases for decisions. There has been a cry in recent years for a return to a more sociocentric and less individualistic orientation in American society (e.g., Etzioni, 1993).

Self-esteem's preeminence was further challenged when Baumeister, Smart, and Boden (1999) described a dark side of high self-esteem. They observed that "the benefits of favorable self-opinions accrue primarily to the self and they are, if anything, a burden and potential problem to everyone else" (p. 241). After examining the evidence in several areas of interpersonal violence, they concluded that "the societal pursuit of high self-esteem for everyone may literally end up doing considerable harm" (p. 275).

Jean Twenge (2006) has argued that we now have a "Generation Me": "Today's young people . . . speak the language of the self as their native tongue. [In this view] the individual has always come first, and feeling good about yourself has always been a primary virtue" (p. 2). Like Baumeister before her, Twenge underscores the problems of self-esteem for healthy family life, including parenting: "Having a baby suddenly means that you have little control over your life—the freedom to which you were accustomed vanishes, and your individual accomplishments are not as valued anymore" (p. 94). Cultivating self-esteem can make it more difficult for us to function as family members.

Seligman (2002) has underscored the limitations of the self-esteem movement: "'Get in touch with your feelings,' shout the self-esteem peddlers in our society. Our youth have absorbed this message, and believing it has produced a generation of narcissists whose major concern, not surprisingly, is with how they feel" (p. 118).

Seligman (2002) also underscores the problems related to quick and easy success:

> The self-esteem movement in particular, and the feel-good ethic in general, had the untoward consequence of producing low self-esteem on a massive scale. By cushioning feeling bad, it has made it harder for our children to feel good and to experience flow. By circumventing feelings of failure, it made it more difficult for our children to feel mastery. By blunting warranted sadness and anxiety, it created children at high risk for unwarranted depression. By encouraging cheap success, it produced a generation of very expensive failures. (p. 217)

The failure of self-esteem to facilitate personal well-being and family functioning should not be understood as a recommendation for self-hate. Depression and despair are destructive; they drain away vast reservoirs of energy. It might be fairer to say that the great American feel-good movement is too simple to sustain human well-being. There is more to full functioning than celebrating ourselves.

A more balanced view of well-being invites us to respect ourselves while cultivating healthy relationships. It should not surprise us that something as important as personal well-being is not as simple as self-appreciation. The good news is that psychology has settled on new and more empirically supported recommendations for personal flourishing that go far beyond the simple prescriptions of the self-esteem movement.

The New Positive Psychology

The failure of the self-esteem movement to provide a foundation for healthy development seemed to leave a vacuum in pop psychology. It was not immediately clear what would replace self-esteem as the foundation for well-being. Then came the positive psychology revolution.

The call to arms was sounded by Martin Seligman in his presidential address at the 1998 conference of the American Psychological Association. He contended that "psychology's focus on the negative has left us knowing too little about the many instances of growth, mastery, drive, and character building that can develop out of painful life events" (Seligman, 1999, p. 561).

Seligman has led the charge to study human thriving. He argues that wellness is more than an absence of sickness. Thriving as a human and a family member is the result of several well-established practices.

Psychology has always had an interest in well-being and mental health. Throughout the history of psychology, scholars and studies have pointed us along a path toward thriving. Prominent among such scholars has been Abraham Maslow, who pointed us toward optimal human functioning. His account of human possibilities was fundamentally optimistic (Maslow, 1970).

Yet much of psychology has been focused on mental illness (Maddux, 2002). "Clinical psychologists always have been 'more heavily invested in intricate theories of failure than in theories of success' (Bandura, 1998, p. 3)" (Maddux, 2002, pp. 14–15). As a case in point, "the illness ideology is enshrined in the most powerful book in psychiatry and clinical psychology—the *Diagnostic and Statistical Manual of Mental Disorders*" (Maddux, 2002,

p. 15). In part because the treatment of mental illness provided funding for practicing psychologists, the field has often focused on illness more than wellness. Positive psychologists argue that the cultivation of strengths may be more important for flourishing than the eradication of mental illness. In fact, Seligman (2002) confronted the idea directly: "I do not believe that you should devote overly much effort to correcting your weaknesses. Rather, I believe that the highest success in living and the deepest emotional satisfaction comes from building and using your signature strengths" (p. 13).

Since Seligman made his call to arms in 1998, there has been an explosion of excellent scholarly contributions to the positive psychology movement. Some of the most important books are listed at the end of this chapter. The bulk of this chapter will summarize some of what has been learned about personal well-being—or flourishing as some call it. Before doing that, a caveat is in order.

Limits of Human Objectivity

Humans are rational beings. We cherish logic and base our decisions on careful reasoning. Yet there is a fly in the cognitive ointment. S. E. Taylor and Brown (1999) describe the human problem:

> Information processing is full of incomplete data gathering, shortcuts, errors, and biases. In particular, prior expectations and self-serving interpretations weigh heavily into the social judgment process. In summarizing this work, Fiske and Taylor (1984) noted, "Instead of a naïve scientist entering the environment in search of the truth, we find the rather unflattering picture of a charlatan trying to make the data come out in a manner most advantageous to his or her already-held theories." (p. 44)

The scientific evidence suggests that we each have two antithetical forces at work within us. Gardner (2008) calls the two systems Gut and Head. Gut, manifest in our feelings, makes snap decisions. "I don't like that person." "That child is defying me." "My spouse is not being fair." Then our minds ("Heads") go to work finding reasons to justify our gut feelings. The problem is that the mind thinks it is being entirely rational even as the conclusions have been hijacked by the gut. You can see what kind of mischief this processing error can create in human relations in general and family relations in particular. We often defend our positions without realizing that they are the creation of self-protective, irrational, and stubborn emotions.

Eventually we can get a serious case of hardening of the categories; we see certain family members as selfish, impulsive, or unfair, and we fail to see their limitations in context of their strengths.

While Gardner (2008) alerts us to the dangers of the irrationality of our judgments, Haidt (2006) warns us about the limitations of our perception that help maintain them. He borrows the term *naive realism.*

> Each of us thinks we see the world directly, as it really is. We further believe that the facts as we see them are there for all to see, therefore others should agree with us. If they don't agree, it follows either that they have not yet been exposed to the relevant facts or else that they are blinded by their interests and ideologies. . . . It just seems plain as day, to the naïve realist, that everyone is influenced by ideology and self-interest. Except for me. I see things as they are. (p. 71)

Haidt (2006) nominated naive realism as the "biggest obstacle to world peace and social harmony" because of the way it makes us so self-assured about our faulty beliefs.

There is more bad news about our imperfect thinking processes. Roy Baumeister (1997) described an intriguing element of our faulty thinking that he calls the myth of pure evil. Under the influence of this myth, we see ourselves and people who are like us as better than we are. At the same time, we see our enemies—and people like them—as worse than they are. Even terrorists and repressive governments see themselves as innocent victims of their evil enemies. The myth of pure evil can create serious mischief in families when there is conflict, whether with a rebellious child or between warring partners. It is easy for each side of the conflict to see their own good intentions and the flawed performance of their adversaries.

Limitations in human rationality can be seen as a devastating problem or a vital invitation. The limitations can lead to endless misunderstanding and conflict or to greater humility and compassion. In families, we can judge and misunderstand each other, or we can listen to and learn from each other. The latter possibility is compatible with Gottman's (n.d.) recommendation that men accept influence from their partners and the recommendation by Smith et al. (1994) that parents tune in to their children's feelings and needs. If solitary humans are to be joined together in enduring relationships, it will be by building bridges between their isolated perspectives.

These observations about the limits of human rationality may not seem to be compatible with a positive psychology. Yet many scholars attest that an emphasis on self (as prescribed by the self-esteem movement) is associated with negative emotional states (Leary, 2004; S. E. Taylor & Brown, 1999). The new positive psychology invites us to recognize that the world does not orbit around us. In fact, all the recommendations of positive psychology point us outward. As we appreciate the world around us, invest our strengths in meaningful work, and serve, we find greater happiness and meaning in our lives.

What are the implications of the above discussion for FLE? One of the most intriguing implications is that we should teach people to be humble—to be open to the views of others. We should also be humble ourselves. It is dangerous for us to impose our own worldview on others without understanding their unique life stories and circumstances. We often teach family members to tune in carefully to the feelings and meanings of other family members (Gottman & DeClaire, 2001). This is also something important for us to do as family life educators.

THE PRACTICAL MESSAGES OF POSITIVE PSYCHOLOGY ●

Seligman (2002) has not only been a founder and leader of the positive psychology movement but also has summarized and organized decades of research on human flourishing. His work can be summarized in a simple model. The foundation of human well-being is savoring. Savoring, however, is not limited to the present. We can savor the past and the future as well as the present. Savoring leads to what Seligman calls "the pleasant life."

The next level of well-being is related to flow (Csikszentmihalyi, 1997), that state of total immersion in challenging tasks that causes us to lose track of time. Flow requires that we deploy our personal strengths and virtues in accomplishing our lives' work. When we use our unique strengths every day, we create what Seligman (2002) calls the good life.

The highest level of well-being is generated by service. The service may be to a person, a group of people, or a specific cause. We may care for the homeless, minister to sick animals, teach the illiterate, or build a playground for children. Service makes life meaningful.

These levels of well-being are considered in greater depth in the balance of this chapter. In addition, we will consider how to translate the findings of research into family life education that can help individuals participate more effectively and joyously in family life.

Before discussing these levels of well-being, we will first make some general comments about well-being. (In this chapter, the word *well-being* will be used almost interchangeably with *happiness, flourishing,* and *thriving.*)

Understanding Well-Being

It is common to imagine that the happiest people are those with the dream lives—who have almost unlimited wealth and all the things that wealth brings with it: homes, cars, travel, luxuries, status, and power. On the personal level, many of us imagine that we will be happier when we finish school, get a job, get a raise, or find love.

This leads to what David Myers (2000) calls the American paradox. Despite real incomes that have doubled in the past 40 years, "we have less happiness, more depression, more fragile relationships, less communal commitment, less vocational security, more crime, and more demoralized children" (p. xi). In an age of plenty, we suffer pangs of purposelessness.

It turns out that happiness is full of contradictions. Many of the things that seemed to ensure it do not. Many of the life strategies that sound boring and trivial hold the keys to well-being. These strategies will be discussed later in this chapter.

There is another surprise in well-being. It appears that half of our typical level of happiness is due to our genetics (Lyubomirsky, 2008). We have a characteristic level of well-being. The happy tend to stay happy. The sullen tend to stay unhappy. Certainly there are day-to-day swings in well-being, but, on average, people hold on to their comfortable level of happiness.

It is true that our circumstances can affect our happiness—but only about 10% of our happiness can be explained by our circumstances. Good weather and nice people do not determine our well-being. They add— or diminish—the luster, but they do not determine the substance of our happiness.

You may recognize that roughly 40% (Lyubomirsky, 2008) of our happiness is not accounted for by the combination of genetics and circumstances. This is where our choices come into play. Each of us makes choices that increase or diminish our well-being. We are not corks on a hostile sea. We may navigate our way to the port that suits us.

In the past decade, there has been a flood of new books that describe what research can teach us about increasing our happiness. At the end of this chapter, I (Goddard) have provided a list of my personal favorites. Most of the remainder of this chapter focuses on those three processes described by Seligman as critical to maximizing our happiness.

Savoring

As mentioned earlier, Seligman (2002) talks about savoring the past, the present, and the future. While all of these can be subsumed under the heading of savoring, we will discuss them separately.

Savoring the present. We humans are wired to notice what is new and different. Things that are familiar fade into the background. While this tendency may help us deal with surprises in our environment, it robs us of happiness.

When something wonderful happens, we take special note. But, within hours or days, it is taken for granted. For example, when any of us first gets a new car, we are ecstatic! Yet, within days, we find ourselves annoyed by the cost of fuel or the hassles of maintenance.

If we want to sustain happiness, we will fight the tendency to take blessings for granted. I (Goddard) have a friend who said to me one day, "This morning when I woke up, I was so glad I could see! And then I went into the kitchen and was amazed by the blessing of running water! Then I wandered to the pantry and felt delighted at all the food I have available." He continued for some time itemizing the seemingly ordinary things that had brought him pleasure that day. That man knows how to savor!

Savoring creates gratitude, which Emmons (Emmons & Shelton, 2002), the leading scholar on gratitude, described as "a felt sense of wonder, thankfulness, and appreciation for life" (p. 460). He observed that

> all in all, setting aside time on a daily basis to recall moments of gratitude associated with even mundane or ordinary events, personal attributes one has, or valued people one encounters has the potential to interweave and thread together a sustainable life theme of highly cherished personal meaning just as it nourishes a fundamental life stance whose thrust is decidedly positive. (p. 466)

Gratitude and savoring cause us to keep cherishing even the ordinary. Bryant and Veroff (2007, pp. 201–204) describe six factors that enhance both coping and savoring.

1. Social support can entail sharing positive feelings and experiences with friends and family.

2. Writing about life experiences can help people organize meaning in their life narratives.

3. Downward hedonic contrast—that is, comparing our lives with the lives of those who are less fortunate than we—can help us appreciate the things for which we once hoped and now enjoy.

4. Humor can help maintain perspective and increase the experience of joy.

5. Spirituality and religion can help people find meaning, purpose, and joy in their lives.

6. An awareness of the fleetingness of experience can remind us to savor sweet moments that will not last.

In Seligman's (2002) pyramid of well-being, savoring is foundational. It leads to what he calls the pleasant life. He contrasts savoring with mind-*less*ness, which "pervades much of human activity. We fail to notice huge swaths of experience" (p. 109). Life is immeasurably poorer when we march through life mindlessly. In contrast, when we savor the simple blessings around us, life is rich!

Savoring the past. The idea of savoring the past may seem odd. What benefit can come from revisiting a history filled with both pain and happiness? Won't time spent in the past merely make us hostages of our disappointments?

The answers are surprising. It turns out that memory is surprisingly malleable. We remember what we rehearse, and we all rewrite history to fit the narrative that we favor. If we like to see ourselves as victims, we can take experiences that lend themselves to that purpose and feature them in our minds and personal narratives.

In support of this idea, Fiske and Taylor (1984) observed that, "instead of a naïve scientist entering the environment in search of the truth, we find the rather unflattering picture of a charlatan trying to make the data come out in a manner most advantageous to his or her already-held theories" (p. 88). We all tend to torture the truth to get it to say what we want.

This process of forming our histories to suit our preferences can work for us or against us. When we focus on the pain and disappointment, we increase and extend the misery. As Seligman (1993) observed, "If your child is abused or if you were abused, my best advice is to turn the volume down as soon as possible. Reliving the experience repeatedly may retard the natural healing" (p. 235). Seligman summarizes the extant research as suggesting that childhood traumas are not particularly formative. "We are not prisoners of our past" (p. 237).

When we focus on the good things in our histories, we create a narrative that sustains joyful living and continued growth. We are happier. We can also rewrite history, filling in empty places and replacing traumas with stories of friendship, growth, and happiness. Many a person has escaped past pains through story books and daydreams.

Seligman (2002) described another way we can feature the gems in our pasts. He suggested that we identify a person who has made a positive impact in our lives. Then we write a letter to that person telling what they did and how it affected us. Take time to craft a heartfelt message. Then, when possible, make an appointment to see the person. Take the letter and, when seated comfortably, read the letter to the person. Read deliberately. Then let the other person react. Reminisce.

Gratitude letters can enrich the lives of the givers and the recipients. The person to whom you read is likely to be overwhelmed with your expression of gratitude. And you will be filled with a sense that your life is blessed.

There are probably people who have had a very positive impact on your life who may be deceased or otherwise unavailable. You can still write a letter. You can imagine yourself reading the letter to the person. You can feel the joy that comes from acknowledging goodness.

Savoring the future. It is common to anticipate the future with fear and dread. Optimism is a better choice. Seligman has written important works about learned optimism (Seligman, 1991) and cultivating optimism in children (Seligman, Reivich, Jaycox, & Gillham, 1995). Seligman's version of optimism focuses on explanatory style—the way in which people interpret their successes and failures. In contrast, other approaches generally focus on expectations for the future. Savoring the future effectively can be advanced by both perspectives. In particular, we focus on a primary enemy of savoring the future: fear—whether that is a fear that we are not capable (as in Seligman) or a fear that the future is gloomy (other approaches).

One example of fear that is particularly pertinent to family life educators is the fear that a child will be abducted. Daniel Gardner (2008), in his intriguing book about fear, observed that, of 70 million American children, about 115 are kidnapped by strangers in a typical year. That means that a child has about one chance in 608,696 of being kidnapped. A child is 26 times as likely to die in a car crash.

We all agree that child abduction is a terrible thing. Gardner's (2008) point is that "the likelihood of a child being snatched by a stranger is almost indescribably tiny" (p. 186). Yet the fear is enormous. The disparity between the probability and the fear is accounted for by our human predisposition to fear (It can protect us from danger!) and the work of the media. We are kept anxious about events that are extremely improbable while neglecting the serious side effects of our fear. The media get our attention and keep it by keeping us worried.

Fear has real consequences. Among other things, many scholars are worried about the exercise and experiences that are denied children because their parents are overly anxious about abduction. We build a culture of fear—water quality, toxins, sharks, immunizations, exotic flus—that may have a real impact on children and their sense of safety. We worry about the wrong things. The greater danger for most children is that they will grow up feeling anxious and lonely. But that does not create a front-page story quite like the rare abduction.

Seligman (2002) recommends positive emotions about the future such as "faith, trust, confidence, hope, and optimism" (p. 83). One way to cultivate such positive emotions is to make specific goals. Rather than coast along hoping for the best, we can make personal resolves to do the things that we are excited about. Maybe you create an article for the newspaper about a subject that is important to you. Maybe you create a curriculum to help couples in your faith community. Maybe you organize a project to repair a playground for neighborhood children. When you are energized by a vision of possibilities and patiently organize your resources to accomplish the task, you are likely to be energized, productive—and happy!

Using Your Strengths

Americans have been famous for their emphasis on self-improvement. For example, Ben Franklin identified 13 virtues and set out to methodically master them (Kurtus, 2005). He found the task to be harder than he expected. It seems that perfecting ourselves is impossible.

Seligman (2002) suggested a different route to well-being. He argued that the good life is not the result of overcoming our weaknesses but the result of using our strengths and virtues.

> I do not believe that you should devote overly much effort to correcting your weaknesses. Rather, I believe that the highest success in living and the deepest emotional satisfaction comes from building and using your signature strengths. (p. 13)

You can see that Seligman's recommendation is a real departure from tradition. Rather than try to make ourselves perfect, we set aside that obsession and learn to use our strengths while managing our weaknesses (Clifton & Nelson, 1992).

The key to this positive approach is discovering our strengths. There are many ways to do that. One way is to use psychological tests such as the Myers-Briggs Type Indicator (I. B. Myers, 1981), True Colors (Lowry & Echols, 2000), or other personality assessments (many versions are available online). Such instruments can help you discover your strengths and preferred way of working.

Another instrument that can help is the VIA Survey of Character Strengths. This instrument is based on the observation (Seligman, 2002, chap. 8) that six virtues have been prized in all major traditions across the past 3,000 years. The six virtues are as follows:

- Wisdom and knowledge
- Courage
- Love and humanity
- Justice
- Temperance
- Spirituality and transcendence

Within those six virtues, Seligman and his team identified 24 strengths of character. So, for example, wisdom and knowledge included curiosity, love of learning, open-mindedness, ingenuity, social intelligence, and perspective. The VIA Survey of Character Strengths includes 240 items to assess a person's strengths (www.authentichappiness.org). Seligman considers each person's top 5 strengths to be his or her signature strengths.

When people design their lives and work to use their strengths, they are more likely to have satisfying lives. Seligman (2002) talks about the fruit of using strengths as "gratifications." He observes that "the defining criterion of gratification is the absence of feeling, loss of self-consciousness, and total engagement. Gratification dispels self-absorption" (p. 119) and provides a powerful antidote to depression. In fact, the field of optimal functioning includes a phenomenon called "flow."

Mihaly Csikszentmihalyi (1997), the guru of flow, has observed that "the normal condition of the mind is one of informational disorder" (p. 26). In contrast to such chaos are those times when we focus our thoughts and energy on a task. "Usually the more difficult a mental task, the harder it is to concentrate on it. But when a person likes what he does and is motivated to do it, focusing the mind becomes effortless even when the objective difficulties are great" (p. 27). Flow happens when high skills and effort meet high challenge. Engagement in the task can become so great that people forget themselves and time.

Naturally, people with different strengths find flow in different activities. One person might find flow in Sudoku while another finds it in woodworking, teaching, scrapbooking, or singing. There are unnumbered ways of entering into flow. To increase such positive experiences in our own lives, Csikszentmihalyi (1997) suggests that we be more mindful in our activities. We can notice how we feel in different activities, times, places, and with different people. We can design our lives to have more flow.

Seligman (2002) helps us identify flow experiences by asking two questions: "When does time stop for you? When do you find yourself doing exactly what you want to be doing, and never wanting it to end?" (p. 114).

It is clear that even a well-chosen career in FLE will not provide uninterrupted flow. Yet each of us can design our lives in ways that challenge us, engage us, and cause us to grow.

Soar with your strengths. Clifton and Nelson (1992) have described five ways to identify our strengths. They recommend that we "Listen for Yearnings" (i.e., notice the kind of activities that draw us). Second, they recommend that we "Watch for Satisfactions." They argue that if any activity "doesn't feel good, you are not practicing a strength" (p. 49). So, when we notice the activities that put us into flow, we're learning important things about our strengths. Third, "Watch for Rapid Learning." The person who thinks that factoring polynomials is fun probably has natural ability and great potential to find satisfaction in that area. He or she may learn quickly and love the process. The fourth and fifth ways are related to each other: "Glimpses of Excellence" and "Total Performance of Excellence." When we find that we can function extraordinarily well in a certain domain, we may have discovered a strength.

Objective measures can help people discover their strengths, but paying attention to our own feelings may give equally valuable data. One program intended to help people discover and use their strengths—and to live flourishing lives in general—is *The Personal Journey*. This is one example of an Extension program designed to help people thrive. In addition to a summary map, *The Personal Journey* provides a series of journaling opportunities to help the user identify strengths and to flourish (http://www .arfamilies.org/family_life/personal/default.htm).

Serving

It is intriguing that the highest level of well-being is attained by serving. This simple prescription is the same one made by grandmothers and Sunday school teachers. Now scientific evidence confirms its importance.

While positive emotions pour from savoring, and productivity streams from using our strengths, the highest level of well-being—what Seligman (2002) calls the meaningful life—springs from finding ways to make the world a better place. "The meaningful life adds one more component [to the good life]: using these same strengths to forward knowledge, power, or goodness. A life that does this is pregnant with meaning, and if God comes at the end, such a life is sacred" (p. 260).

One beauty of service is that each of us can find a way that perfectly suits us. My wife loves to visit the lonely. I like to write about ideas. What is your favorite way of serving?

Apparently it feels good to do good. In an added twist, it apparently feels good to witness acts of goodness. Jonathan Haidt (2003) described a phenomenon he calls "elevation." He provided a definition for elevation, drawing on the words of Thomas Jefferson: "When any . . . act of charity or of gratitude, for instance, is presented either to our sight or imagination, we are deeply impressed with its beauty and feel a strong desire in ourselves of doing charitable and grateful acts also. . . . Now every emotion of this kind is an exercise of our virtuous dispositions; and dispositions of the mind, like limbs of the body, acquire strength by exercise" (qtd. in Haidt, 2003, p. 275).

We have all read books, watched movies, or witnessed in person a person making a noble sacrifice. It is likely that all of us have been lifted by such examples. To quote Haidt (2003), "Elevation is elicited by acts of virtue or moral beauty; it causes warm, open feelings in the chest; and it motivates people to behave more virtuously themselves" (p. 276). It would appear that service is contagious—that is, when we see noble service, we are inclined to act more nobly ourselves.

This principle has application to our own lives as well as our work as family life educators. Not only can we inspire ourselves by studying the lives of good examples, but also we can share good examples with the people we teach and serve. In a parenting class, we can tell stories of people who made personal and professional sacrifices in order to be effective parents. In relationship and marriage education classes, we can share examples of people who sacrificed their own comfort and preferences in order to be the partners they wanted to be.

There is, perhaps, one caveat related to sharing stories of noble examples. If our stories seem to suggest to our students that they should be perfect, we may discourage them. Our stories and instruction must also acknowledge the reality that we all make mistakes. We all struggle. We are all imperfect family members. The healthy balance is to offer inspiring examples while inviting our students to recognize the good things they are already doing and the great things that are possible.

● EDUCATIONAL FRAMEWORKS

What frameworks can help guide family life educators in the promotion of personal well-being? An evolving area of study called Appreciative Inquiry (Mohr & Watkins, 2002) recommends that change agents take a fresh approach to encouraging optimal functioning.

Appreciative Inquiry (AI) expresses the opportunity this way: "Rather than concentrate on breakdowns and malfunctions, we've begun to ask: If the act of studying a system alters it, why not do so in ways that create movement toward peak experiences or successes?" (Mohr & Watkins, 2002, p. 1). The traditional medical approach asks, "What are you doing that is not working?" The positive AI approach asks, "Tell me about a time when you excelled at this process."

The foundation principle of AI may be expressed this way: "Sociological research has shown that when people study problems and conflicts, the number and severity of the problems they identify actually *increase*. But when they focus on human ideals and achievements, peak experiences, and best practices, *these* things—not the conflicts—tend to flourish" (Mohr & Watkins, 2002, p. 2).

The application to family life education is obvious. We often focus on the problems and mistakes that bedevil us. AI invites us to create a new focus in our interactions with clients and students: "Tell me about times when you and your partner felt close and loving. What were you doing and thinking at those times?" Or "Tell me about times when you felt especially effective as a parent. What were you doing and thinking at those times?" Of course the questions can be specific to a lesson or principle. "Today we have talked about showing compassion in our families. Please take a few minutes to think of a time when you effectively showed compassion to a family member. Make a few notes in your class journal. After you have had a few minutes, I will invite you to share with your class partner."

It does not appear that the empirical evidence in support of AI is substantial yet. Still, the whole thrust of positive psychology seems to be consistent with this developing emphasis. Consider these recommendations (Mohr & Watkins, 2002, pp. 5–9) in developing FLE interventions:

1. Choose the positive as the focus of inquiry.

2. Inquire into exceptionally positive moments.

3. Share the stories and identify the life-giving forces.

4. Create shared images of a preferred future.

5. Innovate and improvise ways to create that future.

CONCLUSION ●

Consider the good news. Scholars have discovered countless ways to live better lives. We know enough about flourishing today that any person can map a way to happiness and productivity. We can focus on the positive, cherish every moment, and use our strengths. We can pour ourselves into the lives of others and use our strengths to bring joy to ourselves and those around us.

As we flourish and thrive within our own lives, we can participate more fully and effectively in all areas of life: work, friendship, marriage, parenting, and family life. As we teach FLE, we can help those we serve flourish and thrive so that they enjoy the same benefits in their family lives! What a glorious reward for being a family life educator!

EXPLORATIONS ●

1. How can you help those you teach understand family members in terms of strengths, abilities, and virtues rather than in terms of problems, symptoms, and sickness?

2. Right now, what can you savor? Do you have a view of a beautiful nature scene? Do you feel the blessing of learning and growing? Are you near people you care about? What simple things can you take a moment to savor? As you lead an FLE class, how can you help participants savor?

3. What kinds of activities based on Bryant and Veroff's (2007) six factors might you create to encourage savoring in the people you teach? For example, their first factor, social support, might be taught by inviting the people you teach to think about support they have received and support they offer. They could share stories with each other—offering support to each other as they share.

4. Think about the events of your life. How would you like to tell your life story in a way that is positive? Consider your life history with a theme such as growth, joy, courage, purpose, or service. How could you help the people you serve do this activity successfully?

5. Write gratitude letters. Write letters expressing gratitude to people who have positively affected you. You can send them or keep them for yourself. You can even include people who are no longer alive or in your life. Invite those you teach to do the same and share the results with the class.

6. Exploration: Do you have memories that create problems in your life today? What can you do to move forward beyond those memories? How can you help those you teach do these things?

- "Rescript" difficult memories with positive themes. For example, think about them with a theme of forgiveness (for others or for yourself).
- Sensitive people often review their life histories and see themselves as failures. Instead of considering yourself a failure, view your history in terms of how it helped you grow. What have you learned through your experiences that will help you be the kind of person you want to be in the future?
- Bring understanding and forgiving to heal a damaged relationship in order to move forward.

7. How can you help those you teach better manage their fears and anxieties?

8. What projects do you see yourself undertaking that are most likely to provide flow to you in your life in general, in your work life, and in family life education in particular? Do you prefer to write, teach, lecture, learn, discuss . . . what are the FLE activities that are most likely to use your strengths, challenge you, and satisfy you?

9. Complete the VIA Survey of Character Strengths. Describe how you could use this instrument in a class on personal flourishing or family relationships. For instance, you could invite class members to complete the survey, share their strengths with classmates, and then discuss how their strengths can make their family life both more rewarding and more challenging.

10. Think of times that you have served unselfishly. What were you doing? How did you feel? If you made more room for service in your life, would you be even happier than you are? How can you cultivate more serving in those you teach? The possibilities range from asking them about their service and inviting them to make more room for service in their lives to having a project as a class.

11. Create a lesson in an area of your interest using principles of Appreciative Inquiry to teach principles of positive psychology and guide your students toward better functioning.

12. Journal in response to questions from *The Personal Journey* (http://www.arfamilies.org/family_life/personal/default.htm). Consider what questions or activities you might add to help the people you teach to flourish.

Check out my (Goddard) recommendations for great books on flourishing (in descending order of importance for family life educators):

Authentic Happiness, by Martin E. P. Seligman
Happiness Hypothesis, by Jonathan Haidt
Positivity, by Barbara L. Fredrickson
The How of Happiness, by Sonja Lyubomirsky
The Science of Fear, by Daniel Gardner
What Happy People Know, by Dan Baker and Cameron Stauth
Positive Psychology in Practice, edited by P. Alex Linley and Stephen Joseph
The Handbook of Positive Psychology, edited by C. R. Snyder and Shane J. Lopez
Meanings of Life, by Roy F. Baumeister
Mistakes Were Made, by Carol Tavris and Elliot Aronson
Happiness, by David Lykken
Leadership and Self-Deception, by The Arbinger Institute
Savoring, by Fred B. Bryant and Joseph Veroff
Flourishing, edited by Corey L. M. Keyes and Jonathan Haidt
Finding Flow, by Mihaly Csikszentmihalyi
Character Strengths and Virtues: A Handbook and Classification, by Christopher Peterson and Martin E. P. Seligman
Happier, by Tal Ben-Shahar
Stumbling on Happiness, by Daniel Gilbert
Thanks! by Robert A. Emmons
The Curse of the Self, by Mark R. Leary

CHAPTER 9

MARRIAGE AND RELATIONSHIP EDUCATION

Stephen F. Duncan, Alan J. Hawkins, and H. Wallace Goddard

"Marriage is the first bond of society," declared Roman statesman and orator Marcus Tullius Cicero in 78 B.C. (*De Officiis,* I, 78 b.c., cited in Popenoe, 2001). Since this ancient pronouncement, much scientific data have emerged on just how important marriage is. Recent scholarly summaries have detailed the various social, physical, sexual, and economic benefits of happy marriage to the couple themselves, to the children raised within these unions, and to the broader society (Institute for American Values, 2005; Waite & Gallagher, 2000).

However, the institution of marriage is not completely well. While recent divorce rates (3.5 per 1,000 in 2008; National Center for Health Statistics [NCHS], 2009) are lower than the record rates of the early 1980s (5.1 per 1,000 women in 1981), the general U.S. population still face between a 40% and 50% chance of ending their unions (Bramlett & Mosher, 2002).

Since benefits to adults, children, and society abound when marriages are successful, what can be done to increase the chances of happy, stable unions?

One answer to this question is marriage and relationship education (MRE), an important subspecialty of family life education (FLE). MRE can be broadly defined as any preventative effort to help couples gain knowledge and skills necessary to establish and maintain a healthy couple relationship. Marriage educators work preventively—or, metaphorically speaking, they "work upstream" (Larson, 2004, p. 421)—to help couples anticipate and avoid serious disruption through the learning and practice of marital virtues, science-supported principles, and skills. While earlier scholars distinguished marriage education from marriage enrichment (e.g., see Stahmann & Salts, 1993), more recently, these approaches, when carried out in church and community settings, have incorporated similar elements, and research usually makes no distinction between them (Larson, 2004).

This chapter highlights early beginnings of MRE and various theoretical models used historically to guide preventive interventions to enhance marital quality. We also note several foundational processes at the heart of enduring marriages, identified by some of the leading researchers of the anatomy of healthy marriage relationships, and programmatic frameworks to alert practitioners both to the best content in MRE and best practices. Finally, we discuss various programs and approaches for doing MRE, offer an example of developing an MRE program using text concepts, and note challenges for the future and future directions.

EARLY BEGINNINGS OF MARRIAGE AND ● RELATIONSHIP EDUCATION

MRE enjoys a long and distinguished history. Some of the earliest formal MRE can be traced back to the early 1930s (Stahmann & Salts, 1993), with the earliest known efforts occurring when a premarital education program was established at the Merrill-Palmer Institute. Early premarital counseling established at the Philadelphia Marriage Council included a strong educational emphasis, such as providing information to couples about the realities of marriage and how to anticipate and deal with the potential challenges they might encounter in marriage (Stahmann & Salts, 1993). Churches played a key role in premarital educational efforts through premarital counseling (Schumm & Denton, 1979).

● CURRENT THEORETICAL AND EMPIRICAL FOUNDATIONS AND MODELS FOR PRACTICE

Several theoretical perspectives are used in MRE. Berger and Hannah's (1999) *Preventive Approaches in Couples Therapy* provides a thorough review of the most popular programs and their theoretical underpinnings. Perhaps the most dominant perspective is the cognitive-behavioral perspective, found in 8 of the 13 approaches (see Berger & Hannah, 1999, pp. 12–14). This approach assumes that couples can be taught, in an educational setting, ways of thinking (attitudes and expectations) and behaving (communication and conflict management) that enhance their chances for successful marriage. Several programs eclectically integrate various other perspectives, including social learning, humanistic, communications, and systems approaches.

Marital process research today essentially is threefold, and some of the better known MRE programs, discussed later, make an attempt to integrate these perspectives. One aspect places emphasis on marital disruption and understanding the processes that lead to marital breakdown (e.g., Gottman, 1994). This area of research often focuses on communication processes, how conflict is managed and problems addressed. A second major emphasis addresses the intrapersonal characteristics of spouses and positive interpersonal processes for establishing and maintaining a strong, healthy marriage. According to recent observations (Holman, Carroll, Busby, & Klein, 2008), evidence suggests that researchers are investigating these elements more and more, often referred to as "marital virtues" or "spousal strengths." Some of these virtues or strengths include positivity, friendship, generosity (Fowers, 2000; A. J. Hawkins, Fowers, Carroll, & Yang, 2007), and fairness (Fowers, 2001). Gottman and Gottman's (1999) research has begun to highlight intrapersonal aspects of dyadic interaction, such as fondness, admiration, affection, and respect. A third major emphasis is attention to elements some scholars call "transformative processes in marriage" (Fincham, Stanley, & Beach, 2007, p. 277). These elements include forgiveness (Fincham, 2000; McCullough et al., 1998), commitment (Fowers, 2000; Stanley & Markman, 1992), sacrifice (Whitton, Stanley, & Markman, 2002), and sanctification (Mahoney et al., 1999). Taken together, these intrapersonal and transformative factors become the undergirding for why couples in healthy marriages seek to communicate and handle issues between them respectfully, many factors having little to do with interpersonal skills (Carroll, Badger, & Yang, 2006). Perhaps the best research-based MRE content will come from some intersection among these three emphases.

EXAMPLES OF THE THREE EMPHASES: FOUNDATIONAL • PROCESSES FOR ENDURING MARRIAGES

Working from various theoretical perspectives, several processes have been identified that can arguably be called foundational processes for enduring marriages. These elements derive both from interpersonal processes and intrapersonal traits, those elements of individual character that partners bring to their relationship, and transformative processes that contribute to change and healing in marriage.

Sound marital house theory (Gottman, 1999). Among the most influential of research programs on what makes marriages work derives from the sound marital house theory (Gottman, 1999), and several books have been produced based on this theory, probably most notable the best-selling book, *The Seven Principles for Making Marriage Work* (Gottman & Silver, 1999). Essentially, according to this theory, the two major "staples" evident in well-functioning couples are high levels of positivity and an ability to reduce negativity when dealing with issues.

At the foundation or "ground floor" of this theory is a *deep marital friendship* that occurs away from nonconflict situations. Three components of this friendship include the following:

1. Cognitive room for one's spouse, or knowledge about his or her inner world. This room is expanded through enhanced love maps. A love map is like a mental notebook where individuals collect personal information about their spouse that they want to remember. This notebook includes spouse's dreams, joys, fears, likes, dislikes, frustrations, and worries. It helps partners identify different "points" about their spouse on the map so they know how to love their partner better.

   Couples can use their love maps to show they care. While Gottman's approach is largely cognitive, additional practitioners have suggested how the love maps can guide behavior. For example, clinician Gary Chapman (1992) argues that people have primary "love languages" and that it is important for couples to identify and speak this primary language for loving messages to be received as such. Chapman identifies five major languages of love: words of affirmation, quality time, receiving gifts, acts of service, and physical touch. These languages of love, whether there are five or more (or less), have not been empirically validated (however, see Goff, Goddard, Pointer, & Jackson, 2007, for an early attempt to measure and analyze these concepts). Therapist Richard Stuart (1980) recommends couples engage in "Caring Days" where couples identify sets of loving actions that they would like to receive from their partner. These actions must be specific ("Tell me you love me at least once a day"), positive (not "Don't do this" or "Stop doing that"), small enough to be done on a daily basis (such as "Call me at work during lunch, just to see how I'm doing"), and not related to any recent conflict. Experimental research shows that couples engaging in Caring Days activities significantly enhanced their marital satisfaction (LeCroy, Carrol, Nelson-Becker, & Sturlaugson, 1989). Regardless of which approach couples choose, the principle is for couples to visit openly about how they like to receive love and then agree to do those things often.

2. The second element of the marital friendship is a fondness and admiration system. Couples identify numerous things they admire and appreciate about their spouses, such as characteristics, talents, and things they have done, and keep those things at the forefront of their minds—even posting these characteristics in conspicuous places.

    Respecting one spouse's point of view is an expression of fondness and admiration. Gottman refers to the process of sharing the decision-making power with one's spouse as accepting influence (Gottman, Coan, Carrere, & Swanson, 1998). Accepting influence refers to counseling with and listening to one's spouse, respecting and considering his or her opinions as valid as one's own, and compromising with that person when making decisions together.

    Gottman and Silver (1999) have identified several benefits to husbands if they share power in their marriage relationship. Their wives are far less likely to broach difficult issues in their marriage in a harsh way, increasing marriage survival odds. These husbands are also more likely to become excellent, emotionally intelligent fathers. They maintain dignity and self-respect as they give their spouse respect by allowing them an equal share of power in their stewardships. On the other hand, when husbands are unwilling to share power and decision making with their wives, their marriages have an 81% chance of self-destructing.

3. Turn toward each other instead of away. Our best efforts to connect in marriage can be jeopardized as a result of the failure to respond to another's bids, which Gottman and DeClaire (2001) call "the fundamental unit of emotional communication" (p. 4). A bid can be a question, a look, a gesture, a touch—any single expression that

says "I want to feel connected to you." Gottman's (1999) laboratory studies identified that couples responded to bids for connection in one of three ways: by turning away (e.g., ignoring), turning against (e.g., verbally attacking), or turning toward (actively responding to bids for attention, affection, humor, support). Turning toward one's partner puts deposits in the marital Emotional Bank Account, a personal account where a partner keeps track of how well he or she is connecting emotionally with his or her spouse.

Research shows that how spouses respond to bids for connection affects the relationships in a major way. For example, husbands headed for divorce disregarded their wives' bids for connection 82% of the time, whereas husbands in stable relationships did this only 19% of the time. Wives headed for divorce disregarded their husbands' bids for connection 50% of the time, whereas wives in stable relationships did this only 14% of the time.

With these three foundational elements of marital friendship in place, greater positive sentiments are more likely to be drawn upon generally, which also becomes a resource to help protect the soft underbelly of a relationship during conflict. In the Gottman (1999) laboratory studies, researchers observed couples during conflict situations and assessed the proportion of the interaction balanced between the negative and the positive. They discovered that for couples in stable marriages, the ratio of positive to negative interactions during conflict situations was at least 5 to 1, whereas in couples headed for divorce, the ratio was only .8 to 1. Thus, couples doing well show at least five time more positives than negatives and far less negatives than disrupted couples. Gottman and Silver (1999) call this "positive sentiment override" or the 5 to 1 ratio. When things are positive in the relationship, they are more likely to succeed at making repair attempts when things go awry during discussions. In a 9-year longitudinal study of newlyweds, Gottman et al. (1998) found that positive affect was the only predictor of marital stability or dissolution as well as eventual marital satisfaction of those couples who stayed married. This does not mean that having negativity is all bad or that the goal is to eliminate any negativity (Gottman, 1999). Negativity can inform couples where change is needed for relationship enhancement. The important finding here is that the ratio of positivity to negativity influences marital outcomes and that the better the ratio of positivity to negativity, the better the marriage.

The next level of the theory deals with the *regulation of conflict.* Disagreements crop up even in the best marriages. It is how differences are handled that is an important key to marital success or failure (H. J. Markman et al., 2001). Regulation helps couples establish dialogue, not gridlock, about their perpetual problems. Many styles of dialogue are functional (Gottman, 1994). Many problems do not need solving or cannot be solved; they just need to be discussed well (H. J. Markman et al., 2001). The Gottman approach helps build skills couples need to solve their solvable problems and learn how to physiologically sooth themselves and each other during conflict, to prevent becoming overwhelmed or flooded. They learn how to begin with a softened start-up, while avoiding negative and accusatory remarks, sarcasm, and critical and contemptuous statements. They learn how to make and receive repair attempts, which are anything persons in a discussion do to de-escalate tension so that discussion and solving of a problem can proceed.

The final level of the theory addresses *creating shared meaning*. Shared meaning is built through the meshing of individual life dreams into marital and family mission statements, and couples build and nourish their relationship over time through rituals of connection, goals, roles, myths, narratives, and metaphors. Shared religious faith is one area of ritual that aids in helping couples create a shared "inner life together—a culture rich with symbols" (Gottman & Silver, 1999, p. 243) that bind couples together. "The more you can agree about the fundamentals in life, the richer, more meaningful, and in a sense easier your marriage is likely to be" (Gottman & Silver, 1999, p. 245). "This level then feeds back to deepen and strengthen the foundation of marital friendship" (Gottman, 1999, p. 106). Friendship is also a vital attribute noted in the marital virtues perspective (Fowers, 2001).

Marital virtues perspective. The marital virtues perspective is at least partially a referendum on the heavy emphasis placed on marital satisfaction as the ultimate payoff in marriage and good communication as the key process that leads to it. This approach can largely be summed up by Blaine Fowers (2000, p. 23) when he stated, "As I have observed many different couples, I have become convinced that strong marriages are built on the virtues or character strengths of the spouses. In other words, the best way to have a good marriage is to be a good person." Thus, instead of seeking emotional gratification, the emphasis is on creating a shared life, rooted in commitment and partnership. In a partnership marriage, couples create a shared vision of what they want this shared marital life to be. Couples practice four key virtues: friendship, loyalty, generosity, and justice. Couples become embedded in and active contributors to their social world.

This approach does not argue that important skills such as communication and managing conflict are unnecessary but that they are experienced most effectively in marriage when embedded in a virtue-centered marriage culture. For example, a spouse practices good listening skills because he or she is *patient* and *generous* with his or her time, not because it works to his or her advantage.

Transformative processes. Fincham et al. (2007) note that the marital research landscape is dominated with a focus on risk factors such as conflict to explain marital outcomes. They introduce the idea of "self-regulatory transformative processes" such as forgiveness, sacrifice, sanctification, and commitment and note the emerging research that shows the importance of these elements in predicting marital success.

As an example, marriage scholars Scott Stanley and Howard Markman (1992) have identified two kinds of commitment: *constraint commitment* and *personal dedication.* Constraint commitment comprises "costs and forces that keep marriage together, even if a couple would rather break up" (Stanley, Whitton, & Markman, 2004, p. 498). For example, couples may stay together because of social pressure, the high expense of divorce, or for the sake of the children. Personal dedication, on the other hand, is an intentional decision and desire to stay in a marriage for mutual benefit. It involves "sacrificing for it, investing in it, linking personal goals to it, considering partner's welfare—not solely your own" (H. J. Markman et al., 2001, p. 325). Each type of commitment is important; constraint commitment is more important for the stability of a relationship, and couples can lean on it to weather the storms that are a part of every normal marriage relationship. Personal dedication is more important for fulfillment in marriage. Research shows that personally dedicated couples show a greater priority for the relationship, feel greater satisfaction with giving, and are less likely to seek greener marital pastures (H. J. Markman et al., 2001). Related studies of interpersonal commitment to one's partner, as opposed to marriage as an institution, show additional benefits: greater happiness, better communication, and less destructive behavior during times of crisis (see Stanley et al., 2004, for a review).

Commitments are often shown when couples are involved in unifying spiritual activities, such as active religious involvement within their faith community and prayer, and research shows they bring a number of benefits into their marriages. Couples who practice their faith together are more likely to have less conflict, to reach a mutually satisfying resolution if there is conflict, and to remain committed to each other and the marriage when conflict does occur (Lambert & Dollahite, 2006). Shared religious faith aids in helping couples create a shared "inner life together—a culture rich with symbols" (Gottman & Silver, 1999, p. 243) that bind couples together. "The more you can agree about the fundamentals in life, the richer, more meaningful, and in a sense easier your marriage is likely to be" (Gottman & Silver, 1999, p. 245). Couples who pray together say they feel closer to God, have softer feelings, think about what is best for the couple, and receive help dealing with conflict (Butler, Gardner, & Bird, 1998). Thus, religious activities can have a sanctifying effect on the believers and the couple relationship.

No couple does marriage perfectly, and incidences arise where mutual change, forgiveness, and reconciliation are in order. When mistakes are made, forgiveness and reconciliation processes can heal wounds and restore trust that was lost through mutually trustworthy behaviors (Worthington & Drinkard, 2000).

Thus, when marriage and relationship educators are considering scholarly content from which to draw to create or select programs, they have a wide array of concepts and teachable ideas to select from that address the full dynamic spectrum of marital life, from interpersonal processes such as communication and conflict management to intrapersonal characteristics such as fairness and friendship to transformative processes to keep marriages together during tough times and expedite repair and healing when mistakes are made. The following section provides direction as to how to implement MRE and what to include in it.

● EDUCATIONAL FRAMEWORKS

With content in hand, how shall marriage educators best implement comprehensive programs? Over the past decade, important contributions in the conceptual and practitioner literature have been made to help guide the practice of marriage education. Among these are the Comprehensive Framework for Marriage Education (CoFraME) and the National Extension Relationship and Marriage Education Model (NERMEM).

Comprehensive Framework for Marriage Education (CoFraME). This framework, developed by A. J. Hawkins, Carroll, Doherty, and Willoughby (2004), includes seven dimensions: content, intensity, method, timing, setting, target, and delivery. These dimensions suggest a comprehensive map for the design of potential educational interventions at different levels of the social ecology. The goal of Hawkins et al. is to "offer a framework to help marriage educators think more thoroughly, systematically, broadly and creatively about intervention opportunities to strengthen marriage" (A. J. Hawkins et al., 2004, p. 547).

Content refers to the information being taught to individuals and couples. While relationship skills have received primary emphasis in marriage education to date, it is relatively unknown what kinds of content would be preferred and most helpful to a varied population.

Intensity comprises the intensity level (low, moderate, high) of treatment a couple receives. Interventions can range from pamphlets and informational websites (low level) to multisession, face-to-face couple education (high level). Some researchers and practitioners hypothesize that marriage education needs to be delivered at a higher level of intensity than traditional programs among higher risk groups, such as low-income or other higher risk groups, for them to be effective (A. J. Hawkins et al., 2004).

The *methods* dimension involves how material is taught and learned, the teaching process used to deliver the education material to couples. Many couples reflect many different cultural traditions related to marriage to which a wise marriage educator will be careful to attend.

Timing addresses the question, When does marriage education occur? It refers to the current life stage of the participants. Most marriage education programs and materials focus primarily on engaged and/or newlywed couples. But it is very important to consider higher risk populations at different life stages such as adolescents and transition-to-parenthood couples. Marriage education programs need to increase their attention to adolescents preparing for marriage and to long-lasting marriages as well in order to help prevent problems or keep existing problems from becoming detrimental to the couple.

Setting refers to the location where marriage education is received. Some of these settings may include home-based interventions, familiar community locations (e.g., libraries, churches, schools, and universities), hospitals, or work settings. It may also include media sources such as television, radio, newspapers, and the Internet. With the advent of the iPod, Google phones, DROID, and other technological marvels, the setting can become increasingly flexible and privatized.

It is important that marriage education consider the *target*. Most marriage education materials and interventions have been developed based on the needs of the Anglo population in the United States (A. J. Hawkins et al., 2004; Maldonado-Molina, Reyes, & Espinosa-Hernandez, 2006). It is increasingly important for marriage educators to expand their research on needs assessment to diverse couples in order to customize materials most suitable for the targeted population.

The final dimension is *delivery*. This component deals with the providers of marriage education and how marriage education is disseminated to the public. This may range from "initiatives" led by community advocacy groups to licensed individuals in the human services fields who work with individual couples.

In summary, the Hawkins model provides a comprehensive framework or map for the development of marriage education programs. It attunes family life educators who specialize in MRE to the multiple dimensions needing attention and programming possibilities in their communities.

National Extension Relationship and Marriage Education Model (NERMEM).
While CoFraME is a comprehensive model of marriage education, the
NERMEM (Adler-Baeder et al., 2010) focuses on the content dimension of
MRE. Beginning about 2002, a group of specialists with the Cooperative
Extension System from across the country worked together to identify the
key themes of research on marriage. This group is known as the National
Extension Relationship and Marriage Education Network (NERMEN).
According to the developers of NERMEM, "This research-based, theoretically
grounded and best-practice informed model will help educators design,
deliver and evaluate programs that support healthy couple and marital
relationships. The model presents key patterns of thinking and behaviors
associated with healthy, stable couple relationships and marriages that can
be taught in an educational setting" (Adler-Baeder & Futris, 2008, p. 1).
The work of the NERMEN is unique. Many relationship curricula appear
to be based on the intuitive or implicit models of their creators. Many of
the recommendations are not supported by research (Gottman, 1999). In
fact, marriage scholars have observed that most marriage programs are
loosely connected to research and are rarely evaluated (Adler-Baeder,
Higginbotham, & Lamke, 2004). Even some popular couples programs that
claim to have strong evaluation data actually get only small changes on
a few of the multitude of measured variables (Goddard, Marshall, Olson,
& Dennis, 2010; Jakubowski, Milne, Brunner, & Miller, 2004). NERMEM
attempts to summarize research as a solid foundation for curriculum development. It is not a curriculum itself—though a funded program for training
social workers on MRE based on NERMEM is under development.

TABLE 9.1   NERMEM Core Components

Choose—The central importance of intentionality:

- Decide to make the relationship a priority
- Set limits on thoughts and behaviors that would harm oneself, the partner, and/or the relationship
- Make a sustained commitment to effort in the relationship
- Emphasize individual and partner strengths
- Explore what it means to create a healthy relationship
- Envision a healthy future together

Know—The development of intimate knowledge of partner:

- Develop what you know and believe about a partner
- Move from idealized knowledge to intimate knowledge
- Develop attentive awareness and knowledge of partner's life, thoughts, and feelings
- Understand partner's pressures and needs

- Remember and value meaningful relationship experiences
- Express sincere interest, physical attraction, and emotional closeness
- Self-disclosure and sharing intimate thoughts and feelings with partner
- Share ideas and expectations of a desirable relationship

Care—Demonstrating kindness, affection, understanding, respect, and caring support:

- Expressions of fondness/affection, appreciation, and positive thoughts
- Intentional expressions of kindness and support
- Perspective taking and empathy for partner's view
- Tolerance and making allowances for continuing differences
- Cultivate positive feelings toward partner and relationship
- Soothing troubled or negative feelings
- Being respectful in accepting and valuing differences
- Openness of heart to partner needs and interests
- Being present and accessible to partner
- Listening and turning toward partner in times of challenge or frustration

Care for self—Maintaining physical, psychological, and sexual health and wellness as an individual:

- Develop skills for maintaining physical wellness (e.g., eating, sleep, physical fitness, substance abuse, and individual sexuality)
- Develop effective stress management skills for chronic and acute stressors
- Develop skills for identifying and managing threats to psychological (emotional and mental) well-being

Share—Developing and maintaining friendship and sense of "we"; spending meaningful time together:

- Find and cultivate common interests and activities
- Develop reciprocal exchanges of affection and love with partner
- Spend time together that builds intimacy
- Participate in couple rituals that build the relationship
- Protect the relationship from negative outside influences
- Cultivate a mental awareness, appreciation, and optimistic view of the relationship
- Engage yourselves in a common purpose

Manage—Strategies of engagement and interaction around differences, stresses, and issues of safety:

- Manage differences that occur in values, beliefs, and expectations
- Utilize perspective taking and empathy for partner's view
- Develop a positive emotional climate that is supportive and caring
- Use constructive engagement and interaction strategies
- Manage the stress response during conflicts

(Continued)

TABLE 9.1 (Continued)

- Maintain positivity (more positives vs. negatives) and avoid expression of negative communication patterns (defensiveness, contempt, criticism, withdrawal, etc.)
- Use positive interpretations, judgments, assumptions, and attributions
- Use soothing and supportive behaviors
- Use team-oriented decision-making strategies
- Adopt a willingness to accept influence
- Use forgiveness skills; welcome repair attempts
- Maintain emotional and physical safety

Connect—Engaging social support, community ties, and sources of meaning:

- Draw upon support from a social network
- Cultivate relationships with extended family members
- Participate in a community supportive of your relationship
- Connect to sources of meaning (i.e., spirituality, values)
- Engage jointly in extra-familial organizations and systems
- Identify what is noble outside of the couple and celebrate it
- Identify and invest yourselves in service together
- Offer support/service to others, including external family members

The NERMEN team came up with seven dimensions or components. Those components are listed and described briefly. See Table 9.1 for each dimension and couple practices that derive from them:

- Choose—The central importance of intentionality
- Know—The development of intimate knowledge of partner
- Care—Demonstrating kindness, affection, understanding, respect, and caring support
- Care for self—Maintaining physical, psychological, and sexual health and wellness as an individual
- Share—Developing and maintaining friendship and sense of "we"; spending meaningful time together
- Manage—Strategies of engagement and interaction around differences, stresses, and issues of safety
- Connect—Engaging social support, community ties, and sources of meaning

The full NERMEM report (Adler-Baeder et al., 2010) provides a discussion of the research related to each component. As a family life educator, you may be interested in using the NERMEM as a foundation on which to build a marriage curriculum, book, or program.

PROGRAMS AND APPROACHES ●

Many activities are ongoing to enrich marriages today, which we call traditional MRE and self-directed MRE. Traditional MRE programs are typically fairly intensive, face-to-face, multisession educational interventions, most often taking place in community or church settings. These programs are often first developed at universities, then disseminated through various combinations of commercial and university partnerships. Notwithstanding evidence of their benefits to couples, MRE programs are notoriously underattended, with research suggesting that from 31% to 37% of couples participate in any form of premarital education (National Fatherhood Initiative, 2005; Stanley, Amato, Johnson, & Markman, 2006; Stanley & Markman, 1997). Use goes up with increased availability (Schumm & Silliman, 1997). Hence, scholars/practitioners are calling upon the field to increase the reach of evidence-based MRE programs (Halford, Markman, Kline, & Stanley, 2003; Larson & Halford, in press) and expand the range and flexibility of formats available to couples (Halford, 2004; Larson & Halford, in press).

Self-directed approaches have been emphasized as of late in response to this call. Self-directed approaches are educational interventions initiated and participated in independently by the couple at home, with little or no external professional intervention (Duncan et al., 2009). Self-directed interventions have been identified as among the most common and promising approaches to strengthening marriage (Hawkins et al., 2004; Larson & Halford, in press). Self-directed programs are part of the larger "flexible-delivery" MRE effort, where participants can access psychoeducational material at a time and place that suits them, instead of relying solely on face-to-face contact (Halford, Moore, Wilson, Farrugia, & Dyer, 2004). Examples of self-directed approaches would include books, magazines, Internet articles, structured programs on the Internet, assessment questionnaires, home study programs, DVDs/CDs, and related learning experiences.

In this section, we describe several programs that use either of these approaches and review literature about program effectiveness. (We are indebted to Geniel Childs for her collection of the following programs and effectiveness data.)

Evidence-based programs. Many choices exist for family life educators specializing in MRE to use with their audiences; unfortunately, far more MRE programs exist than have been systematically evaluated. Recently, a team of marriage scholar/practitioners identified several programs that show rigor in the science-based principles taught and in the outcomes they produce in participating couples. In their systematic search for the best programs meeting the EST (empirically supported treatment) designation, Jakubowski et al. (2004) identified 13 programs that had been evaluated empirically with published results. These programs were then placed in one of three categories: efficacious, possibly efficacious, and empirically untested. Programs met the requirements for being designated efficacious if they had been supported by two or more published outcome studies by separate research teams and included control or comparison groups and random assignment. For the designation of possibly efficacious, programs had only one published outcome study or had more than one study done by the same researchers. Programs were considered empirically untested even if some outcome research had been done but no published controlled randomized studies had been done to support them. Four programs were designated as efficacious: Prevention and Relationship Enhancement Program (PREP), Relationship Enhancement (RE), Couple Communication Program (CCP), and Strategic Hope-Focused Enrichment. Three programs were designated possibly efficacious: CoupleCARE, ACME, and Couple Coping Enhancement Training (CCET). The remaining five programs were designated as empirically untested: Structured Enrichment, Marriage Encounter, PAIRS, Imago, Traits of a Happy Couple, and Saving Your Marriage Before It Starts (SYMBIS). We provide a description of four programs, three of them efficacious and one possibly efficacious, that are also among the best known and used: CCP, RE, PREP, and CoupleCARE.

Couple Communication Program (CCP). The focus of CCP is to teach practical communication skills. This includes an emphasis on a collaborative marriage, which includes recognizing the difference between effective and ineffective ways of talking and listening in order to improve the quality of couple communication. Participants are taught skills to help them increase their self-awareness and to carefully tune in to their partner in order to develop productive listening skills, and they are taught a process for "mapping issues" in order to make decisions and resolve conflicts collaboratively. Couple Communication is presented in two formats: five to six sessions in a group with an instructor and other couples for a total of 8 hours of instruction, or six 50-minute sessions with the instructor and one couple.

Relationship Enhancement (RE). The Relationship Enhancement model is based on the assumption that the most effective way to resolve relationship problems, or to enhance relationship quality and satisfaction, is to teach skills for constructively resolving problems in ways that meet the needs of everyone involved. In the RE program, relationship problems are viewed as an inevitable result of the differing beliefs, feelings, needs, and desires of individuals. Relationship problems are also influenced by life events and transitions. The skills taught in RE are intended to bring about change in individuals on a cognitive, emotional, behavioral, and interpersonal level in order to effectively navigate problems that arise. RE is most often presented in a 2-day weekend format or in a multisession format totaling 15 hours of instruction. Workshop groups generally comprise 4 to 10 couples. Program leaders are trained by the National Institute of Relationship Enhancement, and leaders are encouraged to master the skills themselves in order to effectively teach the skills to the participants.

Prevention and Relationship Enhancement Program (PREP). PREP is a well-known MRE program and has undergone fairly extensive effectiveness research. PREP content focuses on training couples in communication, conflict resolution, and problem-solving skills. The goal is to reduce relationship risk factors and build protective factors through these skills. The PREP program addresses topics such as commitment, conflict, gender differences, fun, friendship, and sensuality. PREP is presented in a full-day workshop plus two 2-hour weeknight sessions for a total of 12 hours of instruction. Information is presented through lectures and demonstrations modeling skills and coaching couples in practicing the skills.

CoupleCARE. The focus of the CoupleCARE (2006) program is to help couples recognize and define strengths and vulnerabilities in their relationships and to develop personal and couple goals that will strengthen the relationship. Of particular emphasis is the concept of self-change and the recognition that relationship enhancement is a matter of partners taking the responsibility for changing their own behavior and not their partner's. CoupleCARE is offered in a self-directed format that is generally completed by couples at home. The program is presented in six sessions. It is recommended that couples complete one session per week. A session typically consists of watching a presentation on DVD, completing exercises in the guidebook, followed by a 30- to 40-minute phone call with a professional relationship educator. The program may also be presented in a face-to-face format. CoupleCARE offers a new approach in the area of practice by using a professionally supported, self-directed educational program. Of particular note is the extensive background research on adult education instructional design that went into the development of this program (Halford, Markman, & Stanley, 2008). The content and delivery practices of the program are well linked to how adults learn.

● EFFECTIVENESS OF MARRIAGE AND RELATIONSHIP EDUCATION

Recent studies show that MRE interventions bring measured benefits. In a recent and exhaustive meta-analytic review of 117 marriage and relationship education studies, A. J. Hawkins, Blanchard, Baldwin, and Fawcett (2008) found that MRE produced moderate effect sizes for both relationship quality (from .30 to .36) and communication skills (from .43 to .45). Effect sizes for experimental studies were larger as compared to quasi-experimental studies, and unpublished studies generally produced comparable effect sizes to published studies, suggesting little "publication bias" in the effects of MRE. In a second meta-analysis (Blanchard, Hawkins, Baldwin, & Fawcett, 2009), these researchers found evidence that MRE programs served as universal prevention and as selective or indicated prevention, demonstrating positive effects at longer term follow-ups for well-functioning couples and at postassessment and shorter term follow-ups for more distressed couples. In a third, separate meta-analysis of premarital education programs (Fawcett, Hawkins, Blanchard, & Carroll, 2010), these researchers found that premarital education produced positive effects on communication skills, and these were especially evident when researchers assessed outcomes with careful observational measures. These findings continue the "moderate effect" trend noted in an earlier meta-analysis of both premarital and marital enrichment programs (Giblin, Sprenkle, & Sheehan, 1985). Recent studies (Stanley, 2001; Stanley & Markman, 1997; Williams, Riley, Risch, & Van Dyke, 1999) have also highlighted specific benefits. Some of these benefits include enhanced communication and conflict management skills, more commitment to one's mate, greater positivity in marriage, and reduced chances for divorce (Stanley, 2001; Stanley et al., 2006).

The programs evaluated in these studies were traditional, face-to-face offerings. Other modes of MRE also show effectiveness. For example, Gottman, Ryan, Swanson, and Swanson (2005) experimentally compared five brief interventions and their ability to enhance positive affect during conflict discussions. Three of the interventions were various dosages of workshops, one combined workshops and therapy, and the fifth consisted of having couples read Gottman and Silver's (1999) *The Seven Principles for Making Marriage Work*. This book consists of numerous exercises and homework activities that couples can do together at home without a helping professional. While the workshops and therapy approaches produced greater gains in aspects of communication, results showed that the book intervention significantly increased a husband's ability to influence his wife with positive affect. The researchers concluded, "This means that she is more likely to respond positively to his positivity, increasing the likelihood that they will get into positive affect exchanges . . . simply by the relatively inexpensive intervention of the couple having read the Gottman and Silver (1999) book" (p. 187). However, in this study, the researchers reported that the book intervention also provided "up to three hours of telephone consultation with a doctoral student in clinical psychology" (p. 165) as part of the intervention. Thus, it cannot be determined with certainty how much of the positive gains were due to the book material alone.

Halford et al. (2004) experimentally evaluated the CoupleCARE program, a self-directed, flexible delivery program that consists of a six-unit home study to be completed by couples in about 6 weeks. For each unit, couples watch videotapes and complete individual and couple activities at home and then share a telephone call with a couple educator. Participating couples significantly increased relationship stability and satisfaction and improved relationship self-regulation but failed to improve significantly in communication.

An additional study explored the effectiveness of self-directed, therapist-directed, and assessment-based interventions for premarital couples (Busby, Ivey, Harris, & Ates, 2007). Researchers found that couples using a self-directed workbook of exercises completed over a 6- to 8-week period made no significant improvement. However, the workbook intervention did arrest declines so that couples maintained their high pretest scores at posttest and, to some extent, at a 6-month follow-up. The only contact participants had with outsiders in this case was with a research assistant who contacted them to inquire whether they had completed the exercises and to send them a questionnaire. The assessment-based intervention (where couples take the online RELATE inventory and then complete a six-session series based on the inventory) was better than the therapist-directed (six unstructured 1-hour sessions to discuss the relationship) and self-directed approaches at improving communication and relationship satisfaction and reducing the number of problem areas.

Duncan et al. (2009) experimentally compared web-based marriage education with a traditional, face-to-face intervention and each to a control group. Results showed that the website produced positive changes in relationship satisfaction and empathic communication in participating couples when compared to a control group, even rivaling the effects of a similar-content, traditional multisession marriage education program.

Thus, MRE offered using both traditional workshop and self-directed approaches has been shown to be at least modestly effective with participating couples. The results of these studies of nontraditional modes of

MRE suggest that flexible, self-directed approaches to marriage education can have a modest, positive influence on participating couples, even when compared with more traditional, face-to-face approaches, and even if the benefit is to arrest further relationship erosion.

● EXTENSION SERVICE PROGRAMS AND RESULTS

One example of an Extension MRE program is *The Marriage Garden* (Marshall & Goddard, 2006). This curriculum is based on an early form of NERMEM (Goddard & Olsen, 2004). By using the garden as a metaphor, the program teaches lessons on commitment, personal growth, nurturing the relationship, understanding your partners, solving problems, and serving.

As is true of many Extension programs, *The Marriage Garden* is based in research, provides practical teaching guides, does not require training or certification to use it, and is available free or affordably. The program includes a summary folder and six lesson guides that can be used for self-study, marriage mentoring, or group discussions. The challenge for many Extension programs is that extensive, quasi-experimental evaluations are not available.

In the past, many Extension programs depended on traditional delivery to reach the intended audience. Yet many people are less willing to attend a series of evening classes. In order to reach new audiences more effectively, more than 100 faith leaders across Arkansas were trained in *The Marriage Garden*. The 2-day training included a summary of research findings and an experience of each lesson. Data from posttests and delayed posttests show that the material was perceived as useful and resulted in reports of improved relationships.

Other Extension programs range from online informational units and newsletters to program curricula and state initiatives. For more information about Extension MRE efforts in your state, go to www.nermen.org.

● CREATING YOUR OWN MARRIAGE AND RELATIONSHIP EDUCATION PROGRAM

Many MRE-specializing family life educators today choose from among the many available programs, developed commercially, by universities, by churches, or some combination, and use those programs for their audiences.

Many program developers conduct leader training. Other family life educators choose to develop their own approach, supplemented by the vast resources created by marriage enrichment practitioners. Thus, it is important to know how to recognize a quality program and how to develop one, as well. How does one go about it?

Here's an example of how an MRE program might be created. In this example, we'll integrate ideas from the earlier chapters on designing comprehensive prevention programs (Chapter 2), program evaluation (Chapter 3), instructional design (Chapter 4), marketing (discussed in greater detail in Chapter 16), and the A. J. Hawkins et al. (2004) model from this chapter. Let's imagine we want to create a marriage education program that has both traditional and nontraditional elements. For the sake of discussion, we'll call the program "Staying Together and Loving It." We will take it through Stages 1 to 3 of the development model.

Problem analysis. Our problem analysis concluded that marriages, unless deliberately strengthened, are subject to entropy over developmental time. This is shown by slow declines in marital happiness and results in high levels of divorce. To prevent erosion, intentional marriage building is necessary. We consulted existing research and theoretical literature regarding healthy marital processes, seeking teachable ideas, and identified concepts, principles, and practices regarding commitment, love and friendship, handling conflict, equal partnership, intimacy, and continuing courtship. These ideas formed the basis for goals and objectives. One goal was to enhance dedication commitment of our couples, with an objective that, by the end of a program, couples would report higher levels of dedication commitment as measured by a commitment inventory. Several organizations in the community shared interest with us in strengthening marriages. We established a coalition with the local ministerial association.

In reviewing existing practices in marriage education and in consultation with our partner organization, we tentatively decided to create a moderate-intensity (six 2-hour sessions) program to be offered in an interfaith setting well known in the community. In addition to this traditional setting, we also wanted to increase chances of reaching more people by adapting the program for flexible delivery at home. To support the effort, we thought it wise to propose creating a supportive website and placing information and video clips there that would reinforce the primary concepts of the program. We also wanted to test Marriage Minute Messages, short, 90-second messages to emphasize important points from the series that could be downloaded to iPods, cell phones, and the like. Our thought was to target early married (1–5 years) and engaged couples with low to moderate measured levels of dysfunction. Since we have a large Latino population in our area, we thought this targeted audience should be both Anglo and Latin.

Program design. Next we checked out these ideas with our targeted audience. We organized several focus groups organized by different demographics of interest (by gender, years married, and ethnic origin) to ask them about these plans and to get ideas of their own about how to go about building a marriage education program that they would be excited about. The data from focus groups confirmed our beliefs to focus on commitment, love and friendship, handling conflict, equal partnership, intimacy, and continuing courtship but also gave us many ideas as to how to reach people with this information. We established change objectives for each of the six areas. For example, for the commitment area, our change objective was as follows: Compared to pretest measures, couples will report higher levels of dedication commitment at posttest. We found existing measures that were reliable and valid that we could use as pretest and posttest assessments that also fit our change objectives. Instructional methods followed a component display theory approach. General principles with examples, couple and individual insight activities, interactive questioning, and video modeling of skills were used as change methods. When skills were being taught, techniques for skill training (see Chapter 6) were used.

For the traditional setting, we decided to use trained facilitators, one man and one woman, to lead the traditional groups and trained relationship educators to work with these leaders as coaches. In addition, these relationship educators also worked with the couples who chose a flexible delivery approach. These educators made telephone calls as follow-up. All facilitators and educators would undergo several hours of training in the curriculum. The content and methods used in the program were tailored for the population based on cultural understanding. For example, in addition to the Latin version being translated into Spanish, all facilitators trained would be native to that culture (Snyder, Duncan, & Larson, 2010).

We undertook multiple approaches to recruitment, many of these ideas coming from the target audiences. We identified a couple with a passion for MPE to champion the program. Word of mouth, local radio and television celebrities, announcements in church bulletins, Latin festivals, announcements on the newly created website, and news releases are several of the recruitment strategies used.

Pilot testing. We are now ready to try the developed program and strategies. We decided to pilot test the program at the new community facility. Ten couples participated in each of the versions for English and Spanish speakers. We had participants formatively evaluate their experience in the program and the staff evaluate the implementation processes from their perspective. On the basis of this clientele and staff feedback, we decided to make some changes.

CHALLENGES FOR THE FUTURE AND FUTURE DIRECTIONS ●

Projecting the future is a perilous endeavor. Perhaps the best we can do is project a likely trajectory for MRE based on some important emerging trends. Of course, with change comes challenge. In this final section of the chapter, we make some educated guesses about where MRE is heading in the near future and the likely challenges it will face. To guide our guesses, we return to the CoFraME model (A. J. Hawkins et al., 2004) discussed earlier and apply it to forecasting a variety of specific features of MRE.

Target

MRE practitioners have received criticism for not making a greater effort to provide services to lower income, more disadvantaged, and more diverse populations who perhaps have the greatest need for preventative education to help form and sustain healthy marriages and relationships (Ooms & Wilson, 2004). The past few years, however, have seen a dramatic increase in MRE targeted to lower income and more diverse couples and individuals. This trend is due in large part to increased public funding and initiatives to help more disadvantaged populations (A. J. Hawkins et al., 2009). It is our impression that MRE practitioners have embraced this need to provide more services to those who may need it most. We believe this trend will continue over the next decade. Thus, we will see continued program development and providing of services to lower income couples and individuals and to diverse racial and ethnic groups.

Timing

Until recently, the majority of MRE has been focused on engaged couples and early married couples. We see evidence that MRE will increasingly target youth and young adults. Much research has documented how relationship formation and interaction patterns begin in adolescence and are common in the emerging adult years but that early relationship behavior and attitudes can put young people on problematic paths for eventual marital success (Cherlin, 2009; Whitehead & Pearson, 2006). In states such as Alabama, Oklahoma, Utah, and elsewhere, healthy relationship education programs delivered in high schools have increased. And there is emerging evidence that they can help youth—across racial/ethnic and economic status—learn healthy interaction patterns and avoid unhealthy relationship beliefs (Kerpelman et al., 2010). In addition, MRE practitioners are beginning to reach out to emerging adults who are in romantic and cohabiting relationships to provide valuable educational programming in this period of the life course before most individuals choose to marry but are forming important attitudes, beliefs, and interaction patterns that can affect marriages later on (Rhoades, Stanley, & Markman, 2009). We anticipate that MRE for this important group, offered through community colleges, universities, and elsewhere, will grow in number and quality over the next decade. Also, MRE scholars have pointed out the substantial need for tailored services to remarrying couples (Adler-Baeder & Higginbotham, 2004); remarriages constitute half of all marriages in the United States now and have somewhat higher risks for divorce (Bramlett & Mosher, 2001). Again, we see evidence that MRE practitioners are responding to this challenge and finding success with programs that address the unique circumstances of married and unmarried stepcouples and their families (Higginbotham & Skogrand, 2010). We believe there will be significant growth in this area of the field over the next decade, as well.

Setting

Faith-based organizations have been the most significant setting for providing MRE. This will continue and even grow. We see evidence that religious groups of all stripes are taking even greater interest in helping their congregants prepare more effectively for marriage and also help them nurture and sustain those relationships over time. In addition, there has been a dramatic growth in MRE services for military families. Over the past decade, military couples have experienced higher levels of stress due to multiple deployments in war zones and lengthy separations. The military is responding to these challenges by offering numerous services, including MRE, and there is evidence that these services can reduce divorce rates (Stanley, Allen, Markman, Rhoades, & Prentice, 2010). Such success suggests that the military is likely to increase their investment in MRE over the next decade.

Content

MRE has placed a significant emphasis on helping couples develop better communication and problem-solving skills, consistent with research on the importance of interaction behaviors for relationship quality and stability (Gottman & Silver, 1999). Given the evidence that, in general, MRE is effective in improving communication skills (Blanchard et al., 2009), we do not anticipate that this emphasis will diminish. However, as noted earlier, within this emphasis, there appears to be growing attention not just to specific communication techniques but also to the motivations and virtues behind them. As a result, effective communication training now includes such things as building friendship, expressing forgiveness, and avoiding negative attributions. That is, interaction skills and personal motivations and virtues increasingly are merging. We predict and hope that this friendly and constructive merger will continue to grow over the next decade. In addition, we already see how MRE programs are adapting and tailoring their content to fit the diverse circumstances of various racial, ethnic, cultural, religious, and special needs populations. This appears to be an emerging "best practice" in MRE, and we expect that tailored programming will continue to grow over the next decade. However, future research needs to illuminate better the value of tailored content versus the adequacy of more universal content.

Methods

Because MRE is modifying programming to fit more diverse populations and unique circumstances, pedagogy is also evolving. Traditionally, MRE has involved a great deal of didactic information presentation that is probably well received by the more educated audiences typical of MRE in the past. We see evidence that MRE practitioners are employing more active learning styles in their programs that may be more effective with less educated participants (Dion et al., 2008). Another interesting development in the field has been the proliferation of web-based MRE that facilitates self-guided learning. A generation reared on the web will undoubtedly look more to virtual MRE for help. We do not anticipate that the increasing use of virtual MRE will necessarily reduce the interest in face-to-face, group-based MRE. Indeed, we think these two sources can coexist and reinforce each other. Moreover, we expect that the explosion of social networking and web 2.0 applications will open up intriguing possibilities for creative MRE practitioners. Web 2.0 MRE would be a less didactic, more democratized, and more fluid pedagogical process. The effectiveness of this kind of approach to MRE would become a fascinating future research question.

Dosage

The modal MRE program dosage is about 12 hours (A. J. Hawkins et al., 2009). The evidence is mixed on how dosage is related to the effectiveness of MRE (A. J. Hawkins & Blanchard, 2009). Nevertheless, over the next decade, there will likely be greater variation in dosage. We believe an increase in web-based, self-guided MRE will allow more individuals and couples to consume smaller dosages, perhaps in response to more specific and personal needs. At the same time, we see evidence of programs targeted to more disadvantaged populations programming higher dosages to meet the added stresses and challenges that these couples experience, with some evidence of modest success (Cowan, Cowan, Pruett, Pruett, & Wong, 2009; Dion & Hershey, 2010).

Bright Prospects and Real Challenges

Overall, we see bright prospects for MRE over the next decade. In the United States, Americans still place a high value on creating healthy, stable marriages, although they seem to struggle more than most to form and sustain them (Cherlin, 2009). Those paired forces will create fertile ground for the potential value of MRE. Its reach will include a more diverse and needy audience. MRE for youth and emerging adults will grow, providing more potential to help them avoid problematic trajectories for forming and sustaining healthy marriages. MRE will be available in a wider variety of settings and dosages tailored to more unique circumstances and different learning styles. As a result of these trends, we predict that much larger numbers of individuals and couples will make use of MRE services than has been the case in the past. Indeed, the field of MRE has never been more exciting.

At the same time, the challenges facing the field are real and serious. One set of challenges involves effective response to the growth of services and growing diversity of the participants served. Can MRE practitioners and the scholars who support the field keep up with the demand and provide high-quality preventative services to such a diverse landscape? This will be a big challenge for the field but may also spur an infusion of new talent and energy. Another crucial challenge involves the uncertainty of continued government support. Over the past decade, a handful of states, such as Oklahoma, Utah, and Texas, have committed regular funding to support

MRE (A. J. Hawkins et al., 2009). Also, the federal government under the rubric of poverty prevention has legislated the investment of public funds to support state and community healthy marriage initiatives and MRE demonstration programs. Unquestionably, this infusion of modest public funding and serious government interest has buoyed, energized, and improved substantially the MRE field. Important evaluation research that will mature over the next few years may have some influence on the continuation of this funding stream, either supporting or questioning it. But this funding will also be subject to constant political dynamics. Public support for MRE does not have a large and entrenched interest group. Only time will tell how the current nexus between MRE and public policy will play out. Our powers of prophesy here are inadequate. If funding diminishes significantly or disappears, this may dampen prospects for MRE. Of course, this could also spur innovative ways of supporting the growth and development of the field, as well. MRE practitioners should probably be prepared for either outcome.

CONCLUSION ●

This chapter has reviewed the historical beginnings of marriage and relationship education, its current scholarly foundation and frameworks for practice, different programs and approaches, effectiveness, and challenges and future directions. More opportunities than ever before exist for family life educators to do marriage and relationship education with a widening and increasingly diverse audience. The need for effective MRE is not likely to diminish in the future. We hope eager family life educators will embrace these opportunities.

EXPLORATIONS ●

1. Examine several MRE curricula and other resources (publications, website articles, etc.) to see to what degree they incorporate a contemporary research base, as suggested in the NERMEM model.

2. Attend a Smart Marriages conference or visit the website (www .smartmarriages.com) to become exposed to a wide variety of MRE offerings.

Examine the materials and ideas to which you are exposed and compare them to a research base and other elements of quality FLE. Which programs appear to be science based? Which have plans for implementation? How have the programs been evaluated?

3. Use the CoFraME model to help you design a comprehensive response to MRE needs in your community. How could many of these elements apply to creating an awareness of FLE opportunities in other subject matter areas?

CHAPTER **10**

PARENTING EDUCATION

Heidi E. Stolz

P arents play a key role in children's development. Scholarship on the parent-child relationship almost invariably points to two fundamental components of parenting that are consistently related to child and youth outcomes: (a) a supportive component, including warmth, affection, and involvement, and (b) a controlling component, including provision of structure to the environment, limit setting, monitoring, and supervision (see B. K. Barber, Stolz, & Olsen, 2005, for a review). Specifically, Amato and Fowler (2002) suggest that children and adolescents do best when parents support them, spend quality time with them, avoid harsh punishment, and emphasize communication. Although the research literatures typically refer to these dimensions as support and control, the lay parenting literatures often label them nurture and guidance, respectively. Overall, there is much evidence that higher levels of parental support or nurture combined with higher levels of behavioral control or guidance are related to more positive outcomes for children and families.

Although 60 years of parenting research clearly identifies the important role of parents in promoting children's well-being, effective parenting is not easy. Children and adolescents are faced with opportunities and sometimes pressures to select harmful behaviors. According to the 2005 national Youth Risk Behavior Survey (YRBS; Centers for Disease Control and Prevention,

2005), during a specified 30-day period, 9.9% of high school students reported driving a car after drinking alcohol, 18.5% had carried a weapon, 43.3% had drank alcohol, 23.0% had smoked cigarettes, and 20.2% had used marijuana. In addition, during the 12 months preceding the survey, 35.9% of high school students had been in a physical fight and 8.4% had attempted suicide. Overall, 46.8% of high school students reported having had sexual intercourse, and 37.2% of those sexually active high school students had not used a condom during their most recent sexual encounter. Parents are charged with protecting children from these and many other risks and to do so amid the pressures that accompany changes in the workforce, in family structures, in media messages, and in cultural values, to name just a few. Given that parents are in a key position to positively affect children, yet face significant challenges to daily, positive parenting in our complex and ever-changing society, it makes sense that they would need and benefit from help. In an effort to meet this need, the number of parenting education programs in the United States designed to inspire, inform, and train parents has increased.

● HISTORY AND CURRENT STATE OF PARENTING EDUCATION

To develop some perspective on the topic of this chapter, let's first briefly consider the history of parenting education. Parent education in the United States has existed in some form since at least the early 19th century. The movement began in the 1800s with mothers who met in discussion groups and was expanded in the 1820s through the formation of associations to teach parents how to instill religious and moral values in their children (Croake & Glover, 1977). At the beginning of the 20th century, parent education efforts gained momentum. Family professionals initiated publications and programs to disseminate parenting information (Doherty, 2000). Government responses included the first White House Conference on Child Welfare in 1909 and the 1914 Smith-Lever Act, which began the Cooperative Extension Service. A survey conducted by the U.S. Office of Education in 1930 revealed that almost 400 organizations were conducting some form of parent education (Croake & Glover, 1977). The field of parent education has continued to grow, and currently more than 250,000 professionals, paraprofessionals, and volunteers are serving as parent educators in the United States (National Parenting Education Network, n.d.). Thus, there is a long history of parents both needing and receiving help with their parenting, and over time, both the level of need and the number of people and programs working to meet the need have increased.

UNDERSTANDING EFFECTIVE PARENTING •

Before we can consider various efforts to educate parents about parenting, it is useful to first explore the end state that parenting education hopes to promote. In other words, what do parents need to believe, know, and do to positively affect their children?

Positive Parenting Dimensions and Behaviors: The Scholarship of Parenting

One body of information that helps us better understand what behaviors parenting education programs should strive to promote is published, peer-reviewed scholarship on parenting and the parent-child relationship. Specifically, in this chapter, we will consider two research-supported parenting frameworks that specify the salient components of parenting. First, Baumrind's (1971; see also Maccoby & Martin, 1983) typological framework has occupied a central role in the research literature. From this perspective, two dimensions of parenting are considered key—responsiveness and demandingness. These two dimensions are then used to identify four basic *types* of parenting, which is why this is labeled a *typological* framework. Much research suggests that the authoritative style or type of parenting, characterized by high responsiveness and high demandingness, is associated with positive child and youth outcomes in a variety of domains (Baumrind, 1991; Lamborn, Mounts, Steinberg, & Dornbusch, 1991).

A second parenting framework that sheds light on important aspects of parenting emerged from the early work of Schaefer (1965) and Becker (1964), as well as the later work of Barber and colleagues (B. K. Barber et al., 2005) and Steinberg and colleagues (Steinberg, 1990). This framework suggests that three key dimensions of parenting—support, behavioral control, and (avoidance of) psychological control—each predict specific aspects of youth functioning (B. K. Barber et al., 2005). This is considered a *dimensional* framework because the dimensions are considered separately rather than being combined to create types of parenting. When we consider these two influential frameworks, we find two agreed-upon components or dimensions of positive parenting (responsiveness/support and demanding-ness/behavioral control) and one additional dimension specified only by the second framework (avoidance of psychological control). Given that these three parenting dimensions are supported by decades of research, it is important to briefly consider the parenting behaviors that each dimension comprises and the extent to which parenting education efforts emphasize each dimension.

Responsiveness/support. First, much research supports the notion that consistent, stable emotional connection between parents and children affords children a solid foundation for the development of important social skills. This connection is often measured by children and adolescents' perceptions of parental support. This overarching construct of parental support covers a number of more specific constructs such as attachment, warmth, nurturance, and involvement. Thus, Baumrind's (1971) notion of responsiveness is quite similar to the support construct in the dimensional frameworks. Perceived support from parents has been predictive of school performance (Eccles, Early, Frasier, Belansky, & McCarthy, 1997; M. R. Herman, Dornbusch, Herron, & Herting, 1997), self-esteem (Bulanda & Majumdar, 2009), and social competence (B. K. Barber et al., 2005) in childhood and adolescence. Many parenting education models, as well as specific programs and curricula, attempt to teach parents to increase their levels of support and responsiveness by communicating love and affection for their children.

Demandingness/behavioral control. Second, both identified parenting frameworks reviewed above (Baumrind's typological framework and the dimensional framework suggested by Barber and Steinberg) specify the role of parental behavioral control or demandingness, including supervision, monitoring, and rule and limit setting (Dishion & Loeber, 1985). When parents provide structure around their offspring's behaviors, youth learn to self-regulate and are therefore less likely to engage in antisocial behaviors (Maccoby & Martin, 1983). In addition to active monitoring, overall parental knowledge of how and with whom school-aged children and adolescents spend their time has also been linked to more positive behaviors (see Kerr & Stattin, 2000). Research on youth of various nationalities has indicated that a high level of parental behavioral control, including monitoring and knowledge of adolescents' friends and activities, has a "specialized relationship" (B. K. Barber et al., 2005, p. 57) with decreased antisocial behavior, suggesting that it is the most effective intervention target (with regard to antisocial behavior) at the parental level. As was the case with parental support, many parenting education programs also explicitly seek to teach parents how to develop or maintain an appropriate level of behavioral control.

This is understandable and appropriate, given that many parents seek parent training programs due to the "acting out" behaviors of their children, and research supports this relationship between parental behavioral control and children's externalized problem behavior.

Psychological control. A third important component of parenting is specified by the dimensional framework discussed above. In effect, this framework suggests that to understand parenting, it is helpful to separate the construct of control into two different dimensions. Thus, behavioral control, as discussed above, is quite similar to Baumrind's (1971) idea of demandingness and is generally positive and helpful for children. However, psychological control includes parental controlling behaviors involving shame, guilt, love withdrawal, and other manipulative forms of discipline that are harmful for children and adolescents. Much scholarly work has demonstrated the existence and negative effects of psychological control, which is defined as "control attempts that intrude into the psychological and emotional development of the child (e.g., thinking processes, self-expression, emotions, and attachment to parents)" (B. K. Barber, 1996, p. 3296). Although there is widespread acceptance in the scholarly literatures of the negative effects of psychologically controlling parental behaviors, this parenting dimension perhaps plays a less central role in parenting education programming.

Take a moment to reflect on these three dimensions of parenting that have been supported by decades of research. Consider the parenting you have personally experienced. Did you feel supported? Were appropriate limits set and enforced? Did you have the freedom to express your thoughts and feelings even if they differed from those of your parents? It is hoped that considering these dimensions of positive parenting with regard to your own life helps you see the real-world usefulness of this research and empowers you to help parents with whom you might work take steps toward more positive parenting.

Priority Practices for Parents: The National Extension Parent Education Model (NEPEM)

On the basis of parenting frameworks and research as well as extensive experience with programs for parents, professionals with the Cooperative Extension Service created the National Extension Parent Education Model (NEPEM), a model specifying "critical" or "priority" parenting practices (Smith et al., 1994). This model offers another opportunity for us to better understand the aspects of parenting that are critical to children's well-being and should therefore be targeted by parenting interventions. According to NEPEM, the six priority parenting practices and their descriptions are as follows (Smith et al., 1994, p. 14):

Category	Priority Practice
Care for self	Manage personal stress.
	Manage family resources.
	Offer support to other parents.
	Ask for and accept support from others when needed.
	Recognize one's own personal and parenting strengths.
	Have a sense of purpose in setting child-rearing goals.
	Cooperate with one's child-rearing partners.
Understand	Observe and understand one's children and their development.
	Recognize how children influence and respond to what happens around them.
Guide	Model appropriate desired behavior.
	Establish and maintain reasonable limits.
	Provide children with developmentally appropriate opportunities to learn responsibility.
	Convey fundamental values underlying basic human decency.
	Teach problem-solving skills.
	Monitor children's activities and facilitate their contact with peers and adults.
Nurture	Express affection and compassion.
	Foster children's self-respect and hope.
	Listen and attend to children's feelings and ideas.
	Teach kindness.
	Provide for the nutrition, shelter, clothing, health, and safety needs of one's children.
	Celebrate life with one's children.
	Help children feel connected to family history and cultural heritage.
Motivate	Teach children about themselves, others, and the world around them.
	Stimulate curiosity, imagination, and the search for knowledge.
	Create beneficial learning conditions.
	Help children process and manage information.
Advocate	Find, use, and create community resources when needed to benefit one's children and the community of children.
	Stimulate social change to create supportive environments for children and families.
	Build relationships with family, neighborhood, and community groups.

Developed by Charles A. Smith, Dorothea Cudaback, H. Wallace Goddard, and Judith A. Myers-Walls in collaboration with Extension professionals throughout the United States. This project was supported by the Extension Service, U.S. Department of Agriculture, and the Cooperative Extension Service, Kansas State University, under special project number 92-EXCA-2–0812.

Overall, the reviewed parenting frameworks, scholarship, and NEPEM suggest that parents need to first be in a position to learn parenting (e.g., be able to care for themselves and understand children's development), and then they would benefit from learning how to support and encourage children (including responding to and motivating children) as well as how to guide children (including limit setting and provision of structure) without exerting control on their thoughts and feelings. Last, beyond learning improved parenting behaviors, parents would benefit from learning how to identify, create, and use resources outside of the family for the benefit of their children. Parenting education, broadly defined, includes all efforts to instill in parents a desire to parent well and to provide the knowledge and skills (specified above) deemed necessary to do so.

UNDERSTANDING EFFECTIVE PARENTING EDUCATION •

Having reviewed scholarship on positive, effective parenting and considered the priority parenting practices specified by the NEPEM, we now have a better understanding of the predispositions, knowledge, and behaviors that parenting education programs should attempt to shape and teach, in order to improve the lives of children and adolescents. Although effective parenting programs generally do target one or more of the constructs reviewed above, the specific parenting behaviors or dimensions emphasized, as well as the mechanisms thought to be responsible for behavioral change, differ, based in part on the theoretical underpinnings of the parenting program. Given that these theoretical models shape the content and focus of parenting programming, six theoretical models that inform parenting education are reviewed below, with examples provided of programs stemming from each model. Most of these models are also reviewed succinctly by Myers-Walls (2007) along with a scenario-based quiz to help parenting educators identify which model(s) best reflect their beliefs about parenting.

THEORETICAL MODELS OF PARENTING EDUCATION •

Attachment models. Bowlby's (1969) theory of attachment suggests that attachment to a caregiver is a primal and fundamental form of behavior where people seek the comfort and security of a consistent, attuned, and responsive individual. Parenting education programs grounded in this theory tend to focus on helping parents develop positive forms of attachment with their children by increasing awareness and knowledge about children's emotional needs. Thus, these programs tend to focus primarily on the supportive dimension of parenting, and they tend to focus on infants and young children, given that the early years represent a sensitive window for secure attachment. From this perspective, a solid parent-child attachment provides the foundation for other positive parent and child outcomes. One parenting education program that is grounded in attachment theory is Steps Toward Effective, Enjoyable Parenting (STEEP; Egeland & Erickson, 2004). STEEP attempts to help parents recognize the connections between their past and present relationships and also better understand their infant's feelings. By promoting a secure attachment between infant and parent, STEEP parent educators hope to affect parent-child interactions and relationships into the future.

Behavior modification models. Programs that are grounded in behavioral theories tend to focus on modeling, reinforcement, and punishment. Parents are instructed to identify a goal and establish a reinforcement and/or punishment schedule to shape the child's behavior toward the goal. Thus, parenting education programs grounded in this model tend to focus on parental control more so than support, and they tend to downplay the role of internal states (e.g., children's feelings or motives). Although there is some indication that punishment is ineffective in the long run, and there is concern that these approaches result in behaviors that are externally produced rather than internally motivated, these types of programs have been shown to be effective in two distinct populations—children with learning disabilities (Gates, Newell, & Wray, 2001) and youth engaging in high-risk behavior (Stolz, Vargas, Clifford, Gaedt, & Garcia, 2010). Myers-Walls (2007) suggested that both Assertive Discipline and Confident Parenting are parenting education programs grounded in behavior modification. Another parenting education program grounded in the behavior modification framework is Parent Project (Fry, Johnson, Melendez, & Morgan, 2003), a 10- to 16-week parenting program for self- and system-referred parents of at-risk or out-of-control youth. The program targets parents whose adolescents exhibit behaviors such as running away, drug and/or alcohol use, poor school attendance, or violence. Parent Project facilitators teach parents to influence their children and motivate them to change their own behavior via positive strokes, positive consequences, and negative consequences. Parent Project facilitators also teach parents to consider and inquire about the "5 Ws" (Fry et al., 2003, p. 30), representing "Who," "What," "Where," "When," and "Why" about their adolescents' activities, and to occasionally "Spot Check" (p. 30) to see if their adolescents are doing what they claimed to be doing.

Democratic models. Democratic parenting education models are rooted in Adlerian psychology (Adler, 1927) and in the work of Dreikurs (1964). As such, they emphasize the importance of understanding children's perspectives by reflecting on their cognitive and internal motivation processes. These programs de-emphasize parental power and focus instead on warmth, acceptance, and parental perspective taking. Parents are encouraged to try to understand children's motivation for misbehavior and provide children with explanations about the logical consequences of their behavior. Despite the fact that many well-established parenting programs are grounded in this model, Goddard, Myers-Walls, and Lee (2004) question both (a) the ability of the limited motivational options (attention, power, revenge, inadequacy) to explain the causes of misbehavior as well as (b) the ability of parents to diagnose children's motives, especially in the context of a stressful parenting moment. Myers-Walls's (2007) description of parent education approaches indicates that Systematic Training for Effective Parenting (STEP), Parent Effectiveness Training (PET), Active Parenting, and the Nurturing Program are all grounded in the democratic parenting model. Another parenting program grounded primarily in the democratic model is Parents' Toolshop (Pawel, 2000). This program combines elements of several established programs to create a hybrid, democratic approach. Parents' Toolshop teaches a decision-making model as well as problem prevention skills, problem ownership steps, and tools for addressing both "child" problems and "parent" problems.

Social consciousness models. Another parenting education model identified by Myers-Walls (2007) is the socially conscious parenting model. Programs based on this model are sensitive to the larger social and ecological environment in which parenting occurs and emphasize "social change, empathy, and respect for self and others" (Myers-Walls, 2007, p. 4). Nonviolence, acceptance of diversity, and planned simplicity are values stressed by these programs. Because this framework downplays the role of parental power, these programs tend to focus on parental support more so than behavioral control. Some programs emerging from this framework also suggest and support parenting behaviors that avoid parental psychological control (attempts to control children's thoughts and feelings). Myers-Walls includes Teaching Peace in her list of parenting programs based on this model. Teaching Peace (Arnow, 1995) attempts to help parents foster children's self-esteem, which, in turn, is thought to reduce conflict and prejudice.

Counseling and/or communication models. Another basic theoretical model from which parenting education programs have emerged is the counseling or communication model. Parenting programs based in this philosophical approach focus on empathy and open communication. Thus, they tend to encourage behaviors contributing to the dimensions of parental support, and they discourage the use of psychological control. Perhaps the most well-known program based on this model is Faber and Mazlish's (1999) *How to Talk So Kids Will Listen and Listen So Kids Will Talk.* Based on Ginott's (1965) work, this program helps parents cope with their children's feelings, express their own feelings, and use alternatives to punishment.

Developmental models. Last, many parenting education programs are grounded in a developmental theoretical model (Myers-Walls, 2007). These programs are often considered to emphasize children's "ages and stages." As such, the focus is not on parenting behaviors so much as on parental knowledge of children's development. Programs grounded in this model are based on the assumption that if children's developmental needs are met, parents will be faced with fewer problematic behaviors. One well-established developmental parenting program is Parents as Teachers (PAT). PAT is designed to help parents understand their child's development and their role in facilitating their child's learning from infancy to kindergarten. To accomplish this goal, they provide home visiting services to educate parents and conduct vision, hearing, and developmental screenings of young children.

The six theoretical models reviewed above differ with regard to the parenting behaviors targeted and the explanations for how, exactly, changing that targeted parental behavior will, in turn, change children's lives for the better. Although parenting programs stemming from these models are different and sometimes even contain contradictory messages, all of the approaches have been shown to be effective under certain conditions with certain populations. That points to one of the challenges in parenting education—there is really no "one-size-fits-all" approach to teaching parents. Thus, it is important match each parent to a program with a compatible philosophical foundation (for suggestions and tools, see Heath, 1998; Myers-Walls, 2007).

● QUALITIES AND COMPETENCIES OF AN EFFECTIVE PARENT EDUCATOR

Having a solid understanding of the theoretical foundations of parenting programs helps us to sort programs based on philosophies, assumptions, and goals, thus enabling us to select a program that is theoretically sound and an appropriate match for our audience and outcomes of interest. However, regardless of the theoretical basis of a program, it is unlikely to be optimally effective unless it is delivered by a competent parent educator. Thus, in this section, we will explore what we know about the characteristics and qualities of an effective parenting educator. It has been difficult to develop a set of agreed-upon standards or competencies of parenting educators because people working in this capacity have varied educational backgrounds (both in terms of academic discipline as well as level of education) and work in a wide range of settings (e.g., for profit, nonprofit, schools, hospitals, community service organizations; for a discussion, see Cooke, 2006). Despite these challenges, several individuals and entities have nonetheless attempted to identify the core competencies of parenting educators (i.e., the agreed-upon set of required attitudes, skills, and knowledge) as a first step toward creating professional development opportunities leading to standardized credentials. Two such efforts, reviewed in detail by Cooke (2006), will be described below. If you have a passion for helping others improve their parenting, these are the skills and attributes you might want to consider developing through your coursework, practicum placements, or paid or volunteer work.

Texas Registry of Parent Educator Resources (ROPER). Texas ROPER, in conjunction with the Center for Parenting Education at the University of North Texas, gathered data from 400 professionals across the state of Texas. From these responses, a framework was developed specifying 10 areas that are central to the work of parenting educators (Center for Parent Education, 2004). Within each of these 10 areas, specific attitudes, knowledge, and skills have been identified that are thought to play important roles in parenting educators' ability to effectively train and support parents. The 10 identified areas are as follows:

1. Child and Lifespan Development

2. Dynamics of Family Relationships

3. Family Life Education

4. Guidance and Nurturing

5. Health and Safety

6. Diversity in Family Systems

7. Professional Practice and Methods Related to Adult Learning and Family Support

8. School and Child Care Relationships

9. Community Relationships

10. Assessment and Evaluation

Texas ROPER provides free assessment tools for organizations to use to evaluate their areas of relative strength as well as their training needs with regard to attitudes, knowledge, and skills within each of the 10 areas. The assessment tools, as well as other available online resources, are of use to professionals and family service organizations interested in identifying and improving parenting educator competencies.

National Extension Parent Education Framework (NEPEF). After creating NEPEM, a framework for understanding critical parenting practices that make up the *content* of parenting education, faculty members working within the Cooperative Extension System expanded the framework to also include the *processes* that are central to parenting education. The two components together (content and process) make up the National Extension Parent Education Framework (NEPEF; DeBord, Bower, Goddard, Kirby, Kobbe, Myers-Walls, et al., 2002). According to the NEPEF, the content areas that parent educators should be knowledgeable about are those discussed above as priority practices of parents—care for self, understand, guide, nurture, motivate, and advocate. Thus, there is a planned parallelism given that the areas of knowledge that are thought to be at the core of parental competence are also the areas that parenting educators must thoroughly understand before they can effectively educate parents. The NEPEF model then goes beyond specifying the knowledge-based competencies of parenting educators to describe the process-related competencies, or skills, required of parenting educators. Six process-related skills are identified as follows (DeBord, Bower, Goddard, Kirby, Kobbe, Myers-Walls, et al., 2002, p. 7):

Grow: refers to personal growth as a professional; knowing yourself and understanding how this affects the way you relate to others;

Frame: refers to knowing theoretical frameworks that guide practice in the field of parenting education;

Develop: refers to planning and marketing programs to educate parents, and developing evaluation processed that are part of a total educational effort;

Embrace: refers to recognizing and responding to differences in ethnicity, family type, and belief systems among populations being served;

Educate: refers to being an effective teacher; knowing how to use various delivery methods, helping parents learn, and challenging them to higher parenting goals;

Build: refers to reaching out to build professional networks; being a community advocate; and connecting with organizations to expand the field of parenting education.

Overall, it is important to recognize that parent educator competencies include (a) broad and deep knowledge of theory and research related to children, families, and parenting; (b) an attitude of tolerance, sensitivity, and commitment to parents; and (c) instructional, relational, and professional skills. Once core competencies are further refined, it is believed that comprehensive preparation based on those competencies, focused practice, and opportunities for continuing professional development will increase the quality (Heath & Palm, 2006) and the efficacy (Campbell & Palm, 2004) of parent education.

EFFECTIVE DELIVERY FORMATS ●

In addition to understanding the assumptions and goals of a parenting program (e.g., the theoretical foundation, the targeted parenting dimensions) and the characteristics of the individual responsible for delivering the material, it is also useful to consider the mode of delivery itself. Parent educators use a range of techniques (e.g., seminars, group programs, in-home programs, newsletters, hotlines, referral services, magazines, books, pamphlets, CDs, downloadable MP3s, DVDs, text messaging, and videos) to communicate parenting information to parents. Some techniques focus on information provision, others on support provision, and still others on skills training. Below we briefly consider several general modes of information delivery, along with the evidence of effectiveness of each.

Home visitation. One effective technique for reaching parents is the in-home parent education program. This approach involves a trained individual observing and assisting with child and family issues in the home environment. This technique is often used to work with parents of very young children, and families are generally visited one to four times per month. Home visitation programs have provided parenting education to families who are at risk for certain negative outcomes (Duggan et al., 2000) and parents with intellectual disabilities (Llewellyn, McConnell, Russo,

Mayes, & Honey, 2002). According to the Council on Child and Adolescent Health (1998), home visitation programs "offer an effective mechanism to ensure ongoing parental education, social support, and linkage with public and private community services" (p. 486). In addition, the council notes that "home-visitation programs can be an effective early-intervention strategy to improve the health and well-being of children" (p. 488).

Group parenting classes. Another proven effective technique is the in-person group parenting program. In this approach, parents come together for a specified period of time and receive information regarding some aspect of parenting ranging from how to help children deal with divorce (Shifflett & Cummings, 1999) to how to care for an infant who was once critically ill (Pfander & Bradley-Johnson, 1990). One group program, Common Sense Parenting, led to significant reductions in child behavior problems and improvements in parental problem solving among low- and middle-income parents (Thompson, Grow, Ruma, Daly, & Burke, 1993). Participants in another group program in Australia reported short-term increases in parental competence and longer term reductions in child difficulty (J. G. Barber, 1992).

Newsletters. A newsletter is another technique used to effectively reach parents. This type of parenting information is often distributed by an agency to a particular population, such as single parents (Nelson, 1986) or parents of adolescents (Bogenschneider & Stone, 1997). In a survey of 880 parents in 10 states, Cudaback et al. (1985) examined the usefulness of age-paced newsletters and found that a majority of parents believed the newsletters to be useful in increasing both their self-confidence and their knowledge of child development. In addition, Bogenschneider and Stone (1997) surveyed 796 U.S. Midwest parents of 9th to 12th graders regarding the effects of age-paced newsletters and reported closer parental monitoring by parents who received a series of three newsletters (age paced or generic), as compared to the control group.

Books. The sheer volume of books related to parenting that are available in bookstores or through online book vendors suggests that many parents get parenting information in this format. Unfortunately, there are no known scholarly studies related to the effectiveness of parenting books in shaping parenting behavior. However, one good resource for those who are interested in using books to inform parenting is the *Authoritative Guide to Self-Help Resources in Mental Health* (Norcross et al., 2003). While not based on empirical studies, it includes professional assessments to help both parents and parenting professionals distinguish high-quality self-help resources (including those related to parenting) from those that are inaccurate or even potentially harmful.

Web-based approaches. Newer techniques for delivering parenting information also show promise. For example, parents of young children with disabilities reported that the website SPIES for Parents was "helpful, useful, and responsive to their needs and time constraints" (Cook, Rule, & Mariger, 2003, p. 19). Of course, many other websites provide parenting information as well. This approach has the advantage of being free of cost to anyone with a computer and Internet access as well as free from specific time constraints. However, among the disadvantages are the fact that it is difficult to determine the soundness of the information provided, the information is often insensitive to the particular situation of an individual parent, and the method does little to promote a social context for learning.

Again, as was the case with the various theoretical foundations of parenting education approaches, we have reviewed many options with regard to delivery formats, and all of them have the potential to be effective in certain situations with certain audiences.

POPULATIONS SERVED BY PARENTING EDUCATION •

Having considered the theoretical foundations of parenting programs, the competencies considered necessary for individuals who deliver parent training, and the various delivery formats that are used, we will now reflect on the populations for whom parenting education has been shown to be effective. Certainly individuals with a variety of characteristics and needs have had positive and beneficial experiences in general parenting classes, but sometimes enough parents share a particular, salient characteristic that a targeted approach is warranted. One such shared characteristic is pending divorce. Given that many states either encourage or require parent training for divorcing parents, it is encouraging that Bacon and McKenzie's (2004) evaluation of 10 parent education programs for divorcing parents showed significant improvements on measures of parental conflict across programs. In addition, programs designed for incarcerated parents have also resulted in improved participant attitudes, better understanding of effective discipline practices, and recognition of the importance of children's play (among incarcerated fathers; Maiorano & Futris, 2005) and improvements in attitude, self-esteem, and interactions with children (among incarcerated mothers; Harm & Thompson, 1997). Programs targeting teen parents have demonstrated effectiveness in improving both mothers' parenting behaviors and children's developmental quotient scores (Deutscher, Fewell, & Gross, 2006) and in reducing founded child maltreatment reports (Britner & Reppucci, 1997). Also, programs designed for a specific racial or ethnic group have also been shown to change important aspects of parenting. For example, African American parents of teens who participated in an Adlerian video-based parent education program "exhibited significantly more favorable perceptions of their children's behavior" (Farooq, Jefferson, & Fleming, 2005, p. 29) and developed more authoritative parenting views when compared to those in the control group who did not participate in the program. Programs specifically designed for fathers, court-connected parents, and parents of children with disabilities have also been shown to be effective.

● OVERALL EFFECTIVENESS OF PARENTING PROGRAMS

Overall, there is widespread agreement that parenting behaviors affect children in meaningful ways and that effective parenting behaviors can be taught and learned (Britner & Reppucci, 1997; Reid, Webster-Stratton, & Baydar, 2004). Bunting's (2004) review of research on multiple programs targeting a variety of audiences revealed that parenting programs have been found to improve child behaviors and parent relationships, increase maternal knowledge and self-esteem, decrease maternal depression and stress, and improve mother-child interactions.

Parent training programs have been shown to increase parents' feelings of empathy and to help the parents establish better relationships with their children (Barlow & Stewart-Brown, 2000). Several studies have found that parent training resulted in a decrease in negative parenting behaviors (Britner & Reppucci, 1997; Reid et al., 2004). Additional studies have found fewer conduct problems for the children of parents who completed parent training (McKenzie & Bacon, 2002). One longitudinal study (Reid, Webster-Stratton, & Beauchaine, 2001) showed that, one year after the completion of parenting classes, mothers in the intervention were observed to be more positive, less critical, more consistent, and more competent in their parenting than control mothers. Kaiser and Hancock (2003) noted that "there is systematic evidence over the last 30 years that teaching parents specific strategies to support their children's development can be effective" (p. 9).

Although there is plenty of evidence that parenting education can be effective, the vast majority of parenting interventions are not evaluated. How can one easily find evidence-based parenting programs and curricula? Some indicators of evidentiary basis include positive program evaluation results published in scholarly journals and/or a positive rating by an organization such as the Substance Abuse and Mental Health Services Administration (SAMHSA) or the Office of Juvenile Justice and Delinquency Prevention (OJJDP). SAMHSA (2006) defines evidence-based practice as "a practice which, based on expert or consensus opinion about available evidence, is expected to produce a specific clinical outcome" (p. 1) and lists qualifying programs in the online National Registry of Evidence-based Programs and Practices (NREPP). Similarly, OJJDP rates programs that reduce juvenile involvement in the justice system as exemplary, effective, or promising (OJJDP, n.d.). There are several benefits of using evidence-based parent education programs and curricula. First, evidence-based programs have relatively high implementation fidelity (SAMHSA, 2006), which may reduce variability in parental interpretation of presented information, thereby increasing the likelihood of successfully altering negative parent behaviors and beliefs. Also, by using a curriculum with documented effectiveness, parent educators reduce the risk of inadvertently introducing harm to the family unit. Last, the use of evidence-based curricula enhances the likelihood of receiving federal funding (Wandersman & Florin, 2003).

EVALUATING PARENTING EDUCATION ● RESOURCES AND CURRICULA

A plethora of curricula and other resources exist to help parents improve interactions and overall relationships with their children. This wide variety of choices is likely dictated by the large number of variables that affect parenting education, such as age of children, ethnic and racial diversity of participants, differences in demographic characteristics of parents, and the variety of problems that children may present (Heath, 1998). Although there is no shortage of parent education resources and curricula available, it is often difficult for parenting professionals to know what to consider when selecting a curriculum or other materials. In this section, we draw heavily from Cooke's work (as presented in Stolz, Rector, & Cooke, 2009) to outline steps for evaluating parenting education resources, integrating what we have learned previously in this chapter about effective parenting and effective parenting education.

1. *Consider the parenting outcomes targeted.* What are the overall purpose and specific goals of the program or materials? Are the targeted

parenting outcomes related to the research-based dimensions of parenting (responsiveness/support, demandingness/behavioral control, avoidance of psychological control) and/or the NEPEM critical parenting practices (care for self, understand, guide, nurture, motivate, advocate)?

2. *Consider the theoretical foundation.* What is the theoretical orientation/conceptual basis for the program or materials? If it is difficult to identify the theoretical foundation of a parenting intervention, is there a coherent explanation of how change is expected to occur? Is the theoretical model a good fit with your basic beliefs about parenting?

3. *Consider the parent educator competencies.* There are two aspects of this step. First, what are the qualifications of the authors of the materials? Do they have professional preparation in areas related to parenting and parent education? Second, what do the materials assume about the preparation of the parent educator? Do you have the competencies needed to effectively use this particular resource?

4. *Consider the delivery format.* How will the material be communicated to the audience? Is there reason to think this is an effective delivery format given the change mechanisms specified by the theoretical model, the parenting outcomes targeted, and the needs of the audience?

5. *Consider your audience.* Does this resource match the needs of the parent(s) with whom you will work? Is it targeted to parents with particular characteristics? Do the reading level, analytic requirements, and teaching/learning styles match the abilities and preferences of your audience?

6. *Consider the evidentiary basis of the material.* What documentation exists of the effectiveness of the material? If none, are other evidence-based materials available that meet the goals and needs of the program and participants?

7. *Consider practical issues.* How comprehensive is it? Does it include materials that can be used over several sessions with the parent(s)? Is it easy to obtain? How much does it cost? Can it be used multiple times?

● CONCLUSION

Overall, both the need for parenting education and efforts to meet that need have increased, and there is considerable consensus regarding the parenting outcomes that warrant intervention and assistance. Parent educator competencies (attitudes, knowledge, and skills) have been defined at the general level. Parenting education programs differ in their theoretical foundations, delivery approaches, and populations targeted, creating both opportunities for programs that enhance and enrich parenting as well as opportunities for mismatches between programs and participants. A small percentage of parenting programs has identified the resources necessary for a quality evaluation, and many of those programs have been able to document positive changes in parenting behaviors and/or child and youth outcomes. So, where do we go from here?

First, we need to increase the preservice preparation, professional development, and professional identity of parenting educators. Parenting educators (i.e., people whose paid or voluntary work includes helping others improve as parents) are embedded in a wide range of settings (extension, schools, family service organizations, churches, hospitals, private practice, etc.) and have diverse educational backgrounds. As a result, they are often isolated, difficult to identify, and underresourced. This notwithstanding, they are the best venues for ensuring that parenting scholarship gets translated and applied in a way that results in measurable improvements for real people. Thus, one key future challenge for the field of parenting education involves using the identified core competencies to generate specific training and credentialing opportunities. Several states (e.g., Minnesota, North Carolina, Texas, and more recently New York) have worked to advance this goal, but most states offer no agreed-upon training system, credential, or license for parenting educators. Also, recent research suggests that there is strong support for a national parenting education credential (Stolz, Henke, Brandon, & Sams, in press).

Second, once parenting educators are better prepared to work with parents and better able to market themselves as parenting experts, it is important that we work to identify, reach, and engage audiences. One component of this goal involves altering the deficit perspective of parenting education and creating a culture in which parenting is valued and seeking assistance with parenting is de-stigmatized and normative. Then, parent and child characteristics need to be fully considered in identifying a general model, a specific program, and a delivery approach that is likely to engage parents in a meaningful reflection on their role as parents and encourage them to take positive steps. Although creative delivery approaches may be important in this fast-paced digital age, we need to maintain the goal of sustained contact with parents.

Third, professional parenting educators need a quality message to share with parents. Now more than ever there is a belief that everything one needs to know is just a click away on the Internet. While this democratization of knowledge has many benefits, professional parenting educators need to ensure that the information they share is theoretically sound, research based, and, when possible, evidence based. There is an immense need for more and better studies. Some very popular programs have poor evaluations, some evidence-based programs may be good but not great, and some wonderful programs may not be evidence based due to a lack of resources. Improved and expanded parenting education evaluations, and centralized access to the results thereof, will expand the choices available to professional parenting educators as they seek to engage their audiences.

● EXPLORATIONS

1. Download the Core Knowledge Survey, Attitude Survey, and Skills Survey from the Core Knowledge for Parent Educators and Professionals Who Work With Families website sponsored by the Center for Parenting at the University of North Texas (http://www.coe.unt.edu/cpe/core-attitudes). Rate your own attitudes, knowledge, and skills as a parenting educator. What are your strengths? In what areas would additional training or development be helpful?

2. Interview a parent. Ask about his or her parenting philosophy and goals. Have the parent describe several behaviors that he or she engages in for each critical parenting practice suggested by the NEPEM (care for self, understand, guide, nurture, motivate, advocate). Thinking like a parenting educator, what do you think this parent's strengths are? What would you encourage him or her to consider or try? What theoretical model of parenting education would be a good fit for this parent if he or she was looking for a parenting program?

3. Join the National Parenting Education Network listserv (http://www .npen.org; it's free!) to network with parenting educators from across the United States and Canada and better understand the questions and challenges facing professional parent educators.

CHAPTER 11

SEXUALITY EDUCATION

Susan Calahan

Historically, sexuality education has been a lightning rod for controversy fueled by passion-filled debate surrounding many questions, the most basic of which is, should it even be taught at all, followed by what should be taught, at what age should it be taught, where should it be taught, who should teach it, and does it work? Many concerns factor into this often contentious public discourse, including diverse religious and political view points, health-related perspectives, theoretical foundations, research findings, funding, and personal opinions, to name a few. The challenges associated with teaching sexuality education can seem daunting, yet its importance is validated by Drolet and Clark (1994) with the following:

> Sexuality educators may be the unsung heroes of our day. There is perhaps no other subject so fraught with peril for those intent on providing young people with information and skills in an area of such import to the health and well-being of a nation. Every day, educators are meeting the challenges as best they can, because they believe that teaching young people about sexuality is an enormously important part of preparing them to lead productive and healthy lives. (p. xiv)

While challenges do exist, it also is important to keep in mind that encouraging progress in sexuality education has been made. For example, there is now more research-based, empirical evidence than ever before providing information and verification regarding some sexuality education programs and best practices related to content, design, implementation, instruction, and evaluation.

This chapter will address the following aspects of sexuality education: a brief historical overview, why it is important, contemporary theoretical perspectives used in programming, sexuality education programs, and best practices.

● SEXUALITY EDUCATION HISTORICAL OVERVIEW

Whether through formal education, word of mouth among friends, observation, or unspoken insinuation, learning about sexuality has always been a part of adolescent development. Traditionally, this education most often occurred among peers or in the home. Over time, societal transformations due to industrialization, urbanization, and changes to the traditional family placed increased responsibilities for teaching sexuality education on government and other public organizations such as schools and health agencies. With the assumption of this role has come the ever present conflicts regarding sexuality education and what it is or is not, as well as what it should or should not be.

Community groups such as the YMCA and YWCA provided information on some issues related to sexuality as early as the late 1800s (Bruess & Greenberg, 2009). In the early 1900s, sexuality education was acknowledged as a specific discipline (Yarber, 1994), and common topics for instruction included sexual and social hygiene, preparation for marriage, and parenthood. During this time, most sexuality education took place in school settings.

In 1919 and 1930, advancement continued as the U.S. government supported sexuality education as part of the White House Conference on Child Welfare, and in the 1940s, major national organizations began to call for increased efforts in the area of sexuality education. Sexuality education curricula began to increase as the American School Health Association implemented a nationwide program in family life education in the 1950s, and in 1967, the school-based *Growth Patterns and Sex Education* was published (Yarber, 1994). Another achievement for sexuality education in schools came in 1955 with the publication of a series of five pamphlets on sexuality for young people called the *Sex Education* series. These materials were created and published through the collaborative efforts of the American

Medical Association and the National Education Association and were used extensively throughout the nation (Yarber, 1994).

On the shirt-tails of the youth revolution, the 1960s brought a decade of advances for sexuality education. Sexuality education curricula became less focused on preventing sexual immorality and started emphasizing factual information and nonjudgmental discussion.

This also was the time when efforts aimed at stopping sexuality education were begun by those opposing it, which caused several state legislatures to eliminate or restrict sexuality education, and led to contentious confrontations over the implementation of sexuality education in many communities.

With the 1970s came the promotion of sexual health to enhance individual growth and development, which was a new and different perspective for sexuality education. It incorporated a nonjudgmental approach, focused on student discussions and values clarification, and addressed a more extensive variety of topics, including contraception (Yarber, 1994). Growing concerns over teen pregnancy in the 1970s, coupled with the HIV epidemic of the 1980s, created an urgency for increased efforts in sexuality education, which led to an increase in the number of states with policies requiring or encouraging the teaching of sexuality education. Currently, 21 states and the District of Columbia mandate that public schools teach sexuality education (Guttmacher Institute, 2010).

However, opponents of sexuality education, especially in schools, remained a subject of controversy, and they continued to influence the curriculum in the 1990s and 2000s. One such controversy centered on the fact that any sexuality education program in the United States requesting federal funding must adhere to abstinence-only messages (Kohler, Manhart, & Lafferty, 2008). Sexuality education continued to progress as curricula expanded to include the development of skills such as effective communication, decision making, goal setting, and accessing reliable information rather than content only. In addition, there is now more research regarding sexuality education programs and their effectiveness in preventing STD/HIV infections and teen pregnancy.

The terms *sexuality* and *sexuality education* are not one and the same. Both are multifaceted concepts that could be defined in a variety of ways. Bruess and Greenberg (2009) define sexuality as "a natural and healthy part of who we are. It is not about taking part in sexual behaviors. It is an integral part of everyone's personality and includes cultural, psychological, ethical, and biological dimensions" (p. 4). The Sexuality Information and Education Council of the United States (SIECUS) defines sexuality education as follows: "Sexuality education is a lifelong process of acquiring information and forming attitudes, beliefs, and values about such important topics as identity, relationships, and intimacy. . . . Sexuality education addresses the socio-cultural, biological, psychological, and spiritual dimensions of sexuality by providing information; exploring feelings, values, and attitudes; and developing communication, decision-making, and critical-thinking skills" (National Guidelines Task Force, 2004). As you can see from the definition above, sexuality education is much more than just sex ed. The scope of sexuality education is quite broad. It could be said that our sexuality is more about who we are than what we do.

● WHY IS SEXUALITY EDUCATION IMPORTANT?

Sexuality is an essential part of each person's identity. Learning about our sexuality and achieving sexual health and well-being are lifelong processes that begin at birth and continue throughout our lives. Although parents are the primary sexuality educators of their children, children also receive messages about sexuality from many other sources. Some of them may have more negative than positive impact. Schools and other community-based organizations can be important partners with parents to provide young people with accurate and developmentally appropriate sexuality education.

As children enter adolescence, they are increasingly likely to engage in sexual risk behaviors, making them more vulnerable to sexually transmitted diseases (STDs), including HIV, and unintended pregnancy (Gloppen, David-Ferdon, & Bates, 2010; House, Bates, Markham, & Lesesne, 2010). Youth are becoming sexually experienced earlier. The 2005 Middle School Youth Risk Behavior Survey (MSYRBS) reports that 10% of sixth graders (age 11) have had sex (Shanklin, Brener, McManus, Kinchen, & Kann, 2007). While the percentage of high school students in the United States reporting they had sex decreased 16% between 1991 (54.1%) and 2007 (47.8%), the percentage of sexually active students in 2007 is still high (Centers for Disease Control and Prevention [CDC], 2008).

Approximately 745,000 American females younger than age 20 become pregnant every year, and birth rates among adolescents ages 15 to 19 years increased 3% from 2005 to 2006, the first increase since 1991 (Gavin, Catalano, David-Ferdon, Gloppen, & Markham, 2010a, 2010b). The United States has the highest rates of teen pregnancy and birth among similar countries. In 2006, the teen birth rate in the United States was 41.9 births per 1,000 teens ages 15 to 19. By comparison, the teen birth rate in the United States is one and a half times higher than the teen birth rate in the United

Kingdom (26.7 per 1,000), which has the highest teen birth rate in Europe, and is more than three times as high as the teen birth rate in Canada (13.3 per 1,000) (The National Campaign to Prevent Teen Pregnancy, 2006b).

About one in four (26%) young women in the United States between the ages of 14 and 19 (3.2 million teenage girls) is infected with at least one of the most common STDs. More than 20,000 male and female youth and young adults ages 10 to 24 years are living with HIV/AIDS (Gavin et al., 2010a, 2010b). The 2002 National Survey of Family Growth reports that 54.3% of females ages 15 to 19 had engaged in oral sex with a male, and 55.2% of males ages 15 to 19 had engaged in oral sex with a female (CDC, 2002). One in five adolescents is unaware that oral sex can transmit STDs, and two in five considers oral sex to be safer sex. In addition, about 25% of sexually active adolescents also report engaging in oral sex as a strategy to avoid sexual intercourse, and more than two in five do not consider it to be as "big of a deal" as sexual intercourse. On the other hand, adolescents also report that STDs, HIV/AIDS, and unintended pregnancy are big concerns for them, and nearly one third reported having experienced pressure to have sex. While young adolescents (13- to 14-year-olds) are less sexually active, 80% say they are concerned about sexual health issues, and 75% say they have concerns about sexual violence or other physical violence in relationships (Hoff, Greene, & Davis, 2003).

Furthermore, television, music, movies, magazines, the Internet, and smart cell phones include frequent discussions and portrayals of sexual behavior that affect adolescents' conceptions of sexual attractiveness, romantic relationships, and sexual behavior. Fourteen percent of American teenagers ages 12 to 17 who own cell phones say they have sent sexually suggestive nude or nearly nude images of themselves to someone else via text messaging, and 15% of this same group reported having received sexually suggestive nude or nearly nude images of someone they know via text messaging (Lenhart, 2009b). Among youth in the United States 12 to 17 years of age, 30% of females and 50% to 70% of males have viewed sexually explicit images online. Results from longitudinal studies show that this kind of exposure predicts less progressive gender role attitudes, perpetration of sexual harassment in males, sexual uncertainty, uncommitted sexual exploration (e.g., one-night stands, hooking up, and friends with benefits), and earlier oral sex and sexual intercourse for both males and females (Brown, Keller, & Stern, 2009).

In addition, Chandra et al. (2007) reported that teens who watched high levels of television with sexual content were twice as likely to experience a pregnancy 3 years later when compared to those with lower levels of exposure. And finally, listening to music with degrading sexual lyrics is related to initiation of intercourse and progression to more advanced levels of noncoital sexual activity in youth ages 12 to 17. The same does not seem to be true for music with other sexual lyrics (Martino et al., 2006).

Young people also frequently use media for sexual health information. Studies show about 25% or more of online teens access the Internet to find information about sex, STDs, and pregnancy. A concern with this is the possibility that the information they access and/or receive is inaccurate or misleading (Brown et al., 2009). Along these same lines, adolescents report their top three sources of information about sex are school, friends, and parents (Hoff et al., 2003).

The need for sexuality education is apparent. Young people need accurate information regarding sexuality coupled with opportunities to learn and practice life skills that can help them make healthy and responsible decisions throughout their life.

● CONTEMPORARY THEORETICAL PERSPECTIVES USED IN PROGRAMMING

Building programs on sound theoretical models is an important trait of effective sexuality education prevention programs. Kirby (2007) and others report that a primary characteristic of effective sexuality education programs is that they are based on theoretical approaches that have been demonstrated to positively influence high-risk health behaviors (Kirby & Miller, 2003; The National Campaign to Prevent Teen Pregnancy, 2006a).

The most common theoretical models used in these effective programs fall into four broad categories: developmental models, perceived control theories, attitude/intention theories, and social learning theory (Saunders, 2005). Some of these theories include social and psychological constructs such as social cognitive theory (Bandura, 1986), the social development model (Catalano, Kosterman, & Hawkins, 1996), the theory of triadic influence (Flay & Petraitis, 1994), the theory of reasoned action, the theory of planned behavior, the theory of interpersonal behavior, the health belief model, the value expectancy model, the information motivation behavior model, social learning theory, diffusion of innovation, protection motivation theory, social action theory, cognitive behavioral theory, social inoculation theory, locus of control theory, and self-efficacy theory (CDC, 2009a; Saunders, 2005; Tortolero et al., 2010; Yarber, 1994).

Here are two examples of how theories could be put into practice in a pregnancy prevention program. Locus of control theory suggests that for a given situation, individuals with an internal locus of control are more likely to perceive that they have control in that situation. In contrast, individuals with an external locus of control are more likely to believe that they have little, if any, control in a given situation because forces outside themselves have more control. If a teenager believes she has control over her fertility (internal locus of control), she is more likely to consistently use contraception to prevent becoming pregnant. On the other hand, if a teen believes pregnancy is likely, or not likely, to occur regardless of what she does (external locus of control), she is less likely to take the time to use any form of contraception. Sexuality education programs that focus on knowledge and communication skills have been found to increase participants' internal locus of control. Teens who learn accurate and practical information in conjunction with developing skills to negotiate the use of contraceptives or remain abstinent become empowered to maintain control of their sexuality and sexual activity. While pregnancy prevention programs strive to increase participants' knowledge, learning the verbal skills needed to negotiate with a partner is just as important to strengthening an internal locus of control in this model.

The theory of planned behavior suggests that the best predictor of behavior is the individual's intention to complete that behavior, and the intention is determined by attitudes, social norms, and perceptions of control over the behavior. Programs using this model for program development would choose activities that address the theory components. For example, activities would be selected that strengthen positive attitudes toward abstinence, contraceptive use, and responsibility in relationships. Social norms and how they relate to adolescent sexual behaviors would be taught. Besides discussing what their peers believe about sexual health and teen pregnancy, participants could invite their parent(s) to a group discussion on these issues. For homework, participants could create a list of questions to ask their parents about their values and expectations for teen behavior. Parent responses could be discussed at the next program session. To address perceived control, program activities would help youth identify perceived barriers to remaining abstinent or following safer sex practices and problem solve ways to overcome the barriers (Saunders, 2005).

These theoretical models used individually, or in combination, provide a strong foundation for adolescent sexuality education programs. Programs that incorporate these theories are behaviorally based and usually combine content knowledge with the development of social and interpersonal prevention skills to promote changes in behavior. Programs identified in this chapter as effective and/or promising were developed using one or more of these theories.

● SEXUALITY EDUCATION PROGRAMS

"Having accurate, research-based information on what works to prevent high risk sexual behaviors is critically important information for communities and practitioners trying to make informed decisions about preventing teen pregnancy and STD/HIV infection" (Kirby, 2007, p. 6). The quality and quantity of evaluation research regarding sexuality education programs have increased significantly. Since 2001, there has been a 50% increase in the number of studies measuring program impact for sexuality education. In addition, procedural rigor has improved considerably, and published studies on behaviors affecting teen pregnancy and sexually transmitted disease, including factors affecting these behaviors, also have increased (Kirby, 2007).

Following rigorous evaluative review of literally hundreds of school-based, community-based, and other types of sexuality education programs, Kirby (2007) identified common characteristics found in effective sexuality education. In addition to a strong theoretical base, he suggests that effective programs identify and target specific important sexual antecedents, address the age of the participants and their sexual experience, are culturally appropriate, address social pressures that influence sexual behavior, provide basic accurate information, and increase communication, negotiation, and refusal skills.

Effective sexuality education programs change teens' sexual behavior by addressing the risk and protective factors that influence such behaviors. When talking about the effectiveness of sexuality education programs, it is important to remember that there are many things to consider when looking at what causes teens to participate in high-risk sexual behaviors. Thus, results of effective programs may be modest, but it is unrealistic to expect even an effective program to completely eliminate teen pregnancy or STD infections.

Sexuality education prevention programs typically are described by a number of characteristics that describe their structure, setting, target population, duration, or content (Saunders, 2005). Sexuality education programs can occur in schools as part of the educational curricula; in community agencies such as the American Red Cross, Planned Parenthood, and Boys and Girls Clubs; in health clinics; and in the home. They also can be a part of service learning or youth development programs. Some prevention programs address specific concerns such as preventing pregnancy or becoming infected with an STD or HIV, while others target specific sexual behaviors such as delaying the initiation of sexual activity or increasing the use of condoms or contraceptives. Some programs produce effective results in more than one of these areas.

The approach used in sexuality education programs can be comprehensive or abstinence only. Comprehensive programs encourage abstinence and also provide information about contraception. Abstinence-only sexuality education programs are defined by statute as educational programs with the exclusive purpose of teaching the social, psychological, and health gains that come from abstaining from sexual activity (U.S. Government Accountability Office, 2008). If contraception is addressed in an abstinence-only program, it is done so in terms of failure rates. Except for two programs, there is no strong evidence that abstinence-only education programs are effective in delaying sex (Kirby, 2007). Recently, however, findings from two rigorously evaluated abstinence-only programs have shown positive impacts on delaying sexual activity and/or reducing recent sexual activity (The National Campaign to Prevent Teen and Unplanned Pregnancy, 2010). Most programs with the strongest evidence of success are those that strongly encourage abstinence as the safest choice for teens and also encourage those who are sexually active to use contraception (The National Campaign to Prevent Teen and Unplanned Pregnancy, 2010).

The most comprehensive and rigorous evaluations to determine programs with the strongest evidence of positive impact on sexual behavior, pregnancy, or STD rates have been conducted by Kirby (2007). Table 11.1 provides a listing of the most effective sexuality education programs and identifies the sexual behaviors affected by each program. Some of these programs are described next.

TABLE 11.1   Programs With Strong Evidence of Positive Impact on Sexual Behavior or Pregnancy or STD Rates

Curriculum-Based Programs

A Theory-Based Abstinence-Only Program[10]

AIDS Prevention for Adolescents in School[2,6]

All4You![11]

Becoming a Responsible Teen (BART)[1,4,5,7,8,10,11]

¡Cuidate! (Take Care of Yourself) The Latino Youth Health Promotion Program[1,5,6,7,8,11]

Draw the Line, Respect the Line (implemented with both genders; found effective for boys only)[1,10]

Focus on Kids[11]

(Continued)

TABLE 11.1 (Continued)

Get Real About AIDS[6,8,11]

It's Your Game . . . Keep It Real[10]

Making Proud Choices: A Safer Sex Approach to HIV/STDs and Teen Pregnancy Prevention[1,4,5,7,8,11]

Multidimensional Treatment Foster Care[12]

Positive Prevention[10]

Postponing Sexual Involvement[4,5,9]

Reach for Health Community Youth Service[4,5,8,9]

Reasons of the Heart[4,10]

Reducing the Risk: Building Skills to Prevent Pregnancy, STDs, & HIV[1,4,7,9,10,11]

Safer Choices: Preventing HIV, Other STDs, and Pregnancy[1,4,7,8,9,10,11]

School/Community Program for Sexual Risk Reduction Among Teens[2,4,8]

Seattle Social Development Project[2,4,6,8,10,11,12]

Self Center (School-Linked Reproductive Health Care)[2,4,7,9]

SiHLE: Sistas, Informing, Healing, Living, Empowering (implemented and effective for girls only)[1,2,3,6,7,8,11]

Community Programs

Abecedarian Project[2]

Adolescents Living Safely: AIDS Awareness, Attitudes & Actions[5,6,8]

Be Proud! Be Responsible![5,6,8,11]

California's Adolescent Sibling Pregnancy Prevention Project[2,4,9]

Community-Level HIV Prevention for Adolescents in Low-Income Developments (Teen Health Project)[1,4,8,10,11]

HIV Risk Reduction Among Detained Adolescents[11]

Making a Difference! An Abstinence-Based Approach to HIV/STD and Teen Pregnancy Prevention[10,11]

Poder Latino: Community AIDS Prevention Program for Inner-City Latino Youth[4,6,10]

Parent-Adolescent Programs

Focus on Youth (FOY) Plus ImPact[11]

Keepin' It R.E.A.L.![1,11]

Responsible, Empowered, Aware, Living Men (REAL Men)[10,11]

Clinic Protocols and One-on-One Programs

Advanced provision of emergency contraception (implemented and effective for girls only)[1]

HIV Risk Reduction for African American & Latina Adolescent Women[3,6,7]

HORIZONS HIV Intervention[11]

Project SAFE (Sexual Awareness for Everyone)[3,6,7]

Reproductive Health Counseling for Young Men[1]

Tailoring Family Planning Services to the Special Needs of Adolescents[2,9]

Service Learning

Learn and Serve America[4,12]

Reach for Health Community Youth Service[1,4,5,8,9,10,12]

Teen Outreach Program (TOP)[1,2,12]

Community Programs With Multicomponents

HIV Prevention for Adolescents in Low-Income Housing Developments[1]

Multicomponent Programs With Intensive Sexuality and Youth Development Components

Aban Aya (implemented with both genders; found effective for boys only)[1,11]

Children's Aid Society Carrera Program (implemented with both genders; found effective for girls only)[1,2,4,8,9,10,11]

---

[1]One hundred fifteen program evaluations overall (examined only primary preventions); 15 programs with strongest evidence of success. Criteria for strongest evidence of success: completed or published between 1990 and 2007, conducted in the United States, targeted middle/high school age teens, experimental or quasi-experimental design with appropriate statistical analyses, combined treatment and control group sample size of at least 100, and measured impact on teen sexual behavior (Kirby, 2007).

[2]Decreased number or rate of teen pregnancy, [3]reduced incidence of STDs, [4]delayed initiation of sex, [5]reduced frequency of sex, [6]reduced number of sex partners, [7]reduced incidence of unprotected sex, [8]increased condom use, and [9]increased contraception use. Inclusion criteria: published in peer-reviewed journals, experimental or quasi-experimental evaluation design, at least 100 subjects in treatment and control/comparison groups, data collection for both groups continued after intervention for at least 3 months, and program demonstrated at least two positive behavior changes (postponement or delay of sexual initiation, reduced frequency of sexual intercourse, reduced number of sexual partners/increase in monogamy, increased use or consistency of use of effective methods of contraception and/or condoms, reduced incidence of unprotected sex) among subjects relative to controls or effective in reducing rates of pregnancy, STIs, or HIV in intervention youth, relative to controls (Advocates for Youth, 2008).

[10]Delayed initiation of sex, [11]increased contraception use, and [12]reduced teen pregnancy. Inclusion criteria: completed and published in 1980 or later, conducted in United States or Canada, targeted middle and/or high school aged teens (approximately ages 12–18), included baseline and at least 3 months of follow-up data, measured impact on behavior, included at least 75 people in both the treatment and control groups, used sound statistical analyses, and used an experimental or quasi-experimental design (Suellentrop, 2010).

ADOLESCENT PREGNANCY PREVENTION ●

Service learning programs showed the strongest evidence for reducing teen pregnancy (Kirby & Miller, 2003).

Reach for Health Community Youth Service

The Reach for Health Community Youth Service program builds upon community-based service learning. It includes a health promotion curriculum (Reach for Health) that is based on teenage health teaching modules. The curriculum includes information regarding human sexuality and is delivered to seventh and eighth graders. The health curriculum consists of 40 core lessons that focus on three primary health risks faced by youth: (1) drug and alcohol use, (2) violence, and (3) sexual behaviors that may result in pregnancy or infection with HIV and other STDs. The program is based on the health belief model and theories of social learning (Kirby, 2007).

Teen Outreach Program (TOP)

The Teen Outreach Program (TOP) is a school-based program for 7th to 12th graders linking supervised community volunteer service (minimum 20 hours/year), with a minimum of 1 hour of classroom curriculum activities focusing on developmental tasks and life skills. Approximately 15% of the activities focus on direct sexual health content. TOP students were significantly less likely to become pregnant than control group students. This program is more effective with female than male students and was found to be effective for teens with no previous pregnancies, as well as for teens with a previous pregnancy or birth (Gavin et al., 2010b). Facilitators are trained prior to implementation of the program.

● STDS AND HIV/AIDS PREVENTION

Sistas Informing, Healing, Living, Empowering (SiHLE)

Sistas Informing, Healing, Living, Empowering (SiHLE) is a community-based, small-group, skills-training intervention to reduce risky sex behavior among African American adolescent females. Through interactive discussions in groups of 10 to 12 girls, the intervention emphasizes ethnic and gender pride and enhances awareness of HIV risk reduction strategies, such as abstaining from sex, using condoms consistently, and having fewer sex partners. Through the use of role-plays and cognitive rehearsal, the intervention enhances confidence in initiating safer-sex conversations, negotiating for safer sex, and refusing unsafe sex encounters. Facilitators are trained prior to implementation of the program (Effective Interventions, 2009).

All4You!

The goal of this program is to reduce the risk of HIV, other sexually transmitted diseases, and unintended pregnancy among high school–aged youth who are attending court and community alternative schools. The intervention includes two components: behavioral skills development and community involvement/service learning (NLM Gateway, 2004).

Responsible, Empowered, Aware, Living Men (REAL Men)

Responsible, Empowered, Aware, Living Men (REAL Men) is a group-level, skill-building intervention for fathers (or father figures) of adolescent boys ages 11 to 14. It encourages communication between fathers and sons regarding sexuality and promotes delay of sexual intercourse in youth as well as condom use among sexually active youth. The seven 2-hour intervention sessions emphasize the importance of the father's role in helping teens make responsible choices about sex. The first six group sessions are for fathers only and provide information on how to communicate with adolescents (e.g., increasing awareness of listening skills and teachable moments), general sexual topics important to teens, and information about transmission and prevention of HIV/AIDS (CDC, 2009b).

YOUTH DEVELOPMENT PROGRAMS •

Positive youth development programs help young people strengthen relationships and skills, place them in positive networks of supportive adults, and help them develop hope for their future by providing academic, economic, and volunteer opportunities. Gavin et al. (2010b) state, "It is possible that sexuality education programs provide youth the skills and knowledge needed to refuse sex or to practice safer sexual behaviors, whereas positive youth development programs may provide them with the motivation and confidence needed to use those skills. Exposing youth to both types of programs is likely to be more effective than a strategy relying only on one type" (p. S88). While more research must still be done, early reports are indicating that positive youth development programs may be an effective strategy for promoting adolescent sexual and reproductive health (Gavin et al., 2010b). Several studies have shown that constructs of positive youth development programs, including competence (House, Bates, et al., 2010), connectedness (C. M. Markham et al., 2010), confidence (Gloppen et al.,

2010), and character (House, Mueller, Reininger, Brown, & Markham, 2010), can be protective factors for some adolescent sexual and reproductive health outcomes, including intention to have sex, early sex or ever having sex, contraception and condom use, frequency of sex, and pregnancy.

Children's Aid Society Carrera Program

This after-school program is for 13- to 15-year-olds (3 hours/day, 6 days/week for 350 days/year). The program includes activity, service, and parent involvement. Fifteen percent of the sessions focus on direct sexual health content. Female Carrera youth were significantly less likely than control group youth to have sex under pressure, to have ever had sex, and to have a pregnancy or birth and were significantly more likely to use hormonal contraception at last sex than the control group (Gavin et al., 2010b).

Seattle Social Development Project (Full Intervention)

This school and family program, delivered from first to sixth grades, includes interactive learning, interpersonal skill development, and volunteer parent training. By age 18, youth were significantly less likely than nonparticipants to engage in sexual intercourse and to have multiple sex partners. By age 21, they were significantly more likely to report a later age at first sex, fewer lifetime sex partners, and condom use at last sex. Females were significantly less likely to report a lifetime pregnancy (Gavin et al., 2010b). Teachers receive training that emphasizes proactive classroom management, interactive teaching, and cooperative learning.

● CHILD SEXUAL ABUSE PREVENTION

Approximately 300,000 children are sexually abused every year, and in 90% of such cases, the children know and trust the person who abused them. More than 88% of sexual abuse is never reported (Stop It Now!, 2008). Lyles, Cohen, and Brown (2009) report that one in four girls and one in seven boys will be the victim of some type of sexual abuse before the age of 18.

Nightmares; problems sleeping; sudden or unexplained personality changes; fear of certain places or being alone with an adult; resistance to routine bathing; play acting, writing about, drawing, or having dreams of sexual or frightening images; stomachaches or unexplained illness; using new or adult words for body parts; intentionally harming herself or himself; engaging in adult-like sexual activities with toys, objects, or other children; becoming increasingly secretive around use of Internet or cell phone; developing physical symptoms such as unexplained soreness, pain, or bruises around genitals or mouth; and repeated infections in the genital area are some of the behavioral signs and symptoms related to possible sexual abuse (Stop It Now!, 2008).

There is a movement in child sexual abuse programs that emphasizes primary prevention rather than after-the-fact efforts (Lyles et al., 2009). At this time, however, there are no evidence-based programs that are effective in preventing child sexual abuse (Finkelhor, 2007, 2009). Even though programs may not be effective in preventing child sexual abuse, other program objectives—such as promoting disclosure by victims; preventing negative outcomes after the victimization such as feelings of guilt, self-blame, and shame; and creating a more sensitive environment among adults, other children, and organizations when responding to and helping child victims—could justify implementation of the program (Finkelhor, 2007). The following are some promising child sexual abuse programs.

Who Do You Tell?

This child sexual abuse education program is designed to teach elementary school-aged children basic concepts to help them protect themselves from sexual abuse. The program aims to help children learn how to distinguish between inappropriate and appropriate types of touching. In addition, children are instructed on methods that can be used to communicate instances of abuse to trusted adults. The program is conducted in two 45-minute sessions on consecutive days. In addition, parents are invited to attend an informational session that addresses program content and offers advice on how to speak with children about the covered topics (Promising Practices Network, 2010).

Project Teaching Reaching Using Students and Theater (TRUST)

This program incorporates a series of plays to raise the issues of sexual abuse and violence prevention with students from elementary school through high school. The play *Touch* is specifically designed to introduce the concepts of sexual abuse and its prevention to elementary school-age children. Trained high school students present the play. The play introduces the concepts of the touch continuum (nurturing, confusing, exploitive), the way to say no in uncomfortable situations, and the idea that perpetrators can be strangers or people the children know. An optional pre-play discussion led by the teachers covers terms used in the play, such as the names of various body parts, types of sexual abuse, and adults to whom students can turn to for help. There is also a 15-minute question-and-answer session after the play, which is conducted by the facilitator and actors (Promising Practices Network, 2010).

Safe Child Program

This skill-based program was developed in 1981 and updated in 1994. It teaches children ages 3 to 10 a set of skills to help them prevent sexual, emotional, and physical abuse. The main idea guiding the program is that there are times when children can and must be responsible for their own well-being. At the same time, however, the program emphasizes that a child's security can be enhanced without creating misunderstanding, fear, or anxiety or reducing a child's sense of trust. Children learn how to speak up for themselves, assess and handle various situations, and know where to get help. Children are actively engaged in discussions, games, and role-playing in 10 separate sessions, giving them time to practice these skills. The program has two main focuses. The first is prevention of sexual, emotional, or physical abuse by people known to the child. This is taught in the context of life skills, including communication, choices, asking for help, and decision making. These skills are developed through role-play. The other focus of the program is safety around strangers (Promising Practices Network, 2010). The professional training component of the program consists of an introduction to the program, an overview of the problems of child abuse, techniques for teaching the classroom program, instruction on how to recognize and report abuse, and information for implementation of the program.

ASAP (A Safety Awareness Program)

As children with disabilities are especially at risk for sexual abuse, the goal of this program is to encourage community-based programs and schools to join forces in providing comprehensive prevention and intervention services that reduce the risk of sexual, physical, and/or emotional abuse or exploitation faced by children and youth with disabilities. The program is sensitive to all disabilities. Classroom presentation topics and strategies for educators include "Teaching About Feelings, Touches and Words," "Teaching No-Go-TELL," "Teaching About Body Parts," "Teaching About Sexual Harassment/Bullying," "Role-Play Examples," and "Teaching Healthy Sexuality Education" (SafePlace, 2002).

PARENT-BASED SEXUALITY EDUCATION •

One parenting behavior associated with reduced sexual risk taking among adolescents is parent-adolescent communication about sex (Guilamo-Ramos & Bouris, 2009). When it comes to talking about issues pertaining to sexuality, most parents say it is awkward for them to have such discussions with their children. Some parents are concerned that they do not know enough about sexuality to provide the right information at the right time and oftentimes feel they do not know how to talk about sex with their children. Some parents indicate they are afraid if they talk to their children about sexuality, they actually might encourage them to become sexually active. Talking to their children about sexuality does not encourage early sexual activity; in fact, research shows it could have the direct opposite effect (YouthNet Partners in Reproductive Health and HIV Prevention, 2000). As uncomfortable as it may be, it is important that parents move beyond whatever apprehensions they might have in order to help their children foster healthy attitudes about their sexual development.

Parents should be the primary sexuality educators for their children. Research studies indicate adolescents want to hear from their parents on issues related to sexuality, and parents can have a significant influence on their teenager's sexual attitudes and behaviors (Guilamo-Ramos & Bouris, 2009). In a 2009 survey, 31% of teenagers said their parents most influenced their decisions about sex (Albert, 2009). On the other hand, there also is research showing that parents need help in knowing how to approach sexuality-related issues with their adolescent children (Guilamo-Ramos & Bouris, 2009). A case in point can be found in results from a telephone survey regarding young teens' sexual attitudes and behavior. One thousand teenagers, ages 13 to 16, and their parents participated in the study. Results showed that 85% of the parents surveyed said they speak to their children often about sex and relationships. However, just 41% of their teenage children said they had those same conversations with their parents (MSNBC News, 2004).

The timing of parent-adolescent communications about sex, the content of parental discussions, the frequency of communication, and how parental messages about sex are delivered can help promote effective parent adolescent communication. The timing for when parents should begin talking with their child about sexuality-related topics should be before sexual activity begins. It is also best to avoid putting off conversations waiting for a perfect time, instead taking advantage of teachable moments when spending time with their children. Regarding content, parents are most comfortable talking to their adolescent about abstinence, puberty, and the negative health consequences of teen sex such as avoiding pregnancy, STDs, and HIV. They are less comfortable talking about contraception and condoms. In addition, they are more likely to talk to their daughters than their sons about sexuality-related topics. A single "big talk" about sex is not sufficient. Parents should have frequent multiple conversations with their children and adapt their message to their adolescent's changing needs. Studies show that adolescents whose parents repeat specific sexuality messages report more perceived openness in parental communication about sex, feeling closer to their parents, and a greater ability to talk with their parent about sexuality-related and general topics. The context of communication includes how parents talk and the extent to which they seem knowledgeable, open, and accessible during sexuality-related discussions. In addition, parental expertise, trustworthiness, openness, accessibility, and responsiveness when talking about issues related to sexuality are all associated with adolescents' reduced sexual risk taking (Guilamo-Ramos & Bouris, 2009).

Parental monitoring also has been found to have a strong protective effect on an adolescent's sexual attitudes and behaviors. Parental monitoring includes knowing about their child's whereabouts, friends, and activities and also consists of parenting behaviors that communicate and elicit information about their child's actions. In some cases, adolescents will willingly disclose this information, but in other cases, parents may have to directly ask their child for this information (Guilamo-Ramos & Bouris, 2009).

Another means by which parents can influence their children's sexual attitudes and behavior is by conveying values and attitudes that may discourage sexual activity or promote condom or contraception use among sexually active adolescents. Youth will often adopt the values and attitudes of their parents as their own. Thus, adolescents whose parents model values consistent with healthy sexuality often apply those same values when making their own decisions about sexuality. One of the most protective parental values has been the expression of parental disapproval of sex. When adolescents perceive that their parents disapprove of them engaging in sexual activity, they report a later onset of sex, fewer sexual partners, and decreased sexual activity. In addition, the overall quality of the parent-adolescent relationship is a protective factor against adolescent sexual risk taking. Furthermore, when adolescents feel warm, close, and connected to their parents, they are less likely to engage in unsafe behaviors, including reckless sexual behaviors. This outcome is magnified when parental warmth and love are accompanied by appropriate levels of parental monitoring and guidance (B. C. Miller, 2002; B. C. Miller, Benson, & Galbraith, 2001).

Family-based sexuality education can create opportunities to share family values, provide accurate information to children, build effective decision-making skills, and offset negative and exploitive sexual messages in the media (Gossart, 2007). Currently, there are no empirically supported parent- or family-based sexuality education programs, but some promising programs are available.

Saving Sex for Later

The Saving Sex for Later program is designed for parents in communities where children are at risk of early sexual initiation. It is a theoretical-based and research-based program consisting of three 25-minute audio-CDs containing dramatic role model stories titled *Changing Bodies, Changing Relationships, and Changing Influences and Pressures*. The program is designed to help parents talk to their sons and daughters about sexuality and the importance of delaying sexual initiation. While a full evaluation of this program has not been completed, preliminary results are promising with regards to delaying initiation of sex (O'Donnell et al., 2007).

There's No Place Like Home . . . For Sex Education

This curriculum assists parents in their endeavor to talk openly with their children about sexuality. It addresses when to start, what to say, and how to best express the family values parents want to share with their children. The chapters are age specific and contain relevant and age-appropriate sexuality information, useful strategies, communication hints, and suggested resources to support parents in their efforts. It is available in English, Spanish, and a Native American adaptation (Gossart, 2007).

BEST PRACTICES IN SEXUALITY EDUCATION ●

Effective sexuality education programs address the particular needs of the participants, and thus it is important to determine the needs of the program participants and available resources. One way to accomplish this needs assessment is by asking questions and finding answers. For example, you might ask the following: Are STDs more or less common than pregnancy? What are the most prevalent STDs? What is the incidence of sexual activity? What age did they become sexually active? Do they use condoms or contraception? Are there existing pregnancy and/or STD prevention programs in the community and, if so, how good are they? Are there youth development programs in the community? What kind of staff, organizational, and monetary resources are available? The answers to these questions will help you decide whether you should replicate or adapt an existing program or create a new one. If you determine that you will be replicating or adapting an existing program, Table 11.1 provides a list of highly effective sexuality education programs as a starting point. If, after conducting the needs assessment, you decide a new program must be created, Kirby's (2007) "Characteristics of Effective Curriculum-Based Programs" offers a step-by-step guide to do so. This guide was created based on the rigorous evaluation of hundreds of sexuality education programs. It takes you through the steps of developing the curriculum, content to include, and finally evaluation. You can evaluate the program or curriculum using the Curriculum Evaluation Tool (National Guidelines Task Force, 2004). This evaluation tool addresses such things as concepts and topics covered in the program, teaching strategies that were used, accuracy and relevance of the information, cultural sensitivity, and parental involvement. This tool can be used for evaluating an extensive program or to compare the strengths and weaknesses of several curricula. It can be downloaded and printed from the SIECUS website at http://www .siecus.org/_data/global/images/guidelines.pdf (National Guidelines Task Force, 2004). SIECUS also provides a separate evaluation tool that can be used specifically for evaluating STDs/HIV programs. The STDs/HIV checklist can be downloaded and printed from the SIECUS website at http:// www.siecus.org/_data/global/images/guidelines.pdf (National Guidelines Task Force, 2004). Kirby (2007) has created a comprehensive evaluation guide, "Characteristics of Effective Curriculum-Based Programs," that can be used to evaluate sexuality education programs and/or curricula:

The Process of Developing the Curriculum

1. Include multiple people with expertise in theory, research, and sexuality education to develop the curriculum.

2. Assess needs and assets of the target group.

3. Use a logic model approach that specifies the health goals, the types of behavior affecting those goals, the risk and protective factors affecting those types of behavior, and activities to change those risk and protective factors.

4. Design activities consistent with community values and available resources.

5. Pilot-test the program.

The Contents of the Curriculum

Curriculum Goals and Objectives

6. Focus on clear health goals—for example, the prevention of STD/HIV, pregnancy, or both.

7. Focus narrowly on specific types of behavior leading to these health goals (e.g., abstaining from sex or using condoms or other contraceptives), provide clear messages about these types of behavior, and address situations that might lead to them and how to avoid them.

8. Address sexual psycho-social risk and protective factors that affect sexual behavior (e.g., knowledge, perceived risks, values, attitudes, perceived norms, and self-efficacy) and change them.

Activities and Teaching Methodologies

9. Create a safe social environment for participants.

10. Include multiple activities to change each of the targeted risk and protective factors.

11. Use instructionally sound teaching methods that actively involve participants, help them personalize the information, and are designed to change the targeted risk and protective factors.

12. Use activities, instructional methods, and behavioral messages that are appropriate to the teens' culture, developmental age, and sexual experience.

13. Cover topics in a logical sequence.

The Process of Implementing the Curriculum

14. Secure at least minimal support from appropriate authorities, such as departments of health, school districts, or community organizations.

15. Select educators with desired characteristics, train them, and provide monitoring, supervision, and support.

16. If needed, implement activities to recruit and retain participants and overcome barriers to their involvement (e.g., publicize the program, offer food, or obtain consent).

17. Implement all activities with the highest possible standards of exactness.

Contemporary sexuality education curricula reflect the growing body of research that emphasizes teaching functional sexual health information; developing the necessary interpersonal skills needed to adopt, practice, and maintain health-enhancing sexual behaviors; and shaping group and personal norms that value a healthy lifestyle. In addition, characteristics of effective sexuality education curricula have been identified that address content, instructional processes, implementation, processes, and evaluation. Effective sexuality education:

1. Focuses on specific behavioral outcomes. Curricula should have a clear set of behavioral outcomes with instructional strategies and learning experiences that focus exclusively on these outcomes.

2. Is research based and theory driven. Use instructional strategies and learning experiences that are built on theoretical approaches that have been demonstrated effective in influencing health-related risky behaviors in youth. The most promising curricula go beyond the cognitive level and address the social influences, values, norms, and skills that influence sexual-related behaviors of adolescents. The curriculum should build on protective factors that promote healthy sexual behaviors and reduce risks that contribute to unhealthy sexual behaviors.

3. Addresses individual values and group norms that support health-enhancing behaviors. Instruction strategies and learning experiences help students accurately assess the level of sexual risk-taking behavior among their peers (e.g., how many of their peers are sexually active or are infected with an STD), correct misperceptions of peer social norms, and reinforce health-enhancing values and beliefs.

4. Focuses on increasing the personal perception of risk and harmfulness of engaging in specific sexual health risk behaviors and reinforcing protective factors. Sexuality education curricula provide opportunities for students to assess their actual vulnerability to health problems, risks of engaging in harmful health behaviors, and exposures to unhealthy sexual situations. Sexuality education curricula also provide opportunities for students to affirm health-promoting behaviors.

5. Addresses social pressures and influences. Sexuality education curricula provide opportunities for students to address personal and social pressures for engaging in risky behaviors (e.g., media influences, peer pressure, and social barriers).

6. Builds personal and social competence. Sexuality education curricula build essential skills (e.g., communication, refusal, accessing accuracy of information, decision making, planning, goal setting, self-management) that enable students to deal with social pressures and avoid or reduce risk-taking behaviors. For each skill, students are guided through a series of developmental steps: discussing the importance of the skill, its relevance, and relationship to other learned skills; presenting steps for developing the skill; modeling the skill; practicing and rehearsing the skill using real-life scenarios; and providing feedback and reinforcement.

7. Provides functional health knowledge that is basic, accurate, and directly contributes to sexual health-promoting decisions and behaviors. Sexuality education curricula provide accurate, reliable, medically accurate, and credible information so that students can assess risk, correct misperceptions about social norms, identify ways to avoid or minimize risky situations, examine internal and external influences, make behaviorally relevant decisions, and build personal and social competence. A curriculum that provides extensive information for the sole purpose of improving content knowledge is inadequate and incomplete.

8. Uses strategies designed to personalize information and engage students. Instructional strategies and learning experiences are student centered, interactive, and experiential (e.g., group discussions, cooperative learning, problem solving, role-playing, and peer-led activities). These strategies help students personalize information and maintain their interest and motivation while accommodating diverse capabilities and learning styles. Such instructional strategies include methods for addressing key sexual health-related concepts; encouraging creative expression; sharing personal thoughts, feelings, and opinions; and developing critical thinking skills.

9. Provides age- and developmentally appropriate information, learning strategies, teaching methods, and materials. Sexuality education curricula address students' needs, interests, concerns, developmental and maturity level, and current knowledge and skill levels. Learning should be relevant and applicable to students' daily lives.

10. Incorporates learning strategies, teaching methods, and materials that are culturally inclusive. Curricular materials are free of culturally biased information but also include information, activities, and examples that are inclusive of diverse cultures and lifestyles (e.g., gender, race, ethnicity, religion, sexual orientation, age, physical/mental ability, and appearance). Strategies promote values, attitudes, and behaviors that support the cultural diversity of students; optimize relevance to students from multiple cultures in the school community; strengthen students' skills necessary to engage in intercultural interactions; and build on the cultural resources of families and communities.

11. Provides adequate time for instruction. Sexuality education curricula use adequate time to promote understanding of key health concepts and to practice skills. Short-term or "one-shot" curricula (e.g., a few hours at one grade level) are generally insufficient to support the adoption and maintenance of healthy sexual behaviors.

12. Provides opportunities to reinforce skills and positive health behaviors. Sexuality education curricula build on previously learned concepts and skills and provide opportunities to reinforce health-promoting skills across sexual health areas and grade levels (e.g., more than one practice application of a skill, skill "booster" sessions at subsequent grade levels or in other academic subject areas).

13. Provides opportunities to make connections with influential others. Sexuality education curricula link students to other influential persons who affirm and reinforce health-promoting norms, beliefs, and behaviors. Instructional strategies build on protective factors that promote sexually healthy behaviors and enable students to avoid or reduce health risk behaviors by engaging peers, parents, families, and other positive adult role models in student learning.

14. Includes teacher information and plans for professional development/training that enhance effectiveness of instruction and student learning. Sexuality education curricula are implemented by teachers who believe in what they are teaching, are knowledgeable about the curriculum content, and are comfortable and skilled in implementing expected instructional

strategies. Ongoing professional development and training is critical for helping teachers implement a new sexuality education curriculum or implement strategies that require new skills in teaching or assessment.

CONCLUSION ●

Family life educators can make great contributions teaching sexuality education in a variety of settings. There are highly effective programs that can be replicated or adapted to meet the needs of individual participants. There also are many useful tools to assist in creating and evaluating a new program.

EXPLORATIONS ●

1. Locate a sexuality education program in your area. Use the "Characteristics of Effective Curriculum-Based Programs" to evaluate its effectiveness. Based on your evaluation, would it be effective? If not, what would need to be done to turn it into an effective program?

2. Identify and prioritize the sexuality education needs of your target audience. Use your findings, to determine one or two theoretical models and teaching strategies that could effectively address the needs.

CHAPTER **12**

FAMILY LIFE EDUCATION ON THE TECHNOLOGICAL FRONTIER

Aaron T. Ebata and
Steven A. Dennis

What is history's greatest technological advance? Is it the plow, which gave birth to leisure time and creative thought? Is it the printing press, which fueled education for the masses? Or is it the personal computer and global communication resulting from the massive electronic network known as the Internet? Each arguably has changed the course of history. Each has altered the way families interact and learn about their duties and relationships. In this chapter, we explore the role and effective use of technology in family life education (FLE).

Often when we hear the word *technology*, we imagine electronic devices, computers, software, hardware, or some amazing piece of equipment that has become a tool for humankind. Although such devices qualify as technology in the truest sense, technology has a broader definition. It is the application of science. It is scientific advances applied to commerce, industry, education, and daily life. Technology considers both physical tools and research-based principles. It is both hardware and processes. Because technology and the science of sound instructional principles are addressed elsewhere in this book, this chapter focuses primarily on the technological trends and web development tools and processes that are central to FLE via the Internet and other distance education technologies.

Throughout this chapter, web addresses and links are given as examples. Although all addresses and links were active at the time of publication, the Internet is ever changing. Any discontinued sites or broken links attest to the challenge of providing FLE via the dynamic world of the Internet.

THE TECHNOLOGICAL LANDSCAPE •

Computer Usage and Internet Access

In 1953, only about 100 computers existed in the entire world. They were massive machines that filled rooms yet had less power than many handheld computers today. Since IBM's introduction of the personal computer (or PC) in 1981, the cost, power, versatility, and usage of computers have exploded. Much of the growth can likely be attributed to the rapid expansion of the Internet.

The Internet began as a military project in 1970 but was soon opened up to military contractors and university research partners. By the late 1980s, most universities and many businesses were online. However, it wasn't until the advent of the World Wide Web in 1992 and the commercialization of the Internet by Internet service providers in 1993 that growth rocketed, and the Internet truly became the information superhighway.

In 2007, a Census Bureau report estimated that 73 million households (or 62%) had Internet access (U.S. Census Bureau, 2009). By comparison, in 1997, 36% of households had computers and only 18% of households had Internet access. Amazingly, Internet access had more than tripled in a single decade. The greatest growth has occurred among those connecting via high-speed or broadband connections, such as DSL, cable modems, or satellite systems. The Census Bureau data indicated that in 2007, 82% of households used high-speed connections while only 17% used a dial-up connection. Internet access by modem has declined, particularly in urban settings. Increasing high-speed access has spawned a growth in websites rich with graphics and video. Mobile phones and personal digital assistants (PDAs) with wireless Internet capabilities are further expanding the possibilities of access.

Moreover, both a 2000 Census Bureau study and a 2007 study using a representative sample of American households found that married couples with minor children have higher rates of computer ownership, broadband connections, and Internet usage than other household configurations (Kennedy, Smith, Wells, & Wellman, 2008). Most (93%) of these families had at least one computer, and more than half (58%) owned two or more. Two thirds had a home broadband connection, and 93% had at least one parent who used the Internet, and in 76% of these families, both parents used the Internet. It should be noted that families with children are also more likely to own and use cellular phones. High rates of Internet use are also found among single-parent households (87%) and nonmarried adults with children (90%). These types of families are also more likely to use social networking sites and send text messages to stay connected and manage schedules.

Until recently, "Internet use" was generally defined as using e-mail, sending instant messages, or accessing content on websites. E-mail (87%) and searching for information on the World Wide Web (64%) are the primary uses of the Internet for adults (U.S. Census Bureau, 2001). However, more recent trends (often termed "web 2.0") have included the rise of "user-generated content" or sharing of information, opinions, pictures or videos, and "what I am doing now" through the use of blogs, media-sharing sites (i.e., Flickr and YouTube), social networking sites (i.e., Facebook and MySpace), and status updating services (i.e., Twitter and FriendFeed). For example, 35% of all Internet users used social networking sites in 2008, compared to only 8% in 2005 (Lenhart, 2009a). Most of these users (75%) were between the ages of 18 and 24. Other than age, however, social network users are relatively evenly spread across demographic categories of race, income, education, and geographic location.

In the early part of the decade, some cautioned that unequal access to technology resulted in a digital divide in our society (Roach, 2003; Strover, 2003; U.S. Department of Education, 2003; Van Dijk & Hacker, 2003).Women, minorities, and poor youth and families were disadvantaged in a high-tech world. Ono and Zavodny (2003) found that although the gender gap for access to computers or the Internet disappeared by 2000, women accessed the Internet less frequently and for shorter periods of time. Women appear to be less intense about their online experience. The 2000 Census Bureau survey (U.S. Census Bureau, 2001) found Internet access to be more common in suburbs than in either central cities or rural areas. Households in the West were most likely to have access, and households in the South were least likely. White non-Hispanics and Asians were more likely to have access than Blacks or Hispanics. And finally, while usage and access increased with age during childhood, the trend reversed among adults, with those older than age 65 least likely to either own a computer or have access to the Internet. Undoubtedly, as computers and communication technologies expand, the variety of users, as well as the value of access, will increase.

A 2009 study found that 63% of American homes had broadband connections (up from 55% in 2008) but that the greatest growth in broadband adoption over a 1-year period was among those who were typically seen as being on the "other side" of the digital divide. These included senior citizens (19%–30%), those with incomes less that $20,000 (25%–35%), those with incomes between $20,000 and $30,000 (42%–53%), those with only a high school degree (40%–52%), aging baby boomers (50%–61%), and rural Americans (38% to 46%) (Horrigan, 2009).

It is important to recognize that the Internet and its use are amazingly dynamic. Already these use and access statistics are dated. More individuals and families are connected than ever, and these numbers continue to rise. But while the digital divide may be closing on one front, it will always exist on another. When a new technology emerges, it is first embraced by those with the greatest resources. Only as use and demand increase does it become more affordable and accessible to all. A 2009 study found that the use of status update services (to share immediate updates about themselves or to see updates from others) grew from 11% to 19% of all Internet users over a 5-month period. Moreover, those who drove growth in these services were those who used social networking sites, those who connected to the Internet using mobile devices, and those younger than age 44 (Fox, Zickuhr, & Smith, 2009). Those who own more Internet-connected devices (e.g., laptop, smartphone, game console) are more likely to use status update services than those who have fewer ways to connect to the Internet.

So although the Internet is expanding, some are being left behind. Family life resources distributed solely through the Internet will likely miss many of those with the greatest need. Some lack the money to get connected, and others lack the desire. Some may see no personal benefit to Internet access, or they may lack confidence in operating computers or maneuvering the Internet.

Still, assumptions as to who uses and benefits from web-based programs are being challenged. Several studies have found that seeking parenting information or support on the Internet is more likely among young, unmarried mothers (Radey & Randolph, 2009; Sakardi & Bremberg, 2005). In examining participant ratings of a site with information for families, Steimle and Duncan (2004) found greater changes in self-reported attitudes and behaviors among non-Whites and those with less than college educations. Bowers and Ebata

(2009) found that parents who were in child- or family-focused professions rated their parenting website more highly than more typical parents. In the end, prediction is risky business. The ever-changing nature of the Internet and expanding technologies makes it difficult to project the probabilities and possibilities of FLE on the technological frontier. Nonetheless, recognizing and responding to the cultural changes in learning and information delivery will be essential to the success of FLE in the future.

Learning and Information Delivery in a High-Tech World

Technological changes have and will continue to facilitate cultural changes. Although the way we learn may be tied more to our biology and cognition than technological advances, the context of learning and methods for disseminating information will continue to change. Smith (1999, pp. 31–34) suggests that technology has changed the cultural conditions in the six following ways:

1. The locus of information control has shifted from the expert to the consumer.

2. Learning is becoming anarchistic and chaotic.

3. Information has become a global business.

4. Learning is now embedded in a culture of speed.

5. Infoglut and corresponding information anxiety is a challenge.

6. New technologies create new communication communities.

Each of these cultural changes will shape the responsibilities and methods of family life educators. Let's consider each in greater detail.

1. *The locus of information control has shifted from the expert to the consumer.* Increasingly, the consumer will determine when, where, and how to access information. Experts can no longer organize, package, and deliver information in controlled manners that are based more on their own preferences than the needs and preferences of consumers. With potentially thousands of options, consumers are in control and will access and create information according to their needs and way of thinking.

2. *Learning is becoming anarchistic and chaotic.* In the past, educational resources have been largely linear. They have clear objectives, a

logical plan, and a predictable conclusion. Such resources are neat and tidy and have an obvious start and ending. Increasingly, learning is nonlinear. Hypermedia allow learners to follow multiple paths—each with a different ending. The learning objectives and paths are determined by the interests of consumers. Although customizing the path of learning to meet the preferences, desires, and needs of individual learners sounds appealing, there are concerns. Chen and Dwyer (2003) warn that there is little empirical evidence to show that a hypermedia learning environment improves learning outcomes. In fact, Astleitner and Leuner (1995) suggest that hypermedia may deter learning in several ways. For example, hypermedia make goal attainment less defined. Learners may miss key points because they are distracted by huge amounts of less pertinent or unnecessary information. A learning objective is most easily met when the target is clearly identified. In a hypermedia environment, there may be no specific targeted objective.

In addition, learners may become spatially disoriented by the complex node-link structure of hypermedia. After selecting a few embedded links, learners may lose sight of where they came from, where they are, and where they should go. In short, they become lost in hyperspace. Finally, hypermedia may contribute to cognitive overload resulting from the high memory demand. Although hypermedia may be an ideal structure for information retrieval, it may not be equally effective as a means of knowledge acquisition or learning.

3. *Information has become a global business.* Geographic and organizational boundaries are fast becoming meaningless. Organizations and educators who seek to protect their turf will find there is no turf in the digital world. Consumers can electronically access material from libraries, universities, or organizations around the world with greater speed than they can drive to their county Extension office. Family life educators will find their target audiences spanning the world. To attract consumers, organizations will need to pool resources and expertise in collaborative ways. Already collaborative efforts such as CYFERnet exist (see http://www.cyfernet.org). The CYFERnet website brings together peer-reviewed research-based child, youth, and family resources from all the public land grant universities in the country. Likewise, institutions of higher education are collaborating to offer degree programs. For example, the Great Plains Interactive Distance Education Alliance (GPIDEA; http://www.gpidea.org) offers multi-institution programs in family financial counseling, gerontology, and youth development. The Cooperative Extension Service's development of eXtension (http://www.extension.org) is another example of an interactive learning environment that connects learners with research-based information from land grant

institutions. These connections enable the sharing of research among professionals, as well as provide consumers with credible information prepared for general audiences. Moreover, they direct individuals to local Extension resources or more individualized and interactive online support.

4. *Learning is now embedded in a culture of speed.* In a culture of instant gratification, individuals and families place great value on quick results and immediate access. Whether individuals are trying to lose weight, purchase consumer goods, or expand their learning, it seems that sooner is better. Although distributed learning opportunities increase the likelihood that information will be presented when and how it is needed, the window of opportunity is small in a culture of speed. Family life educators must be ready with accessible resources when the need arises. For example, following the September 11 terrorist attacks on the World Trade Center in 2001, professionals were scrambling to provide parents with resources to help themselves and their children appropriately discuss and cope with the devastating event. The window of opportunity was small. Many excellent resources have been developed since, but fewer were available at the time they were most needed. Hurricane Katrina in 2005 and the economic challenges of recent years have provided additional opportunities for an immediate response to families in need. To be successful, family life educators must be ready when the window of opportunity opens.

5. *Infoglut and corresponding information anxiety is a challenge.* Information on nearly every subject can be easily found in minutes. In fact, peddlers of information no longer wait for people to come to them. Aggressive approaches that use spyware and unsolicited spam messages have added to infoglut of the Internet. Sifting through the enormity of information to determine if it is accurate, credible, and useful is an ominous task. Many have likely asked which of the 350,000 hits to an online search have what they need. Effective search and filtering strategies have become increasingly important. Many professional organizations and academic centers are struggling to find ways to screen, endorse, or implement criteria standards for acceptability. For example, the Child & Family WebGuide (http://www.cfw.tufts.edu) was created by librarians and child development faculty at Tufts University as an effort to help parents and professionals find credible and useful information about family life, parenting, and child development.

Although the technology exists for search engines to search only among preapproved or credentialed sites, it generally has been used only to filter inappropriate content from children (see http://www1.k9webprotection

.com or http://www.opendns.com) or the safety of products (see http://www.tnpc.com), not to ensure the quality and credibility of family life content. After the introduction of web browsers in the 1990s, numerous website awards were created by self-appointed individuals or groups to lend credibility and recognition to websites. But unlike the Oscars, Grammys, or Emmys, web surfers are generally unaware of which awards truly represent a significant or credible honor. In fact, the Web Credibility Project at Stanford University (http://credibility.stanford.edu/) sponsored a study that found that the average consumer paid far more attention to the superficial aspects of sites, such as visual cues, than to its content. For example, nearly half of all consumers (or 46.1%) in the study assessed the credibility of sites largely on visual design, including layout, typography, font size, and color schemes (Fogg et al., 2003). It appears that many consumers believe if it looks dazzling, the content must be good. More rigorous criteria are less common among professionals and consumers. One study found that preservice and in-service teachers considered the credibility and usefulness of Internet resources to be equal to information found in textbooks (Iding, Crosby, & Speitel, 2002). This may or may not be the case.

Fetsch and Hughes (2002) suggest that consumers evaluate the quality of family life content by comparing it to recognized standards or corroborating sources. Consumers should look for biases, emotional appeals, and conflicts of interest that are common to commercial or ad-sponsored sites. Fetsch and Hughes also recommend that consumers be wary of dramatic claims that oversimplify the nature of family life or suggest there is only one way to handle a problem.

6. *New technologies create new communication communities.* News groups and listservs, chat rooms, forums, blogs, and social networking sites and tools have provided new ways for people to meet, discuss ideas, and share their feelings. As with any educational approach, what attracts some may alienate others. Some prefer to discuss ideas and share feelings through the anonymity of the Internet. Others prefer the personalization that comes with face-to-face interaction.

As social networking tools have grown, family life educators have recognized the importance of the context in which information is provided. Knowledge provided by experts might be deemed more valuable because of their academic or professional credentials. However, information also carries value and credibility when it is delivered by friends or family in the context of a caring and trusting relationship or by those who share experiences and values similar to one's own. On the Internet, researched-based knowledge has often been trumped by the individual experiences shared among friends or kindred spirits in an atmosphere of trust. Recognizing this phenomenon, even professional organizations such as the National Council on Family Relations (NCFR) have flocked to the social networking sites to make their presence known. These new communication communities are changing the way family life educators think, research, and market.

Smith's (1999) six cultural shifts are just a beginning. *Change* is the catchword of the technological frontier. The new and expanded communication opportunities provided by the Internet and other technologies are undoubtedly most effective when passed on to the learner in the form of choices. Variety, flexibility, and alternative approaches will help each learner individualize a plan that works best for him or her. Yet within the plethora of choices, it is increasingly important that consumers and family life educators critically evaluate the credibility and usefulness of ever-expanding information.

● ASSESSING THE CREDIBILITY OF ONLINE PROGRAMS FOR FAMILY LIFE EDUCATION

The number of quality family life education websites and intervention and prevention programs continues to grow. Unfortunately, the number of eye-catching websites pushing products or sharing pseudoscience and personal testimonials as undisputed truths has also grown. Information is now disseminated by a wide variety of individuals, organizations, or institutions, and there is no recognized authority that monitors the quality, reliability, and currency of information. Faced with a variety of views, it can be challenging for consumers to distinguish between a credible source and a less reliable source (Zaidman-Zait & Jamieson, 2007). One study claims that nearly 75% of information available to parents online is reliable; however, the gaps between empirically based information and popular print on certain issues (e.g., corporal punishment) could be dangerous to children and infants (Cain, 2008). While 19% of parents say that the Internet improves the way they care for their children, "parents are less vigilant than nonparents in checking the source and sponsorship of the information" (Allen & Rainie, 2002, p. 3).

Research reveals that women are more likely to seek health information online, and they are more concerned about the credibility of the sources (Cotton & Gupta, 2004). A recent study found that "high SES [socioeconomic status] parents were more likely to trust the information on a website if the site was associated with a credible organization (e.g., a university or research organization)" (Rothbaum, Martland, & Jannsen, 2008, p. 123). However, a study of who uses the Women's Health Matters website mirrored the results of the Stanford Web Credibility Project and found that the women's perceptions of the site were influenced by their experience in navigating the site (Marton, 2000). Marton (2000) suggests that design elements cannot be separated from content because "usability" affects perceptions of quality. Website design, frequent updates, language, and resources (e.g., working links to other reliable sites) are also considered important criteria by parents (Zaidman-Zait & Jamieson, 2007).

These studies suggest that those seeking FLE on the web should be able to easily navigate through a site, the information they receive should be easily understood, and they should be able to find the credentials and criteria they need to be assured that the information they obtain is current and from a credible source. More important, educators may need to help "lower skilled" web users choose information that that is "informative, credible, and useful" (Rothbaum et al., 2008).

Assessing the integrity and credibility of information acquired from the Internet may be one of the most pressing skills needed by consumers and family life educators today. The following criteria may be helpful in determining if a website and the information it provides is reputable and research based:

1. *Does it carry legitimate authority?* Is there a reputable person, company, or organization behind the website with recognized authority? Often the domain suffix can be helpful. Information from .edu, .gov, or .org sites may be more reputable than a .com site. Educational institutions, nonprofit professional organizations, and government entities are often in the business of acquiring and disseminating research-based information without the competing goal of profit. Commercial sites designed for profit may be more interested in the advertising opportunities or product sales than the integrity of the information.

2. *Is authorship provided?* When the name of the author is given, the credentials and contact information are usually also given. This requires an author to stand by his or her work and opens the work to challenges or questions, particularly when the author is accessible by e-mail.

3. *What is the purpose of the information?* What action would the author of the information like you to take? Is the information designed to advocate a specific position? Does it sell a product or service? Does it inform

or entertain? Does it serve to link you to an online community or to redirect you to a commercial enterprise? Identifying the purpose of information may help you recognize any bias in the information. Most reputable websites will identify the mission or purpose of the website; it may be important for one to find out how the mission is being carried out or funded.

4. *Has the information been passed through a peer-review process where there is an opportunity for acceptance or rejection?* Online journals or information accepted only after a rigorous review process is generally better information. While not of equal value, even the online reviews generated by consumers or uninvited critics may be useful. More educational sources are following the example of commercial giants such as Amazon in creating these opportunities for informal and ongoing reviews.

5. *Is the information current and accurate?* Does it appear to be updated regularly? Dates should indicate when the information was originally written or created. Information with errors is less likely to have been through a review process or to have been edited for clarity and accuracy by a qualified editor.

6. *Is the information relevant to your specific situation?* Cure-all approaches that provide a single "snake oil" solution for all problems are rarely of significant value. Information that is conveyed cautiously and identifies the specific contexts or conditions is generally more reputable. Individuals should look for specific examples that are similar to their own situation. Quick fixes and single solutions are rarely the answer to family life challenges that are clouded with dozens of interacting variables.

7. *Begin an information search from a trusted portal.* CYFAR (www.cyfernet.org) or eXtension (www.extension.org) and other trusted sites can serve a beginning point for your search. Trusted sites often critically evaluate the links they provide or refer to from their own site (for additional information on website credibility, refer to Fogg's [2002] guidelines for developers in the next section).

While the above list is important for ensuring quality for consumers, it is equally important to developers. As consumers critically question the information they acquire from the Internet, it will be increasingly important that family life educators develop programs that are trusted, personal, timely, and easy to find. In the next section, we explore the development of online programs.

DEVELOPING ONLINE PROGRAMS FOR ●
FAMILY LIFE EDUCATION

As the world population becomes increasingly wired and turns to the web to seek information and learn new skills, having web-based programs may be an essential part of an overall outreach effort. However, without careful planning, a web-based effort can lead to unforeseen problems. We emphasize that the web is a delivery medium that makes it easy to do certain things, but the impact and educational value of a program still depend on the quality of the content and the extent to which the program can effectively fulfill some educational need.

In this section, we apply some of the findings and suggestions summarized in the previous section while outlining practical issues that need to be considered when developing an online outreach effort. First, we examine the advantages and disadvantages of web-based efforts and compare online programs with more traditional programs. We then use a program development model to offer steps that educators should take in designing a web-based program. Next, we address the need for developers to promote, market, and evaluate their efforts. Finally, we conclude by commenting on some developing issues in web-based delivery of FLE.

Why Should Family Life Educators Consider Online Programming?

There are a number of advantages that web-based programming can have compared to more traditional ways of delivering education and information:

- It can be convenient for consumers. A web-based program is potentially available 24 hours a day, 7 days a week. Users can seek information when they need it, at a time and a place that is convenient for them and not the providers.
- An online program can provide support to and enhance other kinds of more traditional efforts such as parenting classes or presentations.
- By using the hyperlinking and multimedia features of the web, online resources can potentially offer richer, more flexible learning experiences or more useful ways of structuring or presenting information.

- A web-based information warehouse can potentially be easier to maintain, update, and distribute compared to print resources.
- A web-based effort can be cost-effective and build on existing resources.
- A web effort can reach new audiences that traditionally may not have been served.

Recent studies have shown that going online to seek information about parenting is common. For example, Radey and Randolph (2009) found that the Internet was the third most common source of information for parents (used by 76%), surpassed only by books and magazines (94%) and family members (80%). Rothbaum et al. (2008) found that 85% of parents in their study reported using the web to find information about children or families (with higher SES parents more likely to do so than lower SES parents). More important, there is preliminary evidence that web-based resources can be an effective way to deliver family life education (e.g., Bowers & Ebata, 2009; Deitz, Cook, Billings, & Hendrickson, 2009; Grant et al., 2001; Na & Chia, 2008; Steimle & Duncan, 2004) and that it may be as effective as face-to-face training in certain circumstances (Duncan et al., 2009).

One of the biggest disadvantages is that an online resource will not reach certain populations. However, some other important challenges or potential barriers need to be considered:

- Online resources are only available when all of the links in the technological chain are working. Thus, all of the following must be in place and operating for a user to be able to use a web-based program: (a) the computer server that houses the site and the network (or Internet service provider) that distributes the information, (b) the Internet network or backbone and nodes through which information passes, (c) the user's Internet service provider, (d) a working telephone or cable lines or unobstructed satellite or radio transmission paths through which digital signals must pass, and (e) the user's computer system. All of these parts rely on electrical power, of course!
- The promise of online support or enhanced programming may promote expectations or demands that are difficult or costly to meet. There is greater pressure to be (or at least appear to be) current and dynamic—with new content appearing regularly.
- Having an online delivery system does not guarantee that the content is useful, is credible, or meets any criteria or standard for quality (technically referred to as "junk").

- New audiences may have different needs and expectations compared to audiences that family life educators have traditionally served and may create additional demands on an educator. Educators may put faith in the importance of certain factors that make a resource credible or useful (e.g., that it is research based), but studies described earlier show that consumers may be using other criteria to make judgments of credibility. Having a web presence means having a *global* presence, which can make it difficult to *limit* one's audience or to handle requests or communications with a broader pool of clients.

In sum, although a good web-based program can be effective and efficient, it may also be costly and difficult to maintain. It may require new resources and expertise to successfully sustain the effort. At their best, web-based resources can effectively engage, educate, inspire, and provide support. They can connect people, provide social support, and enhance skill-building opportunities. At worst, these resources can be dull, be inaccurate, or reinforce myths and misconceptions about family life.

Model and Methods for Web-Based Delivery

An important first step is to consider how a web-based effort fits into the overall educational strategy that an individual or organization might have. In general, a web-based effort can serve to (a) provide support to existing educational offerings (e.g., workshops, printed materials), which might involve supplemental information or opportunities for communication, and/or (b) provide information or educational programs that can stand alone. We focus on three kinds of information or learning experiences:

1. Information that can be used as reference (links, fact sheets, background papers, brochures, documents) where users decide when and how to interact with the materials in an unstructured fashion

2. Structured learning experiences (online classes, curriculum modules, lessons) that provide some kind of planned framework or guided interaction with the materials to achieve some learning goal

3. Opportunities for interactions with an expert, authority, instructor, or other users

Reference Materials

Part of the appeal of the web is the ability to freely make unrestricted choices amid what often seems to be an infinite universe of chaos and anarchy. Being able to find critical information quickly and easily, without having to go through barriers erected by others, is at the heart of this idea. Most websites are designed to provide an archive of information that relies on users searching for, then "picking and choosing," the reference information that they might need. The most common method of delivering this type of content on the web is still text and images. Although there may be links within the text that can easily take users to other sources of information, most of the family life content on the web is essentially electronic versions of what you might see on a printed page. The web can also be used to distribute formatted or illustrated text (brochures, newsletters, etc.) that can be downloaded and saved for viewing or printing. Kidshealth (kidshealth .org) and Parenting 24/7 (parenting247.org) are examples of sites that focus on child development and parenting.

Links to other sources of information are a common and powerful feature of web-based programs. Most websites feature links to other resources on the web, but some sites are primarily designed to refer users to other sources of information. These portals, or directories, are guides to other sources of content. The value of a good directory or portal is that it makes it easier for users to find the kinds of resources that they would find most helpful. Most good portals provide (a) a structure or way of cataloging and labeling sources into categories that can be browsed by a user and (b) a good search feature that lets users enter a set of keywords. Examples of portals for FLE include CYFERNet (www.cyfernet.org), eXtension (http:// www.extension.org), Teen-Link (http://www.teenlink.umn.edu), and the Tufts University Child & Family WebGuide (www.cfw.tufts.edu).

Structured Learning Experiences

Although collections of resources can be helpful, many educators believe that learning certain types of skills or content can be facilitated by more structured experiences that guide or facilitate a student's progress through a sequence of instruction or activities. Examples of structured courses or educational modules include an online marriage class from Utah Marriage (http://www.utahmarriage.org/) and courses on discipline and anger management for parents from Kansas State's WonderWise Parent (http://www.ksu.edu/wwparent/courses/index.htm). The web is also well suited for formal online distance learning coursework that uses many of the tools and methods outlined above. A variety of courseware or authorware is available to schools, colleges, and corporations and provides instructors with tools for constructing or supporting web-based learning (e.g., WebCT, Blackboard, Moodle). Educators have the option of constructing modules or courses that are entirely on demand (essentially a self-study model where the user determines the time and pace of study), in real time (where students may be geographically dispersed but expected to be connected to the instructor and other classmates via technology at a certain time), or some combination of both. The use of synchronous (real-time) and asynchronous (anytime) methods of facilitating participation still assumes that some guided interaction by the instructor, as well as interaction between students, is beneficial for learning.

Opportunities for Interaction

Message boards, discussion forums, chat rooms, blogs, and social networks can facilitate communities of like-minded others trying to find answers to specific questions or problems. The web has the potential to facilitate communities of shared expertise and support while bridging social and geographic barriers. These tools can be used for communication between an educator and a client or user and for communication between users. For issues where there may be many right answers in addition to expert advice (e.g., coping with an infant who won't sleep through the night, trying to manage the stress of caring for a disabled parent, etc.), shared experience can provide a sense of support and can normalize what might be perceived by an individual as an abnormal or an isolated experience.

Program Planning and Development for the Web

In the next few sections, we focus on the issues that educators must address in developing their own web-based resource. We recommend following a typical program development or curriculum development process (outlined in other chapters in this book), with additional consideration given to issues that are unique to the web. For example, Thorndike (2009) reports on a needs assessment of parents and expectant parents attending a pediatric practice as well as a sample of health care providers regarding the potential use of the Internet for treating infant and parental sleep problems, as well as other issues.

There are three basic ways that an educator could develop and build a web-based effort. The first method is to do it yourself. In some cases, individuals or groups of individuals have designed, built, and maintained their own sites as well as provided the content for the site (with some technical support from others or an institution). A good example is the WonderWise Parent (www.ksu.edu/wwparent/index.htm) developed by Dr. Chuck Smith at Kansas State University. One of the major shifts in the past 5 years has been the development of easy-to-use tools that allow anyone to create their own websites and "wikis" (e.g., Google sites, PBworks, SnapPages, Weebly), blogs (e.g., Blogger, Wordpress), and social networks or specialized communities (e.g., Ning, KickApps, Wetpaint).

Despite the proliferation of tools to help those who are not technically inclined, a sustained effort typically requires developing some technical expertise and a passion for creative expression. Most others will (or should) use one of two other methods: (a) hire technical staff and manage the development themselves (or with a team) or (b) outsource the project to experienced designers and programmers.

Whatever method you choose, there are some important issues that you will need to consider and communicate with those who will be developing the effort. Rather than focusing on the specific elements of good design (e.g., aesthetics, ease of navigation, being easy to find by search engines) that we mentioned earlier, here we focus on broader issues of program development for the web. We organize our discussion around a process that should help an educator develop a plan that can function as (a) a strategic road map for keeping track of progress, (b) a document that will serve as the basis for working with a web designer and programmer to develop a more specific set of requirements, and (c) a tool that can be used to describe the effort to stakeholders and potential funders.

The Web Development Process

Like the development of any program or curriculum, the development of a web-based effort will go through stages that connect to other stages. These stages and transactional process would include the following:

- A strategic planning stage, where needs are assessed, overall goals and objectives are identified, and strategic options are considered. Different methods might be considered, along with considerations for how the effort will be managed when the effort is completed, and how it will be evaluated.
- A definition phase, where a preliminary design and prototype might be developed and evaluated by the educator and representatives of the potential audience. During this stage, functional requirements

may be specified and technical needs determined. An estimated budget and tentative timeline or schedule may be outlined in this stage.

- A development phase, where an initial version or prototype is built and content is developed and implemented into the site. Small-scale testing and feedback from users can be used to make modifications in the design, and a "final" model is determined and built.
- An implementation phase in which the website is reviewed and tested and finally launched.
- This cycle is then repeated for the next phase or the next version of the site.

Before meeting with a web designer or developer, it can be useful to prepare a written document that tries to capture your vision of the program in a concise way (in addition to documenting goals, objectives, and methods). Come up with possible names or titles for the program that will clearly convey the site's purpose or contents. You might also consider a short tagline, or subtitle, that clarifies or adds to a user's understanding of the purpose of the site. Next, develop a single-sentence (or short-paragraph) description of the purpose of the site and what a user can expect to find there. This information will be useful to a web designer and can serve as an early draft of materials that can eventually be used in news releases and promotional materials. Next, develop a list of keywords that someone might use to describe and access your site. Finally, make a list of existing sites that you would want a designer to look at because (a) they have elements that appeal to you, (b) they would be sites that have similar content and would compete with your program, or (c) they have elements that exemplify what you do not want to see in your program.

Designing Effective Resources

At a time when almost endless information is at our fingertips and technologies and communication networks are expanding, it is easy to become enthralled with the latest advances in hardware and software. But the effective use of any technology requires that it be applied with sound principles of instruction. Five are suggested here.

1. Develop and market the value of credibility. Today's consumers have numerous access points for information. When competing against the information provided by thousands of others, the sources considered most credible will capture the attention of consumers. Credibility may even be more important in settings of anonymity or minimal personal contact. When developing a website or other resources, Fogg (2002) recommends 10 guidelines for enhancing the credibility:

1. *Make it easy to verify the accuracy of the information on your site.* Use citations and references, and clearly identify source materials.

2. *Show that there's a real organization behind your site.* List a physical address or post a photo of your office.

3. *Highlight the expertise in your organization and in the content and services you provide.* Share the credentials and affiliations of the experts who are on the team. Avoid links to less credible sources. Your site may become less credible by association.

4. *Show that honest and trustworthy people stand behind your site.* Identify the real people behind the work. Share bios that convey their involvement and trustworthiness.

5. *Make it easy to contact you.* Having a physical address, phone number, and e-mail address will show that you welcome personal contact and have nothing to hide.

6. *Design your site so it looks professional.* Pay attention to the layout, typography, images, and consistency in design. Make sure your overall design matches the purpose of the site.

7. *Make your site easy to use and useful.* Find ways to help the user locate information quickly and intuitively. Keep it simple.

8. *Update your site's content often.* People assign more credibility to sites that show they have been recently updated or reviewed.

9. *Use restraint with any promotional content.* If possible, avoid having ads on your site. If you must, clearly distinguish the sponsored content from your own. Avoid pop-up ads.

10. *Avoid errors of all types.* Typographical errors and broken links hurt a site's credibility more than most people imagine. It's also important to keep sites up and running.

2. Engage your learners. Multimedia (audio, video, animation) elements have the potential for being a powerful tool that might engage users, but the advantages and disadvantages of the use of any type of media remain the same regardless of how it is actually delivered. For example, a video of talking heads will probably have the same impact if viewed on the computer as if viewed on TV. The advantage of having video available over the web is that of convenience and potential timeliness. More recently, a variety of software tools (Adobe Presenter and Connect Pro; Camtasia Studio, Screenflow) make it easy to develop multimedia presentations. Moreover, free or low-cost web applications make it easy to then share these as slideshows (e.g., Jing, Slideshare) or videos (e.g., YouTube, Vimeo) over the web. Unfortunately, these tools cannot ensure that these presentations will be effective or even entertaining.

Active learning strategies require something of the learner. Learners can be engaged by audio and video, lively discussions, or hands-on games or activities, but they can also be engaged mentally with thought-provoking questions, captivating stories, or analogies or metaphors. Learners can also participate through role-playing, simulations, or case study analysis. Web-based courses, teleconferencing, web casting, and other technology-based approaches can all be designed with engagement in mind. Whatever the approach or delivery method, effective family life educators will find ways for learners to reflect on or apply the information. Active strategies will increase participant learning. PBSkids (http://pbskids.org/) or goCyperCamp (http://gocybercamp.org/) are excellent examples of websites that promote an interactive experience. Here we define *interactive* as the ability to customize, shape, select, or change information or experience provided by the website based on individual input. Examples include the following:

- Customized features of a website, personalizing an online experience, or getting customized information based on user input. For example, both the Parenting 24/7 and eXtension Just In Time Parenting (www.extension.org/parenting) websites allow parents to enter the birth date of a child to get monthly e-mail deliveries of parenting newsletters that are specific to the age of their child. The Talaris Institute's Parenting Counts website (www.parentingcounts .org) allows users to create a Personal Journal to store and share photos and stories while tracking developmental milestones and accessing research-based multimedia information.

- Quizzes, surveys, questionnaires, or smart guides or wizards that provide a different set of information, advice, or referrals based on a diagnosis of responses from a user. This type of tool might help users narrow down a complex set of paths or choices (like trying to choose a TV or figuring out what a medical symptom might mean or how to deal with a child who bites or how to conduct a program evaluation). The Parent Self-Assessment (PSA; see http://psa.uaex .edu/default.asp) is one example of an assessment tool that channels parents to educational resources based on the assessment profile. Similarly, a variety of assessments at Martin Seligman's Authentic

Happiness website (see http://www.authentichappiness.org) help users learn their signature strengths.

- Gamelike experiences that lead to different outcomes based on choices made during different parts of a story. These structured-choice scenarios might be as simple as a branching story or as complex as a computer game (like the Sims). Games that have non-violent or prosocial story lines or agendas are rare, but there is a growing movement for developing these types of games (e.g., Changemakers.net, Gamesforchange.org).

- Community recommendations and ratings. These might include user recommendations or ratings of different sources of information, advice, or ideas similar to user reviews of books and merchandise found on commercial sites such as Amazon.com or on Epinions.com.

3. Incorporate variety and extend choices. Each learner has a favorite way of learning. By designing educational materials with a variety of learning activities and methods, a richer learning environment is created, especially when learners are given an opportunity to choose among the various options. Levin, Levin, and Waddoups (1999) found that "multiplicity" may decrease efficiency in the short run but may encourage the development of powerful new learning and teaching environments in the longer term. They define *multiplicity* as multiple contexts for learning, multiple instructional media, multiple instructional formats, multiple learning activities, and multiple assessment techniques. Levin et al. believe that multiplicity results in both a broader and deeper representation of content to be mastered. Hence, the very act of choosing one's preferred method of learning may enhance the ownership or personal control and responsibility that individuals feel over their own learning. Centering the locus of control for learning on the individual may ultimately help sustain motivation and inspire continued learning. In short, choice cultivates personal responsibility.

4. Provide learners with instructional maps. In a hypermedia environment, one can easily get lost, but sound instruction in any environment requires a clearly charted course. Using menus, sidebars, summary tables, graphical representations, transitional cues, outlines, video examples, or other content organizers can help learners to clearly identify key points and the direction of the content. Appropriate menus with an easy way back can keep learners from being lost in a sea of embedded menus and hyperlinks. Providing learners with a clear instructional map will help them reach their learning destination effectively.

5. Provide broad support. Smith (1999) noted that "the Internet is a great informer but a poor coach" (p. 33). The methods in which FLE is provided may change, but humans will always need the specific guidance, feedback, and support of mentors and teachers. Similarly, Dhanarajan (2001) warns that commitment to leading-edge hardware and software is not enough. Mastering the tools of distance education technologies requires significant training and support for both the designer and end users to become proficient and master such tools. Although many independent learners have the determination and skill to learn with only minimal support, effective FLE will require more. Speaking of distance education in higher education, Dhanarajan notes,

> A passionate teacher, a personal computer, a server, and connections can spawn an instant course. . . . While these may be excellent for those learners seeking enrichment and personal pleasure who have greater skills to "learn" through cyberspace, they are far from satisfactory for those who are intent on gaining credits and qualification. Such people need an assurance of institutional commitment to provide all the other services of a healthy and supportive learning environment such as access to mentors, libraries, laboratories, assessment, and opportunities to gain recognized credit. A chat room is not a substitute for the range of services provided by committed institutions. (pp. 64–65)

Indeed, the successful family life educators of the future will not only provide a broad level of support to learners but will develop and deliver content in proven ways. Adequate planning and preparation is a must. In the next section, we share more specifically the design and planning considerations for developing a successful online course.

Practical Considerations for Managing Content

The belief that a web-based program will somehow be easier to maintain or manage than some other type of program is a mistaken one. Although web delivery makes certain kinds of tasks easier (or less relevant), many educators who have turned to the web have discovered that these types of programs sometimes take more attention than print materials that can sit on a shelf or a curriculum that is already in use by others. Web users assume that information on the web is dynamic and changing, so it is important for educators to plan for managing change. More specifically, educators need to plan for how the site will be managed once the site is up and running. Specifically:

- Who will be responsible for making decisions about the contents of the site and authorizing changes in the design of the site or its contents (i.e., managing the site)?
- What process or procedure will be used for evaluating existing content and determining the need for revising or developing new content? How often should existing content be evaluated? When do the materials expire? What process will be used to determine when things should be deleted or revised? How often should the site be updated with new content? Who will be responsible for developing, reviewing, and editing new content?
- Who will be responsible for actually putting content online or actually making changes in the design or functionality of the site? Will there be a formal process or procedures for keeping track of which changes need to be made and when and how these changes are accomplished?
- Who will be the primary contact for the program?

The answers to these issues may suggest using a certain type of model for managing the site and may have implications for the actual design of the site itself. For example, sites that will have frequently updated content can be designed so that content can be updated or changed using content management systems (e.g., Drupal) or site management tools (e.g., Adobe Contribute) that make it easy for the less technically inclined to add or change content in certain sections of pages and to prevent accidental damage to the site itself.

Disseminating and Marketing

A web-based program must be promoted like any other type of educational program. Although we would like to believe that the quality of the site will speak for itself, the quantity of information available on the web makes it easy for good information to be hidden unless conscious, strategic efforts are made to promote the program. Efforts could include the following:

- Direct marketing to the primary (target) audience using electronic methods (e-mail announcements, information on other websites that serve the same audience) as well as traditional methods (print announcements using mailing lists, flyers and brochures, media spots, etc.).

- Marketing to secondary audiences that might recommend or provide information about the site to the target audience (other sites, services, providers, consumer guides, reviewers, etc.). For family life educators, this would mean promoting the resource to other professionals, institutions, agencies, and businesses that serve families.
- Integrating social networking features into a web resource that allow others to contribute to or easily share content from the program, creating a presence in existing social networking sites that are already used by those you are trying to reach (e.g., groups or fan pages in Facebook) or participating in online communities as an author or representative of a program.
- Personal appearances, demonstrations, and participation in public and professional events that might garner media attention.

It is useful to think of a marketing effort as a promotional campaign that has several coordinated parts. News releases and media attention can be useful, as many newspaper and television stations have websites that provide additional information and links to viewers who may have seen part of a news article or broadcast.

It is especially important to be able to generate electronic word of mouth so that other websites or individuals provide a link to your resource. In the next section, we discuss different methods of finding and ranking the relevance of particular websites in search results. Two of the most important determinants remain (a) how many other websites refer to you and (b) whether the websites that refer to you are themselves highly ranked.

Evaluating Web-Based Family Life Programs

We have been discussing the potential of web-based programs and have outlined issues and procedures that should be kept in mind when developing web-based family life programs. Although web-based efforts proliferated in the 1990s, there were relatively little published data on the effectiveness of these types of programs (Hughes, Ebata, & Dollahite, 1999; S. N. Morris et al., 1999). Since that time, there has been a slowly growing body of work that has attempted to evaluate web-based programs (Bowers & Ebata, 2009; Deitz et al., 2009; Duncan et al., 2009; Grant et al., 2001; Hughes, 2001; Na & Chia, 2008; Steimle & Duncan, 2004). These studies suggest that the use of the web as a medium for education and outreach is promising, but systematic efforts to evaluate web-based programs are still uncommon and provide unique challenges and barriers.

Steimle and Duncan (2004) have adapted Jacobs's (1988) five-tiered model for evaluating family programs and offer helpful guidelines and recommendations for evaluating web-based programs. Here we summarize some of these recommendations and make additional comments for specific stages.

Tier 1, the *website preimplementation stage*, includes needs assessment, preliminary research, and pilot testing focused on developing and improving a program. This stage might include the use of focus groups, individual interviews, surveys, and walk-through usability studies of prototypes.

Tier 2, the *website utilization stage*, focuses on whether and how a site is being used. The most common method of assessing utilization would be to examine web log statistics that are commonly collected (and often misinterpreted). Originally designed as a means to assess load, traffic, or demand put on a web server (the computer that hosts a website), these statistics have been used to estimate the number of visits a site receives, which parts of a site get the most visits, the time spent on each visit, and where the visitor was previously before coming to the particular site. Hughes (2001) provides a "layman's guide" to the kinds of statistics that are available from web logs and shows how these kinds of data can be used in formative evaluations. He also points out the limitations of web log statistics.

Tier 3, the *visitor satisfaction stage*, involves collecting user information (which could be qualitative or quantitative) that would help improve a program and provide additional information that might complement information on website utilization. The use of web-based surveys or quick feedback ("How helpful was this article?") would be helpful at this stage.

Tier 4, the *progress-toward-objectives stage*, focuses on "determining whether the program is successful in meeting its goals." This might include user reports of knowledge, attitude, or behavioral change or anecdotes and success stories that attribute change to the program. Most of the evaluations cited previously rely on individual self-reports of the usefulness or impact of a web-based program and fall into this category.

Although not addressed by Steimle and Duncan (2004), another object of attention at this stage would be an assessment of how successfully disseminated or visible the site might be. This can be thought of as an assessment of relative impact of a site in comparison to other sites that might have similar objectives. A quick and dirty assessment might include an examination of page rank in a Google search (using keywords that you think should bring up a particular site). It could be argued that this method assesses relevance or visibility by taking into account the extent that other sites link to a target site. For these types of assessments, developers will be faced with trying to make sense of their results. Often, inferences about whether some number or statistic is "good enough" or "needs improvement" can be made only when compared to the ranking, visibility, relevance, or centrality of other sites. Even here, however, the developer will need to define the appropriate universe for comparison. One developer might feel that it is unfair to compare the relative impact or visibility of a site developed by an educational institution (with a meager budget) with a commercial site funded by a major corporation or federal agency. Another developer might reason that consumers may not initially care about these considerations when doing a search on the web and that a site must compete for visibility with all other sites. These developers would have quite different universes for comparison, and while the actual performance of their sites might be similar, their relative performances based on comparisons might be quite different.

Tier 5, the *website impact stage*, focuses on long-term outcomes that might use experimental or quasi-experimental methods. Although a systematic treatment outcome model that uses a pre-post comparison group design with random assignment might be the ultimate test of the effectiveness of a web-based program, Jacobs (1988) points out that only certain types of "mature" programs might warrant this kind of effort. At this stage, a developer might consider what the most appropriate model for evaluation might be by thinking about how one might evaluate comparable or analogous offline programs or resources. For example, if the site provides unstructured, on-demand content that consists primarily of text in short articles, comparable offline analogs might include fact sheets or brochures, newsletters, magazine articles, or popular trade or self-help books. How would these types of resources be evaluated? Would one expect a website to have the same impact as an intensive, long-term intervention that uses multiple methods and supportive relationships with professionals and peers and is based on evidence-based principles?

Most of the evaluations previously noted rely on self-reports of the usefulness or impact of a web-based program by users who have selected to use these programs. A few studies have tried to control for selection by using experimental or quasi-experimental methods. For example, Duncan and his colleagues (2009) compared the impact of a web-based marriage education course to a face-to-face course and a control group; these researchers found that both programs produced comparable positive changes in marriage relationships. After randomly assigning parents to a web-based resource or control group, Deitz and colleagues (2009) found that the parents who used the web resource had greater knowledge of mental health issues relevant to adolescents and reported greater self-efficacy for managing these issues.

● CONCLUSION

For family life educators, the use of technology could make this the best of times but also brings the potential to easily make it the worst of times. While technology provides a wealth of opportunities to both consumers and providers of information, it provides greater power to consumers who can afford to view information as a commodity. An important issue to family life educators and other information providers is whether they can add value to information that could easily be obtained from a variety of sources. In the past, educators may have had the advantage and luxury of relying on certain badges of credibility (educational credential, affiliation with a university or organization, claims of being research based, etc.) or having relationships of trust to market a limited resource to familiar audiences. The increased availability of information makes it essential that educators explore and perhaps embrace some of the methods used by commercial providers and marketers to engage new audiences who will make the final judgment about whether an educational program is credible and useful and whether a provider can be trusted to provide useful information in the future.

● EXPLORATIONS

1. Perform an Internet search on "family life education" or visit some of your favorite family life sites. Using the web credibility criteria outlined in the chapter, assess the credibility of the sites. Which sites do you trust? What could be done to enhance the credibility of the sites?

2. Visit your organization's website. Assess the freshness of the content. Schedule an appointment with the webmaster for your site or one of interest. Ask about policies and procedures for keeping content up-to-date.

3. Develop an evaluation plan for an FLE website or web course that is of interest to you. Using the five-tier approach discussed in the chapter, determine what information needs to be collected at each tier. Consider who and how the information can be collected. Determine an approximate timeline.

CHAPTER 13

WORKING WITH THE MEDIA IN FAMILY LIFE EDUCATION

Tonya Fischio

The Air Force would never send a pilot to fly an F-16 without hours of instruction, study, and training. However, millions of people take a seat in the cockpit of family life having previously only ridden as a passenger. Not only do they lack formal training, but there is no instruction manual in the glove compartment to refer to. While some figure it out as they go, others are headed straight for destruction, hoping to find the eject button before impact.

Unfortunately, family life education (FLE) professionals cannot be at the other end of each headset offering suggestions, guidance, and encouragement. They can, however, use a very powerful communications tool to reach millions of these volunteer pilots—the media.

The most common traditional media outlets include newspaper, magazine, television, and radio. However, over the past several years, very influential "new media" or social media have entered the stage. These new media include blogs, podcasts, Facebook, Twitter, and the next big thing that is inevitably just around the corner.

The new media allow FLE professionals to get their message out to their intended audiences directly without having to go through a gate-keeper (i.e., reporter, editor) who can change the messaging or even stop it by choosing not to run a story. Another advantage of the new media is the ability to use content in multiple formats through RSS feeds. Once you create content, you use it in a Tweet, on your Facebook page, in your blog, and on your website. In addition, any individual who likes the information you post can share it instantly with hundreds of their "friends." The viral nature of this new media makes it a very valuable communication tool.

One of the drawbacks of the new media is that information posted is typically not seen as credible as information distributed through traditional media. It is therefore recommended to use both traditional and new media. Pitch your information to traditional media while spreading the message through new media. If traditional media pick up on your information, then use the new media to spread the story again.

A second drawback is the transitional nature of the new media. The landscape of new media is changing daily with new players coming on the scene trying to push the king off the hill. The rules and etiquette change just as frequently. However, most sound concepts for working with traditional media also apply to the new media and will be the primary focus of this chapter.

● MASS MEDIA AND FAMILY LIFE EDUCATION

Family life educators have a wealth of information that can change lives, strengthen families, and improve society. The challenge comes in getting this accumulated intellect, research, and experience out to those who can implement it in their lives. The mass media are an effective tool family life educators can use. While it has great promise, there are also potential limitations that must be taken into consideration. Part of the promise of mass media is signaled by the amount of family materials available for public consumption. For example, it is estimated that there are over 1,500 parenting books in print, comprising 20% of the psychology market, and over 200 magazines that devote themselves to parenting and family matters (Simpson, 1997). These numbers do not include the magazines that occasionally feature such material. Additional advantages of mass media include the capability to reach many people at once as well as the findings that media can and do influence behavior (Simpson, 1997).

But there are also limitations. As far-reaching as mass media are, they have only the capability to provide a narrow scope. Media are confined by the length of sound bites and print inches. In addition, parenting advice offered through media channels is often confusing and conflicting (Simpson, 1997). Some experts favor a more permissive parenting approach and trumpet their philosophy, while others just as loudly proclaim that parents need to reassert authority. Because of the potential for success as well as failure when using mass media channels, family life educators need specific guidelines to follow as they navigate the challenges and realize the promises of mass media communication.

UNDERSTANDING TRADITIONAL MEDIA: ● WALK A MILE IN THEIR SHOES

Deadlines! Deadlines! Deadlines!

You've been up since 4 a.m. and you're on the air in 30 minutes with a breaking story for the morning news. Your source hasn't returned your calls. It is time to move to Plan B. "Four, three, two, one, and you are on the air." Sorry, missed opportunity for your original source. Next time you won't waste your time calling him to begin with.

Your newspaper story is due to the editor by 4 p.m. To present a well-rounded story, you need a source to represent another viewpoint. Who do you call? Not the guy who interrupted you while you were rushing to meet yesterday's deadline. He insisted on rambling on about a release he just sent that had no relevance to your area of focus. Instead, you remember a source you previously used who returned your phone calls promptly, provided an insightful perspective, and even recommended another source.

Media representatives are always under a deadline—one that is typically measured in minutes and hours rather than days or weeks. And, with increased online presence, journalists are now expected to feed the Internet beast regularly as well (Adalian, 2009).

There is no time for writer's block, pushy publicity seekers, or unresponsive sources. If media representatives leave you a message, call them back as soon as possible. If, however, you are calling for your own purposes, always ask if they are on deadline. If they are, ask when you should call back. The last thing you want to do is annoy media representatives dealing with deadlines. Such actions will most likely get your name remembered—along with a loud alarm shouting, "Royal pain . . . avoid this person!"

It is easier to be respectful of deadlines when you know when they are—so ask. If you don't have the opportunity to ask, generally mornings are best. Unless a media representative indicates otherwise, avoid trying to make phone contact during the afternoon. This is not applicable to contacting bloggers, who are not on deadline and write posts to their blog when the ideas are flowing.

Information Flood

Every day, media representatives are bombarded with information coming from all directions: phone, e-mail, fax, courier, Facebook, and so on. While technological advances have made it possible for the media to gather and share information in a matter of seconds instead of days, these advances have also created a mountain of information for each representative to sift through. As it would take more than a full-time job to carefully review all the information, media representatives have developed strategies to weed out nonessential information. To keep your release from landing in the recycle bin, you need to be aware of the strategies they use and then appeal to their sense of news. The media's first approach to assessing how newsworthy the information is relies on general industry guidelines.

Newsworthy Guidelines

Information has to fit into only one of the following categories to be considered newsworthy; however, the more categories it fits, the more likely it is to receive coverage.

1. *Proximity.* These are "local" stories, where information is relevant to an audience in a specific area or region targeted by the publication or broadcast station. Sometimes media representatives are willing to cover a story that seems out of proximity if a local angle is present. For example, when Arizona implemented a new immigration law, the news was covered on the *TODAY Show* as well as in the local media of several states due to talk of proposed immigration legislation in those areas.

2. *Timeliness.* An event happening today is fresh; one that happened a day or two ago is already old news. Occasionally, major events have a 2-day life span; however, this is the exception rather than the rule. Research published in the current issue of a peer-reviewed journal is timely; a study published in the previous issue is usually past its prime.

3. *Value/importance.* What kind of impact will the information have on the media outlet's audience? How many people will be affected? Who is involved (prominent figures add to newsworthiness)?

4. *Conflict/controversy.* Conflict and controversy are natural magnets for media outlets. While most companies or organizations want to avoid controversy, sometimes it can play to their advantage. For example, while communities were deciding how to deal with the H1N1 virus, Clorox capitalized on the public's fear and increased product sales by touting Clorox Wipes as a way to keep the virus away from your family.

5. *Unusual.* The unexpected, remarkable, rare, strange, and even outstanding people or situations can merit media coverage. A Colorado family's experimental runaway balloon riveted the nation for several hours when authorities feared a child was on board.

6. *Human interest.* Audiences appreciate stories that have an emotional appeal. Often these stories introduce elements the audience can relate to, inspiring them and subtly encouraging action. A mother who chooses to leave her professional career to stay at home with her children may not seem like breaking news. However, when presented with the rising trend of the modern 1950s woman, her transition back into a full-time homemaker role is the perfect human interest story. Many FLE stories may fit well into this category.

Although general guidelines are established to determine how newsworthy a potential article is, you can never escape a certain level of subjectivity. No matter how objectively reporters try to handle information, news decisions are influenced by reporters' backgrounds, previous experiences, and personal judgments. Unfortunately, this leaves you with no guarantee for media coverage. Your job is to make sure your information fits clearly within at least one of the given criteria.

News is tomorrow's history done up in today's neat package. News is the best record we have of the incredible meanness and the magnificent courage of man. . . . News is the timely, concise, and accurate report of an event; it is not the event itself. Mitchel Charney Reporting. (Calvert, 2000, p. 13)

● WORKING WITH THE MEDIA: PLAYING ON THE SAME TEAM

Mutually Beneficial Relationships

"Many reports grow to rely upon credible communicators at universities and nonprofit agencies almost like field correspondents. They count on their sources to keep them abreast of the latest trends and steer them to front-page stories" (Calvert, 2000, p. 15).

Just as you need the media to get your message out, the media need you, but don't expect them to admit it as readily. How do you get media representatives to recognize the value you can contribute to their job as a trusted source they seek after?

The first step is to build a relationship. Identify the local media representatives with whom you want to work and invite them to lunch. Some representatives do not accept lunches or are not allowed to by their employer. In such cases, arrange to meet them without the food or to have a tour of their bureau. One-on-one meetings are the perfect opportunity to put faces with names for both parties. Remember to ask questions. Find out what kind of stories media representatives look for. Are they more interested in human interest stories or only the latest research? Do they like stories that offer advice to the readers? Do they prefer to write feature or a straight news stories? Once you have a greater understanding of what the media representative is looking for, have a conversation about how your organization can help facilitate the representative's needs.

After a relationship is established, it is important to maintain that relationship and become a valuable source. "Great PR people turn themselves into sources rather than gatekeepers. If a PR person is a possible source for a scoop, rather than someone who is there to confirm or deny information, then that PR person is suddenly a lot more important in our world" (Adalian, 2009). You also add value by providing media with everything they need, including all relevant facts, links, photos, graphics, quotations and access to experts, and compelling reasons to write the story (BurrellesLuce, 2009).

A few other media etiquette tips include the following:

- Respond quickly to media inquiries.
- Send thank you cards for coverage received and at other appropriate times.
- Recommend another expert or source when you don't have the information or simply think it would be helpful.

- Tell the truth at all times, without exception (nothing burns bridges with the media more quickly than an untruthful or evasive response).
- Never exaggerate your qualifications, accreditation, or title.

Information Tools

The media are dependent on information they receive from outside sources. There are a variety of tools employed to distribute information to the media. Each tool has its own purpose, advantages, and disadvantages. You must become familiar with the various tools in order to effectively select the one that fits your message. We cover the following tools in this section: press kit, press release, column article, radio program, and letter to the editor or opinion editorial.

Press Kit

A press kit is a package for media representatives of written materials created to introduce and provide background on your company, organization, program, or service. Press kits may be distributed to media representatives prior to a major event, with a release announcing the launch of a new program, when you meet with media representatives during the relationship-building phase, or upon request. A press kit may contain (but is not limited to) the following materials:

- Fact sheet or backgrounder
- Current release
- Biography sheet
- Recent media clips
- Brochures/pamphlets

Fact sheet or backgrounder. A fact sheet is a one-page, brief overview of a company, organization, program, or issue. It must contain the 5Ws and 1H: who, what, when, where, why, and how. Fact sheets are written in third person in a very direct, concise manner, implementing an outline format, with each section of information easily identified (see Figure 13.1). Readers must be able to find the specific information they are looking for without having to read the entire document. You may customize information sections according to your needs.

CONTACT: Tom Holman
(801) 422-6704
RELATE@byu.edu

RELATE

FACT SHEET

PURPOSE

To help strengthen marital and premarital relationships by identifying and evaluating specific strengths and challenges in the relationship.

HISTORY

Developed at the BYU Family Studies Center, RELATE was released in 1997 and is the third version of a comprehensive relationship instrument developed by the Marriage Study Consortium. The first version, called Marital Inventory, was developed in 1980. Tens of thousands of couples and individuals have completed one of the three versions of the question-naire in the last 20 years.

The framework of RELATE is based on the comprehensive review of research regarding the premarital predictors of marital quality from the 1930s to today.

FEATURES

- Covers more than 60 aspects of the relationship and 100% of the pre-marital predictors, **making it the most comprehensive relationship assessment tool of its kind.**

- Evaluates relationships in four major categories: personality and values, support from family and friends, communication and conflict resolution; and family background.

- Provides a four-section report with interpretive graphs, charts, and an assessment of problem areas.

- Easy to take and administer.

COST

$5 per person/$10 per couple

AVAILABLE

Mail: RELATE Institute
1041 L JFSB
Brigham Young University
Provo, UT 84602
Telephone: (801) 422-4359
E-mail: relate@byu.edu
Internet: https://www.relate-institute.org/

Figure 13.1   Sample Fact Sheet

A backgrounder is longer than a fact sheet, provides more details, and is written in a traditional paragraph format rather than the outline format of a fact sheet. The backgrounder may provide additional history of an organization or issue.

Current release. A press kit may contain one general release about the company, organization, program, or issue, or it may contain several releases recently distributed to local media. (More details regarding the format, writing, and distribution of releases are included in the forthcoming "Writing Guidelines" section).

Biography sheet. A biography sheet provides background on an individual who may be a spokesperson, expert, presenter, researcher, or other individual whom a media representative may use as a resource. Information may include current position, educational background, published research or areas of expertise, awards, and professional credentials. "Its purpose is to describe the individual's expertise in a credible way; to make the spokesperson or employee believable in the eyes of the readers" (Derelan, Rouner, & Tucker, 1994, p. 66).

Recent media clips. Media clips are copies of articles that feature information you provide to the media or that mention your organization. If you are distributing the press kit to local media, then local clips are sufficient. However, if you are distributing the kit to national outlets, including only local clips may diminish the impact. Media clips serve to illustrate the newsworthiness of your content. If you intend to distribute a media clip in mass quantities, you need to contact the original outlet and receive permission. Some may require that you submit your reprint request in writing.

Brochures/pamphlets. Include any brochures or pamphlets you have printed about your organization or program. Although these printed materials are general and may target a different audience, they still provide valuable information that the media may find of interest.

Press Release

Writing and distributing a press release to media outlets is the most common method for providing information and breaking into the news network. Although you may be able to pique a media representative's interest in a story or topic through social media posts, it is the press release that provides the media representative with enough substantive material to determine whether or not to write an article.

Make sure all releases fit at least one of the newsworthy categories provided earlier in the chapter. It is also important to follow the standard format for releases, which is presented in this section.

Standard release format. See Figure 13.2 for a sample release using the following format guidelines:

- Use company or organization letterhead. If you do not have letterhead, include the organization's name, address, e-mail, website, and telephone number at the top of the first page.
- Place contact information for the individual handling media inquiries in the top right corner. Include name, phone number, and e-mail address.
- Center a headline that catches the attention and provides insight into the content of the release.
- Use a larger font for the headline than you use for the text. Headlines are also often set in bold type.
- Include the date the information is released and the city of origination in parentheses before the first sentence of the text.
- Indent all paragraphs five spaces.
- Use double spacing.
- Limit the "lead," your door opener, to the first one or two paragraphs.
- The body of the release fills in all remaining details. It typically applies the principle of the inverted pyramid, providing information in descending order of importance.
- Limit the release to two pages when possible, printed only on one side.
- At the bottom of page 1, center "-more-," indicating there is an additional page. If you choose to ignore the two-page limit, continue to center "-more-" at the bottom of each page except the final page.
- Include the page number (i.e., -2-, 2-2-2, or Page 2) at the top of each page following the first page.
- Center "###" at the bottom of the final page, indicating there is no more information.

Headline. The headline is a short, catchy summary of the information presented in the release. It does not have to be written as a complete sentence, and it does not include a period at the end. Headlines are the bait to entice media representatives into reading the release. Media representatives may scan several releases, reading only the headlines.

CONTACT INFORMATION

Elizabeth Thompson
MRDAD.COM
Visit Our Site
866-836-6255
Email us Here

New Book Gives Men the Tools and Support
They Need to Be the Best Dads Ever

Announcing the release of the essential resource for new dads. This new book gives dads the tools, support, and encouragement they need to be the best dads possible.

(San Francisco, CA—June 14, 2004) Fatherhood expert Armin Brott's groundbreaking book, THE NEW FATHER: A DAD'S GUIDE TO THE FIRST YEAR, has been completely revised, updated, and expanded. The new edition features the latest research on hundreds of topics, from what's going on at the hospital right after childbirth to how a dad can support his partner when she's having trouble breastfeeding. THE NEW FATHER: A DAD'S GUIDE TO THE FIRST YEAR includes updated advice for dads in the military and others who are separated from their babies, information on preemies and multiples, and specific guidance for adoptive, divorced, and older dads. It also provides invaluable information and practical tips on such issues as:

- The baby's physical, intellectual, verbal, and social development
- Understanding fathers' emotional and psychological development
- Analyzing the baby's temperament
- Planning finances and choosing the right life insurance policy
- Understanding how the new mom is feeling and how the baby will change your relationship
- Being involved even if you're only able to see your baby for a short time every day
- Juggling work and family
- Introducing the baby to reading, music, and even art

  "Becoming a father is one of the most dramatic changes a man will ever experience," says Brott. "And the first year of fatherhood is critical, because that's when the initial bonds between father and child form and the foundation of a lifelong relationship is built."

  Written with the same thoroughness, accessibility, and humor that have made Brott's NEW FATHER series the most popular fatherhood books in the country, THE NEW FATHER: A DAD'S GUIDE TO THE FIRST YEAR (paperback, $12.95, hardcover, $18.95) incorporates the latest scientific research, the author's personal experiences, and those of the hundreds of new dads he's interviewed. The series, which also includes the best-seller THE EXPECTANT FATHER, is the gold standard in its field. And with over one million copies sold, Brott's books are the essential resource for new dads—and moms—everywhere. For additional information, review copies, or to schedule an interview with Armin Brott, contact Elizabeth Thompson at MrDad.com

# # #

Figure 13.2   Sample Press Release

Lead. If the headline is the bait, then the lead is the hook. From the lead, media representatives determine if the information is newsworthy and significant enough to investigate. The lead must raise public need, concern, or interest and leave media representatives eager for more information. If you don't have a good lead, you might as well not waste your time writing the remainder of the release, because no one will look at it.

There are two kinds of releases and thus two kinds of leads—the straight news story and the feature story. A release for a straight news story is direct and to the point. Straight news stories and leads are good for conferences, conventions, professional meetings, awards, new developments, some research, and other breaking news. The lead for such a story should contain the 5Ws and 1H: who, what, where, when, why, and how. The most important of these six elements should be included in the first paragraph; the remaining elements may follow in the second paragraph. The lead should contain the climax or conclusion of the story, allowing subsequent paragraphs to fill in the details. Supporting materials may include examples, quotes, statistics, and other facts that build the story. Write a release knowing that you will most likely not get in the last word as most readers stop long before the last paragraph.

Historical Note: The media first implemented the concept of the inverted pyramid during the Civil War as field correspondents sent their stories via telegraph. After numerous stories were interrupted due to the enemy cutting communication lines or the system simply malfunctioning, correspondents began sending the most vital information over the wire first. This allowed important information to be relayed to the waiting public regardless of whether or not some of the supporting details were received.

(Anderson & Itule, 2003, p. 44)

A feature story or soft news must also answer who, what, where, when, why, and how; however, this information does not necessarily need to be included in the feature's lead. Features are commonly about people, which lend them perfectly to marriage, family, and human development stories. When writing a lead for a feature story, search for a human interest angle that the audience can relate to. You want to make them feel and generate emotion as much as possible. An effective feature lead uses narrative, descriptive language, and mental imagery, composing words to develop a picture in the audience's mind. However, be careful not to use too many descriptive or flowery words. Strong verbs are often more effective than an abundance of adjectives. Once the lead captures attention, the supporting information paragraphs must follow with the details.

Following is an example of a feature lead that captures its audience's attention and draws them into the story:

> With a wave of the wand and a dance in the night, Cinderella found herself in the arms of Prince Charming and they lived happily ever after . . . maybe. We missed the follow-up story, but according to the 20 years of research, the fantasy was most likely locked in the attic with the glass slippers.
>
> While many enjoy their Cinderella moment as they are swept off their feet, they often find that marriage doesn't chase their problems away with the stepmother. Unresolved issues linger longer, much longer, than the echoing of the wedding bells.

You may also use anecdotes or create a scenario to capture the reader's attention. If you can involve the readers in the story, they are more likely to read on to the next paragraph. As a feature lead typically cannot stand alone, make sure to indicate its significance. The remaining body of the release often presents the information in descending order of importance.

Quotations. Quotations are an essential element to every release. An actual statement from an expert or third party lends credibility to the presented information. Media representatives often look for interesting sound bites to add interest and personality to a story. By providing them with such sound bites, you are more likely to get your message across your way. A direct quotation is the only information from your release that has to be printed verbatim if the media representative chooses to use it. To increase the likelihood of a quotation's inclusion in a media story, write specific, vivid, descriptive statements that reflect the source's personality. Make sure the quotation contains accurate information and that it is easy to understand. If a statement sounds too academic, uses jargon not familiar to the average reader, or belabors a point, it will not be used. Incorporate a quotation into the first page of a release and continue to moderately use them throughout. Use transition paragraphs to lead into a quotation as well as to separate two quotations.

Distribution. Once a release is written, share it. Time the distribution of a release to go out simultaneously through both social media and traditional media. For social media, post it immediately to your website so search engines may begin to pick it up. Use RSS feeds so any subscriber gets an immediate update. Send out a Tweet and post a teaser to your Facebook fan page all driving your audience back to the full release on your webpage. Allow the viral nature of social media to spread the word.

Identify which type(s) of traditional media you want to distribute your release to: daily newspapers, weekly community papers, magazines, specialty publications, television/radio, and so on. Each type of media has advantages and disadvantages.

Daily newspapers have a greater circulation and reach a broad range of people; however, the number of subscribers who actually read the paper daily is significantly lower than the circulation numbers imply. Also, of those who do read the paper, studies indicate that they read approximately one fourth of the paper, skipping a majority of information. Dailies are also inundated with information, causing many stories to go uncovered.

Weekly community newspapers have a smaller circulation, but they have a more loyal audience. Weeklies are also more likely to print a release verbatim, as they have a smaller staff and do not receive the mounds of publicity seekers knocking at their door.

Magazines have a longer shelf life than newspapers—typically 3 to 5 weeks. Feature stories frequent magazine pages, and the articles are typically longer, allowing for greater detail or more sources.

Specialty/trade publications directly target your audience. Also those reading the publication are often actively seeking information.

Television will summarize your information into a sound bite lasting between 30 and 90 seconds. Due to the limited time, television stories focus on the highlights and have to eliminate much of the detailed information. Television is also interested in strong visuals.

Radio seeks a local connection to the issues it covers and often allows sources to share their message points by participating in a live, on-air talk show program. However, if your information is simply covered in the news segment, it is subject to the same time limitations as in broadcast television news (approximately 30 seconds or five sentences).

Once you have determined the type(s) of media you want to distribute your release to, create a media list with name, address, phone number, and e-mail address. This information may be found online or through Bacon's media guides found in many libraries. If your library does not have a copy, you may order your own at cision.com.

There are also newswire services, such as PR Newswire, willing to distribute your release for a fee. Contact your local PR Newswire representative through the company's website, e-mail, or toll-free number: www.prenewswire .com, information@prnewswire.com (telephone 1-888-776-0942).

Newspaper Column Article

As an expert, you can work with your local newspaper to print a regular column on a given general topic (e.g., family, marriage, parenthood). If the paper agrees to run the column after they have seen a sample of your writing, be prepared to generate fresh ideas constantly. You can't just decide one week that you are too busy or that you don't have an idea to write about. You are committed. Once you have agreed to write a regular column, start keeping an idea folder for those times when your mind is in a drought for ideas.

Column articles often offer advice insights, answer questions, and sometimes simply entertain with anecdotes and personal experiences related to the topic. A column is a great opportunity to share your personal yet professionally informed opinion with a large number of people whom you otherwise would never reach. Column writing is casual, like a letter from one friend to another. Always promote your column on your Facebook and Twitter accounts.

Column articles are similar to blogs in many ways. If you are going to go through the effort to write a weekly column, with minimal additional effort, you can also share your expertise through a blog.

You may be surprised at the impact a simple column article may have. One family life educator had a regular biweekly article called "Family Matters" that was sent out via university communications services and ran in an average of 13 Montana newspapers per release, as well as in a few regional papers. His photo accompanied the articles, so he was occasionally recognized as he traveled the state. At a conference in Billings, a marriage and family therapist from a remote rural area approached the educator and told him that articles the educator wrote were leading people to realize that changes in family life were needed and they were coming to the therapist for counseling.

Radio Programs

Radio programs are short, prerecorded informational segments or a question-and-answer program focusing on a specific topic. For example, Zion's Bank of Utah records a radio program featuring a different local business each day. The program does not promote the bank other than mentioning that it is the sponsor of the program. Another example is Intermountain Health Care recording a daily health tip.

Radio scripts follow a basic structure, including an introduction, a teaser or headline, the main information or advice, a billboard, and a closing, including identification. Here is an example of a prerecorded radio script:

From the Montana State University Extension Service, here's Steve Duncan with a tip on balancing work and family.

Ever feel bombarded when you come home at the end of a hard day? Try taking 15 minutes to unwind before attacking the new demands of home. It may be one of the best things you can do for your family. The shift from work to family is largely mental, but there are some physical things you can do to help it along.

Before you leave work, make a list of everything you need to do the next day. This will help you leave those tasks behind and clear your mind of home activities.

Have a pre-dinner snack such as fruit, vegetables and dip, cheese and crackers, or a cup of soup. This will stave off that starving feeling and you won't have to jump immediately into preparing dinner.

Play your favorite music, get a cool drink, and relax while you read the mail.

Walking, bike riding, swimming, or playing tennis may offer time with your spouse or children, as long as it relaxes you.

I'm Steve Duncan, Family and Human Development Specialist, with the MSU Extension Service.

Letter to the Editor or Opinion Editorial

If you have a strong opinion about a specific topic, especially one covered in a publication's editorial pages or by a radio talk show host, you're always welcome to submit a letter to the editor. As with all press materials, there is no guarantee that your letter will be printed or read on the air. If the editor does decide to include your letter, it will be printed or read verbatim. Keep all letters to the editor short. Get directly to your point of view and don't ramble. Sign the letter and include your city of residence.

Opinion editorials are similar to letters to the editor because you have control of the content. One advantage of an opinion editorial is that you can expand on your point of view and little more with 500 to 750 words. One disadvantage is that op-ed articles are harder to place. Not all papers include space for them. Check the paper you want to send an op-ed to. If it has an op-ed section, send it with your title, affiliation, and contact information at the end of the op-ed.

● WRITING GUIDELINES

Regardless of the communications tool(s) you select to distribute to the media and reach your end target audience, you need to follow some basic writing guidelines. First, all media materials are written according to the

Associated Press (AP) Stylebook. Some common AP rules include not using a comma before the last item in a series of three or more, spelling out all numbers fewer than 10, not capitalizing official titles such as president or vice president of individuals in a company if the title follows the given name, and using only an individual's last name after the first reference. These are only a few of the hundreds of guidelines listed in the stylebook. Copies of the *AP Stylebook* are available at most bookstores. You can also write and request to purchase a copy from Associated Press, AP News Features Department, 450 W. 33rd St., New York, NY 10001.

Second, write tight, short, and clearly. Sentences should average 15 to 20 words. Once you get 30 or more words in one sentence, you start to sacrifice readability. Break up long sentences with more periods. If this is not possible, use a dash or colon to create a bite-sized thought. A sentence shorter than 20 words may be used on occasion if it adds impact, but be careful not to lose your message. Keep your paragraphs short as well. Media outlets print most information in columns. A long paragraph can seem uninviting in such a narrow space. Pick up a newspaper and look at the length of the paragraphs. Although they vary from one sentence to several sentences, they remain relatively short. Remember, space is a premium, so there is no place for redundancy, an abundance of adjectives, or nonessential information.

Third, use common, simple words. Two simple words are often more readable than one complex or technical word. This is sometimes difficult for individuals who are used to writing for peer-reviewed journals. Remember, when writing for the media, your audience is not composed of colleagues who are familiar with the topic and issues. Rather, you are trying to reach individuals, parents, and families who may have no background related to the topic but who are interested in and need the information. If there is a word that you would not typically use when talking outside of work, then don't use it when writing for the media.

Fourth, use the active voice, where the subject acts upon the object. The active voice can help keep your sentences short as well as maintain interest. It is always better to demonstrate an action rather than just tell about it. Also, active verbs invite the reader into the story more than *to be* verbs.

Finally, edit and rewrite all press materials. There is always a better way to write a sentence or explain a concept. Don't become so attached to your first draft that you can't scrap it for a better one. As you read through your press materials, look for ways to shorten, simplify, and add action. Imagine that you'll receive a dollar for every word you eliminate without changing the meaning. It may surprise you how many wasted words were in the first draft. Double-check all facts and name spellings.

Robert Gunnings (1968): Ten Principles of Clear Writing

1. Keep sentences short on the average.
2. Prefer the simple to the complex.
3. Prefer the familiar word.
4. Avoid unnecessary words.
5. Put action into your verbs.
6. Write the way you talk.
7. Use terms your reader can picture.
8. Tie in with your reader's experience.
9. Make full use of variety.
10. Write to express, not to impress.

Broadcast writing employs many of the same basic writing guidelines as print; however, there are a few differences. Primarily, broadcast writing is written for the ear, not the eye. It has a very limited amount of time to capture and maintain the audience's attention while simultaneously giving information. Visual images are created with words to help the audience experience the story, not just hear it. Simple, direct visual language paints word pictures.

When writing for broadcast, facts are not presented in descending order but rather are incorporated into a complete package that holds the audience's attention throughout. It is essential that the information is presented in a fluid, easy manner for the viewer or listener to follow. Scripts must also be written for easy reading by the broadcaster. Other writing guidelines that pertain to television and radio writing include the following:

- Use a conversational tone and write as if you were talking to a friend. You need to write with simple, common words that the viewer or listener will understand the first time. Broadcast audiences do not have the option to go back and reread information they missed or did not understand as print audiences do.
- Keep all sentences short. In print you want to vary the length of your sentences for interest. However, using short sentences in broadcast ensures that the meaning is not lost.
- Simplify and round off complicated numbers. "Three and a quarter million dollars" is easier for viewers or listeners to hear than is "three

million, two hundred and forty-three thousand, nine hundred and seventy-five dollars" ($3,243,975).

- Use the phonetic spelling of uncommon or complicated words and names. Viewers and listeners will never see the phonetic spelling, but it helps the broadcaster pronounce it properly.
- Summarize statements instead of using quotation marks.
- Place the title of an individual before his or her name.
- Avoid abbreviations to eliminate confusion. Only use acronyms that are more common than the actual name (i.e., FBI, NCAA, CNN). When it is necessary to use a common acronym, place a hyphen between each letter (i.e., F-B-I).

Writing for Television and Radio

First Sentence:
The Grabber: Summarize the story in one sentence in a way that entices the viewer or listener to want to hear and see more.

Second Sentence:
Visualization: Describe the video the viewer sees on the screen for television or use words to create the video in the listener's mind for radio. Enhance the visual image or create the visual image.

Third Sentence:
The Facts: List the important facts about what happened in a short sentence.

Fourth Sentence:
The Setup: Set up the sound bite or actuality. In radio, you need to use the person's name and title so we understand from whom we'll hear and why we should care. In television, you can use a blind lead.

Sound Bite or Actuality: Select the portion of the interview to tell the story. This should not run longer than 10 to 20 seconds. It should not contain facts, because the reporter can tell the facts. It should contain emotional or editorial statements the reporter cannot make.

The Fifth Sentence:
The Big Finish: Summarize what will happen or what will likely happen in the future because of the foregoing information.

Source: Courtesy of Robert Walz, KUTV Channel 2 reporter and BYU Professor of Communications.

● MEDIA INTERVIEWS

Now that you have learned how to build relationships with media representatives, catch their attention with newsworthy information, select the right press materials, and write clearly, you can sit back and relax, right? Sure, you can, that is, until a media representative calls you wanting a "live" interview. Those beads of sweat appearing on your forehead are for a good reason. You have seen too many people stammer around not knowing what to say or, worse yet, get trapped by an unexpected, leading question. The thought of vice presidential candidate Sarah Palin's notoriously bad interview with Katie Couric in 2008 heightens the fears of any new prospective interviewee. What if you make a mistake or sound dumb? Fear is a natural reaction to a request for an interview, but it is a manageable fear with a little research and preparation.

Research

Start by researching the interview medium and environment. Television and radio interviews may be live, with no editing, or taped, allowing the producer to edit at will. Live interviews are more intimidating because there is no room for mistakes. Everything you say and do is seen and/or heard by the audience. However, this may also serve as an advantage, as the producer cannot edit out any comment you want the audience to hear. A taped interview may not make you as nervous, but many of your comments will be cut. You may be disappointed when a half-hour interview results in a 30-second sound bite.

Television

Television interviews are shorter than other media due to the fast-paced nature of television. Each story typically lasts from 30 to 90 seconds. In a television interview, you must pay attention to your appearance and mannerisms.

Radio

On a radio talk show, there are many interruptions. You have to pause for every commercial as well as for scheduled news or traffic and weather breaks. You will also have to listen to the talk show host's comments and opinion in between his or her questions. Many shows allow listeners to phone in with comments and questions. While many callers make valuable contributions, be prepared for the occasional caller who may take you off guard.

Print

Interviews for print media are typically a little longer than broadcast, as the media representative is allotted more space to elaborate on a topic. Some journalists prefer to interview in person, but more are conducting interviews over the phone and asking sources to fax or e-mail additional information. With more time for interviews and more space allotted for the story, you are also more likely to have many of your message points included in the story. Unfortunately, in print media, there is also a greater likelihood of a journalist misquoting you than when you are taped for television or radio. For this reason, it is wise to inform reporters that you are taping the conversation, and they are welcome to reference the recording when they write the story.

Next, research the interviewer. Review material previously produced by the interviewer to get a feel for the type of stories they present. Do they primarily cover controversial issues? Are their stories fair and well rounded or leading and somewhat biased? Do they have a reputation for getting the dirt and asking all the tough questions? It is also appropriate to directly ask interviewers what type of a story they are preparing and who else they are interviewing. Once you understand the direction media representatives want to take the story, you can begin shaping your message.

Preparation

Target Audience

Determine your primary, target audience. Be specific—a "general" audience does not exist. Think about who you want to hear your message so you can direct all comments to the audience rather than the media. If the story is about children coping with divorce, are newlywed couples your target audience? Probably not.

Self-Interest

Once you determine your target audience, identify the audience's self-interest in relation to the topic. What motivates them? Using our first example of children coping with divorce, you decide your target audience is divorced parents or parents in the process of getting a divorce. Their self-interest is dissolving a marriage with the least amount of emotional damage to their children. Now you can develop specific message points tied to the target audience's self-interest.

Primary Message Points

Although you may have many facts you would like to share with your target audience, it is important to try to limit your main message points to three. These three points are what you want your audience to remember if they don't retain anything else. Main message points are not the details but rather general statements that may serve as headings or memory joggers for your supporting information. To help the audience remember your three primary message points, tie them in to the audience's self-interest and repeat them often in an interview. Politicians and talking heads are usually well trained on message repetition and can serve as good examples. The next time you watch a news program, listen to how frequently the individual being interviewed repeats the same sentence. Media representatives often try to elicit a different response by altering the question slightly. However, a well-trained spokesperson will not fall for this trick but will rather stick to the message point and repeat it until the interviewer moves on. The more you repeat a message point, the more likely the audience is to remember and the less likely you are to get off track or to make a comment you regret later. Although you want to stick to your message points, you may support them with additional information, including examples, anecdotes, statistics, and quotes. Remember to repeat, repeat, repeat.

Who is in control of the interview is up to you. Although the interviewer asks the questions, your answers direct the flow of information. If an interviewer tries to take a story in another direction than you prefer, simply come back to your message points. Answer the interviewer's question, followed by a main message. Following are a few examples:

- "Yes (the answer), and in addition (message point)."
- "No (the answer); let me explain (message point)."
- "I don't know about that, but what I do know is (message point)."

Even with repetition, a lot of information is given in an interview. It is important to help your audience remember the main message points by emphasizing and summarizing them. For example:

- "That is interesting, but I think it is most important to remember . . ."
- "It boils down to this . . ."
- "Let me emphasize . . ."
- "It is critical to remember . . ."

Interview Control

To reiterate a main point from the previous section, when you are in an interview situation, get your message points across. An answer plus a key message equals your response. To ensure that the integrity of your message is maintained, it is acceptable to tape an interview. Taping an interview is like taking out misquote insurance. Although it doesn't guarantee that your words will never be taken out of context, it does extend a safety cord for recourse. If this does happen to you, request a retraction or correction statement.

Also, keep your cool at all times. Never act defensive when an interview turns hostile or you are put on the hot seat. If you stay in control and stick to your message points, you maintain credibility with the audience. In addition, know when to stop talking. Experienced media representatives have mastered the power of the "silent pause." They have found that when they allow silence to linger, human nature taunts the individual they are interviewing to fill the pause. It is during these ramblings that the media obtain their juiciest quotes and the interviewee pulls away from message points and may speculate or make a statement that he or she later regrets. Once you have answered the question and stated a key message, then stop and wait for the next question, regardless of how long the silence hangs (it's probably not as long as you think it is anyway).

You need to maintain a high level of energy throughout an interview. A low-key response may be fine in a normal conversation, but it appears negative and boring in a radio or television interview. You should also maintain eye contact with the interviewer and sit erect or even lean forward slightly. Don't fidget; it's annoying. You can, however, use natural hand movements, just not so many that it distracts from your message. Also, don't forget to listen. If you're too busy thinking of what you're going to say next instead of listening, you may miss the boat and say something unrelated or, worse yet, miss an opportunity for a better comment than the one you're rehearsing in your head.

Finally, people wonder what to wear for an interview. Dress in your typical business attire for a print or radio interview. Dress conservatively for a television interview. You don't want what you wear to distract from your message. If you choose to wear a print, keep it simple and unobtrusive. Although it might not be comfortable for a man, allow the station to apply makeup if they offer. You'll be glad you did when you see yourself on the television.

Interview DON'Ts

1. Never say, "No comment." "No comment" means "guilty" to most people who hear it.
2. Never say anything off the record. Assume all microphones are live. The most important rule is to never say anything you don't want to see on TV or read on the front page of a newspaper.
3. Never lie to a reporter.
4. Never lose your temper. Be polite but firm.
5. Never use profanity or slang. Don't tell jokes. Don't say anything that could even remotely be construed to be off color, sexist, or racist. Don't comment on anyone's age, religion, or politics. Tell jokes only if they are self-deprecating.
6. Never say "uh." Drop all the "uhs" from your speech.
7. Never wave your hands. Don't bob and wave your head around. Sit still.
8. Never answer hypothetical questions. Don't speculate. Be specific. Stick to what you know.
9. Never comment on what others have said—particularly if you haven't seen or heard it. Don't verify something that might not be true.
10. Never use doublespeak, government-speak, or jargon. Use numbers in an interesting way. Make your information easy to understand. Personalize your information. Relate it to the reporter or the target audience. Humanize it.
11. Never talk to a reporter without doing your homework. Prepare. Turn the interview into a "sales call."
12. Never stop talking after you've answered a yes or no question. Keep going. Say something like, "Yes, but you should also know . . ." or "No, but let me elaborate. . . ."

Interview DO's

1. Do your homework before you talk to a reporter. Be prepared for the reporter's worst questions with three positive points you want to get across. Practice what you want to say. Remember, you're selling your activity. Talking to a reporter is an "opportunity."
2. Speak in short sentences using plain English. For TV and radio, think in terms of 20- or 30-second answers. This ensures that the reporter will use what you say.

3. Smile. Act like you enjoy what you're doing. Call reporters by their first name; reach out and physically touch the reporter. Look interested in what you're doing.

4. Tell a positive story. You do a lot of good things; tell the reporter about your three positive points.

5. If you don't know the answer, say, "I don't know." If you do know the answer and can't tell it now, tell the reporter when you can give him or her the answer. Refer the reporter to someone who does know the answer or offer to find out who does.

6. If a TV station offers you makeup, accept it. The TV camera will add 10 years and 10 pounds. Remember, the TV pros all wear makeup.

7. Dress conservatively and simply. Be remembered for what you said, not what you wore. Ignore this rule if you're a rock star.

8. Stop talking when you've made your point. Let the reporter worry about empty air space. Stick to your subject. Don't speculate.

9. If a reporter asks several questions in a row, pick the one you want to answer. Or, ask the reporter to repeat the question.

10. Have show-and-tell material. A simple pie chart works well. Have a videotape? Take it too.

11. Take advantage of the opportunity at the end of the interview when the reporter asks if there is anything you'd like to add. Repeat your three positive points and summarize.

SOURCE: Calvert (2000, p. 107).

CONCLUSION ●

Communicating FLE messages through media channels represents tremendous opportunities to reach large audiences. Knowledge of the media and skill at drafting messages for targeted public via print, radio, television, and new media is necessary if family life educators are to have the greatest impact for good.

EXPLORATIONS ●

1. Read the following headlines. Determine which stories are newsworthy and identify the standard criteria you applied to make your decision.

    a. Parenting Workshop to Be Held at Panguitch Civic Center

    b. Las Vegas Chapel of Love Reports an Increase in Wedding Ceremonies

    c. The Modern Day Woman Is Returning Home to a '50s Ideal

    d. Families Beating the Economic Downturn With Staycations

2. Change the following sentences to the active voice:

    a. The shy child was shunned by the kids at the playground.

    b. The premarital assessment will be completed by the couple before they marry.

    c. They were focused on each other's problems before receiving counseling.

3. Simplify and clarify the following sentence: A ubiquitous example is the use of clinical and psychometric diagnoses to account for student's lack of learning.

4. Write a 30-second radio script on a topic related to your field of study. You may elect to write a script for a radio PSA or a radio program.

5. Given the following information:

    a. Identify the target audience.

    b. Identify the three primary message points.

    c. Write an interesting lead that grabs the reader's attention.

Your state is now offering covenant marriage, a legally distinct kind of marriage, in which the marrying couple agrees to obtain premarital counseling and accept more limited grounds for divorce. The covenant marriage laws delineate that marriage is more than just a mere contract between two individuals. The belief is that without marriage, there would be no foundation of family in society and no civilization or progress to follow. The movement intends to promote and strengthen marriages, reduce divorce, curb childbearing outside of marriage, discourage cohabitation, and bolster marriage as an honorable, desirable status. As a law, covenant marriage was technically written neutrally with respect to religion, but it quickly became marked as a religious form of marriage due to its sacred historical background.

CHAPTER 14

WRITING FOR THE LAY AUDIENCE

The written word forms a conversation between a writer and a reader. At times the words may feel like a stern lecture. Other times the conversation may seem pointless, dense, or wrong-headed. Yet, at best, the written conversation expresses the writer's soul, engages and enriches the reader, and builds a bridge between both.

This first part of this chapter will provide suggestions for effective writing. The latter part of the chapter will provide samples of excellent writing in very different styles.

PURPOSES OF WRITTEN MATERIAL ●

I (Goddard) was asked to evaluate a short web course on parenting that was intended for a general audience. Several considerations seemed important in evaluating any stretch of writing.

What is the target audience like? For example, is the audience primarily first-time parents of newborns? Or are there likely to be many readers who are parents of school-age children or teenagers? Are the readers seeking general information, or are the parents seeking answers to specific problems because the website caters to parents of problem teens?

What do the parents already know? What is their previous experience with this website or other parenting materials?

What are the objectives of the course or article? The obvious answer may be "to give parents information that will help them be more effective." But the article may have additional objectives. Maybe a primary objective is to motivate the reader to be a regular visitor to the website. Maybe the article is intended to promote a certain book, program, or product. Maybe the article is intended to challenge a common idea that is presumed to undermine the parents' parenting efforts.

Unfortunately, our writing experiences for university classes often have a very different objective: to prove to professors that we know more than we do. In service of that cause, we may write in great depth and length, using technical jargon and barely related references. Those practices are rarely effective in writing for professors and will surely be unhelpful in writing for a real-world audience.

Evaluating the Course

The title of the course that I reviewed was Identifying Your Parenting Style. The website was designed to help primarily parents of teens who were in trouble. I assumed that the course would provide some process for identifying the readers' parenting style and challenges and would make recommendations for more effective parenting. I was surprised to find that the course was focused on summarizing Diana Baumrind's work. It defined and frequently used terms such as *authoritative, authoritarian,* and *laissez-faire.* The objective seemed to be to enable parents to name and describe Baumrind's categories of parenting.

Such depth and jargon may be more appropriate for a college course than for a lay audience, especially since the terms can be confusing. In writing for a lay audience, we usually want to provide readers with clear understanding and move them fairly quickly to action steps. Extensive background information may not be necessary.

There are many ways to approach the subject. I have a colleague who uses objects to illustrate parenting styles: The marshmallow parent may be sweet but melts under heat and squishes under pressure; the jawbreaker parent may be tough but is brittle and inflexible; the tennis ball parent is flexible but has reasonable boundaries. The useful question is not whether those categories map perfectly onto research designations but whether the idea will be clear, memorable, and useful in moving parents toward actions that are supported by research.

Another approach is to discuss important parenting dimensions. The central dimensions in child guidance are (a) warmth, nurturance, and support, together with (b) monitoring and firmness (see Peterson & Hann,

1999). An effort to educate parents might describe ways to be both warm and firm.

While research provides the skeleton of our recommendations, our real-life experience provides the flesh. From our experiences, we draw stories, metaphors, and an intuitive sense of ways to apply the research. For example, in writing for a lay audience, we might observe that most parents find either warmth or firmness to come more naturally. We can use our strength while developing and managing our weaker side.

TIPS ON WRITING ●

It is tempting to hope that there is some tidy formula for writing effectively for lay audiences. Just as in all processes with humans, there are sensible steps but no magic formulas.

Rico and Volk (1999) have described a "natural" process to turn thoughts into written words. This approach may be especially helpful for those who are daunted by a blank page.

For those who have the words but want guidelines, LaRocque (2003) may be useful. She provides a dozen guidelines to good writing such as keep sentences short, avoid pretensions (don't write as if you were writing for a professor!), use active verbs, and get right to the point. In addition to the dozen guidelines, LaRocque also provides useful help on storytelling. Her book is filled with practical examples from her experience as a writing coach.

In addition to the guides described above, there are other recommendations that make your writing more likely to be effective.

Read Widely to Develop Your Own Style

To become an effective writer, it is useful to be an active reader. Read articles from newspapers and magazines. Note what works for you and what doesn't. Save those that you consider to be both most effective and most similar to the voice you want to develop.

You may favor a lively and irreverent style such as Dave Barry's (1991): "So most married couples, even though they love each other very much in theory, tend to view each other in practice as large teeming flaw colonies" (p. 208).

Carol Tavris's (1989) writing is clear and richly visual: "The individualism of American life, to our glory and despair, creates anger and encourages its release; for when everything is possible, limitations are irksome. When the desires of the self come first, the needs of others are annoying. When we think we deserve it all, reaping only a portion can enrage" (p. 69).

Many readers enjoy the writing of Sam Quick (Quick & Lasueur, 2003): "Peace is still possible in the hustle and bustle of modern life, but it thrives on the quiet times. Preferably in the morning before the activities of the day claim you, cultivate a state of inner quietness. You might read briefly from an inspirational source, enjoy a period of meditation and prayer, or keep a journal about something wonderful and close to your heart" (p. 1).

You may choose to write with the power and directness of Martin Seligman (1991): "Freud's speculations were built on very little observation and a very free use of imagination. He claimed that depression was anger turned against the self. . . . For all its hold over the American (particularly the Manhattan) imagination, I have to say that this view is preposterous" (pp. 10–11).

Some of the passages above were written for an educated and informed audience. They may be too complex for some of the people we serve with family life education (FLE). In many cases, FLE is written to an eighth-grade reading level. LaRocque (2003) has written about writing with simplicity and clarity. She argues that "short words are small, strong, and suited to story telling. . . . We should trust them more" (p. 31).

Each of the authors above has developed a voice that is distinctive and effective for his or her purpose and personality. Martin Seligman would probably not succeed at efforts to write Dave Barry's humor columns. Dave Barry does not have the technical knowledge or disposition to write a thorough treatise such as Tavris has written. Reading widely can help us find and develop our own voices, whether it is closer to one of those above or one very different.

Some writers use a more formal style; some use a more conversational one. Some write objectively. Some feel comfortable with a personal and disclosing style. Just as in all relationships, we use our unique style to deliver a message that speaks to our audience.

It is tempting to recommend one process of writing. Many people recommend a thorough outline. There are others who prefer to let the material lead them to unexpected places. It takes hundreds of hours of experience to develop a writing voice.

In the latter part of this chapter are samples of very different styles of writing about family. You may get ideas for your unique style by examining these samples.

Know Your Audience

It makes a great deal of difference whether your audience is readers of a metropolitan newspaper, a technical company newsletter, or an elderly homemakers' book of hints. It is important to know the audience. But even a thorough demographic profile is not enough. What are the current issues? What is their history (e.g., what are the articles they have previously read? What historical cohort are they a part of?)? What is the culture of their group?

Clearly there are no simple or easily accessible answers to these questions. That is why it is wise to ask questions of members of the group and those who have worked with them or written for them.

I (Goddard) have written articles that I thought were clear and direct. A helpful editor has responded with a multitude of questions: "Who is this person? Why should we trust him?" "What does this word mean in this context?" "What is the background to this idea?" We may get so accustomed to communicating with our professional peers that we lose touch with the language of our audience. A good editor can alert us to communication failures. It can also be useful to have our material read by members of the target audience who are brave enough to be honest.

In some cases, you may be writing for a low-literacy audience. While all the suggestions for writing for lay audiences in general apply to writing for this audience, there are special considerations in writing effectively for those with limited literacy. For additional information on writing for low-literacy audiences, see specialized instructions, such as Gaston and Daniels (n.d.).

In one case, I (Goddard) was asked to prepare a message for Title I parents in a poor, rural Alabama school district. In preparation, I drove to the community, walked around the neighborhoods, asked questions at a convenience store, and interviewed a mother of two children in the school. The experience was humbling. I may know something about research on parenting, but if I do not understand my audience, I am not very likely to help them. Their day-to-day challenges and experiences are very different from mine. I know my message was humbler and I think it was more helpful because of my efforts to understand the audience.

Clearly Define Your Purpose

Very often we have something we want to say but we are not quite sure what it is. It is more a flurry of impressions than a distinct message. Try to express in one sentence exactly what you would like your audience to know, feel, and do. For example, with a workplace newsletter, your objective might be to "challenge old ideas in the area of couple relationships so that the readers will be anxious for more information as delivered through future columns."

In addition to the single-objective statement, it is often very useful to identify two or three supporting ideas per article or chapter: "1. Readers will understand the limitations of frank communication for improving relationships. 2. Readers will understand the importance of kindness in relationships. 3. Readers will be encouraged to identify three ways to effectively show kindness."

Write Simply and Clearly

For our colleagues, it may be effective to write, "Research shows that marital quality and stability is primarily related to the occurrence and maintenance of positive feelings, interactions, and behaviors that promote attraction, closeness, and personal support of another person." How would you communicate the same idea to a lay audience?

The idea could be communicated with a simple statement: "Strong marriages come from finding positive ways of being together." It might also be useful to use an anecdote to illustrate.

Another example: "The famous religious thinker Martin Luther once declared, 'Marriage is the school of love.'" The same idea might be communicated more clearly with the words "Marriage can help us learn valuable lessons about love."

Still another example: "William James, known by some as the father of modern psychology, once stated, 'The deepest craving of human nature is the craving to be appreciated.' In marriage, we long to feel that our partner respects and appreciates us. How can marital partners meet this craving for appreciation in ways that build and strengthen the relationship?" Instead, we could simply ask, "Do people like to be appreciated? How can you show appreciation that supports your partner?"

We can use word-processing programs to help us write simply and clearly. For example, in Word 2007, use the Spelling and Grammar check with the option "readability statistics" checked to assess Flesch-Kincaid reading levels. Aim for a 9th- to 10th-grade reading level.

● EXAMPLES OF EFFECTIVE WRITING

As you read the following examples of writing for a lay audience, notice the distinct characteristics of each piece. Consider those factors that would make it effective for some audiences and less effective for others. You will note that some of the passages are written in a more professional voice and others in a more conversational voice. As you study them, you will probably find that one or more of them feel very comfortable to you. Look for writing that uses a voice you might like to use.

Martha Beck, from *The Joy Diet* (2003), pp. 92–93, 192–193

These days, I'm less like a nurturing, nondirective therapist than a skydiving instructor who stands at the open door of an airplane and methodically shoves terrified students into thin air. Experience has taught me that the way to a joyful life is always fraught with fear, that to find it you must follow your heart's desires right through the inevitable terrors that arise to hold you back. If you don't do this, your life will be shaped by fear, rather than love, and I guarantee, the shape will be narrow and tiny compared with your best destiny.

I once had a client named Pierre who wanted very much to find the right woman but was terrified of rejection. We were both thrilled when Pierre met Emily, the aerobics instructor of his dreams, and their first three dates went beautifully. Then catastrophe struck, at least from Pierre's perspective: Emily called to say she'd have to take a rain check on their next evening out, because her uncle had died and she had to go out of town for the funeral.

"Pretty obvious what's going on, isn't it?" Pierre said after telling me this.

"Um, well, I guess so," I said. "Her uncle died. She has to go to the funeral."

Pierre snorted derisively. "Oh please. It's my hair. She figured out I'm losing my hair." He was so convinced of this that he was planning to end the relationship.

I reacted so strongly to Pierre's biased interpretation of his interaction with Emily (I think I laughed out loud for a full minute) that he decided to do a little research before he passed judgment. He found a website for the newspaper in the town where Emily's uncle had supposedly lived and died. Sure enough, they had run a recent obituary for someone with Emily's surname, and the funeral was on the very day she had claimed to be attending it. Pierre's relationship was back on.

H. Wallace Goddard, an excerpt from "The Cat Door" in *The Great Self Mystery* (1995), a five-part program intended to help adolescents discover and use their gifts

Kesha studied the room wide-eyed. Never had she seen so many gadgets. Sam laughed at her. "Haven't you ever seen a lab before?" Kesha shook her head in amazement. "What do all these things do?"

(Continued)

(Continued)

"My mom's an inventor," Sam explained. "She thinks of new ways of doing things. Like this." Sam led Kesha to a table covered with motors, metal rods, wires, and miniature doors. "Mom is developing an automatic door for cats to enter the house."

Kesha half scowled and half smiled. "That seems so silly."

"Maybe. But even the electric can opener seemed pretty silly years ago," Sam replied.

"But what if some other animals come along? The door will open and you'll have families of armadillos and skunks and possums in the house!"

Sam shrugged. "That's what inventing is all about, I guess. Trying to find some ways to solve old problems without making new ones."

As they continued through the lab, Kesha marveled at all the projects. "And your mom does this for a living?"

"That's right. She has a lab right here in our home and she invents."

"I love the creative part of this, but . . . " Kesha hesitated, "how does her inventing pay all the bills?"

"That's a good question for you to ask her sometime." Sam led the way from the lab through the living room to the kitchen." Here, have a cookie."

Kesha eyed the cookie suspiciously. It looked like a normal chocolate chip cookie. "So, Sam, are you going to be an inventor like your mom?"

Sam looked surprised. "Oh, no! I'm not an inventor! I'm very different from my mom! Mom has all kinds of new ideas and she's great with machines."

"So . . . what are you good at?"

"Hmmmm . . . " Sam thought for a long time. "That's a good question. I'm not sure. But I know I am no good at inventing."

Martin E. P. Seligman, excerpt from Chapter 11, "Love," from *Authentic Happiness* (2002), pp. 185–186

Work can be a source of a level of gratification that far outstrips wages, and by becoming a calling, it displays the peculiar and wondrous capacity of our species for deep commitment. Love goes one better.

The tedious law of *homo economicus* maintains that human beings are fundamentally selfish. Social life is seen as governed by the same bottom-line principles as the marketplace. So, just as in making a purchase or deciding on a stock, we supposedly ask ourselves of another human being, "What is their likely utility for us?" The more we expect to gain, the more we invest in the other person. Love, however, is evolution's most spectacular way of defying this law.

There is a time in life (later, we pray, rather than sooner) that we all go into a tailspin. We age, sicken, or lose our looks, money, or power. We become, in short, a bad investment for future payouts. Why are we not immediately set out on the proverbial ice floe to perish? How is it that we are allowed to limp onward, enjoying life often for many years beyond these times? It is because other people, through the selfishness-denying power of love and friendship, support us. Love . . . is the emotion that makes another person irreplaceable to us. Love displays the capacity of human beings to make commitments that transcend "What have you done for me lately?" and mocks the theory of universal human selfishness. Emblematic of this are some of the most uplifting words it is ever vouchsafed for a person to say: "From this day forward, for better, for worse, for richer, for poorer, in sickness or in health, to love and to cherish until death do us part."

Bill Doherty, from *Take Back Your Marriage* (2001), p. 105

I think of long-term marriage like I think about living in my home state of Minnesota, in Lake Wobegon, perhaps. You move into marriage in the springtime of hope, but eventually arrive at the Minnesota winter with its cold and darkness. Many of us are tempted to give up and move south at this point. We go to a therapist for help. Some therapists don't know how to help us cope with winter, and we get frostbite in their care. Other therapists tell us that we are being personally victimized by winter, that we deserve better, that winter will never end, and that if we are true to ourselves we will leave our marriage and head south. The problem of course is that our next marriage will enter its own winter at some point. Do we just keep moving on, or do we make our stand now—with this person, in this season? That's the moral, existential question we face when our marriage is in trouble.

A good therapist, a brave therapist, will help us to cling together as a couple, warming each other against the cold of winter, and to seek out whatever sunlight is still available while we wrestle with our pain and disillusionment. A good therapist, a brave therapist, will be the last one in the room to give up on our marriage, not the first one, knowing that the next springtime in Minnesota can be all the more glorious for the winter that we endured together.

John Gottman, from Chapter 8, "Strengthening the Foundations" in *Why Marriages Succeed or Fail and How You Can Make Yours Last* (1994), pp. 224–225

Finding the Glory in Your Marital Story

One sure sign of a strong marriage is a couple's tendency to "glorify" the struggles they've been through together. In interviews, we found that a stable couple will describe their marriage in terms of a worthwhile journey, a saga in which they face adversity and become closer because of it. They tell detailed stories about certain traumas or intense experiences that bonded them to one another. They say they've come through troubled times feeling more committed and hopeful about their relationship.

It's not that couples who glorify their marriages actually faced more troubles than less stable pairs. But they seem to garner more meaning and inspiration from their hardships than others might.

The point is that stable marriages become even stronger in the telling of the tale. Stable couples' stories serve to bolster their faith in one another and their union.

Charles A. Smith, author's description of *Raising Courageous Kids* (2004)

Too often in this perilous world we hear the faint drumbeats of approaching danger, a call beckoning those whose hearts are filled with hate. Yet at the moment when these merchants of misery release inexplicable pain in the world, men and women with courageous hearts appear. Their heroism rekindles hope and reminds us that good will and decency remain alive.

Alana Franklin rescues a six-year-old boy from a gunman who invaded his home. *Fallon Richards* pulls a bed-ridden elderly man from his bed to safety during a fire in his mobile home. *Terreatha Barnes* leaps into a runaway vehicle containing two preschool children and brings it to a halt by pushing on the brake with her hands (breaking her jaw as she does so). What do these three individuals have in common? Other than being courageous females, Alana, Fallon, and Terreatha were all eleven or twelve years old. Their example shows us that the same heart that prompted passengers on Flight 93 to rise up against their captors, firefighters to march up the steps of the World Trade Center, and two men to bring a woman in a wheelchair down 70 floors at the WTC to safety, beats inside young people as well.

We are not born with courage. Threads of power, devotion, integrity, honor, and valor were combined and woven into the tapestry of our lives from the moment we were born.

H. Wallace Goddard, excerpt from
"Something Better Than Punishment" (1994, pp. 1–2)

When we think of discipline, we may think of threats and punishment. They may be the most common ways that parents deal with their children's misbehavior.

What is wrong with threats and punishment? One thing that is wrong with them is that they teach children bad things. Can you think of some bad things that are taught to children by the use of threats and punishment?

Consider threats. It is common for parents to get frustrated with their children and yell at them. "If you do that one more time I'm going to whip you, young man!" "I've told you a thousand times. If I have to tell you once more . . ." Threats are bad because they insult children. They are likely to make the child feel dumb and put-down. The child may feel angry with the parent for treating him that way. Threats are also bad because they may tell the children that we yell a lot but we never do anything. Consider the following story.

> A mother was loading her children in the car to go to the store. Just as she got them all in the car, the neighbor came over to talk to her. As the two ladies talked, the children became restless. One of the boys began to climb out the car window. The mother yelled for him to get back in the car. Then she returned to talking with the neighbor. The boy sat in the window and played. The mother yelled at him to get in the car and threatened to spank him. He sat still while his mother yelled at him, but as soon as she returned to talking, he climbed out the window onto the hood of the car. The mother continued to talk to the neighbor.

> This boy did not think his mother was very serious. She yelled a lot. But she never did anything—unless she became really angry. It's common for parents to be yelling, "Don't touch that!" "Leave her alone." "Go away." Using threats may teach children that parents are unkind and that they don't mean what they say.

There are also problems with punishment. Sometimes parents punish because they are angry. They may spank their children in anger. What does spanking teach a child? For many children it teaches that the world is a cruel place. It may also teach them that parents are mean. It may teach them that it is all right for big people to hurt little people. Those are not the things we want to teach our children. The most effective parents rarely or never use spanking.

When a parent spanks a child for bad behavior, the parent may think that making the child suffer teaches him or her not to do bad things. What it usually teaches the child is to feel

(Continued)

(Continued)

angry or unsafe. Or it may teach the child not to do bad things when the parent is around. But it does not teach the child to be helpful or to have self-control or to feel safe.

There is something better than making children suffer. It is teaching. We want to teach our children that rules are important, that people can work together and solve problems without using physical means.

Teaching is more than talking. It includes how we act. In this publication are some ideas to help you more effectively teach children respect for rules. You can use these suggestions to find better ways to discipline your children—ways to be sure you are helping, never harming your children. You can help your children develop into strong, caring people you will be proud of. [Five principles of guidance follow.]

Haim Ginott, excerpts from Chapter 1, "The Code of Communication: Parent-Child Conversations" in *Between Parent and Child* (Ginott, Ginott, & Goddard, 2003, pp. 5–8)

Children's Questions: The Hidden Meanings

Conversing with children is a unique art with rules and meanings of its own. Children are rarely naive in their communications. Their messages are often in a code that requires deciphering.

Andy, age ten, asked his father, "What is the number of abandoned children in Harlem?" Andy's father, a lawyer, was glad to see his son take an interest in social problems. He gave a long lecture on the subject and then looked up the figure. But Andy was not satisfied and kept on asking questions on the same subject: "What is the number of abandoned children in New York City? In the United States? In Europe? In the world?"

Finally it occurred to Andy's father that his son was concerned not about a social problem, but about a personal one. Andy's questions stemmed not so much from sympathy for abandoned children as from fear of being abandoned. He was looking not for a figure representing the number of deserted children, but for reassurance that he would not be deserted.

Thus his father, reflecting Andy's concern, answered, "You're worried that your parents may someday abandon you the way some parents do. Let me reassure you that we will not desert you. And should it ever bother you again, please tell me so that I can help you stop worrying."

On her first visit to kindergarten, while her mother was still with her, Nancy, age five, looked over the paintings on the wall and asked loudly, "Who made these ugly pictures?" Nancy's mother was embarrassed. She looked at her daughter disapprovingly, and hastened to tell her, "It's not nice to call the pictures ugly when they are so pretty."

The teacher, who understood the meaning of the question, smiled and said, "In here you don't have to paint pretty pictures. You can paint mean pictures if you feel like it." A big smile appeared on Nancy's face, for now she had the answer to her hidden question, "What happens to a girl who doesn't paint so well?"

Next Nancy picked up a broken fire engine and asked self-righteously, "Who broke this fire engine?" Her mother answered, "What difference does it make to you who broke it? You don't know anyone here."

Nancy was not really interested in names. She wanted to find out what happened to children who break toys. Understanding the question, the teacher gave an appropriate answer: "Toys are for playing. Sometimes they get broken. It happens."

Nancy seemed satisfied. Her interviewing skill had netted her the necessary information: This grown-up is pretty nice, she does not get angry quickly, even when a picture comes out ugly or a toy is broken, I don't have to be afraid, it is safe to stay here. Nancy waved good-bye to her mother and went over to the teacher to start her first day in kindergarten.

—◆—

Carol, age twelve, was tense and tearful. Her favorite cousin was going home after staying with her during the summer. Unfortunately, her mother's response to Carol's sadness was neither empathic nor understanding.

CAROL (with tears in her eyes):   Susie is going away. I'll be all alone again.
MOTHER: You'll find another friend.
CAROL: I'll be so lonely.
MOTHER: You'll get over it.
CAROL: Oh, Mother! (Sobs.)
MOTHER: You're twelve years old and still such a crybaby.

Carol gave her mother a deadly look and escaped to her room, closing the door behind her. This episode should have had a happier ending. A child's feelings must be taken seriously, even though the situation itself is not very serious. In her mother's eyes a summer separation may be too minor a crisis for tears, but her response need not have lacked sympathy. Carol's mother might have said to herself, "Carol is distressed. I can help her

(Continued)

(Continued)

best by showing that I understand what pains her. How can I do that? By reflecting her feelings to her." Thus she would have said one of the following:

"It will be lonely without Susie."

"You miss her already."

"It is hard to be apart when you are so used to being together."

"The house must seem kind of empty to you without Susie around."

Such responses create intimacy between parent and child. When children feel understood, their loneliness and hurt diminish. When children are understood, their love for the parent is deepened. A parent's sympathy serves as emotional first aid for bruised feelings.

When we genuinely acknowledge a child's plight and voice her disappointment, she often gathers the strength to face reality.

Shirley Jackson, from *Life Among the Savages* (1997), p. 1

Our house is old, and noisy, and full. When we moved into it we had two children and about five thousand books; I expect that when we finally overflow and move out again we will have perhaps twenty children and easily half a million books; we also own assorted beds and tables and chairs and rocking horses and lamps and doll dresses and ship models and paint brushes and literally thousands of socks. This is the way of life my husband and I have fallen into, inadvertently, as though we had fallen into a well and decided that since there was no way out we might as well stay there and set up a chair and a desk and a light of some kind.

● CONCLUSION

The best-written materials read naturally and effortlessly. What is hidden behind the text is the time spent gaining the knowledge, finding a voice, writing the ideas, and refining them. There is no royal road to effective writing. It takes thoughtful effort.

EXPLORATIONS ●

1. If you were designing a web course for families such as those described at the beginning of this chapter, what knowledge of parenting do you think is most important for them to have? How would you make it memorable? What strategy would you use to help the parents apply the knowledge to their parenting challenges?

2. Identify samples of writing that speak to you. Describe characteristics of the voice in those samples.

3. Select a family topic on which adult family members are likely to have an interest. Have each member of the class write an 800- to 1,000-word article on that subject as if it were being prepared for a local newspaper (or some other agreed-upon outlet). After each person has had a few days or a week to prepare the article, make enough copies for your class members or colleagues. Share them. Discuss the strengths and limitations of the various pieces. As a follow-up activity, refine your article and submit it to a print source.

4. Discuss with a classmate or colleague your reactions to the several writing samples. What do you like about each? Do you have some other sample of writing that especially appeals to you? How would you describe the style you have developed or hope to develop?

PART V

PROMOTING, MARKETING, AND SUSTAINING FLE PROGRAMS

CHAPTER 15

CREATING EFFECTIVE COLLABORATIVE PARTNERSHIPS

With all the challenges facing families today, wise family life education (FLE) professionals realize that they cannot fully address these concerns singlehandedly. We need the help of like-minded others. How do we go about bringing our contributions to the collaborative table and synergize with them to effectively serve families in our communities?

Stated succinctly, "Community-based organizations, [family life educators], and agencies that share common goals can expand their outreach and effectiveness through collaboration, partnerships, linkages, and networking. Educational . . . needs of . . . families are interrelated and complex. Since no one system alone can effectively address the multiplicity of needs and problems of families, the collaborative process is a recognized and practical approach. The collaborative process involves agencies, corporations, and volunteer groups working together to provide comprehensive approaches to the complex problems of families. From this process, new alliances, partnerships, and networks evolve, and ultimately benefit . . . audiences" (Cooperative Extension System [CES], 1991, p. 4).

There are many ways to work together to address family issues. Because effective collaboration is a key characteristic of strong, sustainable community-based programs, as noted in Chapter 2, we devote special attention to working together collaboratively in this chapter. We begin by defining the collaborative process in addressing complex family issues and discuss its advantages and challenges. We next present a taxonomy for working with others (ranging from networking to full collaboration) and strategies for building effective collaborative partnerships. Finally, we provide a discussion of principles for successful collaboration and examples of effective collaborative partnerships in action.

At the conclusion of the chapter, readers will have the opportunity to select a family life topic reflecting a community need (e.g., better parenting of young children) and create a community linkage plan that pulls together important stakeholders (e.g., parents, preschool teachers, Head Start representatives), decision makers (e.g., legislators), and agency representatives (e.g., child protective service agencies) to address the topic.

● DEFINING THE COLLABORATIVE PROCESS

Problems facing families today rarely involve simple, silver bullet solutions. No one group or discipline can effectively or successfully address the multiplicity of needs and problems of families (CES, 1991). Family concerns that attract the preventive attention of family life educators have multiple causes, with both risk factors and protective factors occurring at different levels of the social ecology (see Chapter 2; Bronfenbrenner, 1986). Because family issues are multilevel and multidisciplinary in scope, the best solutions to address them are likewise multifaceted and holistic. For example, a family-serving organization with the goal of helping parents balance work and family will have less success on its own than it would have if workplaces joined it by adopting family-friendly policies and radio stations provided helpful balancing hints to commuting parents. Not surprisingly, therefore, many individuals and groups recommend working together to form strong problem-solving relationships to enhance the benefits to children, youth, families, and communities (Borden & Perkins, 1999; CES, 1991; Extension Committee on Organization and Policy [ECOP], 2002). In fact, more and more initiatives at the local, state, and federal levels expect multiple-sector agencies to collaborate (Borden & Perkins, 1999). While it may not be possible in terms of time or resources to address all problems from a systemic perspective and work at multiple levels simultaneously, the most effective and comprehensive FLE offerings would address both risk and protective processes at several closely interrelated levels of the human ecology (Bogenschnieder, 1996).

Collaboration has been defined as "a process through which parties who see different aspects of a problem can constructively explore their differences and search for solutions that go beyond their own limited vision of what is possible" (Gray, 1989, p. 5). All parties bring to the collaborative table their own knowledge, training, understanding, and experiences; collaboration is a process whereby those strengths and gifts are placed on the table and fused with others. Effective collaborations are full partnerships, where all parties throw down institutional, disciplinary, and agency barriers and individual agendas to develop a shared vision, common goals, and strategic plans. The players "invest a relatively equal amount of tangible and intangible resources" to the partnership (Ritter & Gottfried, 2002, p. 7). Leadership is shared, and the successes of respective partners are interdependent (Evans et al., 2001). If the ultimate goal in FLE is the restructuring of existing programs and services toward comprehensive, integrated service delivery for families, then full collaboration represents the ideal situation (Melaville & Blank, 1991).

ADVANTAGES OF COLLABORATION ●

There are many advantages that accrue when family life educators work together collaboratively with like-minded others to address the needs of families.

Opportunity to Bring Together a Wide Range of Expertise on Behalf of Clientele

Family issues are complex, and all members of a collaboration, with their unique training and experiences, will bring a different view of the problem and solution. The varied perspectives release the group from parochialism of perspective that can result within a single agency or disciplinary focus. Ideally, the collaboration also includes members of the targeted audience, who bring with them their own experiences and expertise that need integration into the professionals' views.

Decisions at Every Level of the Program Are Better

At every level of program design, decisions are made about content, process, and so on. Because the problem or concern is likely to be fully defined and details not missed and multiple perspectives drawn upon, programmatic solutions are likely to garner better results.

Can Harness and Combine Financial and Human Resources

When integrated FLE services to families is the goal, a collaboration allows for various agencies to allocate a portion of their funds and a portion of the time of employees to addressing the issue.

Enhance Likelihood of Community Buy-In

When many sectors join together collaboratively, a community sees that efforts go beyond the work or ideas of one person or group. With many community sectors represented and included, participation levels increase.

Increase Likelihood of Institutional Change

Members of collaborative partnerships can establish goals within their own organizations to institutionalize the participation of personnel in collaboration through line-item budgets and work plans that include ongoing participation, human and financial, in collaborations serving families.

Increase Likelihood of Program Dissemination

Members of collaborations bring with them their own clientele, which become instant clientele of the collaboration. Thus, participation is multiplied as the collaboration grows.

Improves the Quality of Programs and Is Worth the Effort

As part of its effort to evaluate efforts across its funded programs, the Children, Youth, and Families at Risk (CYFAR) Evaluation Collaboration conducted surveys of Extension Service professionals in 45 states and territories in late 1997 and early 1998. Respondents were asked if working together rather than alone improved work and if it was worth the effort. When asked how strongly they agreed with the statement "Working with other extension staff has improved our programs for children, youth and families at risk," 78% agreed or strongly agreed. When asked whether collaboration with other community, county, state, and federal organizations is worth the effort, 82% agreed or strongly agreed that it was.

CHALLENGES TO COLLABORATION ●

A decision to collaborate is not without its challenges. These challenges must be recognized and addressed if a collaborative partnership is to work effectively and be sustained over time. Here are several challenges that need attention (Meek, 1992a):

Turf Issues

Sometimes members of collaborations become concerned with getting credit or owning for themselves a particular domain. As a popular saying goes, "It is amazing how much can be accomplished when no one cares who gets the credit." For fullest accomplishment, turf protection and mistrust must be overcome. If collaborative partners mistrust each other, they will not be willing to share resources or be receptive to one another's ideas. Most of the advantage of working together will be lost; in fact, there may be a negative outcome.

One such negative outcome occurred when a successful program designed to help families transition from public assistance to self-sufficiency was blocked from expansion and permanence when a previously collaborating group decided on competing for grant dollars against the collaboration. The outcome was the closing down of the successful program in that area and the subsequent limiting of services the program provided to needy families.

When individuals and groups join a collaboration, they typically are committed at the outset to the ethic of working together harmoniously, sharing power, program ownership, and other resources. The processes that follow of creating a shared vision, mission, and strategic plan are often all that is needed to reduce turfism. Turf battles do occur, however, and when they concern substantive issues in the collaboration, such as goals, resources, or methods, they can usually be resolved with ordinary problem-solving strategies (e.g., identify and clarify the concern, suggest solutions, choose one a collaboration thinks will work, carry out the solution) (Meek, 1992b). Of course, full collaboration requires the goodwill and cooperation of all collaborating organizations. If one organization refuses to cooperate, it cannot be coerced. It can only be invited.

Reaching Consensus

It takes time to reach agreement on a general course and direction, followed by specific goals, objectives, roles, and other related decisions.

Sometimes partners lack the authority to make decisions on behalf of their sponsoring organization and must return to get clearance for their involvement. Depending on how well the collaboration communicates or how often it meets, decision by consensus could make acting on a problem slow and ineffective.

Similar to overcoming turfism, a key to consensus building is the strategic planning process that first begins with the creation of a shared vision that truly incorporates the diversity of perspectives represented. A shared vision provides a strong foundation for a collaboration, and once it is in place, achieving consensus on mission, goals, and objectives receives impetus.

In facilitating the planning for a local healthy marriage initiative for Hispanics, a strategic planner first defined and gave examples of vision statements. He then asked members of the budding collaboration to answer four questions to probe their perspective (adapted from Callor et al., 2000):

Vision Statement: A written statement that describes the community as it could be at some future point.

Examples:

A community committed to putting family first.

Married couples love, support, and respect one another.

All children and youth live in families that promote their positive development.

Answer the following:

Where do you hope the Healthy Marriage Initiative will be in 5 years?

What is the purpose of the initiative? What problem does it address?

What do you hope the initiative will offer over and above what other programs offer?

Write your vision statement.

The resulting two-part vision statement read: Married couples living together in love and respect who support each other and their children; Communities that empower couples with knowledge, attitudes, skills, and resources necessary for successful marriage.

Limited Resources

It is possible that otherwise valuable partners will decide not to collaborate because they lack the finances to do so. Such potential partners are faced with the decision of devoting resources to a collaboration or keeping the funds within their own organization to address their own high-priority projects. If a collaboration is funded through extramural funds, where partners' involvement is paid for by those dollars, these concerns can be partially overcome. Otherwise, a looser connection among the partnership that does not involve the sharing of financial resources may be advised.

Divergent Views

As efforts toward reaching consensus ensue, some may adopt a policy position that is inconsistent with one of the partners and may cause the partner to be uncooperative, ineffective, or to simply drop out. Preventively, these challenges can be addressed through establishing core values of the collaboration during the visioning process, among which might be stated, "We honor and value the unique gifts, talents, and perspectives each individual, group, and organization brings to the collaboration." The core values guide the development of the ground rules a collaboration might adopt, which might include an occasional reminder to members to respect and hear one another's views.

Member Difficulties

Members in crisis may cause cooperation to decrease. Human service organizations are often at the top of agencies targeted for budget cuts. Thus, collaboration member agencies may suffer challenges of their own, such as the elimination of their own jobs. As organization administrations change, so too may the attitude of the participating organization toward the collaboration, which may pose problems if the new administrator does not favor or does not understand the nature of the collaboration.

For a collaboration to be successful, it must have sustained, committed membership. Extracting written commitments from individuals, groups, and organizations indicating their commitment of time, people, and revenue may be necessary. In addition, collaborations will want to develop membership guidelines governing terms of office and replacement of members (Bergstrom et al., 1995).

A COMMUNITY LINKAGES FRAMEWORK •

While there is much to be desired in full collaborative partnerships to comprehensively address family concerns, it would be inaccurate to suggest that full collaboration is necessary or best for every program. There is a variety of ways of working together for families in communities, and certainly some problems, goals, or issues may benefit from more limited partnerships. The level of partnership selected depends mostly on the purposes of the program (Betts et al., 1999). Family life educators should ask themselves, What level of collaboration is necessary for program success?

A useful model describing the levels of collaboration is the Levels of Community Linkages model, developed by the National Network for Collaboration (Bergstrom et al., 1995), showing a continuum of possible levels of partnership in projects, as well as the purpose, structure, and process of such linkages. Other authors (e.g., Melaville & Blank, 1991) have also discussed a variety of approaches in working together. We present an adapted model in Table 15.1 and discuss it below.

Networking

At the network level of partnership, the purpose of the relationship is dialogue toward mutual understanding, passing along information that is helpful to each other's work. While it is possible that networkers are part of groups that have similar goals, goal similarity is not a prerequisite to networking. This level of working together is entirely appropriate if all one wants to do is to let one know what the other is doing. For example, one community organized a services network for Hispanic families, meeting each week to provide each other with information about services each organization offered, to calendar upcoming events, and to discuss needs. Family life educators might only need or want to network, when at this point all they want to do is inform others of the services they provide and share ideas during networking meetings.

Cooperation

Relationships move from networking to cooperation when organizations begin to match needs and efforts to avoid overlap. They work to help each other realize their goals but do not change the basic services they provide or the rules that govern their organizations (Melaville & Blank, 1991, p. 14). For example, while two family life educators operating in the network's organizations may very capably provide parenting education, cooperating family life educators might decide that one should specialize in programs for parents with children birth through age 11 while the other might focus on parents of adolescents. They would refer clientele to one another.

TABLE 15.1   Levels of Community Linkages

Levels of Partnership	Purpose	Structure	Process
Networking	Dialog and understanding Share information between agencies	Loose/flexible link Roles loosely defined Community action is primary link among members	Low-key leadership Minimal decision making Little conflict Informal communication
Cooperation	Match needs/limit overlap of services	Central body of people as communication hub Semiformal links Roles somewhat defined Links are advisory Group leverages/raises money	Facilitative leaders Complex decision making Some conflict Formal communications within the central group
Coordination	Share resources to address common issues or create something new	Central body of people consists of decision makers Roles defined Links formalized Group develops new resources and joint budget	Autonomous leadership but focus on issue Group decision making in central and subgroups Communication is frequent and clear
Coalition	Share ideas and resources over a multiyear period	All members involved in decision making Roles and time defined Links formal with written agreement Group develops new resources and joint budget	Shared leadership Decision making formal with all members Communication is common and prioritized
Collaboration	Build a program together to accomplish a shared vision and impacts	Consensus used in shared decision making Roles, time, and evaluation formalized Links are formal and written in work assignments A full partnership	Leadership high, trust level high, productivity high Ideas and decisions equally shared Highly developed communication

SOURCE: Adapted from Bergstrom et al. (1995); Betts et al. (1999); Melaville and Blank (1991).

Coordination

From cooperation to coordination involves increasing the depth of interdependence of partners. In addition to doing what cooperators do, coordinators also share resources (human and/or financial) to address issues of shared concern or to create something new by virtue of the association. Typically, the associations are temporary and time limited. Thus, if family life educators' effort and involvement are intended to be short-lived, coordination may be the appropriate level of partnership. For example, members of an ongoing youth services network who had concerns about higher risk youth in the inner cities met together to identify issues facing the youth. The group decided to elicit the help of family and human development Extension specialists to conduct a survey of youth attitudes and behaviors corresponding with these issues. The specialists summarized the findings into a reader-friendly report, complete with tables and recommendations based on the findings. From recommendations, the specialists suggested various FLE program offerings that could be used to address the identified needs.

Coalition

Coalitions essentially involve long-term coordination. Members share ideas, leadership, and resources over several years. In the aforementioned example, the youth agency network becomes a coalition simply as it continues to remain in existence over many years and continues to address youth needs as they arise. The family life educators brought in to help address the needs would continue in their advisory role.

Collaboration

Perhaps the feature that most distinguishes a collaboration from other levels of linking together is the focus on building a program together to accomplish a shared vision and outcomes. Parties gather together from conceptualization stages, creation of a shared vision and mission, and strategic plans, continuing on through the implementation and evaluation of programs. They recognize and honor unique contributions and share credit for accomplishment (ECOP, 2002). Collaboration is ideal when the needs of an FLE audience require a seamless, comprehensive response. For example, one family-based program designed to prevent child abuse involved an initial home visit to assess needs, which could vary from parenting skills to knowledge of nutrition to housekeeping skills. Drawing on resources collected and developed by the collaboration, the home visitors proceeded to provide the in-home education to empower the families.

ASSESSING THE EFFECTIVENESS OF YOUR COLLABORATION ●

Effective collaborations have key characteristic processes (Borden & Perkins, 1999). Once a collaboration is in place in a community, family life educators can take steps to evaluate the strength of an FLE collaboration. Each of the following 13 factors (Borden & Perkins, 1999) can be rated on a scale of 1 to 5 (1 = strongly disagree to 5 = strongly agree) to assess how well a collaboration is functioning:

- *Goals*. The collaboration has clearly defined goals. It has developed a shared vision and mission, strategic plan, and intended outcomes. The strategic plan is followed carefully and referred to and updated annually.
- *Communication*. The collaboration has open and clear communication. There is an established process for communication between meetings.
- *Sustainability*. The collaboration has a plan for sustaining membership and resources. This involves membership guidelines relating to terms of office and replacement of members.
- *Research and evaluation*. The collaboration has conducted a needs assessment and has obtained information to establish its goal, and the collaboration continues to collect data to measure goal achievement. They share these evaluation data with members of the collaboration, stakeholders, and funding agencies.
- *Political climate*. The history and environment surrounding power and decision making is positive. The political climate may be within the community as a whole.
- *Resources*. The collaboration has access to needed resources. Resources refer to four types of capital: environmental, in-kind, financial, and human.
- *Catalysts*. The collaboration was started because of existing problem(s), or the reason(s) for collaboration to exist required a comprehensive approach.
- *Policies/laws/regulations*. The collaboration has changed policies, laws, and/or regulations that allow the collaboration to function effectively.

- *History.* The community has a history of working cooperatively and solving problems.
- *Connectedness.* Members of this collaboration are connected and have established informal and formal communication networks at all levels.
- *Leadership.* The leadership facilitates and supports team building and capitalizes upon diversity and individual, group, and organizational strengths.
- *Community development.* This community was mobilized to address important issues. There is a communication system and formal information channels that permit the exploration of issues, goals, and objectives.
- *Understanding community.* The collaboration understands the community, including its people, cultures, values, and habits.

● GETTING STARTED: STEPS FOR CREATING EFFECTIVE COLLABORATIVE PARTNERSHIPS

Visit With Parties Who Share Goals and Interest

Inventory the organizations in the community (and state, depending on the scope of the program) and identify those that share similar goals and interests to those of your organization. Arrange an opportunity to meet with them to discuss jointly working together. If your interest is in parenting education, what other groups or individuals share the goal of helping parents effectively nurture their young?

Agree On Desired Outcomes

In the process of discussion and synergizing your ideas with your collaborative partner, agree on outcomes that members of the group are jointly committed to. One outcome a parenting collaborative group might target is "Equip parents with effective, positive child guidance tools and, in the process, substantially reduce use of corporal punishment as a discipline strategy."

Have a Shared Vision, Mission, and Strategic Plan for Achieving Outcomes

Although, as noted in Chapter 3, arriving at a shared vision takes time, such a process is important to invite the commitment of all collaborative parties. Once that is achieved, the next vital step is the development of a mission statement (where we define what the organization is and does) and a strategic plan (specific steps the program will take to achieve the desired outcomes, in line with the project vision and mission).

Pool Resources (Human and Financial) and Jointly Plan, Implement, and Evaluate Programs

The best collaborative partnerships approach the ideal of seamlessly fusing parties together. Participating agencies devote a substantial amount of the parties' time and job effort to the collaboration. After the preliminary work of creating the vision, mission, and strategic plan is accomplished, the parties continue to work together to put the flesh on the skeleton of the program, including development of the materials, implementation and dissemination of materials, and determining whether the program accomplished targeted outcomes.

Involve Participants in the Collaboration

A serious weakness in many family life educational efforts is the failure to include the target audience in predevelopment stages of a program. As a result, such programs are destined to fail from the beginning (see Chapter 16 for a fuller discussion). However, in addition to assessing participant needs, it is also critical to involve them in the collaboration, where the participant voice can be heard not only with respect to how an FLE program is developed but also how it is implemented and evaluated.

Focus On Participant Needs and Outcomes

The felt and ascribed needs identified during needs assessments conducted at the program predesign stages become the focus of attention and effort. Without meeting participant needs and achieving intended outcomes, the program will fail.

Build Ownership at All Levels (Local, County, State, Etc.)

The antidote to turfism is shared ownership. Shared ownership is fostered through full participation of all parties at the visioning and strategic planning stages, and each participant is delegated individual responsibility for the outcomes of the joint effort (Melaville & Blank, 1991).

Recognize and Respect Strengths of Members

Each member of the collaboration will bring unique strengths, perspectives, and skills to share as part of the project. Taking time to appropriately acknowledge the contributions of each member of the group for good ideas and so on is an important part of building positive morale among group members. For collaborations to thrive, a perceptive and cooperative facilitator is a key resource.

● EXAMPLES OF EFFECTIVE FAMILY LIFE EDUCATION COLLABORATIONS

As you will recall from Chapter 2, effective collaboration is an important component of effective, sustained, community-based FLE programs. Many community partners are involved. Below we present two examples of effective FLE collaborations that use many of the principles and steps outlined above.

Alabama's Begin Education Early and Healthy (BEE) Program

The Begin Education Early and Healthy (BEE) program (Abell, Adler-Baeder, Tajeu, Smith, & Adrian, 2003) targets geographically isolated, limited-resource (low-income and/or limited-education) families with pre-school-age children (2–5). The key thrust of the BEE program is to assist parents in becoming more effective in meeting their goals for the development and well-being of their children. Specific goals of the project are to increase parental capacity to (a) provide appropriate guidance, emotional support, and involvement in school readying behaviors; (b) initiate contact and interact productively with community services related to children's health; and (c) develop effective coparenting relationships across a variety of family forms and structures.

The project envisioned communities in Alabama where children and youth can lead positive, secure, and productive lives. The mission statement reads, "Sharing parenting information about early childhood education and development with rural, underserved families to increase parents' abilities to guide and nurture their young children's learning readiness."

The BEE program uses one-on-one parenting education modules and a unique van-based delivery system as its core programming content. These modules focus on providing parents education in support of their effectiveness as caregivers and first teachers of their young children, as well as parents' health literacy and coparenting relationships. Health modules address the development of knowledge and skills that parents need to interact effectively with the health care system, to follow the instructions and advice provided, and to use complementary components of the health care system. Learning module objectives focus on building strengths among participant families through the development of practical knowledge and decision-making skills that form and sustain healthy adult relationships, family relationships, and nurturing environments for children.

Delivery of the core BEE program is done by a trained paraprofessional BEE educator, who recruits and works one-on-one with caregivers and at least one child age 2 to 5. Up to 15 families are recruited and are enrolled for 10 weekly, 1-hour sessions. Each family attends their sessions aboard a van, renovated to be a classroom on wheels, which travels to their homes. On the BEE van, the child takes part in hands-on developmentally appropriate activities while the educator and the parent discuss parenting and child development. BEE health and relationship modules are delivered in a group setting in faith-based or community-based locations identified through the work of the BEE collaboration coordinator. Potential group leaders or educators are recruited and identified by community agencies and organizations and trained to conduct learning modules by project co-directors with the assistance of the BEE collaboration coordinator.

Three counties (Wilcox, Macon, and Perry) were selected as sites for the BEE project. These counties are located in Alabama's Black Belt, an area defined by its fertile black soil that was once the backbone of the state's agricultural economy but is now plagued by pervasive poverty and economic stagnation. Extension and community leaders in these counties have shown an interest in grassroots efforts designed to address communitywide concerns and recognition of the need to develop more cohesive community collaborations to address families' security, health, and educational needs.

Key groups in the BEE program are the BEE advisory boards, critical for expanding community involvement and collaboration. These boards involve community members in advising program staff and serve as a mechanism for involving the broader community in creative support and expansion activities.

Educating Families to Achieve Independence in Montana (EDUFAIM) Program

The Educating Families to Achieve Independence in Montana (EDUFAIM) program (Duncan et al., 2003) is a second example of an effective collaborative. Formed to help families make transitions from public assistance to self-reliance, EDUFAIM is designed to help limited-resource families gain the knowledge, attitudes, and skills needed for effective family resource management and progress toward a self-supporting lifestyle.

This collaboration first began with simple discussions among parties interested in improving the plight of limited-resource families in Montana. In early 1995, specialists at the Montana State University Extension Service met with the Department of Public Health and Human Services (DPHHS) public assistance directors to discuss working together for limited-resource families. Initial meetings focused on nutrition education and food resource management, since most of the state dollars available at that time for the education of limited-resource families were earmarked for nutrition programs. However, it was clear that Montana families coming off public assistance needed more than nutrition education to make a successful transition to self-sufficiency. Extension and DPHHS parties both concluded that many public assistance families now needed educational aid in a number of areas as they made the transition from welfare dependence to self-sufficiency. They decided to seek grants to fund such a transition program in Montana. They were successful in obtaining a State Strengthening grant from the Children, Youth, and Families at Risk Initiative (CYFAR) of the Cooperative State Research, Education, and Extension Service (CSREES). The state-level collaborative partnership had been forged.

While state-level partnership is important, without local collaboration and buy-in, a program will falter. The next step was to select local community sites. State partners contacted county Extension agents and their county welfare directors to assess the level of interest and community buy-in to EDUFAIM. To be selected, sites needed to demonstrate interest and buy-in and have a community infrastructure that would allow for the collaboration of many agencies to carry out the work. In addition, in an attempt to reach the most resource-poor areas of the state, the percentage of children living in poverty at the selected sites needed to meet or exceed 20%. Two sites were selected initially, serving five rural Montana counties.

Specific educational program content for EDUFAIM is determined by the needs identified and prioritized by individual families and communities. Program areas may include, but are not limited to, nutrition and health (e.g., preventive health education, maternal and infant nutrition, food preparation, healthy and low-cost food shopping and food safety), individual and family development (e.g., parent education, building family strengths, balancing work and family, building self-efficacy and positive expectations, managing stress), resource management (e.g., time management, money management, consumer skills), community development (e.g., small business development), and housing (e.g., housing affordability and availability, protection of housing investment, health-related environmental issues within the home).

Upon entry into the program, families develop a family investment agreement (FIA). The FIAs list the kinds of EDUFAIM courses families believe they need to help them move toward greater self-sufficiency. Classes are taught in small group settings or one-on-one, as needed, by local EDUFAIM staff consisting of an EDUFAIM family educator assisted by an EDUFAIM program aide. The family educator is a professional holding a master's degree with considerable experience working with limited-resource families. Program aides are paraprofessionals indigenous to the limited-resource population who have real-life experience in public assistance. This combination of professional and real-life experience is likely to form the basis of strong, caring associations between educators and participants (Giblin, 1989). The family educator and program aide work collaboratively with the local community advisory council for FAIM, consisting of agency representatives, volunteers, and members of the target audience.

Local staff are supported with educational materials and training, evaluation, and computer technology by the state EDUFAIM team. This team comprises resident and Extension faculty representing 10 disciplines—family science, nutrition, adult development, adult education, child development, family economics, community development, housing, youth development, and computer technology. Each site has two computers, one for office use and one for public use. These computers provide Internet connectivity, allowing access to many web-based resources for their clientele and the ability to stay connected with other professionals locally and nationally. Specialists assist sites by pointing community EDUFAIM staff to resources that help support them in their work with limited-resource audiences.

The state EDUFAIM team is in turn supported by college deans, department heads, Extension administration, and state directors of the DPHHS, who together have developed a shared vision and strategic plan for addressing the educational needs of at-risk families in Montana, using EDUFAIM as a vehicle. The vision of the EDUFAIM program is "Supportive Montana communities that empower families to develop skills, knowledge and competencies necessary for managing family resources and progressing toward a self-supporting lifestyle." In connection with this vision, the EDUFAIM mission statement reads as follows: "EDUFAIM is a collaborative effort of the Montana State University Extension Service, Department of Public Health and Human Services, and Community Advisory Councils that provides educational programs to empower FAIM and other at-risk families in attaining knowledge and developing skills necessary for managing family resources and progressing toward a self-supporting lifestyle." This vision and mission statement forms the basis of a comprehensive strategic plan for its accomplishment. The vision, mission, and strategic plan are reviewed and updated annually, and course corrections are made when needed.

In turn, local EDUFAIM staff and community advisory councils have developed their own vision, mission, and strategic plan that are in line with the state vision. They likewise hold regular meetings to review and update their plans.

The federal liaison external to the project termed the EDUFAIM project a "model of collaboration" (Woods, 1998). Several specific collaboration strategies have been used with success in EDUFAIM; five are listed below.

Shared Vision

From the outset, in participating communities, EDUFAIM has been viewed as the catalyst to coordinate the variety of necessary programs to help remove barriers to employment and to help families become self-supporting. Everyone at the table shared the vision that this collaboration would produce superior results.

Focus on Participants' Needs

The collaboration has been working in part because everyone has strived to keep in mind that collaboration exists to meet participant needs in the most effective way possible. Participants were interviewed during the design phase of EDUFAIM to learn from them what they needed to become self-reliant. Their responses, plus their representation as members of community advisory councils, helped form EDUFAIM's entire structure, service delivery approach, and strategic plan.

Use of Most Knowledgeable and Experienced Resources

The partnership used the most knowledgeable and experienced resources in the community. Each of the participating organizations and agencies at the local level selected a top member of their team to guarantee a horizontal collaboration among "equals." This was done because it has been their experience that hierarchical collaborations do not work. Because of this egalitarian arrangement, the EDUFAIM partnership was able to recognize and respect their limitations and defer to the core competencies of other collaborators. As a result, EDUFAIM staff participated in an extremely strong referral network.

Compensation Arrangements Discussed in Advance

Issues of ownership were discussed openly. At one site, ownership issues started to become a concern when Welfare-to-Work monies became available and there was the potential for interagency competition. However, because of the shared vision and focus on the needs of individuals, community agencies were able to come together to write the grant, and all compensation arrangements were completely and satisfactorily resolved.

Responsiveness to Clientele

Program leaders discovered throughout the growth of their program that they needed to respond quickly to the needs of clientele and be as flexible in providing services as possible. They found it essential to their success that their working environment was responsive and the communication paths streamlined. Modern technology (i.e., e-mail, faxing, cell phone) helped them to perform optimally with their collaborators and participants.

CONCLUSION ●

Given the social problems landscape, there are many opportunities for family life educators to make a difference in communities. Wise FLE professionals realize that their strength and effectiveness with their educational audience are multiplied as they work together with like-minded individuals. This chapter presented several ways to work with others, focusing on the establishment of collaborative partnerships, and provided a few examples of such partnerships in action. One of us alone is never as powerful as all of us together.

EXPLORATIONS ●

1. Detail a collaboration plan for your program. The essence of collaboration is to gain community ownership and support of the program, coordinating or collaborating with other agencies and existing efforts in the community to avoid duplication.
- Identify those persons, agencies, and organizations that would likely share the vision of your program and be interested in similar

outcomes. This will be your steering or advisory group. Describe how you will ensure the diversity of the group.

- Describe how you would initiate a collaboration among the members of the committee. How would you go about creating a shared vision, mission, and strategic plan to direct your program? How will you resolve concerns about program ownership (turf issues)?
- Describe how you will coordinate, collaborate, partner, network, and so on with other agencies and existing efforts in the community to avoid duplication and extend your reach.

2. Make a list of the kinds of programs family life educators might foster in a community. Identify which efforts might be best approached through networking, cooperation, or other means, including working alone. Assess the advantages and disadvantages of each approach.

3. Scan your community for examples of FLE programs. Identify the projects according to their level of partnership. Make plans to visit several programs and their leaders and observe how effective the level of partnership works, given the program's purpose.

CHAPTER 16

MARKETING FAMILY LIFE PRINCIPLES, PRACTICES, AND PROGRAMS

I n the movie *Field of Dreams* (P. Robinson, 1989), a voice whispers to the lead character, "If you build it, they will come." Eventually, he discovers that the "it" he is to build is a baseball diamond in the middle of a cornfield on his farm. This diamond becomes a place where the late, great ones gather to play ball. Not only do the players show up, so do the crowds!

In contrast, traditional family life education (FLE), especially that which takes place outside school classroom settings, suffers from "underwhelming participation" (Bowman & Kieren, 1985). Although no reliable figures exist for outreach FLE as a whole, studies of participation in marriage preparation programs have found that only 36% of couples who married in the past 5 years received church-affiliated premarital counseling (Stanley & Markman, 1997). One reason for underinvolvement of participants may hinge on the way FLE programs, principles, and practices are marketed. It is still the FLE professionals themselves, rather than potential clientele, who sense the need and appreciate the benefits of FLE the most. How can we foster a greater application of principles and practices and participation in programs?

Outreach family life educators can learn much from the field of social marketing to help answer these questions. Marketing emphasizes understanding target audiences through research, as a prelude to or concomitant with program development, in order to tailor the programs to the needs of the audience and thus facilitate their acceptance (Kotler & Bloom, 1984, cited in Levant, 1987). Marketing aims at understanding the motivations and underlying values of target audiences in order to encourage widespread adoption of targeted behaviors.

Most businesses and organizations exist only because of their markets (Calvert, 2000). Businesses that ignore consumer needs soon die. It is suspected that FLE programs not designed to meet specific needs of the target population will meet a similar fate (Duncan & Marotz-Baden, 1999). Effective businesses and organizations often spend a significant amount of money to persuade persons in these markets to buy their product. The field of outreach FLE has a different "product" to sell than most businesses: knowledge, principles, and practices important for enriching individual, marriage, and family life. How can family life educators create a market for FLE principles and programs? How do we motivate audience participation in FLE programs? How do we motivate adoption of desired behaviors? How should programs be produced, priced, placed, and promoted, with what partners, and with what funding to reach the target audience most effectively?

Drawing upon the original 4 Ps of marketing (product, price, place, promotion) and integrated with additional Ps of social marketing (publics, partnership, policy, purse strings; Weinreich, 1999), we present a discussion of principles and some practical strategies for helping to answer this question, using relevant family life examples. At the end of the chapter, readers use the integrated Ps of marketing to devise a marketing plan of their own.

● THE SOCIAL MARKETING MIX

Social marketing as applied to FLE involves the use of consumer marketing principles to encourage the adoption of a behavior, principle, or practice that will benefit individuals, families, and society as a whole. We distinguish this kind of marketing from traditional forms of marketing in that the target goal is the strengthening of individuals, marriages, and families in their relationships.

Katz (1988) suggests that marketing decisions may be analyzed along four dimensions: product, price, place, and promotion. Marketing research links the 4 Ps as the framework for data collection on which marketing decisions are subsequently based (Katz, 1988). Marketing research quantifies and qualifies the nature of client needs and monitors the effectiveness of the process of satisfying those needs. If clients' needs are not satisfied, revisions begin with the 4 Ps (Katz, 1988).

Product

Product is the total package of professional services that is delivered to the client. The quality of these services may be an important factor in the client's decision to participate in a program. The services should have consistently high quality (Kotler & Roberto, 1989) in order to maintain a loyal clientele. In addition to the services themselves, a social marketing perspective also identifies the "product" as the behavior or cluster of behaviors we want participants in FLE to adopt. For example, parenting educators may want participating parents to adopt specific parenting practices, such as better listening and communicating with their youngsters. Leaders of a marriage workshop may want couples to intentionally attend to the "little things" in marriage, such as calling their spouse from work on occasion and making special time for intimacy.

Assessing the Target Audience

An important part of designing a product, in fact in addressing all eight of the Ps of marketing, is to first identify and become knowledgeable about the target audience. Assessing target audience needs ensures that the resulting educational programs are relevant to individuals and families throughout the life span and are based on the identified needs of such families (L. H. Powell & Cassidy, 2007). Identifying the specific target audience is aided by first segmenting the population (Kotler & Roberto, 1989). Some of the factors by which an audience might be segmented include, but are not limited to, the following (Kotler & Roberto, 1989; Weinreich, 1999):

- *Geographic region:* County, city, or SMSA (Standard Metropolitan Statistical Areas—a standard Census Bureau designation of the region around a city); size; density (urban, rural, suburban); climate
- *Demographic:* Age, gender, family size, family life cycle, income, occupation, education, religion, race/ethnicity, social class, language, literacy
- *Psychographic:* Lifestyle, personality characteristics, values, conceptions of social norms

- *Attitudinal:* Attitudes, opinions, beliefs, and judgments about product; benefits sought and barriers avoided; readiness stage (unaware, aware, informed, interested, desirous, intending to buy)
- *Behavioral:* Product user status, usage rate, occasion for use, other health-related activities

The segment should be of practical importance to the target audience, the knowledge of which would enhance the potential of developing a product tailored for that need. For example, a balancing work and family program developed with large urban area business parents in mind may likely be largely irrelevant to a rural, farm family audience also interested in harmonizing their work and family life. Once a target audience has been clearly identified, the next step is to find out from them what issues trouble them, to assess needs and the ways such a need might be addressed. For example, if we wanted to help working parents better balance work and family, we may want to first find out what concerns they have about balancing work and family, how important they feel it would be to do something about it, and what kind of balancing product would appeal to them the most. "To have a viable product," writes Weinreich (1999), "people must first feel that they have a genuine problem, and that the product offered is a good solution to that problem" (p. 10).

A variety of methods can be used to assess the needs of a target audience. Much can be learned about an audience through collecting secondary research, which does not require any face-to-face contact. Secondary research data comprise data that are already available, usually found in scholarly works such as journals and books, but also general social surveys conducted within the community of residence of the target audience. In addition, there are data sets available at the local, state, national, and international levels that help to identify needs associated with membership in a target audience. To further tailor a program to the needs of a specifically targeted audience usually requires the collection of additional data from the intended audience themselves, or primary data collection. Methods of data collection of this sort include telephone or face-to-face interviews and larger scale surveys of the target population. For example, the Oklahoma Marriage Initiative (Johnson et al., 2002) conducted a large-scale social survey from which they learned valuable information regarding Oklahoman attitudes regarding a number of factors but also marriage education, and this information was then used to determine how to proceed with their outreach efforts. To increase their participation in marriage preparation, young adults have been surveyed in college classroom settings to understand their perceptions of marriage preparation programs from a marketing perspective (Duncan, Box, & Silliman, 1996; Duncan & Wood, 2003). Vital information was learned in these studies addressing how a marriage preparation program might be produced to attract a larger, more diverse audience of young adults.

A primary prevention framework (Dumka et al., 1995) suggests the importance of consulting the target group through focus groups in order to enable program developers to adapt educational program content and processes to the needs, conditions, values, beliefs, and expectations of the audience (Dumka et al., 1995; Morgan, 1996; Morgan, Krueger, & King, 1998). Focus groups are small discussion groups normally consisting of 6 to 12 participants of similar or varied characteristics, depending on the interests of the researcher (Fern, 1982, and Morgan & Spanish, 1984, cited in Lengua et al., 1992). The expressed needs of the focus groups are incorporated into the various elements of program design, including topics, selection of change objectives, length and breadth of program, cost, and recruitment and retention strategies (Dumka et al., 1995).

One approach to conducting focus groups as a method of assessing the family life educational needs of the target audience is illustrated by Duncan and Marotz-Baden (1999). Data collected from county Extension agents and other sources led to the identification of "balancing work and family" as a major family program initiative in Montana. Surveying the research literature revealed that while balancing work and family was indeed a dilemma, the data were badly biased toward urban dwellers. Seriously lacking were data regarding the rural family's experience with the issue, indeed whether it was an "issue" at all. To assist in answering this question for Montanans, county Extension agents led focus groups in six different regions of the state (northwest, southwest, north central, south central, northeast, and southeast). Focus group participants were recruited using a methodology adapted from Community Action Planning (Schaaf & Hogue, 1990) called a "People Matrix." The People Matrix is a tool to assist focus group leaders in identifying and recruiting a broad mix of categories of persons in a community. For the purposes of this study, the authors were interested in recruiting parents from various personal and vocational categories who were likely to be consumers of balancing work and family information. Persons who fit these categories were invited by the county agent facilitators to participate in the focus groups. Participants within each region were recruited from different geographical sites (north, south, east, west), from different cultures (Hispanic, Native American, White, other), and from different age categories (young adult, middle adult, older adult).

Following the 4 Ps of marketing, an interview schedule was adapted from Lengua et al. (1992). Participants were asked 11 open-ended questions to probe concerns they had about balancing work and family, how programs might be produced, priced, and promoted, and where they might be held, consistent with a marketing perspective. Results revealed that indeed balancing work and family was an important issue and suggested that a preferred balancing work and family program would involve a modest time investment, be low cost, and involve the workplace, the community, and family members, among other elements. The program would teach personal skills, resource management, meal planning, and relationship skills that would help participants address their work-family concerns.

The target audience research process will also reveal the methods whereby family life educators can best help participants reach product goals. For example, in regard to information on balancing work and family, researchers (Duncan & Marotz-Baden, 1999) asked focus groups, "How would you like to get this information? What methods would you like to see used?" Respondents were interested in a variety of methods outside of the traditional FLE workshop. The only major theme that emerged was that the methods used not take much time away from family. Options most frequently noted were mini-classes; workshops (short, concise) in a relaxed atmosphere offered during the day at the workplace or during kids' school hours; reading materials for study at home (newsletters, news articles) containing short, quick tips at appropriate reading level; audiotapes; videos; radio spots; and support groups. The involvement of community organizations such as the chamber of commerce, churches, and employers was seen as important.

"Positioning" the Product

In addition to understanding the needs of a target audience, family life educators also need to position their product to maximize its appeal to clientele (Weinreich, 1999). Part of this involves having the target audience help identify the benefits of following the FLE principles and practices and why pursuing these benefits is better than the alternatives, for example, doing nothing. These benefits are integrated into how we reveal the product to the public. They need to be able to answer the question, "What's in it for me?" For instance, continuing on with the balancing work and family example, if the end product of a program is "greater harmony between work and family settings," what benefits would accrue from greater work-family harmony? Some that may be listed include a stronger marriage, stronger relationships with children, less guilt, more time for family recreation, and greater personal peace.

Price

Price, the fee for services rendered, is determined after examining several interacting factors, such as the cost of offering the product, the price of the competitor's product, the target population's sensitivity to prices, objectives of the organization (profitability vs. market penetration), and capacity to supply services (Kotler & Roberto, 1989; Weinreich, 1999). But it also includes various tangible and intangible costs a client must face in order to receive the intended benefit from the product (Weinreich, 1999). In a balancing family and work workshop series, such costs include the time and energy invested in a workshop, transportation to and from the workshop, competing activities (such as a favorite TV program scheduled at the same time as the workshop), child care costs (if necessary), and the monetary cost of the class. Participants may also need to face the barriers that might stand in the way of actively harmonizing work and family, such as a lack of knowledge about time management, lack of motivation to spend more time and energy at home instead of at work, and a concern about losing status at work if one becomes more family focused. One aspect of human motivation related to price is that the target audience must view the benefits of FLE as outweighing the costs of participation. These benefits include knowledge gains and emotional and psychological benefits (Kotler & Roberto, 1989).

For example, when developing a parenting workshop series for lower income parents with young children, a sliding scale as a fee for services or scholarships could be provided by local businesses to allay the financial costs of programs. Child care services might also be provided at no cost through volunteer partners to likewise reduce the actual and perceived costs of participation. While longer programs tend to be the most effective programs, an assessment could be made of target audience perceptions as to how long participants would be willing to commit to a program. Regardless of how effective it might be, if a program demands more than an audience will give, the size of the audience is likely to be diminished.

Once real and perceived costs are understood, an important question is this: How can we best position the FLE product so that it minimizes the perceived costs and the barriers associated with its adoption? Some parents feel overwhelmed with the dilemma of balancing family and work, wondering how it possibly can be done. Tips for parents might include the following: Spending 30 minutes of one-on-one a day can be done; it's not as difficult as you think—just take them to the store with you.

Direct questioning can also provide important data. As part of target audience surveys, family life educators can ask questions such as, "How much time and money would you be willing to spend on a program like this?"

Place

Place describes the physical location where services are offered to users. Convenience for clientele may be a key issue in participation in programs. Place includes a variety of "locations": Extension offices, shopping malls, at-home education (e.g., videos, Internet), or even mass media approaches. Some research indicates that the most favored locations for outreach FLE programs would be in familiar locations—common gathering places for community members (Duncan et al., 1996; Levant, 1987), such as libraries, churches, and universities. One study (Duncan & Marotz-Baden, 1999) asked participants in a balancing work and family focus group, "Where would be the most convenient place to have a program like this?" Familiar community sites (Extension office, library, community centers, schools, courthouses, churches) where a group already meets were preferred. Presentations to organizations also attracted interest. There was a clear preference for programs to be available where parents already are, specifically the workplace or at home (take-home packets and videos), and programs that used new technologies (interactive TV and computer).

Kotler and Roberto (1989) recommend three considerations in terms of place: access, security, and appearance.

Access

FLE services should be easily and conveniently accessible, be they services available at workshop locations or over the Internet. There should be convenient hours of operation, such as an appropriate time for maximum accessibility for whoever the target audience is. The location should be conveniently accessible, as close to the target audience as is possible. Some research (Duncan et al., 1996; Levant, 1987) suggests that maximum distance from home should be within 15 miles. Yet audiences with transportation barriers may need additional help to get to a workshop even if only a moderate distance away from home. Other aspects of accessibility include staff who are not too busy to be responsive to the needs of clientele and not having to wait long to receive the needed assistance.

Security

Part of what family life educators should do is create a climate of safety for all participants. Clientele want a place that is safe. Family life educators can take steps to ensure that the place selected for a workshop ensures the physical safety of participants. Beyond physical safety is the importance of emotional safety of participants. Most FLE in face-to-face settings goes beyond information giving to the sharing of feelings. Participants need to feel that an FLE group is, emotionally, a safe haven. Facilitators can do much to create such a climate, as noted in Chapter 5. Participants should feel assured that their dealings will be kept private. Such safety can be emphasized as facilitators emphasize privacy as part of the ground rules for an FLE group.

Appearance

Aspects of appearance are also important. Recent research on an FLE website revealed that appearance was an important consideration for potential users (Steimle & Duncan, 2004). The appearance of physical facilities and educational material, be they print publications, videos, CDs, or websites, sends a message regarding the professional nature and quality of the service.

To probe "place" issues during a target audience survey or focus group, family life educators could ask participants, "Where would be the most convenient place to have a program like this?" However, beyond a physical location of services, place also refers to the locations where the target audience is most likely to make decisions about the product (Weinreich, 1999) or the specific practices family life educators wish the intended audience to adopt. For example, for a program promoting harmony between work and family settings, where are some of the places that could be used to get the message across? Some of those might include workplace newsletters to employees, television public service announcements during evening programming, and radio spots during the noon hour and commute times.

Promotion

Promotion is the method of bringing awareness of the service to the service user. Promotional activities, including advertising and word of mouth, must sustain an image of propriety and respectability in order to expand services to a larger target audience (Katz, 1988). It includes the integrated use of advertising, public relations, promotions, media advocacy, personal selling, and entertainment approaches (Weinreich, 1999).

Of the variety of promotional approaches that could be used, research shows that marketing through personal communication, or word of mouth, is the most effective way of getting a target population to adopt a specific action (Kotler & Roberto, 1989; Weinreich, 1999), such as attending a parenting workshop series. Personal promotional approaches, including word of mouth and personal invitation by mail or telephone, are the preferred way of hearing about program offerings, according to some studies (see Duncan et al., 1996; Duncan & Marotz-Baden, 1999; Levant, 1987). Word-of-mouth communication can be done by the clientele themselves but also by identifying influential individuals and organizations who can act as opinion leaders, including neighbors, community leaders, radio and television personalities, spouses of governmental officials, and newspaper columnists, as well as by featuring well-known and influential personalities giving testimonials in promotional materials. Word-of-mouth communication is especially effective when it follows a mass communication about the subject (Kotler & Roberto, 1989).

In addition, if timed right, a promotional message is likely to have strong conversational value. For example, a program designed for parents of adolescents would wisely use a promotional strategy that hit on the salient points for parents with teenagers (e.g., how do we help our teens make good choices even when we're not around?). Material on the workshop might be distributed on an evening at the school when many parents are likely to be around and have the potential for conversing about the topic such as after an athletic event.

Targeting of the promotional message to a developmental stage is also important. Family life educators will want to promote the program to those parents who are likely to be most interested in the program. For example, parents of newborns will likely not be very interested in learning how to handle the terrific twos, so giving them this information at the hospital would likely not be effective.

The research you conduct with the target audience will be the most effective and reliable source of deciding what mix of promotional sources to use. Family life educators can ask the target audience questions such as, "What is the best way to let you know that a program like this is available?"

In addition to the personal approaches noted earlier, one assessment study of balancing work and family needs (Duncan & Marotz-Baden, 1999) noted, in response to this question, additional preferred promotional approaches, including the media (newspaper, radio, newsletter, posters), employers, and community agencies. Other methods of promotion noted in the marketing literature (Weinreich, 1999) for family life educators to consider include advertising (e.g., television or radio commercials, billboards, posters, brochures, grocery bags, fast-food restaurant placemats), public relations (e.g., press releases, letters to the editor, appearances on talk shows), promotions (e.g., coupons for attending parenting seminars), media advocacy (e.g., press events designed to encourage policy change, such as reducing fees for marriage licenses if couples complete marriage education), personal selling (e.g., direct mail campaigns), special events (e.g., health fair or conference displays), and entertainment (e.g., dramatic presentations, songs, television shows).

Beyond the traditional marketing mix, social marketing adds four additional Ps: publics, partnership, policy, and purse strings (Weinreich, 1999).

Publics

For an outreach FLE program to be maximally successful, it needs to be sensitive to the variety of publics that potentially will influence or be influenced by the program. Thus, *publics* refers to groups both internal and external to the program (Weinreich, 1999). The primary group external to the program that family life educators want to influence is, of course, the target audience, those who we want to adopt the principles and practices we teach. However, at least three additional secondary groups are important in marketing considerations. The first group comprises persons in the near environs of target audience clientele who have an influence on the target audience's opinions. These persons might include the target audience's partner, parents, relatives, friends, or coworkers. For example, in addition to promoting a marriage preparation program to committed couples in a community, word of the opportunity might also be shared with parents and recently married couples who can encourage involvement. A second group might be public policy makers, such as legislators—city and state government officials whose position makes them influential in creating the environment conducive to acceptance of the behavior change one seeks to bring about. For example, laws have recently been passed in the state of Florida requiring high school students to receive some form of relationship education prior to graduation, with the end behavioral goal of moderating marital distress. Such efforts undertaken in other states might begin by seeking buy-in and authorship of a bill by a state legislator. Still another group includes those defined as gatekeepers who have some control over access to public messages that encourage the primary group to adopt a behavior, such as media professionals (public service directors at radio and television stations, local reporters in various media), health professionals, and business owners. In Arkansas, public television station buy-in to the idea of effective parenting was necessary to free up considerable time for broadcast of the popular *Guiding Children Successfully* program series.

Thus, winning the buy-in of these secondary target audiences prior to the launch of major FLE initiatives is critical in hastening the acceptance of a program.

The development team of an FLE program may be quite energized about a program. Beyond them, it is necessary to also win over others internal to the program. This group comprises staff at all levels of an organization but especially staff members providing the direct services and the administrators. This kind of buy-in can be achieved by bringing internal staff together to jointly establish a shared vision, mission statement, and strategic plan. For example, one program designed to help lower income families (the primary target audience) move from public assistance to self-sufficiency (Duncan, et al., 2003) first sought the buy-in of its Extension Service, its Department of Public Health and Human Services, and university department heads and deans before launching its initiative into the state. These groups met together to jointly create a vision, mission, and strategic plan. Strong buy-in to the program was a prerequisite to communities being selected to participate in the program. The selected local communities likewise met together to establish their own vision, mission, and strategic plan that was closely aligned with the state-level plan.

Partnership

As discussed in Chapter 15 on collaboration, most issues facing families are much larger in complexity than any one organization can handle on its own. Partnership is strategically wise from a marketing perspective in that persons will likely have more confidence in a program that partners with others who have expertise with more than just one group. Teaming up with others not only extends human and financial resources but also usually increases access to the target audience (Weinreich, 1999). The task for family life educators is to think of other groups who share the same goals.

For example, if you desired to conduct a program to address strengthening marriage at the time of transition to parenthood, you could offer the program on your own. Or you might do as some family life educators did: partner with the state's largest health care organization and offer a low-dosage program called Marriage Moments as part of existing childbirth education classes. Whereas offering the material separately may have been possible, doing it in partnership with an existing agency and infrastructure already used by many new parents has reached far more parents than other more traditional ways of offering the program ever could.

Family life educators may want to think about the various organizations they could partner with to expand their reach. Organizations that have similar goals to family life educators might include school systems, the governor's office, local government offices, businesses (especially after they are shown how strong marriages and families positively influence profitability), state and local agencies, and higher education institutions. Given the many possible roles family life educators may play, they may feel least comfortable in the role of marketing expert. As family life educators consider who to partner with, it may be wise to include those persons and organizations with marketing savvy, such as businesses and public relations persons.

Policy

For some FLE principles and practices to become maximally integrated into a culture, it may require more than a public service announcement campaign with website material. Sometimes policy change at a higher level is necessary to produce the kind of community support necessary to bring about targeted attitudinal and behavioral change. Culture change as well as individual change is sometimes necessary. Family life educators might ask if there are any changes in policies or legislation necessary in order to bring about the change they desire.

While corporal punishment is the subject of some controversy in both the scholarly and lay communities, some argue that for child abuse to be eliminated requires the legislative prohibition of spanking by parents, notwithstanding that the vast majority of parents have used the approach. An FLE initiative on effective parenting with a specific objective to eliminate spanking among participating parents may find that accomplishment of that objective is quite elusive without help from greater powers—namely, the state. To increase the likelihood that couples consciously prepare for marriage may require a shift in public policy. For instance, some states have proposed a discount on marriage license fees if couples complete marriage preparation through their religious organization. Family life educators might present brown-bag seminars on balancing work and family, yet the goals of such programs are likely to be sabotaged if the workplace lacks flexibility in when or where employees must work.

Purse Strings

A variety of sources may be considered to help fund outreach family life educational efforts, including the direct costs to consumers. Most FLE programs are not fully funded by participant fees. Wise family life educators give consideration to the funding of their efforts, especially long-term funding that ensures sustainability of the service. The resources identified as part of the partnership created can form an important source of sustaining funds, especially if the partnership progresses to form a true collaboration, as discussed in Chapter 15. Beyond that, family life educators will need to seek funding from a variety of other sources to maintain the program, such as state and federal agencies, foundations, and donors who are committed to strengthening families. Some FLE efforts sell a product in addition to providing a service as a way to keep the outreach self-sustaining. For example, the RELATE premarital assessment tool (www.relate-institute.org) is the first of its kind, totally online assessment device offered at a nominal price that is designed to sustain the website.

● CRAFTING MARKETING MESSAGES TO FOSTER CHANGE

In the movie *Field of Dreams* (P. Robinson, 1989) discussed at the beginning of this chapter, the closing scene features a long line of interested persons heading to a desired location. Something motivated them within to make the decision to come to the soon-to-be-famous cornfield baseball diamond. Perhaps ideally, family life educators would have many levels of institutional support promoting FLE, making it likely that a target audience will participate. For example, some have even argued for passage of laws necessitating marriage preparation as a requirement to receive a marriage license. Laws of this sort make it easier for targeted behavior (such as attendance at marriage preparation and the subsequent beneficial behaviors) to be performed by the target audience. Laws passed prohibiting smoking in public places certainly have made it more difficult for smokers to light up. With few exceptions, outreach FLE rarely enjoys the same kind of institutional encouragement that accompanies other health behaviors and hence must rely more on persuasive means to attract its audience (exceptions would be mandated attendance such as court-ordered parenting classes or coparenting classes for divorcing parents). This being the case, it is critical that social marketing messages be crafted based on an understanding of human nature and behavior change theories (Weinreich, 1999).

While theories suggesting approaches for developing social marketing messages in FLE do not exist, several theories have been used in the field of health and social behavior that can provide a basis for such messages. Some of the most widely used theories include the health belief model

(Strecher & Rosenstock, 1997), theory of planned behavior (Ajzen, 1991), social cognitive learning theory (Bandura, 1986), stages of change theory (Prochaska & DiClemente, 1983), and the diffusion of innovations model (Rogers, 1983). Rather than consider each theory separately, we present a synthesis of characteristics derived from these and other behavior change theories that must be present in a program's messages and intervention, or already be present in the target audience, in order to effect behavior change (Weinreich, 1999).

In describing the characteristics, we will use the marketing of marriage preparation programs as an example. The target audience is engaged heterosexual couples. The product we want them to adopt is a serious, concerted effort toward marriage preparation, leading to enhanced marital outcomes.

Characteristic 1: Believe That They Are at Risk for the Problem and That the Consequences Are Severe

Let's take a couple from the target audience, John and Janet, both in their mid-20s. John just proposed marriage and Janet accepted. They are very much in love and optimistic about their future together. However, both of them come from families where the parents have divorced; likewise, their parents' parents also terminated their marriage. While they are aware of research communicated through media reports suggesting that couples whose parents had divorced are at heightened risk for marital disruption, John and Janet downplay any concerns, insisting their marriage will be much different.

Let us imagine you have announced a marriage education initiative in your community. The initiative includes many facets and educational resources, comprising brochures and bulletins, marriage workshops, a website, and referrals to marriage and family therapists as needed. What social marketing messages might be designed to encourage targeted audiences to feel the need for the program, leading them to invest in some aspect of your program offering? Marketing messages would need to convince John and Janet that because of their family backgrounds, they are at increased risk for marital trouble. The increased risks, shown in higher levels of mismanaged conflict, poor communication, and heightened negativity, can lead to the death of a marriage relationship, or divorce. Once a couple's awareness of risk is heightened, a call to action should be included, such as including a telephone number or website in promotional materials as a doorway for obtaining more information or registering for a workshop.

Characteristic 2: Believe That the Proposed Behavior Will Lower Its Risk or Prevent the Problem

Once John and Janet are aware of their increased risk, they still must be convinced that investment in a marriage education offering will provide what they need to effectively reduce risks or alleviate potential problems altogether. A marketing message designed to produce this belief might list the various benefits of marriage preparation, such as enhanced ability to manage conflict, higher dedication to one's mate, and greater positivity, as well as a reduced chance for divorce. They might be persuaded to become involved when they learn that participation ups their chances for outcome success by 30% compared to nonparticipants (Carroll & Doherty, 2003).

Characteristic 3: Believe That the Advantages of Performing the Behavior (Benefits) Outweigh the Disadvantages (Costs)

John and Janet have grown up in a culture that has actively perpetuated myths about marriage (Larson, 1988)—such as preparing for marriage should just come naturally, that no special knowledge or skill is necessary—which scholars identify as the myth of naturalism (Vincent, 1973). Besides, Janet and John say, all this serious thinking, assessment, and analysis takes all the romance out of the process. Somehow Janet and John need to be convinced that spending some serious preparation time for their marriage will not remove the good things about the relationship but will only serve to enhance them, including the romance. A marketing message of this sort might acknowledge the myth of naturalism up front (e.g., some think it takes no special knowledge, character, or skill to have a great marriage) and then point to the enhanced benefits among couples who have taken the time to learn how to strengthen their relationships (e.g., "At first, learning to really listen to Barbara seemed like going through the motions. But now I really *know* her, and we feel closer to each other than I ever imagined").

Characteristic 4: Intend to Perform Behavior

According to the theory of planned behavior (Ajzen, 1991), behavioral intention is the strongest predictor of behavior. Intentionality is influenced by three major factors:

- *Attitude toward the behavior.* This involves the person's weighing the positive and negative consequences of the behavior, similar to Characteristic 3.
- *Subjective norms about the behavior.* What significant others think about the behavior and how motivated a person may be to fulfill these perceived expectations play a role.
- *Perceived behavioral control.* This involves a person's perception of the power of external factors to either help foster or distract from the behavior.

To maximize the likelihood of John and Janet participating in some form of active marriage preparation, it is necessary to build their intention to take action. We could try to change their attitude by emphasizing the positive consequences of participation (e.g., better management of conflict, more positivity) and downplaying the negative consequences (e.g., 2 hours a week for 6 weeks is nothing compared to a lifetime of increased happiness in marriage). The positive consequences might be demonstrated by a couple whose actions toward one another make plain the benefits accruing from marriage preparation. John and Janet might be persuaded toward involvement if people important to them (e.g., such as a recently married friend couple who had been involved and benefited from it) recommended their participation. Finally, they might be more likely to be involved if we made their involvement easier, such as offering the program as part of something they were already doing (e.g., as a class in a church they both attend).

Characteristic 5: Believe That They Have the Ability and Skills to Perform the Behavior (Self-Efficacy)

While the benefits of marriage preparation can be trumpeted loudly, John and Janet must believe they have the wherewithal to gain those touted benefits for themselves. In essence, they must possess a sense of self-efficacy, acknowledging to themselves, "Hey, I can do that! I can have that kind of marriage, too." We might promote their self-efficacy by first providing peer models of the behavior, such as attendees of marriage preparation programs who, like them, have accentuated marital risks and were skeptical that marriage preparation could enhance their relationship, and what they now realize having gone through the experience and how it benefited their marriage.

Characteristic 6: Believe That the Performance of the Behavior Is Consistent With Its Value System and Self-Image

Although John and Janet are skeptical about the claims touting the benefits of marriage preparation, they are strong believers in the importance of marriage and see themselves as married to each other permanently. Marketing messages that relate to how important marriage is to society, how most people desire marriage for the companionship and intimacy it can bring, and the benefits of facing life together as a couple rather than alone might build this characteristic. Messages with this in mind can then be crafted to show how marriage education provides the knowledge and skills that enable our marriages to start off on the right foot.

Characteristic 7: Perceive Greater Social Pressure to Perform the Behavior Than Not to Perform It (Social Norms)

Janet and John wonder if many people are actually interested in focused marriage preparation or if it is just an interest of a very small minority of people. Wise marketers of marriage preparation programs can emphasize the research that reveals that a high percentage of young adults report interest in and a need for marriage preparation (e.g., Duncan et al., 1996). Social norms marketing messages found in promotional materials might read like this: "Eighty-eight percent of young adults say marriage preparation is important: How about you?"

Characteristic 8: Experience Fewer Barriers to Perform a Behavior Than Not to Perform It

We need to minimize or eliminate in their minds the barriers to John and Janet's participation in marriage preparation. It is important to give attention to at least three possible barriers (Weinreich, 1999):

- Physical barriers (e.g., ease of access of materials, transportation, money)
- Emotional or psychological barriers (e.g., fear of social disapproval for participating in marriage preparation; fear of exposing relationship weaknesses or raising doubts about marriage)

- Social or cultural barriers (e.g., the only people who attend marriage preparation are problem couples admitting they can't make it on their own; promoting equality in marriage in a culture that specifies constrained gender roles)

CONCLUSION ●

Outreach FLE, currently receiving growing but still underwhelming involvement from the public, will remain a fairly empty field of dreams unless family life educators do a better job of applying the principles of social marketing to their work. The eight Ps of social marketing have been discussed with family life educational examples, along with integrating these ideas into the psychological underpinnings of human behavior. We hope our reach can extend even beyond our dreams as we seek with understanding to reach an ever larger audience.

EXPLORATIONS ●

1. Use the ideas in the chapter to devise a marketing plan for your outreach FLE program. Consider the following questions, adapted from Weinreich (1999), as you craft your plan:

Target Audience
- Identify your primary target audience, segmenting as appropriate. Also, identify others in the secondary audience (influencers) you might want to involve in marketing your program, such as relatives of the target audience, media professionals, public figures, and sports heroes.
- Discuss briefly how you would research the needs of the primary target audience. What information is essential for your research? What primary and secondary data collection approaches would you use to gather that information?

Program Goals
- What specifically do you want to accomplish with your target audience? How many in the target audience will adopt the targeted behavior?

Product

- What is the product or behavior you are asking the target audience to adopt?
- What are the key benefits the target audience would receive from adopting the product?
- What is the competition for your product in the target audience's eyes? Competition in FLE might include other FLE offerings or simply competing activities (such as a favorite program on TV held at the same time as a workshop) or no desire to learn ("I already know how to parent effectively! No one can tell me what I don't already know").
- How is your product different from and better than the competition's?

Price

- What are the costs or other barriers that the target audience associates with the product?
- How can you minimize the costs or remove the barriers?

Place

- What are the places in which the target audience makes decisions about engaging in the desired behavior?
- Where do target audiences spend much of their time?
- How will the target audience receive the product? How can existing delivery systems be used, such as a company newsletter, school website, or a toll-free hotline? What approaches to product dissemination will be most efficient for reaching target audience members?

Promotion

- Which communication channels do target audience members pay the most attention to and trust the most?
- What promotional techniques (e.g., marketing tools and strategies, media and community contacts) are the best for conveying your message?
- Who are the most credible spokespeople to address your target audience?

Publics

- Who are the people or groups (in addition to primary and secondary target audiences) outside your organization whose support you need for your program to be successful?

- Who are the people or groups inside your organization whose support you need for your program to be successful?

Partnership
- Which are the most promising organizations to join forces with?

Policy
- What types of policies (organizational or governmental) should you address in your social marketing program?

Purse Strings
- From which organizations will you seek further funding, if necessary?

2. Choose a program topic and desired product or targeted behavior. For each of the characteristics derived from the synthesis of behavior change theories that must be present in a program's messages and intervention, devise marketing messages designed to motivate change in participants toward accomplishment of your program's product.

CHAPTER 17

NARRATIVES OF FAMILY LIFE EDUCATORS

I n Chapter 6, we spoke of personal narrative as an effective way to teach family life education. Stories from one's own life or from the lives of others have an emotional quality that reaches deeper into the heart of the reader and listener. It makes the abstract concrete. It makes it real. In the same way, we believe that sharing the perspectives of actual family life educators would be a great way to enhance understanding of what this career actually entails. Their experiences can mentor, inspire and encourage us, give direction to our own professional pathways, and perhaps provide a beginning professional network.

Some years ago, some thoughtful scholars compiled a work titled *Pioneering Paths in the Study of Families: The Lives and Careers of Family Scholars* (Peterson & Steinmetz, 2002). This volume was devoted to autobiographical essays by scholars in family studies and child development from a variety of disciplines. While we won't attempt to accomplish what they did in a single chapter, we can attempt to address questions like those often asked of us: What do family life educators do? How did you get involved in family life education (FLE)? What about it do you find most rewarding? What about working in FLE is most challenging to you?

This chapter provides a real-life look into professional family life education from the perspective of several family life educators themselves. First we describe the many venues and settings where family life educators can be found. We then follow with the profiles of persons who are working in many of these settings. Afterward we share our own pathways into the profession of family life education.

WHERE DO FAMILY LIFE EDUCATORS WORK? VENUES, SETTINGS, AND PROFILES

Family life educators work in a variety of venues and settings (National Council on Family Relations [NCFR], 2009a). Three broad venue categories include the following:

- ***Practice***—teaching, education, program or curricula development
- ***Administration***—leadership or management, organizing, coordinating
- ***Promotion***—public policy, lobbying, advocating for system change and awareness

Beyond these three broad categories, family life educators are found in numerous settings, many of which are described below, along with the employment opportunities available at each setting (Gilliand & Goddard, 2006; NCFR, 2009a):

- *Government and public policy.* Family specialists are needed at this level to help sensitize governmental systems to the needs of families, as most policies have familial impact, for good or ill. Job possibilities at this level include family policy analyst; child, woman, or family advocate/lobbyist; departments of child and family services; juvenile justice; international family policy advocate; or international human rights advocate.
- *Community-based social services.* Social services comprise government agencies (such as departments of child and family services or entities of similar names) or nonprofit agencies (such as those funded by United Way). Job possibilities at this setting include Big Brother/Sister case worker, family service agent, senior center program provider, institutional social service specialist, children's service provider, department of family services coordinator, department of family services case worker, youth development program specialist, adoption agent, and many others.

- *Health care and family wellness.* Families come in contact with this system at many points in their lives. It includes services for human well-being performed by a variety of practitioners. Job possibilities in this setting include public health program director/specialist, hospital family support specialist, child life specialist, nutrition counselor/educator, prenatal and maternity specialist, holistic health care specialist, long-term care administrator, and hospice care worker.

- *Military family support.* The U.S. military recognizes the need to support families. There may be programs and counseling offered through religious services held by the base chaplain. There are also Family Support Centers on nearly every base of every branch of the military. These centers offer a variety of resources and services for families. Job possibilities include chaplain, family support center director, family support specialist, and military family educator.

- *Faith communities.* Many faith-based organizations provide family-oriented services. Job possibilities include clergy, family mentor, family life educator, parent educator, and youth worker.

- *Entrepreneur.* Some family life educators with business and marketing savvy (and a taste for risk taking) find a great way to strengthen families is through entrepreneurship (starting a business) or social entrepreneurship (starting a nonprofit organization). They become owners of businesses who create and disseminate products and services to families, owners of nonprofit organizations, and owners of social enterprises.

- *Family intervention.* Family life educators are often found in settings serving families in ways that push beyond mere information giving and processing of feelings. Counseling is one of the most common careers for family life educators. Conversely, some counseling professionals also obtain FLE training and Certified Family Life Educator (CFLE) certification and do both counseling and education in their professional setting, thus working in prevention and remediation simultaneously. Job possibilities include licensed professional counselor, licensed marriage and family therapist, case manager for family treatment plans, crisis and hotline services, court-mandated parent education programs, divorce mediation, abuse protection services, and drug and alcohol prevention counselors.

- *Writing and communication.* Some family life educators become excellent media people with the gift of communicating family concepts to the masses in an accessible manner. Job possibilities include curriculum and resource development, public service radio and television programming, and newspaper and magazine journalism on social issues affecting children and families.

- *Business, consumer, and family resource services.* Some family life educators seek careers in business, helping the business sector be more responsive to the changing needs of families. Job possibilities include corporate childcare administrator, employee assistance specialist, family financial counseling and planning specialist, family resource management specialist, family business consultant, and human resource specialist.

- *Education.* Family life educators are found in teaching environments interacting with the very young to the very old: early childhood education, the public educational system, universities and colleges, and community-based educational programs. Job opportunities include preschool teacher, preschool director, Head Start, child development public school teaching in family and consumer sciences (requiring state certification), cooperative extension county educators and state specialists, university teaching and research in family science departments, and teaching family life education programs in the community (e.g., parent education, marriage education, sexuality education, aging programs).

Below we profile several family life educators who are currently working in a number of these settings. These profiles first appeared in the booklet, *Making a Difference: Your Guide to Strengthening Marriages and Families,* published by the Family Life Education Institute (Gilliland & Goddard, 2006). We made contact with the creators of *Making a Difference* and received permission to use the original survey data and profiles collected first in 2002. We then contacted several of the profiled persons and received updates and permission to use their profiles in this chapter.

In the concluding section of this chapter, we describe our own pathways into the profession of family life education. We hope our stories, like the profiles of these professionals, energize you to identify your place in the critical work of family life education.

Community-Based Social Services—Denise Dunn

Denise Dunn, M.S., CFLE, is Executive Director of Housing Services for Eaton County in Mulliken, Michigan. Her job mission is to assist people with low or moderate incomes, including those with disabilities, to obtain safe and affordable housing. In doing so, she helps provide an environment that encourages and supports the attainment of economic self-sufficiency. Denise is a Certified Family Life Educator with a bachelor's degree in family life education and a master's degree in family and consumer sciences.

We asked Denise how she got involved in family life education. She said,

I was working on a B.A. in education and was struggling to find classes as a non-traditional student who had to work to support 3 children when I discovered the Family Life Education program at Spring Arbor College (it is now a university). I was impressed with the fact that I would be able to work with adults who wanted to learn information to better their lives and decided to change my major and attend Spring Arbor in their non-traditional degree program. My internship involved working with the families, whose children I had in my classroom (as a paraprofessional instructional aide) during the summer months, on parenting and educational learning activities. This situation was some-what of a selfish internship as I would have these same students back in the fall. It was my hope that this intervention would improve the child's learning in the fall and improve their behavior as well. What I learned was that I did not want to pursue a Master's in Social Work, but rather work as an educator in some capacity. Just before graduation I was offered a position with a large, downtown church as their Program Director which included program development from birth to death. This opportunity suited my educational visions for myself at the time. This particular church had a homeless mission program and I became very interested in the homeless. Once again, the Lord moved me to make a change and my current position as Executive Director became available and was offered to me.

Some of the rewarding aspects of this job, according to Denise, "have been those items surrounding meeting people's self-sufficiency educational needs so that they can make informed decisions for themselves. These items include home buyers education, budgeting, buying insurance, under-standing credit and credit repair, landlord/tenant law, and foreclosure pre-vention. To me these very basic areas improve lives daily and can do so almost immediately." She enjoys "watching people make positive changes that impact their lives."

She also notices how the work stretches her staff.

The most challenging aspect of her work "is finding the time to develop programs for the emerging needs as quickly as people need them along with all of the reporting that is required by my multiple funding sources which provide the financial support for the office." But she finds this kind of work is a great way to learn about other people. Understanding non-profit organizations is a plus asset in this work. "I currently have 2 employees who are working toward a B.A. in Family Life Education. I could use an office full of people with this background."

Entrepreneur, Government, and Public Policy—Aaron Larson

Aaron Larson, B.S., CFLE, describes himself as a "social entrepreneur." He holds a bachelor's degree in family science. Aaron serves as Director of the National Healthy Marriage Institute (http://www.healthymarriage-weightloss.com). The National Healthy Marriage Institute is a nonpartisan, nondenominational social enterprise organization dedicated to developing products and resources to strengthen marriages and families. Its vision is to help more children, women, men, and communities access the benefits associated with healthy marriages. Aaron has created numerous products to help strengthen marriage, long-distance parenting and grandparenting, and even has pioneered a combination weight loss/marriage education program.

Aaron got involved in family life education

when I figured out that it is easier to make changes from the inside out rather than the outside in, meaning it is easier to strengthen families from the inside rather than from the outside. So I started looking for ways that I could empower families with the skills and insights that they could use to make positive changes inside their families.

Even from his undergraduate years, Aaron looked for novel ways to reach audiences. While taking a senior-level family life education course, Aaron and some of his classmates did life skills education for the inmates at the nearby prison. One of the inmates approached Aaron afterward and said, "The judge says I need a parenting class. Can you do one?" Aaron set about creating 100 ideas for inmates to stay in touch with their children and with the facilitation of his earliest FLE mentor, Shirley Klein, was able to teach male inmates about fathering. It was in this setting where Aaron tried out some of his earliest ideas about "long-distance fathering" that later found their way into the *Dads at a Distance* and *Moms Over Miles* booklets he now produces (see http://www.fambooks.com/daads.htm). It wasn't easy to make a go with these booklets initially, and for a while he had bundles of them sitting in his apartment instead of in clients' hands. That changed when, with several of his booklets in tow, Aaron displayed his goods identified with "Helping Deployed Dads" at a conference for Army Community Service Center staff. He now provides booklets to deploying dads and moms in all of the U.S. services and in Canada. In the process of being successful as an entrepreneurial FLE, Aaron recommends additional training in business marketing. He says you've got to "be willing to take risks and think outside the box."

While building his business, Aaron gave over the daily running of the business to a sister-in-law (also an FLE) and spent 18 months as a healthy marriage specialist in the Administration for Children and Families of the U.S. Department of Health and Human Services, working as a government appointee for then President George W. Bush's Healthy Marriage Initiative, an initiative that continues as of 2010. In his role as a healthy marriage specialist, Aaron became aware of the myriad policies and programs available for strengthening marriage and helped create a strategic plan and the Request for Proposals (RFP) sent out nationally. The Healthy Marriage Initiative provided $300 million in federal funding during its first 5 years of existence. While Aaron delighted in working on the initiative, he was less excited about working in a federal system. "It's the federal system and all the rumors about it being a bureaucracy are true," he said.

Aaron says the most rewarding aspect of his work as a family life educator is "knowing that the work I do has the opportunity to help hundreds of thousands of families around the world experience a little more of the joy and happiness of family life and less of the pain and misery. I have found that helping people strengthen their marriages and families brings me great joy." As for the most challenging aspects of this work, Aaron adds,

> By far the most challenging aspect for me is trying to figure out different ways to help people prevent family problems. It's like trying to convince people paddling down a smooth river that I have some skills I can teach them to navigate the upcoming rapids. From their perspective they don't see the rapids and the river they are on doesn't have any major rapids so they don't need what I have to offer. Besides, they are doing just fine as is. Prevention is a tough sell, but if we can pull it off there will be a lot less need for the intervention side.

Family Interventions—Melissa Vogel

Melissa Vogel, M.S., LMFT, LCPC, CFLE, established the HealthWorks Family Center in Soda Springs, Idaho. Melissa holds a bachelor's degree in family and human development with minors in psychology and social work, as well as a master's degree in family and human development, with an emphasis in marriage and family therapy. As a licensed marriage and family therapist in private practice and as a family life educator, she has conducted both counseling and educational classes for over 30 years in the center she established. She also contracts with a number of agencies and writes grants for funding, writes parenting curriculum, and provides in-service training for schools. She has also taught marital relations, child development, and family crisis classes at the university level. For the past several years, Melissa has been the Mental Health Director for the eight-county Southeastern Idaho Critical Incident Stress Management (CISM) team. In this role, she helps provide critical incident management training for employers, schools, and first responders.

We asked Melissa how she got involved in family life education. She said,

> I started my career as a preschool teacher headed for a degree in Early Childhood Education. I worked as a consultant to The Consumer Product Safety Commission doing public education and media work. After hearing me on a radio interview I was hired to provide parenting workshops for a junior college. Those jobs allowed me to work part-time while I raised my own children. I became increasingly interested in working with parents, as I felt I could make a greater impact on the lives of children. This led me to change my major so as to focus on child development and family dynamics. I found myself drawn toward the field of mental health and obtained my M.S. in Marriage and Family Therapy.

Melissa began her professional work by approaching referral sources and asking what they needed. For example, she would ask judges what programs they were frequently wishing for so they could order to them. Melissa had taught community parenting classes for over 35 years. She notes that "many of my students are initially court-ordered and angry to be in class. Having them connect with their peers, repeat the class several times voluntarily, and report positive change in their parenting behaviors is very rewarding."

We asked Melissa what she considers the most rewarding aspect of her work as a family life educator. She responded, "Parents are so appreciative of information, support. They find themselves often overwhelmed by issues that did not exist during their childhood, such as computer and cell phone use. Advances in brain science and research in other areas of child development bring a wealth of exciting information to share with parents. I also enjoy working with parents who have taken 'life detours' and are in the process of reinventing themselves and creating a better life for their children. I get great satisfaction from knowing my work with parents has an intergenerational 'ripple.'"

The most challenging aspects of this work, according to Melissa, are "teaching evening classes, sometimes low attendance, and shifts in funding." She also mentioned there is considerable "unpaid time required to 'sell' programs, write grants, and implement projects. Each of these projects have their own protocols, reporting forms, etc."

Education—Stephanie Jones

Stephanie Jones, M.S., CPE-I, works as an Extension Associate in the Department of 4-H Youth Development and Family & Consumer Sciences at North Carolina State University (NCSU). In 2007, she became the first graduate of a Master of Science degree program in Human Development and Family Studies (with a specialization in family life and parent education) jointly administered by North Carolina State University and University of North Carolina at Greensboro. First coming to Extension as a Program Associate in Brunswick County, she now works part-time at the state level (she telecommutes and works from home), providing support to the graduate teaching faculty in the degree program, coordinating graduate certificate programs for the Department of 4-H and Family & Consumer Sciences, and working on special projects. Stephanie also has obtained early childhood credentials and received specialized training in several parenting education programs and provides service to local, state, and national organizations and initiatives focused on family life education. Specifically, she serves as the Credentialing Chairperson for the North Carolina Parenting Education Network (NCPEN) and also on the Professional Preparation and Recognition System Committee for the National Parenting Education Network (NPEN).

Stephanie's pathway into family life education began with an interest in people. "I've always been interested in people and their behavior. In fact, I actually enjoy sitting and just observing people. It was my interest in people that propelled me to get a degree in history." While in college studying history, she also took classes in the social sciences. She "found that classes in child psychology and sociology of marriage and the family really interested me. Since I was married and parenting, it seemed natural to me to add family life and parenting to the subjects I was studying. I began to read about family life and parenting for pleasure and for the betterment of my own family."

Her interest in family life education was also spurred on by her family background. "I grew up in a faith tradition where marriage and family are highly valued. It was in part due to my desire to live out these values that led me to seek employment in an occupation that allowed me to work with families." Shortly after, Stephanie began working for her county's Cooperative Extension Service.

Stephanie indicated that the most rewarding aspects of her work as a family life educator are "to have a part in the education of burgeoning family life professionals and to continue to learn from experts in the field. . . . I get a lot of satisfaction from knowing that my service is helping support family life educators and is contributing to advancing the field." Stephanie also noted positive spillover into her own family. "I have broad base of knowledge and a repertoire of skills to use with my own family." While such knowledge and skills can be enriching to families, Stephanie notes it can also present challenges. "I find that knowledge doesn't always easily translate to applying skills, especially when dealing with those closest to you. And because of the breadth of my knowledge I find that I sometimes overanalyze my own children and family."

The most challenging aspect of her current work as a family life educator "is juggling the demands of my job with my family life. My job vies for my time and attention, but so does parenting four daughters, ages 17, 15, 13, and 5, and a maintaining my marriage. I'm grateful that I can work with a university from a remote location and continue to make my family life a priority. At some point in the future I would like to again provide direct services to families. I hope that when that time comes the field will have evolved and that the necessary structures will be in place to enable me to be able to make a living wage doing the work that I love and believe in."

Not-for-Profit Organizations, Writing, and Communication—Julie Baumgardner

Julie Baumgardner, M.S., is the President and Executive Director of First Things First (FTF; http://firstthings.org/), a grassroots agency dedicated to strengthening families in Chattanooga, Tennessee. Julie holds a bachelor's degree in Psychology and a master's degree in Community Agency Counseling. She has also been trained in several models of marriage education, including PREP, PREPARE/Enrich, FOCCUS, and The Marriage Breakthrough and several parenting curricula. At FTF, Julie directs 10 full-time employees where, besides teaching seminars, she works to promote family-friendly workplace policies and increase community awareness of the importance of strong marriages and families through public service campaigns. Prior to joining FTF, she was the regional marketing manager for a group of hospitals and also worked as a social worker and program director for a child and adolescent program at a psychiatric hospital.

The success of the FTF initiative has sparked interest in duplicating the FTF model in cities across the country. Although they focus on the Hamilton County area, due to the uniqueness of their community initiative model organization, Julie and her FTF team have provided technical assistance to hundreds of communities nationwide. She says, "We are dedicated to strengthening families through education, collaboration, and mobilization. We have three goals: to reduce divorce and out-of-wedlock pregnancies and increase father involvement in the lives of their children." She describes her work atmosphere as "fast paced!!!!!" She speaks frequently both locally and nationally on healthy marriage and family issues. She serves on the national advisory board for the Coalition for Marriage, Family and Couples Education.

In addition to her providing FTF leadership, Julie writes a weekly column on family issues in the *Chattanooga Times-Free Press* that reaches thousands. She also hosts a monthly talk show on public television discussing topics relevant to marriage and family. These offerings are accessible on the FTF website.

We asked Julie the most rewarding aspects of her work as a family life educator. She said, "I love helping people learn skills that will strengthen their relationships. I love watching people 'get it' when we are teaching skills, whether it is communication, conflict resolution, father involvement, etc."

When asked about drawbacks of her work, Julie says she honestly doesn't know of any. "I get energized when I work in this area. It is my passion. If you are passionate about helping build strong marriages and families, I would highly recommend [this type of work]."

Health Care and Family Wellness—Melissa NewMyer

Melissa NewMyer, M.S., works as a Child Life Specialist at The Children's Hospital at Emanuel in Portland, Oregon. Melissa holds a bachelor's degree in Marriage, Family, and Human Development and a master's degree in Counselor Education. She is a Nationally Certified Counselor (NCC), Licensed Professional Counselor (LPC), and a Registered Play Therapist (RPT), in addition to being a CFLE and Certified Child Life Specialist. For six years, Melissa worked full-time as a Child Life Specialist, but since 2007 and two daughters later, she has worked at the hospital as an on-call Child Life Specialist. Her specialty at the hospital is to help children and their families cope with hospitalization and illness. Some of the things she does on the job are listening to music with a patient, showing a child that he or she can still play while in bed, and teaching a family member that his or her sibling still likes the same things even though the sibling doesn't have any hair.

We asked Melissa how she got involved in family life education. During her senior year, she learned about the Family Life Educator Certification through the National Council on Family Relations. As a Marriage, Family, and Human Development major, she learned she was already well on the path to completing the education required to become a CFLE. So she stayed an additional summer term after graduation to complete the education necessary for this certification. "My primary title where I work is Child Life Specialist so family life education fits in as I work with a hospitalized child and their family."

We asked Melissa what she considered the most rewarding aspect of her work. She said,

> I love to see the resiliency of families. Having a child with a critical illness or injury can be one of the most stressful things for a family to endure. However, in these moments we often are able to see how capable and amazing parents and children can truly be. It is most rewarding to watch a family successfully conquer such a challenge and become better and stronger because of it.

She also loves it "when the kids come back to visit and don't want to see the doctors or nurses but ME!"

In terms of the most challenging aspects of this work, Melissa adds that the "hospital can be stressful at times, with beeping machines, crying patients (or nurses) and frustrated doctors, nurses, patients, and families. It can be very emotionally draining working in such an intense setting. A child's hospitalization can range from less than 24 hours to weeks or even months." Some of the challenges she notes are related to the perceived relative status in the medical community of a Child Life Specialist. "Sometimes others don't see the value of child life, or simply think I 'just play' with kids all day." Also, "It can be challenging to see the impact of family life education when many of the families I see, I only have contact with on a short-term basis." In addition, there aren't a lot of positions available; "If I wanted to change organizations, I would have to relocate or if I wanted to relocate, there wouldn't necessarily be positions available where I wanted to go." She also sees little chance for advancement, as well: "I am employed as a Child Life Specialist now. The only other place to go would be to direct a child life program, and there are even fewer positions for coordinators and directors."

Even so, Melissa indicates this work "can be very fulfilling and fun . . . I like families, and kids, and I like helping people," she says.

Military Family Support—David Jones

David Jones, M.S., CFLE, works full-time as a Program Manager with the Army National Guard Family Readiness program. He supervises several Family Readiness Support Assistants in a trainer-of-trainers capacity. The word *readiness* has been inserted in these military job titles to emphasize the preventive aspects of this work. David conducts training webinars regularly, providing ongoing human resource and content training for his assistants. Broadly, these readiness support assistants help families prepare for military life through education about the resources available, through relationship education programs such as marriage and parenting education, and through teaching how to navigate deployment and relocation. In addition to his very busy program management responsibilities, David works part-time as a chaplain with the Utah Army National Guard. He holds the rank of captain. David has a bachelor's degree in Marriage, Family, and Human Development and a master's degree in Family and Human Development, with specific coursework in family life education.

We asked David how he got involved in family life education. After completing his undergraduate degree, he had the good fortune to be hired in the Utah National Guard Family Program Office, as the Assistant Director and then Director. His role was to educate commanders, soldiers, and families on the importance of readiness for military life, the resources available, and how to maintain relationships during military separation. This early work launched him into a career of managing and directing military family programs with the National Fatherhood Initiative and the Army Guard, during which time he developed many educational resources. More recently, he has combined his managing, directing, and program development expertise with a military career as a chaplain.

We asked David to share what he considered the most rewarding aspect of his work as a family life educator. He described it as "seeing the light bulb switch on when a concept taught to a Family or Soldier is grasped. In facilitating Marriage Seminars as a Chaplain, I've seen walls that have been put up for years be torn down as new relationship skills are learned."

David describes the most challenging aspects of this work as "marketing, marketing, marketing. Even with the best of teaching skills and programming, it is only as good as how well it can get into the hands of the target audience. If they don't know about it, it does no good. Family life educators need to know how to market in engaging and successful ways."

PATHWAYS INTO THE PROFESSION OF FLE—THE AUTHORS ●

In this text, we have strived to share expertise gained through collective experience about family life education in outreach settings. Until now we haven't taken opportunity to share how and why we got involved in FLE. We conclude this chapter by sharing our individual pathways into the profession.

Steve's story. When I first entered college, I had aspirations to be a professional musician. I first majored in Jazz Improvisation. I had a dream to be a professional drummer and work in the inner circle of musicians in Los Angeles who did concerts and recording sessions with leading artists. My drum teacher had lived the life of an inner-circle professional musician in California, but he was also a realist. He explained that it takes about 7 years of effort to break into the inner circle, if you are good enough, and during that interim time, you are hunting for odd jobs and for food. His question to me was this: What kind of family life do you want to have?

That question made me think of the strong and varied family life I had experienced. My father died in an auto-pedestrian accident when I was 3. I spent the majority of my upbringing in a single-parent family. And we had hung together well. It wasn't until I was 13 that my mother remarried, which brought additional challenges. But we had weathered those well, too. Notwithstanding many challenges, I had a wonderful upbringing. I decided that the life of a professional musician was not for me, as it would make unlikely my idea of strong family life. Instead I switched to a focus on music education and took an intermission from my education for missionary service to Japan.

I returned home with changed professional aspirations and desires. Among them was a deepened desire to work with families and a hunger to learn anything and everything about families, especially marriage. I voraciously consumed many of the classics summarizing research and theory about marriage and family. In my other classes, I did assignments or gave speeches on family issues. Initially I decided to pursue graduate study in marriage and family therapy; it didn't really matter what bachelor's degree I received. Ultimately I graduated with a degree in Speech Communication with a Music minor, doing my final senior project on family communication.

I enrolled in a master's degree program in family sciences with an emphasis in Family Life Education. This was the first time I had heard those three words in order. An adviser explained I could complete a more general degree at the master's level and then pursue a therapy degree at the doctoral level. During my master's program, I took a few therapy classes but didn't feel at home there, professionally. At the same time, I was having my first in-depth exposure to the preventive side of helping families. I became thrilled with the idea of helping individuals and family members, through educational means, gain the knowledge, skills, and attributes needed to enjoy the quality of family life they want. I credit my first family life education mentor, Joel Moss, with igniting my passion for prevention.

During my Ph.D. program in Family Studies, I assisted Extension specialists Dena Targ and Judy Myers-Walls. They were the first to introduce me to the idea of taking the university to the people where they live and work. Unexpectedly, my first professional position was as an Extension Family and Child Development Specialist at Auburn University. I loved getting the good news of quality family life out to the people. I enjoyed writing articles, traveling the state giving presentations, writing news columns, and giving media interviews in an accessible manner for people who may never come and learn at a university.

While I loved my work at Auburn, I loved the idea of being closer to family more, so I found another Extension position in Montana, spending over 7 years there. While in Montana, I especially enjoyed creating interdisciplinary programs such as Balancing Work and Family and EDUFAIM: Educating Families to Achieve Independence in Montana and writing a popular news column, "Family Matters."

My current position at Brigham Young University as a Professor of Family Life provides the opportunity to continue to extend knowledge beyond the college campus but also to teach students how to do it, too. Today's technology has provided the opportunity to reach numbers of people not possible with traditional family life education. I've been involved in creating a website called Forever Families (www.foreverfamilies.net) and developing a television series, *Real Families, Real Answers,* which was nominated for a Rocky Mountain Emmy award.

Working as a career family life educator has given me more joy personally and professionally than I ever supposed it would or thought that I deserved. It is a work like no other.

Wally's story. After getting a bachelor's degree in Physics and Math Education, I began teaching public school. In addition to the expected classes, I was soon teaching folklore, yearbook, photography, journalism, filmmaking, gifted and talented, and even English literature. I also served as a media director. Some of the "broadening" of my career was due to being in a rural school. But much of it was due to my love of creative challenges.

After a dozen years in the public schools, I wanted more challenges. I wanted to be learning every day! I returned to school and got a Ph.D. in Family and Human Development. When I began my program, I didn't even know about family life education. I only knew that I wanted to be a good husband and father and that I wanted to help people.

When I graduated, I applied for several jobs that seemed to fit my training and interests. I was offered the job as a Family and Child Development Specialist with the Alabama Cooperative Extension Service at Auburn University. My first trainer was Steve Duncan, the first author of this book. I'm grateful for his help in getting started as a family life educator.

I loved my work creating programs and traveling the state of Alabama as an itinerant preacher of family happiness! I couldn't imagine a more satisfying career. In Alabama, we created programs like Principles of Parenting and The Great Self Mystery. Then the Covey Leadership Center (now Franklin-Covey Company) invited me to join them as they worked on the book, *The 7 Habits of Highly Effective Families.* I learned a lot—but must admit that I love community family life education more than the corporate world.

Ultimately, I found another job as a family life educator, this time in Arkansas. Since arriving here, we have created a TV series called *Guiding Children Successfully* and a series of family programs, including The Personal Journey, The Marriage Garden, The Parenting Journey, See the World Through My Eyes, and Managing Stress. I love the opportunity to take powerful research and translate it into practical programs (for more info, go to www.arfamilies.org).

One of the satisfying projects we completed in Arkansas was training ministers all over the state on marriage and parenting. We provided them with summaries of research and walked them through our programs over the course of the 2-day trainings. I'm convinced that working with faith communities and schools are two important ways we can reach people today.

I have also enjoyed writing books. I never imagined myself as an author, yet it is another way of getting powerful messages to people who need them. I helped revise Ginott's classic *Between Parent and Child* as well as write *Soft-Spoken Parenting* and *The Marriage Garden*. Even writing for web magazines has been an interesting way of reaching both secular and religious audiences.

I never imagined how much I would learn in this career. And I never dreamed how satisfying family life education could be. When we have the opportunity of helping people break through to greater understanding and appreciation in their families, we are truly fortunate! I hope you have just as much joy and growth in family life education as I am having!

● CONCLUSION

From these narratives, we realize there are many opportunities, venues, and settings in which to do family life education. Each professional takes a different pathway in the sharing of his or her gifts and passion in FLE. We hope these stories help you find your place.

● EXPLORATIONS

1. Spend some time reflecting on the profiles of these family life educators. Do any of their experiences speak to you? Then think about the who, what, and how of family life education for you, now that you have heard from those who have experience in the field.

- WHO: What audience would you like to work with the most? Consider type, age group, and circumstances (e.g., couples preparing for marriage, married couples, new parents, parents with young children, parents of adolescents, youth, college-age students, grandparents, single parents, stepfamilies, families of children with special needs, etc.).
- WHAT: On what specific topic would you like to share specialized knowledge and skills with your chosen audience? What topic energizes you the most (e.g., marriage preparation, marriage enhancement, communication and problem solving, child development, discipline and child guidance, money management, family stress, dealing with aging and death, work and family balance, life skills, etc.)?

- HOW: How do you want to convey this knowledge and teach these skills to your audience (e.g., products—books, DVDs, brochures, Internet site, magazine, television shows, or services—workshops, programs, events)?

2. Using the venues and settings information from this chapter, do an inventory of the various venues and job opportunities for family life educators in your community. Identify the FLE-oriented agencies and create an annotated discussion of the kinds of work a family life educator could do there. Identify both pre-graduation opportunities and post-graduation opportunities. Create a plan of action to contact these potential employers.

CHAPTER 18

IMPROVING THE PRACTICE OF FAMILY LIFE EDUCATION

Nearly two decades ago, in her concluding chapter of Volume 1 of the *Handbook of Family Life Education*, Margaret Arcus asked, "What issues and problems need to be addressed and what critical challenges must be surmounted if the [family life education] movement is to continue to serve families well?" (Arcus, 1993, p. 229). In this epilogue chapter, we ask a similar question: What are the practical issues that need attention if family life education (FLE) is to be successful in strengthening individuals, couples, and families where they live and work, well into the 21st century?

Many would say that these are both the best of times and the worst of times. Families face unprecedented stress. Yet FLE has powerful new allies with new discoveries in FLE and technological resources. While the field will continue to grow and be refined, we have tools today that can be used to make important differences for those we serve.

To us, there are five issues that require attention: professionalization, program rigor, program effectiveness, marketing, and reaching the neediest audiences. We give special attention in this concluding chapter to the professionalization of FLE. The remaining areas have also been developed as themes in various chapters in this book. We revisit them here for emphasis.

PROFESSIONALIZATION OF FAMILY LIFE EDUCATION ●

Major efforts need to continue to be made to increase the value and understanding of FLE as a profession, and these understandings yet need institutionalization within community consciousness. There is too little information about what family life educators are and do and why the public should care. Efforts are being made to address these deficits. One major effort toward professionalization of FLE has been the certification of family life educators. Perhaps the most comprehensive and notable effort in the field has been the Certified Family Life Educator (CFLE) program sponsored by the National Council on Family Relations, as discussed in Chapter 1. Other professional organizations have been engaged in broad-based certification that have relevance for family life educators. For example, the American Association of Family and Consumer Sciences offers a certification in family and consumer sciences (CFCS).

Even though the theoretical importance of certification for the development of the discipline of FLE has been demonstrated (Cassidy, 2003), and the benefits of certification for applicants and the field are touted (see www.ncfr.org), convincing others of its practical importance has proven to be quite a different matter. For example, in 2001, the National Council on Family Relations (NCFR) commissioned the Human Resource Research Organization (HumRRO, 2001) to conduct a market analysis that, among other things, asked employers to report their preference for hiring certified family life educators over those not certified. Respondents completed a survey by mail or via the Internet. Only 7% of the potential sample responded to the survey, seriously limiting the usefulness of the data. However, findings revealed that only a small minority of potential FLE employers (2.7% of mail survey respondents; 11.5% of Internet respondents) expressed a current preference for hiring certified family life educators, with a larger minority (13% of mail survey respondents; 30% of Internet respondents) expressing a preference for hiring certified family life educators in the future. Evidently, the need for credentialed professionals in family life has not risen to the felt need of credentials for those in social work or clinical professionals, where such credentialing is part of a state's statutes and community consciousness. More work remains to be done to demonstrate convincingly the benefits of certification to potential employers, family life educators, and the public.

A related alternative to broad-based certification for family life educators is the movement to recognize professional development in an FLE subspecialty, such as parenting and marriage education. In the same market analysis cited above, employers were asked to report the extent to which they would favor employees with either certification as a parenting educator or a marriage educator. There was greater preference for the parenting educator certification, perhaps because the respondents were more familiar with the field of parenting education than marriage education. However, before such efforts with other certifying approaches were made, the marketing study findings indicated that NCFR should continue to support the CFLE credential and do so solidly before taking on other credentials (Cassidy, 2003).

Some groups are not waiting for national professional organizations to act on specifying a course and direction in subspecialty professional development and certification. In 2002, a group of eight family life and human development Cooperative Extension specialists began to ask what knowledge and skills parenting educators need to be effective with parents and children. The result of these discussions is the National Extension Parenting Educators' Framework (NEPEF; DeBord et al., 2002), comprising six *content* dimensions drawn from the National Extension Parent Education Model (Care for Self, Understand, Guide, Nurture, Motivate, Advocate) and six *process* dimensions (Grow, Frame, Develop, Educate, Embrace, Build), each discussed in Chapter 10. Developers see NEPEF as a framework for helping to tailor existing degree programs in colleges and universities but also as a structure for credentialing programs. For example, in North Carolina, through focus groups, parenting educators helped design a four-level credentialing system. To become credentialed, parenting educators must demonstrate they have education and experience with each of the NEPEF areas in addition to references and a personal statement with their application. The North Carolina Parenting Education Network has taken this on as part of building the field. Its vision is that court judges and others will begin to recommend that parenting education be delivered by credentialed parenting educators. North Carolina now has over 114 credentialed parenting educators (Karen DeBord, personal communication, March 4, 2010).

Networking provides another opportunity to strengthen the profession of FLE. The profession and service to clientele benefit when we can share and learn ideas from other family life educators locally, statewide, nationally, and internationally, with whom we are bound by a common vision and mission. An example of the kind of networking that needs to take place is the National Parenting Education Network (NPEN; www.npen.org). This organization promotes four tenets: networking, to facilitate linkages among practitioners; knowledge development, to expand the base of research and knowledge and increase its accessibility; professional growth, to address issues such as ethics, standards, certification, and education; and leadership among parenting educators and with policy makers, media, and the public. NPEN has been a catalyst for states to establish their own networks.

Another movement in the professionalization of FLE is training in specific FLE program curricula, either commercial or university based. For example, Smart Marriages (www.smartmarriages.com) posts both a substantial listing of program resources and sponsors pre- and postannual conference training in many different programs for couples, parents, and families. Family life educators can take advantage of this training and incorporate it as part of their programming repertoire. Increased professional capabilities make family life educators more useful to their clientele and put them in a position to promote FLE. Of course, professional training opportunities such as these need to be screened for their credibility and programs for their design (as discussed in Chapter 2). Yet many outstanding programs exist where family life educators can be trained in specialty programs that bring them independent professional recognition. We applaud these movements because we believe they will hasten the speed at which family life educators can be recognized for their expertise. We invite national professional organizations to underwrite such options for their membership.

Colleges and universities can expand their content and practical training in FLE in concert with the times. With the venues of FLE becoming increasingly diverse, it is clear that training programs in FLE need to adapt to adequately prepare students to enter frontline FLE positions in communities as members of nonprofit agencies and other organizations with community FLE missions, as well as prepare them for teaching FLE in high school and college settings. While the principles guiding FLE are similar, the practices differentiating outreach FLE and classroom-based FLE are significant. For example, few academic programs help budding family life educators develop skills at working with the media, networking and collaboration, or developing FLE Internet sites.

Just as there has been a lack of standards to guide the development of quality FLE programs, the field of family life education has long suffered for lack of a unifying credo to guide professional behavior (see Brock, 1993). Recent efforts have sought to overcome this deficit. The Minnesota Council on Family Relations (2009) has accomplished remarkable work in this area. Their effort integrates three theoretical approaches used in ethical decision making: relational ethics (what elements should guide my practice with clientele), ethical dilemmas (how does a good family life educator respond to situations involving abuse and other issues), and virtues (what characteristics embody a good family life educator). From this effort has emerged a long-awaited code of ethics for family life educators who become certified through the National Council on Family Relations. It is focused on the family life educator's relationship with parents and families, children and youth, colleagues and the profession, and the broader community. Persons applying for provisional or full Certified Family Life Educator, or veteran CFLEs as well, must submit a signed copy of the CFLE code of ethics. This code, plus the background information that led to its creation, is in Appendix E.

While we think having a code of ethics is an important step in professionalization, a limitation is that it does not have the same power as professional licensure to motivate adherence to standards of behavior. In addition, the signing of the code of ethics works on the honor system—no one evaluates the FLE professional against the ethical statements. The ethics code is only enforceable, and lightly so, through the National Council on Family Relations. Other family life educators who are unconcerned about certification are free to conduct themselves as they will.

Beyond certification, improved networking, training in specialty programs, expanded academic offerings, and adherence to an ethical code, family life educators can build the profession of FLE by being more proactive about their line of work. Cassidy (2003) suggests several ways this can be done.

Promote and Support Standards of Practice

Becoming certified as a family life educator or some other subspecialty helps to accomplish this. Among other things, certification increases credibility as a professional by showing that the high standards and criteria needed to provide quality FLE have been met. The designation can be included in one's resume, on professional stationery and business cards, and the instructional material one uses.

Educate Employers and the Public

As discussed in Chapter 16 on marketing, family life educators are in need of marketing themselves to a perhaps inattentive public. They need to take the opportunity to explain what family life educators are and do, what their academic training prepares them to do, and why having certification is critical in a world of ideas with questionable foundations about families.

Partner Family Life Education With Other Intervention Services

Family life educators might seek to offer their prevention programs as an adjunct to the counseling services offered by the same agency. For example, a married couple might be directed to family life educators for relationship skill building while using the counseling sessions for clinical issues.

Family Life Educators as Providers in Response to Legislation

Occasionally, a public policy may be enacted that opens the door for increased FLE involvement. For example, one legislative proposal provided a discount on marriage license fees if couples completed a marriage education course. Family life educators could be identified as providers of such a course.

A final effort with the promise of increasing the awareness of family life educators as unique professionals has just begun. NCFR has been working with the Department of Labor (DOL) to create a new job classification. The new occupation is to be titled Certified Family Life Educator. According to Dawn Cassidy (2004), NCFR Certification Director, once a CFLE is part of the DOL's classification system, statistics such as employment settings, educational requirements, and salaries can be more reliably collected, enabling the NCFR to more accurately track and promote the profession of family life education.

PROGRAM RIGOR ●

Over a decade ago, Arcus and colleagues (1993a) expressed concern about a weak scholarly basis for programs. As we mentioned in Chapter 2, "In the area of family life, there is an explosion of information, some credible and some incredible, even implausible. Many persons are willing to be called a family 'expert' through bringing forth armchair theories and ideas of their own design. In contrast, FLE programs must be grounded in the best current scholarship if they are to enjoy credibility" (p. 33).

Recent decades have hosted a revolution in our understanding of family process. New insights into development and well-being challenge old notions of self-esteem (e.g., Baumeister, 1992; Seligman, 2002). Old recommendations in couple relationships have been dramatically altered (e.g., Gottman, 1999). Scholars of parent-child relationships are developing an integration of nature and nurture approaches (e.g., Maccoby, 2002). Yet many of these discoveries do not get beyond a small group of scholars. The greatest discoveries need to find their way to the homes, minds, and practices of family members everywhere.

Since the Arcus et al. (1993a) writing, important advances have been made and models recommended to encourage the development of FLE programs that have strong scholarly foundations (Bogenschneider, 1996; Dumka et al., 1995; Hughes, 1994). In addition, a number of FLE resources have been developed that are founded on solid research (see example programs in Chapter 9). Helping family life educators develop and enhance skill in developing scientifically rigorous programs has also been a major emphasis in this book. Yet there continue to be family life resources developed for the general public that have questionable scientific foundations, some of which earn considerable money for the authors. This undermines the credibility of the profession of FLE while failing to provide value to those who pay the bills. Family life educators will advance the trustworthiness and usefulness of the field to the public to the degree they follow rigorous practices in the design, implementation, and evaluation of their programs.

For FLE to truly make a difference in communities, more programs need to be developed systemically, that is, to be comprehensive and multilevel in focus. To make a meaningful difference for families will require more than a single program focused at a single level. To be sure, this kind of systemic programming is complex and expensive. However, more and more of our programs should consider educational intervention at more than one level. For instance, reduction of marital risks and promotion of strengths requires interventions at different levels of the social ecology: individual (e.g., reducing personal beliefs in marital myths), couple (e.g., dealing calmly with couple differences and challenges), community (e.g., provision of marriage education programs in religious and non-religious community settings), and national (e.g., the establishment of family-friendly policies). In addition, a comprehensive approach would entail the provision of interventions of differing levels of involvement at the personal/couple level dependent on clientele need, ranging from basic information (e.g., marriage fact sheet or video) to couple therapy (Doherty, 1995).

PROGRAM EFFECTIVENESS ●

A key question for FLE among the public is this: Does it work? There is a need to do better evaluations to better answer that question. Many programs are developed without first assessing the needs of the targeted audience and then marketed without evidence that they really work. The importance of assessing needs prior to or concomitant with program development was emphasized in Chapters 2 and 16.

Once FLE resources are developed in concert with up-to-date scholarship and input from the targeted audience, they need rigorous evaluation appropriate to their developmental stage, as emphasized in Chapter 3. Chapter 3 provided many helpful guides for improving the quality of FLE evaluation. Among them is the importance of linking program processes from visioning to goals to objectives to program activities to evaluation items.

There are still too many programs doing evaluations that don't match the maturity level and objectives of FLE programs, limiting the ability to answer important questions about program effectiveness. This circumstance must change if FLE is to become embedded in communities as an indispensable component of strengthening families.

For example, we don't know what kinds of programs work best for what populations, in the short term and the long term, although the pleading for this kind of evaluation has persisted for years (e.g., Carroll & Doherty, 2003, Guerney & Maxon, 1990). We can begin to answer this question even at the formative stages of program evaluation (e.g., Steimle & Duncan, 2004). In addition, we know almost nothing concerning the comparative effectiveness of programs. Little is also known to what degree FLE actually may make matters worse instead of better (e.g., Halford, Sanders, & Behrens, 2001).

Evaluation sophistication must also increase. The better the evaluation, the more that family life educators can declare with confidence to funders and the public that their program accomplishes its vision and mission. Combining multiple methods of program evaluation and quantitative and qualitative approaches, using approaches that follow best evaluative practices, and, as appropriate, publishing them in leading journals are important directions to take. Certainly as programs become mature, family life educators are wise to spend considerable funds demonstrating the impact of the program and communicating findings in understandable ways to decision makers and the public, as well as professional audiences.

● MARKETING OF FAMILY LIFE EDUCATION PRINCIPLES, PRACTICES, AND PROGRAMS

As mentioned in Chapter 16, it is still the FLE professionals themselves, rather than potential clientele, who sense the need and appreciate the benefits of FLE the most. We must do a better job of marketing FLE principles, practices, and programs if the field is to grow in communities.

To apply these principles requires family life educators to first and consistently assess the needs of the target audience, as emphasized in Chapter 16. This audience will tell us most about how important the issue is and how to best reach them with the FLE information we seek to share with them.

As we continue into the future, family life educators will need to give increasing attention to when, where, and how programs will be offered. They will need to move beyond traditional modes of delivery of FLE and expand efforts in other areas. For example, the Internet is a primary "place" where FLE currently and in the future will take place, and this book devotes some emphasis to its use. While some important recent discoveries have been made concerning the relative effectiveness of web-based FLE versus traditional FLE (Duncan et al., 2009), much more needs to be known. As this and other resources are developed, we will need to take care that the quality of the educational experience is not sacrificed. Other places that likely will experience increased emphasis are mass media (multimethod such as radio and TV public service announcements with corresponding evaluation), piggybacking FLE with other content areas (such as intertwining marriage education with childbirth education), and home visits to higher risk clientele needing a one-on-one tailored approach.

Also, when considering traditional FLE, it is clear from some research that audiences prefer short programs. Yet longer programs tend to produce the strongest, most reliable effects on participants. More thoughtful attention must be given to the economy of a program, making it more efficient without reducing effectiveness. For example, can programs be trimmed to the bare-necessity elements of programs that are responsible for producing the greatest benefits?

More effective assessment of educational needs together with precision education may allow users to get the information they need in a format that works for them just as they need it. While growing technological resources will enable new options, it seems clear that family life will always be a uniquely human enterprise.

Finally, as family life educators, we must work harder to position the strengthening of families at the forefront of public attention. Polls suggest we could be successful with a well-coordinated social marketing effort. According to one recent international poll conducted for the World Congress on Families II, most of the world's citizens agree that the family is the fundamental unit of society (Wirthlin Worldwide, 1999). Recent U.S data reported that 92% of Americans agree we can only go forward in this country if families are strengthened (Wirthlin Worldwide, 2000). Using research to frame the health of families as a public health issue may be an important step in the development of social marketing messages. For example, studies show that poor social relationships are as damaging to physical health as cigarette smoking (House, Landis, & Umberson, 1988, cited in Doherty, 1997). It is likely that few in the general population are aware of this research. Knowing such facts may promote greater interest in strengthening their family through education.

REACHING DIVERSE, UNDERSERVED AUDIENCES •

Potential FLE audiences are becoming increasingly diverse. For example, between 1980 and 2000, the minority population grew 11 times faster than the White, non-Hispanic population. While the general population witnessed a 24% growth, there was a corresponding 31% growth among African Americans, 142% among Latinos, and 204% among Asian and Pacific Islanders (Hobbs & Stoops, 2002, cited in Wiley & Ebata, 2004). If trends continue, family life educators can expect the White middle class, as a proportion of their anticipated FLE audience, to decrease in size. To be effective, family life educators will need to carefully examine their personal values and biases in response to growing diversity, as well as assess program goals and objectives, content, teaching methods, and marketing strategies for their fit with the specific audience (Myers-Walls, 2000; Wiley & Ebata, 2004).

There is also evidence that the populations most needful of FLE, including ethnic minorities, are being underserved. For example, individuals and couples who participate in premarital education tend to be at lower risk for marital distress and dissolution (Carroll & Doherty, 2003; Sullivan & Bradbury, 1997). Where the needs are greatest, the opportunities for positive outcomes and impacts increase. We must do a better job in reaching those who are most in need of FLE.

We agree with the four categories of strategies proposed by Wiley and Ebata (2004) to improve family life educators' efforts to reach underserved audiences. First, efforts must be made to increase access of underserved audiences to existing FLE resources. It is possible that the underserved audience simply does not know about the resources ("Did you know that the parenting group meets at the elementary school every Thursday evening at 7:00 p.m.?"), which begs the question of how well materials are being marketed to them. Second, assuming access to a resource, we need to carefully select the resource, making sure it is sensitive to the unique characteristics and needs of the underserved audience. A program for parents in general may not be the program of choice for father strengthening. The third strategy involves modifying the resources or services to fit the audience. Modifying a resource may require language and cultural sensitivity adjustments. Finally, it may be necessary to develop a program from the ground up, because existing programs or modifications thereof are simply inadequate to address the needs of the underserved audience.

For family life educators to more effectively carry out their charge to strengthen families among an increasingly diverse citizenry, they will need enhanced professional training. College and university degree programs will need to give increasing attention to diversity training. Citizens of a diverse society need greater sensitivity to different worldviews. Certification criteria may need reexamination; professional associations can play an important role in the in-service training of its membership (Wiley & Ebata, 2004).

● CONCLUSION

In this book, we have attempted to provide background for the essential skills needed for effective community FLE. We have spoken about the need for a working philosophy to guide our work as family life educators, for programs to be scientifically designed as well as service oriented, and for curricula and programs to follow after established quality guidelines. We have addressed evaluating and creating significant learning experiences that engage audiences using a variety of methods. We have written about the important role of media and use of technology in FLE, as well as building sensitivity to diversity, a need for collaboration, and marketing family life educational principles, practices, and programs. Finally, we have highlighted some important areas of concern as we try and move FLE into the future.

We hope all of this helps us improve our craft and capabilities to strengthen individuals and families with whom we have the chance to work. We wish you every success in the vital work of FLE.

EXPLORATIONS ●

1. Do a personal inventory of your professional strengths and potential in reference to the various skills and ideas presented in this volume. Consider how to best use your strengths. Select an area where you would like to grow in the coming months. You might devote extra study time to the area, observe the work of admired models, practice the skill, or meet with a mentor. Develop in that area until you are comfortable that it has become a strength.

2. If you have not already done so, join a professional association that supports and provides linkages to other family life educators, such as the National Council on Family Relations and the American Association for Family and Consumer Sciences. Study articles in the journals sponsored by these organizations that have particular relevance to work as family life educators.

3. Seek opportunities for state and local networking with family life educators. Check to see if affiliates of NPEN are located in your state and how you can connect with them. Or consider starting your own association with like-minded individuals.

APPENDIX A

A Statement of Principles

H. Wallace Goddard
and Charles A. Smith

This appendix is quite different from the chapters in this book. While all the chapters amass the scholarly thinking and evidence behind certain practices, this appendix lists, describes, and applies a set of principles. These principles are much like assumptions. They may fit with the informed good sense of many scholars and practitioners, but we do not undertake to prove them. We suggest that they be used as discussion points in clarifying thinking or developing programs. In considering program coverage and recommendations, the principles can act as a helpful guide.

For example, when outlining a program for teen parents, planners might examine this list of principles. They might identify those with special application to the specific audience and objectives of the program. They might consider how to honor all the principles in the process of developing the program. The same kind of reflection might be done in designing activities for the program.

The principles can also guide our own development and professional practice. We must grow if we are to help those we serve to grow. Consider those areas where you would like to make greater application of principles in your practice of family life education (FLE).

THE PRINCIPLE OF ORDER: BEHAVIOR HAS ● PREDICTABLE CONSEQUENCES

Elaboration: The laws of nature and the laws of relationships follow systematic principles. By working with the laws, we get the outcomes we seek. A farmer who fails to provide wise and consistent attention to his crops is likely to harvest more weeds than grain.

Marriage example: A couple that tries to operate over the years on initial infatuation without continued investments of understanding and connection is likely to drift apart. A person who chooses to blame is likely to experience alienation.

Parenting example: Children who do not have a close personal relationship with at least one adult who talks to them, loves them, and respects them as special people are likely to grow up emotionally and socially limited. It is important for children's development that there be adults who interact positively with them.

FLE application: Family members who fail to gain knowledge and act deliberately are likely to have more family problems than if they seek information and act intentionally. To affect outcomes, it is important to understand the laws of development and apply them. Family life educators can appeal to people's intuitive sense of this law in marketing programs by asking, "Do you want your family outcomes to be left to chance?"

THE PRINCIPLE OF EMPATHY: A FUNDAMENTAL ACT OF ● CARING IS TAKING TIME TO LOOK AT THE WORLD THROUGH ANOTHER PERSON'S EYES

Elaboration: Our fundamental separateness as humans cannot be overcome without the effort to understand the feelings and unique experiences of those we care about. A fundamental act of hostility or indifference is to fail to see or try to see the world from another person's perspective.

Marriage example: It is common in marriage to interpret partner behavior based on its effect on us. Until we take time to discover what that behavior means to the partner, we do not understand our partner and cannot respond helpfully.

Parenting example: When a child comes home from school feeling humiliated by a bad experience, we can increase our intimacy and show support for the child by taking time to understand what that experience means to the child. The parent begins with "Tell me what happened" and follows by restating the child's experience in words that lets the child know that the parent can relate to the child's experience.

FLE application: This principle not only undergirds the content of much FLE but is vital in the delivery of FLE. Participants can be expected to respond more positively to facilitators who are compassionate and understanding. The same principle may be applied in dealings with ourselves. When we interpret our own lapses in patient, empathic ways, we are less likely to get discouraged (see Seligman, 1991).

● THE PRINCIPLE OF AGENCY: PEOPLE ARE FREE TO MAKE CHOICES

Elaboration: No one can make a person think, feel, and usually even act in ways contrary to that person's choices. A person's choices can be better understood by knowing the past but are not bounded or dictated by what has gone on before.

Marriage example: A partner's anger does not require our reaction in kind. We can choose to be reflective, understanding, and helpful rather than angry, resentful, or spiteful.

Parenting example: Parents can help children recognize their options and make choices based on their values rather than thoughtless, automatic reactions.

FLE application: Much of FLE—and self-help in general—invites participants to make choices. One way humans create problems for themselves is by telling themselves victim stories in which they suffer at the hands of others. Another is to create villain stories in which other people are especially bad and take away our power of choice. A third kind of story is helpless stories, where we see ourselves as powerless.

There is some truth in all of these stories. We do suffer from other people's misdeeds. We do work with some people who are very difficult. We do not have complete control of our experience.

But the key to growth in any setting—family, community, or work—is using the power we do have. Rather than feeding the monster stories that make us—or those we serve—feel powerless, hopeless, and resentful, we can identify our space for action and act within it (see Patterson, Grenny, McMillan, & Switzler, 2002).

THE PRINCIPLE OF MOMENTUM: THE PATTERN OF ONE'S ● LIFE IS DEFINED BY THE ACCUMULATION OF CHOICES

Elaboration: Patterns of choices have a cumulative effect. Some choices are made more difficult because of a pattern of previous choices. The person who has often chosen anger as the reaction to differences of opinion may find that reaction becoming automatic.

Marriage example: The emotional bank account is a good example of the principle of momentum. Those partners who consistently invest in the relationship through acts of thoughtfulness, kindness, and consideration will have an account balance superior to those who make only sporadic deposits or regular (or periodic) withdrawals.

Parenting example: Children can be taught to be aware of momentum. One small act of kindness can lead to another, and then to another, until kindness becomes interwoven in the pattern of a person's life.

FLE application: A participant in a workshop may be very discouraged at the difficulty of a new approach. The new skill can be compared to a new language. It may be learned slowly and used imperfectly but, persisted at, can become natural over time. Some family life educators recommend overlearning, that is, practicing a new skill until it becomes automatic (see Gottman, 1994). This is a way to develop momentum in a different, more helpful direction.

THE PRINCIPLE OF LOSS: SOMETIMES THE BEST CHOICE TO ● SUSTAIN AND AFFIRM LIFE REQUIRES RISK OR SACRIFICE

Elaboration: It is easy to suppose that good choices are always easy. That is not always true. Good usually entails some cost. For example, the willingness to stand up for principles may entail the loss of certain friendships.

Marriage example: Some people avoid close relationships because of the risk of being hurt. The fact is that we can limit our risk and manage our investment, but in so doing, we limit the potential for growth and intimacy.

Parenting example: Close relationships are based on the willingness to give and share with another person. One loses, or risks losing, something in order to gain something even more important—the respect and affection of another person. When parents allow children time to tie their shoes on their own, parents are slowed down. When a parent allows a teen the opportunity to drive the family car, the parent risks damage to the car and injury to an inexperienced driver.

FLE application: It can actually be reassuring to participants that there is risk in undertaking new skills. "No one does this perfectly. We all goof up more or less often." In a counterintuitive finding by Wilson and Linville (1982), students who were told that it was normal to experience some failure as they adjusted to a new process (in their case, university education) actually performed better than those who were not told. It can be reassuring that failure does not signal unique stupidity or ineptitude. It may only mean that we are learning and growing.

● PRINCIPLE OF INTEGRITY: ACTING CONSISTENT WITH INTERNAL PRINCIPLES OF RIGHT AND WRONG AND OUT OF COMPASSION FOR ALL LIFE BUILDS HEALTHY RELATIONSHIPS

Elaboration: A sense of right and wrong is the accumulated wisdom of experience with life. The key is to put these moral concepts into action and monitor their application in terms of how they affect oneself and others.

Marriage example: A man who tells his wife he loves her and works to show his love in his actions toward her is likely to have a strong relationship with her.

Parenting example: Parents may emphasize the importance of consistency between what their children say and do. If children, for example, say they will or will not do something, they are obligated by integrity to follow through consistently. In a similar way, when parents make a promise to a child, parents assume the obligation to do as they said, no matter how challenging it might prove to be.

FLE application: Participants who are evaluating any particular course of action in family life might consider two questions: "Is this action likely to get me what I want? Does this action show respect for the other people involved?" According to Hoffman (2000), humans can develop an internalized concern for others when they are treated with empathy and taught to understand the feelings of others. We can invite participants to draw on their own inner voices of compassion by asking, "What do you feel best about? In your heart, what do you think would show respect for that person?"

THE PRINCIPLE OF MOVEMENT: LIFE IS MOVEMENT ●

Elaboration: Short of cryogenic freezing, humans do not hold still. Life cannot be captured in a shadow box. People move actively toward one set of goals or another. The key is to move briskly and wisely toward carefully chosen goals. To stop growing is to die.

Marriage example: Relationships do not coast to bliss. Failure to invest in a relationship entails moving toward other goals, whether they are as vacuous as television watching or as demanding as career development. In any case, we move either toward or away from each other.

Parenting example: Children are growing and changing every day. Knowing a child means rediscovering him or her afresh in each encounter.

FLE application: It is popular to observe that the only constant is change. In FLE, we can teach people to use change as an ally rather than an enemy. Some of the difficulties in children (colic, diapers, and tantrums) will be outgrown with a little patience and perspective. Some of the difficulties in marriage (severely limited resources, tiredness) pass if we are patient. Rather than let today's discontents become the theme of our family story, we can learn to move forward while watching for sunnier weather (see Gottman, 1994).

THE PRINCIPLE OF GOODNESS: THERE IS AN INCLINATION IN ● THE HUMAN SPIRIT TOWARD LIFE-SUSTAINING BEHAVIOR

Elaboration: Healthy human beings fight to protect and preserve life. Healthy human beings flinch at the sight of suffering and waste. While decay is real, so also is the drive toward goodness, connection, and growth.

Marriage example: There are strong survival instincts that partners have for their relationship. When those instincts are swamped by despair and hopelessness, the relationship may end. However, even when discouragement is strong, the flames of hope can be fanned into new warmth, especially when determination is joined with fresh ideas.

Parenting example: Young children smile and reach out during the first months of life. The parent can encourage that inclination by responding warmly and sensitively to the child.

FLE application: Some scholars have argued that inborn empathy is the basis of moral development (see Hoffman, 1983). If that is true, there is a solid basis for believing that humans can learn to live together. Family members who learn perspective taking may be able to move beyond competitive thinking to cooperative efforts. Family life educators who show compassion for participants can help participants show compassion to other family members (see Chapter 6 in this volume and Maddux, 2002).

● THE PRINCIPLE OF CHAOS: THE WORLD IS NOT ALWAYS TIDY

Elaboration: It is wise to make allowances for imperfection and untidiness in life and relationships. Expecting Hollywood endings in all life struggles sets a person up for disappointment.

Marriage example: We never know our partners completely. We never work together perfectly. There are irresolvable differences in every relationship. Insisting on perfection guarantees disappointment. Accepting differences, even unpleasant ones, encourages more peace and better cooperation.

Parenting example: As we work with children, we make allowances for the inconvenience and challenge of living with little people who will not fit tidily into our adult schedules. Parents who adjust their schedules and expectations in order to synchronize with their children will find greater harmony and growth. Also, despite our good intentions and best efforts, some problems will remain.

FLE application: There certainly is untidiness in FLE. Many participants do not understand (or do not accept) our recommendations or may implement them imperfectly. Any growth is incremental. Family life educators are wise to calibrate expectations. It may be helpful to think about the whole context in which participants live and to acknowledge the challenges of change (for ideas on change processes, see Prochaska, Norcross, & DiClemente, 1994; for ideas about limits on human change, see Seligman, 1995).

THE PRINCIPLE OF READINESS FOR CHANGE: PROBLEMS ARE ● BEST SOLVED WHEN FAMILY MEMBERS ARE MENTALLY AND EMOTIONALLY READY TO GROW AND WHEN FAMILY MEMBERS ARE FEELING SAFE AND VALUED

Elaboration: True and enduring change cannot be achieved through physical or psychological force. Individual perspectives have to be respected and problems addressed at a time when those involved can listen, think, and learn. We cannot impose growth.

Marriage example: Marital conflict is more likely when partners are tired, frustrated, unhappy, hungry, or upset. To attempt to address chronic marital differences when people are in such a state may be like trying to read the paper while sitting in a burning house. There is wisdom in approaching differences when we feel peaceful—when we are under the influence of our nobler nature.

Parenting example: Children do not learn well or gladly when they are tired. Bedtime is not the best time to confront misbehavior and teach limits. Children learn best when they are alert and when we approach them with respect and kindness.

FLE application: It is natural to use a medical model in working with participants in FLE. We diagnose their failings and make specific recommendations. The challenge in working with humans is that the focus on problems can make people feel discouraged or resistant. Seligman (2002) has challenged such medical approaches: "I do not believe that you should devote overly much effort to correcting your weaknesses. Rather, I believe that the highest success in living and the deepest emotional satisfaction comes from building and using your signature strengths" (p. 13). Participants in our FLE efforts may be helped more by appreciation and encouragement of their strengths than by incisive diagnosis of their shortcomings. At the very least, our positive relationship with participants provides us the trust capital that will make us better change agents when participants are prepared to change.

● THE PRINCIPLE OF DISCOVERY: THERE ARE ALWAYS MORE POSSIBILITIES THAN OUR PERSONAL EXPERIENCES SUGGEST

Elaboration: No one person has sufficient experience to know everything about a problem. No one person can see all points of view. That is why it is vital for us to learn from each other.

Marriage example: Many couple conflicts involve imposing our personal "musts" on the relationship. "We must get up early." "We must celebrate the holidays elaborately." "We must have a large house." When we are truly open to other people's experiences and perspectives, we discover many roads leading to growth, intimacy, and satisfaction.

Parenting example: Rather than dictate behavior to children, we can help them discover options. Children should not be flooded with more choices than they can process. But they can be helped to discover multiple pathways through life. In addition, there are many different ways to successfully raise a child.

FLE application: If the only valued tools in an FLE experience are those held by the facilitator, there are likely to be many problems that don't get fixed. The most capable family life educators draw on the life experience and creative thinking of the participants. Each participant brings a unique set of tools and perceptions.

● THE PRINCIPLE OF SYNERGY: WHEN WE ACT TOGETHER, WE DISCOVER POSSIBILITIES THAT NONE OF US WOULD DISCOVER ALONE

Elaboration: When people turn from proving they are right to working toward joint possibilities, they often discover remarkable options. Our differences have important clues to guide our growth and discovery. When we work alone, we limit our reach.

Marriage example: For vacation, he wants to go fishing with the kids. She wants to visit her mother. They can fight about the virtue of their respective preferences. Or, working together, they can discover a better way. Maybe he will find a fishing hole near her mother's place. Maybe she will visit her mom at a different time. There are surprising possibilities when we join creative forces.

Parenting example: Even when parents feel that they cannot allow a child to participate in a certain activity, they can ask the child to suggest alternatives. They can join the child in exploring possibilities. "What would be an activity that we might both feel good about?" The principle of synergy suggests that making children our partners makes for more successful problem solving.

FLE application: This is the 3rd Space concept that is discussed in Chapter 7, "Working With Diverse Audiences." It is also the concept effectively popularized by Stephen R. Covey (1989). Those who are not bounded by their own poverty of options but who effectively draw on the wealth of possibilities in the group are likely to be effective family life educators.

THE PRINCIPLE OF LEGACY: OUR ULTIMATE WELL-BEING ● DEPENDS ON MAKING AN INVESTMENT IN OTHERS

Elaboration: Under the sway of the self-esteem movement, many have determined to meet their own needs at all costs. The self becomes the standard of judgment. Yet generativity and integrity in life depend on the investments we make in other people and in relationships. When we live only for ourselves, we never discover the satisfactions that come from service.

Marriage example: Rather than see marriage as a partnership where two relatively autonomous adults share some part of their lives as long as it is profitable, we can see marriage as the place where flawed and imperfect people commit to join and help each other in a journey. Marriage can be more than a convenient and pragmatic partnership; it can be a commitment to being together, growing together, and serving together. In serving we grow.

Parenting example: When children are involved in service, they are less likely to have serious adjustment problems. Children can be involved in helping others in many ways. In the early years, they may join their parents in visiting the sick, elderly, or lonely. As they get older, they may contribute their own energy and talents to improving life for those in their circle of experience who are in need.

FLE application: Erikson (1963) recognized generativity as one of the great accomplishments of adulthood. While many participants will come to FLE with some measure of sorrow and disappointment, we can invite them to "find the glory in their [family] story" (Gottman, 1994, p. 224). Perhaps they have not triumphed, but certainly they have grown. In fact, Gottman recommends several ways that couples can strengthen their futures by celebrating the best of the past.

● THE PRINCIPLE OF EVIL: THERE IS POTENTIAL FOR EVIL IN PEOPLE

Elaboration: To ignore evil is to be unprepared for the challenges of life. Each of us can be forgiven for an occasional self-serving pursuit of personal goals. None of us is totally selfless. Some individuals, though, twisted by harmful conditions during their formative years, have made the choice to commit themselves to self-serving goals, destructive behavior, and indifference to human suffering. Although not inherently "evil," children who are not treasured, nurtured, and loved can become inhumane. Even though individuals with this destructive personality are a distinct minority, their presence has to be acknowledged and understood.

Marriage example: Partners in a relationship can cherish each other knowing that there is an element of danger in the world. Their marriage can provide solace and comfort and provide a secure base for managing any threats to family well-being.

Parenting example: In the absence of active, committed adults in their lives, children are not likely to develop their potential for compassion and caring. They may even become brutish and heartless.

FLE application: Some people have suffered in ways that make immediate growth through FLE unlikely. They may need help getting unstuck. Wise family life educators learn when to refer participants to mental health professionals (see Doherty, 1995).

● EXPLORATION

Create a set of principles to which you subscribe. The principles may be modified from this list or be a very different set. Consider how the principles you have chosen or developed would guide your efforts as a family life educator in areas where you plan to work.

APPENDIX B

Family Life Education Content Areas: Content and Practice Guidelines

1. FAMILIES & INDIVIDUALS IN SOCIETAL CONTEXTS ●

An understanding of families and their relationships to other institutions, such as the educational, governmental, religious, and occupational institutions in society.

Research and theories related to: Structures and Functions; Cultural Variations (family heritage, social class, geography, ethnicity, race & religion); Dating, Courtship, Marital Choice; Kinship; Cross-Cultural & Minority (understanding of lifestyles of minority families & the lifestyles of families in various societies around the world); Changing Gender Roles (role expectations & behaviors of courtship partners, marital partners, parents & children, siblings, & extended kin); Demographic Trends; Historical Issues; Work/Leisure & Family Relationships; Societal Relations (reciprocal influence of the major social institutions & families, i.e., governmental, religious, educational, & economic).

Practice—A CFLE is prepared to:

- Identify the characteristics, diversity, & impact of local, national, & global social systems
- Identify factors (e.g., media, marketing, technology, economics, social movements, natural disasters, war) influencing individuals & families from both contemporary & historical perspectives.

- Identify factors that influence the relationship between work & family life
- Identify social & cultural influences affecting dating, courtship, partner/marital choice & relationships, family composition, & family life
- Recognize the reciprocal interaction between individuals, families, & various social systems (e.g., health, legal, educational, religious/spiritual)
- Assess the impact of demographics (e.g., class, race, ethnicity, generation, gender) on contemporary families

● 2. INTERNAL DYNAMICS OF FAMILIES

An understanding of family strengths and weaknesses and how family members relate to each other.

Research & theories related to: Internal Social Processes (including cooperation & conflict); Communication (patterns & problems in husband-wife relationships & in parent-child relationships, including stress & conflict management); Conflict Management; Decision-Making and Goal-Setting; Normal Family Stresses (transition periods in the family life cycle, three-generation households, caring for the elderly, & dual careers); Family Stress & Crises (divorce, remarriage, death, economic uncertainty & hardship, violence, substance abuse); Special Needs in Families (including adoptive, foster, migrant, low income, military, & blended families as well as those with disabled members).

Practice—A CFLE is prepared to:

- Recognize & define healthy & unhealthy characteristics pertaining to:
  1. Family relationships
  2. Family development

- Analyze family functioning using various theoretical perspectives
- Assess family dynamics from a systems perspective
- Evaluate family dynamics in response to normative & non-normative stressors
- Evaluate family dynamics in response to crises

- Facilitate & strengthen communication processes, conflict-management, & problem-solving skills
- Develop, recognize, & reinforce strategies that help families function effectively

3. HUMAN GROWTH & DEVELOPMENT ●
ACROSS THE LIFE SPAN

An understanding of the developmental changes (both typical and atypical) of individuals in families across the lifespan. Based on knowledge of physical, emotional, cognitive, social, moral, and personality aspects.

Research and theories related to: Prenatal; Infancy; Early and Middle Childhood; Adolescence; Adulthood; Aging.

A CFLE is prepared to:

- Identify developmental stages, transitions, tasks, & challenges throughout the lifespan
- Recognize reciprocal influences
  - Individual development on families
  - Family development on individuals
- Recognize the impact of individual health & wellness on families
- Assist individuals & families in effective developmental transitions
- Apply appropriate practices based on theories of human growth & development to individuals & families

4. HUMAN SEXUALITY ●

An understanding of the physiological, psychological, and social aspects of sexual development across the lifespan, so as to achieve healthy sexual adjustment.

Research and theories related to: Reproductive Physiology; Biological Determinants; Emotional and Psychological Aspects of Sexual Involvement; Sexual Behaviors; Sexual Values & Decision-Making; Family Planning; Physiological & Psychological Aspects of Sexual Response; Influence of Sexual Involvement on Interpersonal Relationships.

Practice—A CFLE is prepared to:

- Recognize the biological aspects of human sexuality
  - sexual functioning
  - reproductive health
  - family planning
  - sexually transmitted infections (STIs)
- Recognize the psycho-social aspects of human sexuality
  - characteristics of healthy & ethical sexual relationships
  - interpersonal dynamics of sexual intimacy
  - risk factors (e.g., substance abuse, social pressures, media)
- Address human sexuality from a value-respectful position

● 5. INTERPERSONAL RELATIONSHIPS

An understanding of the development and maintenance of interpersonal relationships.

Research and theories related to: Self and Others; Communication Skills (listening, empathy, self-disclosure, decision making, problem-solving, and conflict resolution); Intimacy, Love, Romance; Relating to Others with Respect, Sincerity, & Responsibility.

Practice—A CFLE is prepared to:

- Recognize the impact of personality & communication styles
- Recognize the developmental stages of relationships
- Analyze interpersonal relationships using various theoretical perspectives
- Develop & implement relationship enhancement & enrichment strategies
- Develop & implement effective communication, problem-solving, & conflict management strategies
- Communicate aspects of relationships within the context of their developmental stages

6. FAMILY RESOURCE MANAGEMENT ●

An understanding of the decisions individuals and families make about developing and allocating resources including time, money, material assets, energy, friends, neighbors, and space, to meet their goals.

Research and theories related to: Goal Setting and Decision-Making; Development and Allocation of Resources; Social Environment Influences; Life Cycle and Family Structure Influences; Consumer Issues and Decisions.

Practice—A CFLE is prepared to:

- Identify personal, familial, professional, & community resources available to families
- Recognize the reciprocal relationship between individual/family/community choices & resources
- Apply value-clarification strategies to decision-making
- Apply goal-setting strategies & evaluate their outcomes
- Apply decision-making strategies
- Apply organizational & time management strategies
- Apply basic financial management tools & principles
- Inform individuals & families of consumer rights, responsibilities, & choices of action/advocacy
- Apply stress management strategies

7. PARENTING EDUCATION & GUIDANCE ●

An understanding of how parents teach, guide, and influence children and adolescents as well as the changing nature, dynamics, and needs of the parent child relationship across the lifespan.

Research and theories related to: Parenting Rights and Responsibilities; Parenting Practices/Processes; Parent/Child Relationships; Variation in Parenting Solutions; Changing Parenting Roles Across the Life Cycle.

Practice—A CFLE is prepared to:

- Promote healthy parenting from a systems perspective
- Promote healthy parenting from a child's & parent's developmental perspective
- Apply strategies based on the child's age/stage of development to promote effective developmental outcomes
- Identify different parenting styles & their associated psychological, social, & behavioral outcomes
- Promote various parenting models, principles, & strategies
- Evaluate the effectiveness & appropriateness of various parenting strategies
- Recognize various parenting roles (e.g., father/mother, grandparents, other caregivers) & their impact on and contribution to individuals & families
- Recognize parenting issues within various family structures (e.g., single, blended, same-sex)
- Recognize the impact of societal trends on parenting (e.g., technology, substance abuse, media)
- Recognize the influence of cultural differences & diversity
- Identify strategies to advocate for children in various settings (e.g., schools, legal system, healthcare)
- Recognize the various pathways to parenting & their associated issues & challenges, (e.g., assisted reproduction, adoption, childbirth, blending)

● 8. FAMILY LAW & PUBLIC POLICY

An understanding of legal issues, policies, and laws influencing the well being of families.

Family and the Law (relating to marriage, divorce, family support, child custody, child protection and rights, and family planning); Family and Social Services; Family and Education; Family and the Economy; Family and Religion; Policy and the Family (public policy as it affects the family, including tax, civil rights, social security, economic support laws, and regulations).

Practice—A CFLE is prepared to:

- Identify current law, public policy, & initiatives that regulate & influence professional conduct & services
- Identify current laws, public policies, & initiatives that affect families
- Inform families, communities, & policy makers about public policies, initiatives, & legislation that affect families at local, state, & national levels

9. PROFESSIONAL ETHICS & PRACTICE ●

An understanding of the character and quality of human social conduct, and the ability to critically examine ethical questions and issues as they relate to professional practice.

Research and theories related to: Formation of Social Attitudes and Values; Recognizing and Respecting the Diversity of Values and the Complexity of Value Choice in a Pluralistic Society; Examining Value Systems and Ideologies Systematically and Objectively; Social Consequences of Value Choices; Recognizing the Ethical Implications of Social and Technological Changes, Ethics of Professional Practice.

Practice—A CFLE is prepared to:

- Demonstrate professional attitudes, values, behaviors, & responsibilities to clients, colleagues, & the broader community, that are reflective of ethical standards & practice
- Evaluate, differentiate, & apply diverse approaches to ethical issues & dilemmas
- Identify & apply appropriate strategies to deal with conflicting values
- Demonstrate respect for diverse cultural values & ethical standards

● 10. FAMILY LIFE EDUCATION METHODOLOGY

An understanding of the general philosophy and broad principles of family life education in conjunction with the ability to plan, implement, and evaluate such educational programs.

Research and theories related to: Planning and Implementing; Evaluation (materials, student progress, & program effectiveness); Education Techniques; Sensitivity to Others (to enhance educational effectiveness); Sensitivity to Community Concerns and Values (understanding of the public relations process).

Practice—A CFLE is prepared to:

- Employ a variety of current educational strategies
- Employ techniques to promote application of information in the learner's environment
- Create learning environments that are respectful of individual vulnerabilities, needs, & learning styles
- Demonstrate sensitivity to diversity & community needs, concerns, & interests
- Develop culturally-competent educational materials & learning experiences
- Identify appropriate sources for evidence-based information
- Develop educational experiences
  - needs assessments
  - goals & objectives
  - content development
  - implementation
  - evaluation/outcome measures
- Promote & market educational programs
- Implement adult education principles into work with families & parents
- Establish and maintain appropriate personal and professional boundaries

From the National Council on Family Relations (2009b). *Family life education content areas: Content and practice guidelines*. Retrieved April 21, 2010, from www.ncfr.org. Used by permission.

APPENDIX C

Family Life Education Program Resource Review Form

Use this form to assess the level of quality of outreach family life education (FLE) resource materials, including curricula, videos/DVDs, websites, and other resources. Not all items will apply equally to all resources.

Reference Information

Title: _____

Author: _____

Source: _____

Intended Audience. Please note the audience for which the resource is intended. (Check all that apply.)

____ Parents (Type _____)
     (Single, Step, Adoptive, Teenage, All, etc.)
____ Children (Age Range and/or Family Type) _____
____ Married Couples
____ General Public
____ Other (Specify:_____)

Delivery Method. Indicate the type of resource. (Check all that apply.)

____ News release
____ Short brochure

_____ Long brochure
_____ Slide/video/DVD
_____ Program curriculum
_____ Website
_____ Other _____

Ratings of the Resource. Please rate the educational resource on the following dimensions. Keep in mind the intended resource and the type of delivery method when making these ratings.

	Low/Poor			High/Excellent		
Content: Theory and Research						
1. Prevention/intervention theory is clearly stated.	1	2	3	4	5	N/A
2. Resource is based on current research findings.	1	2	3	4	5	N/A
3. Resource includes the major and/or most important research resources.	1	2	3	4	5	N/A
4. Resource accurately uses the findings from research (or other sources).	1	2	3	4	5	N/A
5. Resource clearly presents the findings from research and other sources.	1	2	3	4	5	N/A
6. Resource draws appropriate implications from the research and other sources.	1	2	3	4	5	N/A
7. Resource notes limitations of research findings and conclusions.	1	2	3	4	5	N/A
Content: Context						
8. Contextual information regarding the families' involvement in relevant settings (school, work, child care, church) is appropriately considered.	1	2	3	4	5	N/A
9. Culture and social class influences are appropriately considered.	1	2	3	4	5	N/A
10. Political, economic, and other macrosocial influences are appropriately considered.	1	2	3	4	5	N/A

Content: Practice

11. Resource adds something new to the practice/intervention approaches on this topic/issue.	1	2	3	4	5	N/A
12. Resource builds on appropriate existing program resources (e.g., other programs, professionals, clinical research).	1	2	3	4	5	N/A
13. Resource accurately uses finding from clinical research/ practice.	1	2	3	4	5	N/A
14. Teaching/intervention strategies and techniques are based on clinical research/practice.	1	2	3	4	5	N/A
15. Resource notes current limitation of clinical/practice knowledge in regard to this program/topic.	1	2	3	4	5	N/A

Comments:

Instructional Process: Teaching Plans	*Low/Poor*			*High/Excellent*		
1. The topic is important for the intended audience.	1	2	3	4	5	N/A
2. There are clear goals and objectives for instruction or the interactive/teaching elements of the website.						
3. Activities/interactive features fit the goals and objectives.	1	2	3	4	5	N/A
4. Activities/interactive features are appropriate for the intended audience(s) (age group, family type, gender, ethnic group).	1	2	3	4	5	N/A
5. Directions for conducting (or doing online) teaching or learning activities are sufficient.	1	2	3	4	5	N/A
6. A variety of activities and teaching formats are used.	1	2	3	4	5	N/A
7. Balance between giving information, discussion, and learning activities is achieved.	1	2	3	4	5	N/A
8. Structured and/or unstructured approaches are used appropriately.	1	2	3	4	5	N/A
9. Sufficient time is allowed to cover topics/activities (not too much or too little).	1	2	3	4	5	N/A
10. The structure of the content is logically organized and easy to follow.	1	2	3	4	5	N/A
11. Teaching aids (visuals, materials, handouts, etc.) are appropriate.	1	2	3	4	5	N/A
12. Potential teaching/practice problems are discussed and solutions suggested.	1	2	3	4	5	N/A

(Continued)

(Continued)

13. Appropriateness of the length of the resource for the topic and the intended audience.	1	2	3	4	5	N/A

Instructional Process: Presentation

14. Appropriate readability for the intended audience.	1	2	3	4	5	N/A
15. Appropriateness of the examples for the intended audience.	1	2	3	4	5	N/A
16. Attractiveness of the resource for the intended audience.	1	2	3	4	5	N/A
17. Appropriate portrayal of a range of racial/ethnic groups.	1	2	3	4	5	N/A
18. Appropriate portrayal of a range of family types.	1	2	3	4	5	N/A
19. Effectiveness of pictures/graphs, etc.	1	2	3	4	5	N/A
20. Quality of the overall design and layout.	1	2	3	4	5	N/A

Comments:

Implementation Process		*Low/Poor*			*High/Excellent*	
1. General information in regard to using the program is provided.	1	2	3	4	5	N/A
2. Appropriate audience for program is outlined.						
3. Limits are provided about audiences that would not be expected to benefit from the program.	1	2	3	4	5	N/A
4. Marketing/recruitment materials and suggestions are provided.	1	2	3	4	5	N/A
5. Logistical issues in implementation are clarified.	1	2	3	4	5	N/A
6. Budget issues are explained clearly.	1	2	3	4	5	N/A
7. Community or agency issues in implementation are explained.	1	2	3	4	5	N/A
8. Potential implementation problems are discussed and solutions suggested.	1	2	3	4	5	N/A
9. If appropriate, staff or volunteer training guidelines are sufficient.	1	2	3	4	5	N/A
10. Background material and/or resources are provided to implementers/trainers.	1	2	3	4	5	N/A

Comments:

Evaluation	Low/Poor			High/Excellent		
1. Evidence of needs assessment process with appropriate audience(s) is provided.	1	2	3	4	5	N/A
2. Utilization data are provided.	1	2	3	4	5	N/A
3. Accountability procedures are provided to track utilization of the program.	1	2	3	4	5	N/A
4. Results of client satisfaction are provided.	1	2	3	4	5	N/A
5. Procedures for assessing client satisfaction are provided.	1	2	3	4	5	N/A
6. Feedback from staff trainers, other stakeholders is discussed.	1	2	3	4	5	N/A
7. Procedures for obtaining feedback from staff trainers and other stakeholders are provided.	1	2	3	4	5	N/A
8. Evaluation of critical program features is provided.	1	2	3	4	5	N/A
9. Effectiveness of the program for specific audiences is clear.	1	2	3	4	5	N/A
10. Limits of the effectiveness of the program are clear.	1	2	3	4	5	N/A
11. Guidelines for impact evaluation are provided.	1	2	3	4	5	N/A
12. Evaluation tools (formative and summative) are provided.	1	2	3	4	5	N/A
13. Summative evaluation tools are tied to goals and objectives.	1	2	3	4	5	N/A

Comments:

Overall Evaluation of the Resource

_____ This resource should not be used at all.
(Describe the major problems.)

_____ This resource would be useful with the following modifications.
(Describe the needed modifications.)

_____ This resource would be useful in the following circumstances and with the following audiences.
(Describe circumstances and audiences.)

SOURCE: Adapted from Hughes (1994, 1997).

APPENDIX D

A Selection of Favorite Movie Clips for Family Life Education

Marriage Preparation

1. *Ever After* (1998), "Is there only one perfect mate?" clip. This question is raised by Prince Henry to Leonardo da Vinci. Ask participants to think about the answer Leonardo gave the prince, how they would answer that question, and how researchers would answer that question. Do we have more guidance today about how to select a mate than they did in Leonardo's day? Is it better, worse, or just different?

Marriage

1. *Fiddler on the Roof* (1971), "Do You Love Me" clip. Use to illustrate differences between perceptions and practices of marriage then (in Teyve's time) and now. Ask participants to think of examples of "married love" from the clip. Were there examples of commitment, devotion, service, and sacrifice? How did love manifest itself in the clip? How would you contrast to the manner that love is talked about nowadays?

2. Show scenes from Disney films, such as *Cinderella* (1950) and *Sleeping Beauty* (1959), where the heroines meet princes and fall instantly in love (with barely a "hello") and are shown in the end marrying these men they hardly know and yet somehow "live happily ever after." Discuss how the media and society can distort an appropriate understanding of marriage preparation and mate

selection. Then show the video *Fanny's Dream* (2000), a very different fairy tale about marital happiness.

3. Show scenes from the film *Runaway Bride* (1999). Possible scenes: Richard Gere's "ideal proposal" acknowledging there will be challenges during married life; scenes where Richard Gere's character discovers Julia Robert's character's tendency to lose herself in relationships (shown by her egg "preferences") and then the scene where she tries to discover her true self, including what kind of eggs she really likes.

4. *UP* (2009). This tender love story contains a wordless segment showing the evolution of a relationship over time, with early attraction, courtship, marriage, and, later on, handling tragedy and dealing with death. A nice discussion starter on how relationships can evolve over time and facing challenges together.

Family Strength Building

1. *Fiddler on the Roof* (1971), "Tradition" clip. To illustrate the role traditions play in family unity, development of personal identity, and a sense of responsibility. This movie can also be used to demonstrate what can happen to families if traditions become so rigid that they lead to intolerance.

2. Show the scene from the film *Les Misérables* (1978) (with Anthony Perkins) where Bishop Bienvenu gives Jean Valjean the silver Jean had actually stolen from him in order to prevent Jean going back to prison. Discuss compassion with the class and its impact on people—those who are compassionate and those who receive their compassion. The most obvious effect on Jean was powerful and immediate—he would not return to prison. However, deeper results are likely as well. (Ask participants for their ideas as to what these could be.) For example, his faith in humankind was restored, his hope for the future was brightened, and he was blessed by the love he, no doubt, now felt for the bishop; he was essentially reborn to a new life of goodness and love rather than hate, anger, and violence. Discuss the sacrifice the bishop had to make in order to be compassionate. Discuss the relationship of this story to the need for love and compassion at home.

3. Show segments from *Life Is Beautiful* (1998) to depict family love and compassion. Examples include the husband picking flowers for his wife from cracks in sidewalks; the wife's devotion to her

husband shown by her joining him in a concentration camp; although separated at the camp, the husband's efforts to communicate love by opening the window and playing her favorite song; the father's protection of his son by turning the concentration camp experience into a game.

4. *The Incredibles* (2004). Scene where Helen catches Bob as he sneaks back from playing "Superhero." The couple begins to argue and conflict escalates, unknowingly in the presence of son Dash and daughter Violet. Good as a more lighthearted demonstration of escalation in communication, as well a door opener to talk about effects of escalation on children.

Parenting

1. *Mary Poppins* (1964), "Grind at that Grindstone." Show scenes to illustrate the importance of parental involvement with children and spending time together as a family. Show the scene where Bert (Dick Van Dyke) has just completed sweeping the Banks's chimney, then gives Mr. Banks some advice about his "little tykes" when he sings "You've got to grind, grind, grind at that grindstone." Ask for class/participant impressions of the clip. Discuss the pressures fathers (and mothers) feel to succeed in the world of work and the "time bind" that is a reality. Also discuss what can happen when time with children is not prioritized, as Bert says "though childhood slips like sand through a sieve."

2. Show a "parental nurturing" clip from *Sixteen Candles* (1984): scene where the father nurtures Sam when she is going through a hard time and can't sleep by listening and talking with her.

3. To illustrate the importance of preparing for parenthood, show a video clip from *Penny Serenade* (1941). This humorous scene depicts a couple bathing an infant whom they have just adopted. It is evident that the couple knows little about caring for babies.

4. Show clips that illustrate different types of parenting styles: authoritative (*The Sound of Music* [1965], where Captain von Trapp whistles for his children), permissive (*Charlie and the Chocolate Factory* [2005], the squirrels and nuts scene), indifferent (*Matilda* [1996], the scene where her parents sign over her custody to Miss Honey), and authoritative (*Friendship's Field* [1995], opening scene).

5. *Hook* (1991), two scenes: Scene 1—the scene that opens at the daughter's play and concludes with Dad showing up late to the baseball game; Scene 2: the troubling phone call from America and Dad yelling at the kids, followed by a pointed discussion between husband and wife about Dad's lack of involvement. Great illustration of how parenting suffers from work and family imbalance.

Family Crises

1. Use several snippets from the ending of *Shadowlands* (1993) to illustrate the family crucible of grieving for a loved one. First, the "Golden Valley" scene to show the good times in the marriage. Then the scene after the wife's cancer returns and she is dying at home. Then a brief clip after his wife's death of C. S. Lewis struggling with the meaning of it all and digging into his faith to accept it. Finishing with the ending scene with C. S. Lewis and his stepson talking about how they miss their mother/wife and grieving for her. These clips allow for a discussion of grief using a neutral example.

2. *A Series of Unfortunate Events* (2004), the "Railroad Stop" clip. Count Olaf deliberately stops at a railroad crossing, cross the tracks, and locks the car doors so that the Baudelaire children cannot get out. The children are facing a stressor event! How will they handle it? This clip is useful to illustrate the ubiquitous ABC-X model of family stress. Violet, Klaus, and Sunny pool their collective resources (B) in response to their entrapment (A) all the while encouraging each other (C), which ultimately leads to success in redirecting the train away from them. Talk about how family resources and strengths can help them overcome adversity.

Several modern films depict crucible experiences and the ways individuals and families deal with them and may be valuable to discuss in class, such as *Steel Magnolias* (1989), *Lorenzo's Oil* (1992), *Stepmom* (1998), *My Life* (1993), *Regarding Henry* (1991), *Life Is Beautiful* (1998), *Deep End of the Ocean* (1999), and *Beaches* (1988).

Gender Issues

1. If you want to illustrate many gender issues in the modern world, show some clips from *Mr. Mom* (1983).

APPENDIX E

Ethics and Family Life Education

F or decades, the field of family life education lacked an official ethics code, but no longer. Here we briefly chronicle the more recent efforts that eventually led to the development of an officially recognized Family Life Educators Code of Ethics, which is now part of the education of all family life educators who desire to be certified as a family life educator by the National Council on Family Relations (NCFR). For greater detail about these processes, we direct you to the excellent chapters (Chapters 20, 24, and 25) in NCFR's compendium, *Family Life Education: Integrating Theory and Practice* (Bredehoft & Walcheski, 2009).

The Need for the Ethical Standard

Brock (1993) announced the need for ethical standards for family life educators. He made the persuasive argument that because there are instances where family life educators can do harm, professional conduct should be guided by professional standards in much the same way as are doctors, social workers, and marriage and family therapists. Such an ethical code is a sign that a professional field is established (Cassidy, 2003).

Ethical Principles and Guidelines

The "Ethical Principles and Guidelines for Family Scientists" were drafted by the Family Science Section of National Council on Family Relations (NCFR) and unanimously approved at the April 1998 meeting of the NCFR

Board of Directors (Adams, Dollahite, Gilbert, & Keim, 1998). These guidelines were meant to be educational and sensitizing to those who consider themselves family life educators and family scientists rather than an enforced legal code. The guidelines invite family life educators and family scientists to think critically about ethical issues. While ostensibly created with family life educators in mind, most of the principles apply to family research scientists working in university settings. Thus, a credo designed exclusively for family life educators was still yet to come.

Minnesota Council on Family Relations (MCFR) Efforts

A pioneer of the current ethics code was the Ethics Committee of the Minnesota Council on Family Relations (MCFR). This group has studied ethical thinking and behavior for parent and family life educators since 1992. In their extensive research, they collected an initial needs assessment from Minnesota parent and family life educators, created and conducted several experimental workshops and field tests to identify guidelines and virtues, and consulted professionals from other fields on professional ethics. Ultimately, the MCFR (2009) developed *Ethical Thinking and Practice for Parent and Family Life Educators*. This document represents a unique integration of different ethical perspectives (Palm, 2009). These include relational ethics, a principles approach, and virtue ethics.

Relational ethics. Relational ethics essentially asks, What principles shall guide my interactions with clientele and other family life educators? This approach focuses on the importance of relationships in any kind of interaction. It stresses understanding relationships as the foundation from which ethical decisions should be made, suggesting that a careful examination of the network of relationships that parent and family life educators encounter is the first step toward applying principles and finding a solution. Relational ethics is also seen as a call for action, meaning that caring relationships should be a constant goal and consistently worked toward by periodic evaluation to understand the state of a particular relationship. Emphasis is put on process and content for moral behavior. General guidelines for developing healthy, caring relationships with the different groups certified family life educators work with are incorporated in each section of the Code of Ethics (Bredehoft & Walcheski, 2009).

Principles approach. Similar to the relational ethics approach, this framework emphasizes specific principles, set as the ideal level of practice in order to achieve and maintain healthy relationships, both between the certified family life educator and the public as well as among families they are helping. These principles were developed inductively through workshops to be used to guide family life educators in responding to ethical dilemmas. The principles approach essentially asks, How shall I deal with ethical dilemmas that arise in my practice of FLE?

Virtue ethics. Virtue ethics asks, What characteristics are important for me to embody as a family life educator? While many characteristics may be seen as important as a family life educator, the MCFR group ultimately decided on three virtues (Palm, 2009, p. 194):

- Caring (the disposition to support the well-being of family members as decision makers in their own lives)
- Prudence or practical wisdom (the ability to understand competing needs in complex situations and make decisions based on reflection and consultation with peers)
- Hope/optimism (the disposition to focus on the strengths and positive potential of family members and other individuals and to maintain a positive attitude in the face of adversity)

With minor adaptations, MCFR guidelines became the officially recognized Family Life Educators Code of Ethics, which is now part of the education of all family life educators who desire Certified Family Life Educator (CFLE) certification.

Family Life Educators Code of Ethics

Preamble

Family life education (FLE) is the educational effort to strengthen individual and family life through a family perspective. The objective of family life education is to enrich and improve the quality of individual and family life by providing knowledge and skills needed for effective living. FLE emphasizes processes to enable people to develop into healthy adults and to realize their potential. Family life education helps people to work together in close relationships and facilitates the ability of people to function effectively in their personal lives and as members of society. While various professionals assist families, it is the family life educator who incorporates a family-systems, preventive, and educational approach to individual and family issues.

Family life education includes knowledge about how families work; the inter-relationship of the family and society; human growth and development throughout the life span; both the physiological and psychological aspects of human sexuality; the impact of money and time management on daily life; the importance and value of education for parenting; the effects of policy and legislation on families; ethical considerations in professional conduct; and a solid understanding and knowledge of how to teach and/or develop curriculum for what are often sensitive and personal issues.

A professional code of ethics provides guidelines when confronted with challenging and difficult ethical dilemmas. They serve notice to the public, and profession, as to the principles and values that will guide decision making under such circumstances. The ethical principles put forth in this Code of Ethics are standards of conduct, which Family Life Educators consider in ethical and professional decision making.

Ethical Principles for Parent and Family Life Educators

I. Relationships With Parents and Families

1. I will be aware of the impact/power we have on parents and family relations.

2. I will strive to understand families as complex, interactive systems where parents have the primary responsibility as educators, nurturers and limit-setters for their children.

3. I will respect cultural beliefs, backgrounds and differences and engage in practice that is sensitive to the diversity of child-rearing values and goals.

4. I will help parents and other family members recognize their strengths and work with them to set goals for themselves, their children, and others.

5. I will respect and accept parents and other family members for who they are, recognizing their developmental level and circumstances.

6. I will support and challenge parents to continue to grow and learn about parenting and their child's development.

7. I will communicate respectfully and clearly with all family members.

8. I will communicate openly and truthfully about the nature and extent of services provided.

9. I will support diverse family values by acknowledging and examining alternative parenting practices that support healthy family relationships.

10. I will include parents/other family members as partners in problem solving and decision-making related to program design and implementation.

11. I will be proactive in stating child guidance principles and discipline guidelines and encourage non-violent child rearing.

12. I will create data privacy and confidentiality guidelines respectful of family members and protective of their legal rights.

13. I will provide a program environment that is safe and nurturing to all family members.

14. I will ensure that all family members have access to and are encouraged to participate in family education.

15. I will support family members as they make decisions about the use of resources to best meet family needs.

16. I will support healthy interpersonal relationships among all family members.

17. I will encourage family members to explore their values and promote healthy sexuality in their family.

II. Relationships With Children and Youth

1. I will treat children and youth with respect and sensitivity to their needs and rights as developing persons.

2. I will strive to understand children and youth in the context of their families.

3. I will do no harm to children and youth and insist on the same from others.

4. I will advocate for children and youth and their best interests at the same time that we work with the parents and other family members.

5. I will provide environments that are respectful of children and youth and sensitive to their developmental and individual needs.

6. I will support the right of all children and youth to have access to quality education, health and community resources.

III. Relationships With Colleagues and the Profession

1. I will value and promote diversity in staff.

2. I will provide staff with policies and support systems for addressing difficult situations with family members, colleagues and others.

3. I will follow data privacy policies that meet legal standards and are based on respect for family members.

4. I will follow the mandatory reporting of abusive family behavior in a respectful and prudent manner.

5. I will define our role as parent and family life educators and practice within our level of competence.

6. I will recognize the difference between personal and professional values in our professional interactions.

7. I will support the ongoing development of a knowledge base that guides us towards ethical and effective practice.

8. I will be committed to ongoing professional development to enhance our knowledge and skills.

IV. Relationships With Community/Society

1. I will be knowledgeable about community resources and make and accept informed, appropriate referrals.

2. I will be aware of the boundaries of our practice and know when and how to use other community resources for the benefit of family members.

3. I will communicate clearly and cooperate with other programs/ agencies in order to best meet family needs.

4. I will advocate for laws and policies that reflect our changing knowledge base and the best interests of parents, families and communities.

5. I will respect and uphold laws and regulations that pertain to our practice as parent and family life educators and offer expertise to legal authorities based on professional knowledge.

By my signature below, I verify that I have read these ethical principles and that they will guide my professional practice as a Certified Family Life Educator

_____

Print Name

_____

Signature/Date

This signed document should be submitted along with the CFLE Abbreviated Application and the CFLE Exam Application.

SOURCE: Drawn from the Minnesota Council on Family Relations (MCFR). (2009). Ethical thinking and practice for parent and family life educators. Minneapolis: Minnesota Council on Family Relations. Used here by permission.

REFERENCES

Abell, E. E., Adler-Baeder, F., Tajeu, K., Smith, T. A., & Adrian, A. M. (2003). *Begin education early and healthy (BEE): Strengthening rural Alabama families*. Retrieved from http://www.cyfernet.org/databases/cyfarreporting/Public/narratives/display.asp

Adalian, J. (2009). *Bulldog reporter's daily dog*. Retrieved November 18, 2009, from website:http://www.bulldogreporter.com/ME2/Audiences/dirmod.asp?sid=&nm=&type=Pblishing&mod=Publications%3A%3AArticle&mid=8F3A7027421841978F18BE895F87F91&tier=4&id=6E0DA6A3426D4D6892ED85D64E9AA8A3&AudID=213D92F8BE0D41BB62EB3DF18FCCC68

Adams, R. A., Dollahite, D. C., Gilbert, K. R., & Keim, R. E. (1998). *National Council on Family Relations: Ethical principles and guidelines for family scientists*. Retrieved from http://www.ncfr.org/gov/ethicguide.asp

Adler, A. (1927). *Understanding human nature*. Oxford, England: One World Publications.

Adler-Baeder, F., Behnke, A., Brotherson, S., Futris, T. G., Goddard, H. W., Higginbotham, B., et al. (2010). *The National Extension Relationship and Marriage Education Model*. Unpublished manuscript, University of Georgia Cooperative Extension, Athens.

Adler-Baeder, F., & Futris, T. G. (2008). *The National Extension Relationship and Marriage Education Model (NERMEM)*. Retrieved February 24, 2010, from http://www.nermen.org/documents/2_specialannounce_web.pdf

Adler-Baeder, F., & Higginbotham, B. (2004). Implications for remarriage and step-family formation for marriage education. *Family Relations, 53,* 448–458.

Adler-Baeder, F., Higginbotham, B., & Lamke, L. (2004). Putting empirical knowledge to work: Linking research and programming on marital quality. *Family Relations, 53,* 537–546.

Administration for Children and Families. (n.d.). *ACF mission*. Retrieved June 14, 2004, from http://www.acf.hhs.gov/acf_about.html#mission

Advocates for Youth. (2008). *Science and success, second edition: Sex education and other programs that work to prevent teen pregnancy, HIV & sexually transmitted infections*. Retrieved April 15, 2010, from www.advocatesforyouth.org

Ajzen, I. (1991). The theory of planned behavior. *Organizational Behavior and Human Decision Processes, 50,* 179–211.

Alabama Cooperative Extension Service. (1996). *PEP leader's manual*. Auburn, AL: Author.

Albert, B. (2009). *With one voice (lite): A 2009 survey of adults and teens on parental influence, abstinence, contraception, and the increase in the teen birth rate*. Washington, DC: The National Campaign to Prevent Teen and Unplanned Pregnancy. Retrieved April 23, 2010, from TheNationalCampaign.org

Allen, K., & Rainie, L. (2002). *Parents online*. Retrieved September 14, 2009, at http://www.pewinternet.org/~/media//Files/Reports/2002/PIP_Parents_Report.pdf.pdf

Amato, R. P., & Fowler, F. (2002). Parenting practices, child adjustment, and family diversity. *Journal of Marriage and Family, 64,* 703–716.

Anderson, D. A., & Itule, B. D. (2003). *News writing and reporting for today's media* (6th ed.). New York: McGraw-Hill.

Arcus, M. E. (1993). Looking ahead in family life education. In M. E. Arcus, J. D. Schvaneveldt, & J. J. Moss (Eds.), *Handbook of family life education* (Vol. 1, pp. 229–246). Newbury Park, CA: Sage.

Arcus, M. E. (1995). Advances in family life education: Past, present, and future. *Family Relations, 44,* 336–344.

Arcus, M. E., Schvaneveldt, J. D., & Moss, J. J. (1993a). Family life education: Current status and new directions. In M. E. Arcus, J. D. Schvaneveldt, & J. J. Moss (Eds.), *Handbook of family life education* (Vol. 2, pp. 199–213). Newbury Park, CA: Sage.

Arcus, M. E., Schvaneveldt, J. D., & Moss, J. J. (1993b). The nature of family life education. In M. E. Arcus, J. D. Schvaneveldt, & J. J. Moss (Eds.), *Handbook of family life education* (Vol. 1, pp. 1–25). Newbury Park, CA: Sage.

Arcus, M. E., & Thomas, J. (1993). The nature and practice of family life education. In M. E. Arcus, J. D. Schvaneveldt, & J. J. Moss (Eds.), *Handbook of family life education* (Vol. 2, pp. 1–32). Newbury Park, CA: Sage.

Arnow, J. (1995). *Teaching peace*. New York: Perigree.

Astleitner, H., & Leuner, D. (1995). Learning strategies for unstructured hypermedia: A framework for theory, research, and practice. *Journal of Educational Computing, 13,* 387–400.

Bacon, B. L., & McKenzie, B. (2004). Parent education after separation/divorce: Impact of the level of parent conflict on outcomes. *Family Court Review, 42*(1), 85–98.

Bandura, A. (1986). *Social foundations of thought and action: A social cognitive theory*. Englewood Cliffs, NJ: Prentice Hall.

Barber, B. K. (1996). Parental psychological control: Revisiting a neglected construct. *Child Development, 67,* 3296–3319.

Barber, B. K., Stolz, H. E., & Olsen, J. A. (2005). Parental support, behavioral control, and psychological control: Assessing relevance across time, method, and culture. *Monographs of the Society for Research in Child Development, 70*(4).

Barber, J. G. (1992). Evaluating parent education groups: Effects on sense of competence and social isolation. *Research on Social Work Practice, 2,* 28–38.

Barlow, J., & Stewart-Brown, S. (2000). Understanding parenting programmes: The benefit for parents of a home-school linked programme. *Journal of Primary Care Research and Development, 2,* 117–130.

Barrera, I., & Corso, R. M. (2003). *Skilled dialogue: Strategies for responding to cultural diversity in early childhood.* Baltimore: Brookes.

Barry, D. (1991). *Dave Barry talks back.* New York: Crown.

Baumeister, R. (1992). *Meanings of life.* New York: Guilford.

Baumeister, R. F. (1997). *Evil: Inside human violence and cruelty.* New York: Freeman.

Baumeister, R. F., Smart, L., & Boden, J. M. (1999). Relation of threatened egotism to violence and aggression: The dark side of high self-esteem. In R. F. Baumeister (Ed.), *The self in social psychology* (pp. 240–279). Philadelphia: Psychology Press.

Baumrind, D. (1971). Current patterns of parental authority. *Developmental Psychology Monograph, 4,* 1–103.

Baumrind, D. (1991). The influence of parenting style on adolescent competence and substance use. *Journal of Early Adolescence, 11*(1), 56–95.

Beck, M. (2003). *The joy diet.* New York: Crown.

Becker, W. C. (1964). Consequences on different kinds of parental discipline. In M. L. Hoffman & W. W. Hoffman (Eds.) *Review of child development research* (Vol. 1, pp. 169–208). New York: Russell Sage Foundation.

Belsky, J., Lerner, R., & Spanier, G. (1984). *The child in the family* [e-book]. Reading, MA: Addison Wesley/Addison Wesley Longman.

Berger, R., & Hannah, M. T. (1999). Introduction. In R. Berger & M. T. Hannah (Eds.), *Preventive approaches in couples therapy* (pp. 1–27). Philadelphia: Brunner/Mazel.

Bergstrom, A., Clark, R., Hogue, T., Perkins, D., Slinski, M., Iyechad, T., et al. (1995). *Collaboration framework: Addressing community capacity.* Washington, DC: National Network for Collaboration, Cooperative State Research, Education, and Extension Service, U.S. Department of Agriculture.

Betts, S. C., Marczak, M. S., Marek, L. I., Peterson, D. J., Hoffman, K., & Mancini, J. A. (1999, March). *Collaboration and evaluation: Application of research and evaluation for community-based programs.* Tucson: University of Arizona Extension Service.

Blanchard, V. L., Hawkins, A. J., Baldwin, S. A., & Fawcett, E. B. (2009). Investigating the effects of marriage and relationship education on couples' communication skills: A meta-analytic study. *Journal of Family Psychology, 23,* 203–214.

Bodenmann, G., Pihet, S., & Kayser, K. (2006). The relationship between dyadic coping and marital quality: A 2-year longitudinal study. *Journal of Family Psychology, 20,* 485–493.

Bogenschneider, K. (1996). An ecological risk/protective theory for building prevention programs, policies, and community capacity to support youth. *Family Relations, 45,* 127–138.

Bogenschneider, K., & Stone, M. (1997). Delivering parent education to low and high risk parents of adolescents via age-paced newsletters. *Family Relations, 46,* 123–134.

Borden, L. M., & Perkins, D. F. (1999). Assessing your collaboration: A self-assessment tool. *Journal of Extension, 37*(2). Retrieved from http://www.joe.org/joe/1999april/tt1.html

Bornstein, M. H. (Ed.). (2002). *Handbook of parenting: Vol. 4. Social conditions and applied parenting.* Mahwah, NJ: Lawrence Erlbaum.

Bowers, D., & Ebata, A. T. (2009, November). *Evaluating the use and impact of an online resource for parents.* Paper presented at the annual meeting of the National Council on Family Relations, San Francisco, CA.

Bowlby, J. (1969). *Attachment and loss* (Vol. 1). New York: Basic Books.

Bowman, T., & Kieren, D. K. (1985). Underwhelming participation: Inhibitors to family enrichment. *Social Casework, 66,* 617–622.

Bramlett, M. D., & Mosher, W. D. (2001). First marriage dissolution, divorce, and remarriage: United States. *Advance data from vital and health statistics, no. 323.* Hyattsville, MD: National Center for Health Statistics.

Bramlett, M. D., & Mosher, W. D. (2002). Cohabitation, marriage, divorce, and remarriage in the United States. *National Center for Health Statistics* (Series 23). Available at http://www.cdc.gov/nchs/data/series/sr_23/sr23_022.pdf

Brammer, L. M., & MacDonald, G. (1999). *The helping relationship: Process and skills.* Boston: Allyn & Bacon.

Brazelton, T. B. (1992). *Touchpoints.* Reading, MA: Addison-Wesley.

Bredehoft, D., & Cassidy, D. (1995). College and university curriculum guidelines. In D. Bredehoft & D. Cassidy (Eds.), *Family life education curriculum guidelines* (2nd ed., pp. 12–14). Minneapolis, MN: National Council on Family Relations.

Bredehoft, D. J., & Walcheski, M. J. (Eds.). (2009). *Family life education: Integrating theory and practice.* Minneapolis, MN: National Council on Family Relations.

Britner, P. A., & Reppucci, N. D. (1997). Prevention of child maltreatment: Evaluation of a parent education program for teen mothers. *Journal of Child and Family Studies, 6,* 165–175.

Brock, G. W. (1993). Ethical guidelines for the practice of family life education. *Family Relations, 42,* 124–127.

Brock, G. W., Oertwein, M., & Coufal, J. D. (1993). Parent education theory, research, and practice. In M. E. Arcus, J. D. Schvaneveldt, & J. J. Moss (Eds.), *Handbook of family life education* (Vol. 1, pp. 1–25). Newbury Park, CA: Sage.

Bronfenbrenner, U. (1979). *The ecology of human development.* Cambridge, MA: Harvard University Press.

Bronfenbrenner, U. (1986). Ecology of the family as a context for human development: Research perspectives. *Developmental Psychology, 22,* 723–742.

Brown, J. D., Keller, S., & Stern, S. (2009). Sex, sexuality, sexting and SexEd: Adolescents and the media. *The Prevention Researcher, 16*(4), 12–16.

Bruess, C., & Greenberg, J. (2009). *Sexuality education: Theory and practice* (5th ed.). Boston: Jones and Bartlett.

Bryant, F. B., & Veroff, J. (2007). *Savoring: A new model of positive experience*. Mahwah, NJ: Lawrence Erlbaum.

Buboltz, M. M., & Sontag, M. S. (1993). Human ecology theory. In P. G. Boss, W. J. Doherty, R. LaRossa, S. K. Steinmetz, & W. R. Schumm (Eds.), *Sourcebook of family theories and methods: A contextual approach* (pp. 419–448). New York: Plenum.

Bulanda, R., & Majumdar, D. (2009). Perceived parent-child relations and adolescent self-esteem. *Journal of Child and Family Studies, 18,* 203–212.

Bunting, L. (2004). Parenting programmes: The best available evidence. *Child Care in Practice, 10,* 327–343.

BurrellesLuce. (2009, September). *Potent PR in an altered media world*. Retrieved November 23, 2009, from http://www.burrellesluce.com/newsletter/2009/september_2009

Busby, D. M., Ivey, D. C., Harris, S. M., & Ates, C. (2007). Self-directed, therapist-directed, and assessment-based interventions for premarital couples. *Family Relations, 56,* 279–290.

Butler, M. H., Gardner, B. C., & Bird, M. H. (1998). Not just a time-out: Change dynamics of prayer for religious couples in conflict situations. *Family Process, 37,* 451–478.

Cain, D. (2008). Parenting online and lay literature on infant spanking: Information readily available to parents. *Social Work in Health Care, 47,* 174–184.

Callor, S., Betts, S. C., Carter, R., Marczak, M. S., Peterson, D. J., & Richmond, L. S. (2000). *Community-based project evaluation guide*. Tucson: University of Arizona Extension Service.

Calvert, P. (Ed.). (2000). *The communicator's handbook*. Gainesville, FL: Maupin House.

Campbell, D., & Palm, G. F. (2004). *Group parent education: Promoting parent learning and support*. Thousand Oaks, CA: Sage.

Carroll, J. S., Badger, S., & Yang, C. (2006). The ability to negotiate or the ability to love? Evaluating the developmental domains of marital competence. *Journal of Family Issues, 27,* 1001–1032.

Carroll, J. S., & Doherty, W. J. (2003). Evaluating the effectiveness of premarital prevention programs: A meta-analytic review of outcome research. *Family Relations, 52,* 105–118.

Cassidy, D. (2003). The growing of a profession: Challenges in family life education. In D. J. Bredehoft & M. J. Walcheski (Eds.), *Family life education: Integrating theory and practice* (pp. 44-55). Minneapolis, MN: National Council on Family Relations.

Cassidy, D. (2004, Spring). Directions. *CFLE Network, 16*(2), 1.

Catalano, R. F., Kosterman, R., & Hawkins, J. D. (1996). Modeling the etiology of adolescent substance use: A test of the social development model. *Journal of Drug Issues, 26,* 429–455.

Center for Parent Education. (2004). *Core knowledge for parent educators and professionals who work with families*. Denton: University of North Texas. Retrieved April 15, 2010, from http://www.coe.unt.edu/cpe/core-attitudes

Centers for Disease Control and Prevention. (2002). *Key statistics from the national survey of family growth, S listing.* Retrieved April 23, 2010, from http://www.cdc.gov/nchs/nsfg/abc_list_s.htm# oralsexmalefemale

Centers for Disease Control and Prevention. (2005). *Youth risk behavior surveillance—United States.* Atlanta, GA: National Center for Chronic Disease Prevention and Health Promotion.

Centers for Disease Control and Prevention. (2008). *Youth risk behavior surveillance: United States, 2007.* Morbidity and Mortality Weekly Report Surveillance Summaries; 57 (No. SS-4). Retrieved April 7, 2010, from http://www.cdc.gov/mmwr/PDF/ss/ss5704.pdf

Centers for Disease Control and Prevention. (2009a). *Best evidence: Focus on youth (FOY) plus ImPACT.* Atlanta, GA: Author. Retrieved April 23, 2010, from http://www.cdc.gov/hiv/topics/research/prs/resources/factsheets/FOY-ImPACT.htm

Centers for Disease Control and Prevention. (2009b). *Best evidence intervention.* Atlanta, GA: Author. Retrieved April 23, 2010, from http://www.cdc.gov/hiv/topics/research/prs/print/best-evidence-intervention.htm

Chandra, A., Martino, S. C., Collins, R. L., Elliott, M. N., Berry, S. H., Kanouse, D. E., et al. (2007). Does watching sex on television predict teen pregnancy? Findings from a national longitudinal survey of youth. *Pediatrics, 122,* 1047–1054.

Chapman, G. D. (1992). *The five love languages: How to express heartfelt commitment to your mate.* Chicago: Northfield.

Chen, W.-F., & Dwyer, F. (2003). Hypermedia research: Present and future. *International Journal of Instructional Media, 30*(2), 143–148.

Cherlin, A. J. (2009). *The marriage-go-round.* New York: Knopf.

Chibucos, T. R., & Leite, R. W. (2005). *Readings in family theory.* Thousand Oaks, CA: Sage.

Christopher, S., Dunnagan, T., Duncan, S. F., & Paul, L. (2001). Education for self-support: Evaluating outcomes using transformative learning theory. *Family Relations, 50,* 134–142.

Clifton, D. O., & Nelson, P. (1992). *Soar with your strengths.* New York: Dell.

Cochran, M., & Woolever, F. (1983). Beyond the deficit model: The empowerment of parents with information and informal supports. In I. Sigel & L. Lagosa (Eds.), *Changing families* (pp. 225–245). New York: Plenum.

Coie, J. D., Watt, N. F., West, S. G., Hawkins, J. D., Asarnow, J. R., Markman, H. J., et al. (1993). The science of prevention: A conceptual framework and some directions for a national research program. *American Psychologist, 48,* 1013–1022.

Coles, R. (1997). *The moral intelligence of children.* New York: Random House.

Cook, R. S., Rule, S., & Mariger, H. (2003). Parents' evaluation of usability of a website on recommended practices. *Topics in Early Childhood Special Education, 23,* 19–27.

Cooke, B. (2006). Competencies of a parent educator: What does a parent educator need to know and do? *Child Welfare, 85,* 785–802.

Cooperative Extension System. (1991). *Reaching limited resource audiences.* Washington, DC: Author.

Cotton, S. R., & Gupta, S. S. (2004). Characteristics of online and offline health information seekers and factors that discriminate between them. *Social Science & Medicine, 59,* 1795–1806.

Council on Child and Adolescent Health. (1998). The role of home-visitation programs in improving health outcomes for children and families. *Pediatrics, 101,* 486–489.

Covey, S. R. (1989). *The seven habits of highly effective people.* New York: Simon & Schuster.

Cowan, P. A., Cowan, C. P., Pruett, M. K., Pruett, K. D., & Wong, J. J. (2009). Promoting fathers' engagement with children: Preventative interventions for low-income families. *Journal of Marriage and Family, 71,* 663–679.

Crews, R. J. (2002). *Higher education service-learning sourcebook.* Westport, CN: Oryx Press.

Croake, J. W., & Glover, K. E. (1977). A history and evaluation of parent education. *The Family Coordinator, 26*(2), 151–158.

Cronbach, L. J., & Furby, L. (1970). How we should measure "change"—Or should we? *Psychological Bulletin, 74,* 68–80.

Csikszentmihalyi, M. (1997). *Finding flow: The psychology of engagement with everyday life.* New York: Perseus.

Cudaback, D., Darden, C., Nelson, P., O'Brien, S., Pinsky, D., & Wiggins, E. (1985). Becoming successful parents: Can age-paced newsletter help? *Family Relations, 34,* 271–275.

Curran, D. (1989). *Working with parents.* Circle Pines, MN: American Guidance Service.

Czaplewski, M. J., & Jorgensen, S. R. (1993). The professionalization of family life education. In M. E. Arcus, J. D. Schvaneveldt, & J. J. Moss (Eds.), *Handbook of family life education* (Vol. 1, pp. 51–75). Newbury Park, CA: Sage.

Dail, P. W. (1984). Constructing a philosophy of family life education: Educating the educators. *Family Perspective, 18*(4), 145–149.

DeBord, K. (1989). Creative teaching: Simulations, games, and role playing. *Journal of Extension, 27*(2). Retrieved June 13, 2003, from http://www.joe.org/joe/1989summer/tt1.html

DeBord, K., Bower, D., Goddard, H. W., Kirby, J., Kobbe, A. M., Myers-Walls, J. A., et al. (2002). *National extension parenting educators' framework.* Retrieved April 1, 2010, from http://www1.cyfernet.org/ncsu_fcs/NEPEF/index.htm

Deitz, D. K., Cook, R. F., Billings, D. W., & Hendrickson, A. (2009). Brief report: A Web-based mental health program: Reaching parents at work. *Journal of Pediatric Psychology, 34,* 488–494.

Derelan, D., Rouner, D., & Tucker, K. (1994). *Public relations writing: An issue-driven behavioral approach* (2nd ed.). Englewood Cliffs, NJ: Prentice Hall.

Deutscher, B., Fewell, R. R., & Gross, M. (2006). Enhancing the interactions of teenage mothers and their at-risk children: Effectiveness of a maternal-focused intervention. *Topics in Early Childhood Special Education, 24*(4), 194–205.

Dhanarajan, G. (2001). Distance education: promise, performance and potential. *Open Learning, 16*(1), 61–68.

Dion, M. R., Devaney, B., & Hershey, A. M. (2003, November). *Toward interventions to strengthen relationships and support healthy marriage among unwed parents.* Paper presented at the Annual Meeting of the National Council on Family Relations, Vancouver, BC.

Dion, M. R., & Hershey, A. M. (2010). Relationship education for unmarried couples with children: Parental responses to the Building Strong Families Project. *Journal of Couple and Relationship Education, 9,* 161–180.

Dion, M. R., Hershey, A. M., Zaveri, H. H., Avellar, S. A., Strong, D. A., Silman, T., et al. (2008). *Implementation of the Building Strong Families program.* Washington, DC: Mathematica Policy Research, Inc. Retrieved from http://www.mathematicampr.com/publications/PDFs/bsfimplementation.pdf

Dishion, T. J., & Loeber, R. (1985). Adolescent marijuana and alcohol use: The role of parents and peers revisited. *American Journal of Drug and Alcohol Abuse, 11,* 1–25.

Doherty, W. J. (1995). Boundaries between parent and family education and family therapy: The levels of family involvement model. *Family Relations, 44,* 353–358.

Doherty, W. J. (1997). *The scientific case for marriage and couples education in health care.* Retrieved from http://www.smartmarriages.com/hpmarr.html

Doherty, W. J. (2000). Family science and family citizenship: Toward a model of community partnership with families. *Family Relations, 49,* 319–325.

Doherty, W. J. (2001). *Take back your marriage.* New York: Guilford.

Doueck, H. J., & Bondanza, A. (1990). Training social work staff to evaluate practice: A pre/post/then comparison. *Administration in Social Work, 14*(1), 119–133.

Dreikurs, R. (with Soltz, V.). (1964). *Children: The challenge.* New York: Hawthorn.

Drolet, J. C., & Clark, K. (1994). Preface. In J. C. Drolet & K. Clark (Eds.), *The sexuality education challenge: Promoting health sexuality in young people* (pp. xi–xiv). Santa Cruz, CA: ETR Associates.

Duggan, A., Windham, A., McFarlane, E., Fuddy, L., Rohde, C., Buchbinder, S., et al. (2000). Hawaii's healthy start program of home visiting for at-risk families: Evaluations of family identification, family engagement, and service delivery. *Pediatrics, 105,* 250–259.

Dumka, L. E., Roosa, M. W., Michaels, M. L., & Suh, K. W. (1995). Using research and theory to develop prevention programs for high-risk families. *Family Relations, 44,* 78–86.

Duncan, S. F., Box, G., & Silliman, B. (1996). Racial and gender effects on perceptions of marriage preparation programs among college-educated young adults. *Family Relations, 45,* 80–90.

Duncan, S. F., Dunnagan, T., Christopher, S., & Paul, L. (2003). Helping families toward the goal of self-support: Montana's EDUFAIM program. *Families in Society, 84,* 213–222.

Duncan, S. F., & Marotz-Baden, R. (1999). Using focus groups to identify rural participant needs in balancing work and family education [Electronic version]. *Journal of Extension, 37*(1). Retrieved from http://joe.org/joe/1999february/rb1.html

Duncan, S. F., Steed, A., & Needham, C. M. (2009). A comparison evaluation study of Web-based and traditional marriage and relationship education. *Journal of Couple & Relationship Therapy, 8,* 162–180.

Duncan, S. F., & Wood, M. M. (2003). Perceptions of marriage preparation among college educated young adults with greater family-related risks for marital disruption. *The Family Journal, 11,* 342–352.

Dunnagan, T., Duncan, S. F., & Paul, L. (2000). Doing effective evaluations: A case study of family empowerment due to welfare reform. *Evaluation and Program Planning, 23,* 125–136.

Eccles, J. S., Early, D., Frasier, K., Belansky, E., & McCarthy, K. (1997). The relation of connection, regulation, and support for autonomy to adolescents' functioning. *Journal of Adolescent Research, 12,* 263–286.

Effective Interventions. (2009). SIHLE. Retrieved April 23, 2010, from http://www.effectiveinterventions.org/files/ SIHLE_Procedural_Guide_8–09.pdf

Egeland, B., & Erickson, M. F. (2004). Lessons from STEEP: Linking theory, research and practice for the well-being of infants and parents. In A. J. Sameroff, S. C. McDonough, & K. L. Rosenblum (Eds.), *Treating parent-infant relationship problems: Strategies for intervention* (pp. 213–242). New York: Guilford.

Elias, J. L., & Merriam, S. B. (1995). *Philosophical foundations of adult education.* Malabar, FL: Krieger.

Elliott, M. (1999). Classifying family life education on the World Wide Web. *Family Relations, 48,* 7–13.

Emmons, R. A., & Shelton, C. M. (2002). Gratitude and the science of positive psychology. In C. R. Snyder & S. J. Lopez (Eds.), *Handbook of positive psychology* (pp. 459–471). New York: Oxford University Press.

Erikson, E. H. (1963). *Childhood and society.* New York: Norton.

Etzioni, A. (1993). *The spirit of community: Rights, responsibilities, and the communitarian agenda.* New York: Crown.

Evans, G. D., Rey, J., Hemphill, M. M., Perkins, D. F., Austin, W., & Racine, P. (2001). Academic community collaboration: An ecology for early childhood violence prevention. *American Journal of Preventive Medicine, 20,* 22–30.

Extension Committee on Organization and Policy (ECOP). (2002, February). *The extension system: A vision for the 21st century.* New York: National Association of State Universities and Land-Grant Colleges.

Faber, A., & Mazlish, E. (1999). *How to talk so kids will listen and listen so kids will talk.* New York: William Morrow.

Family Support America. (2003). Retrieved from http://www.familysupportamerica.org/content/home.htm

Farooq, D. M., Jefferson, J. L., & Fleming, J. (2005). The effect of an Adlerian video-based parent education program on parent's perception of children's behavior:

A study of African American parents. *Journal of Professional Counseling, Practice, Theory, and Research, 33,* 21–34.

Fawcett, E. B., Hawkins, A. J., Blanchard, V. L., & Carroll, J. S. (2010). Do premarital education programs work? A meta-analytic study. *Family Relations, 59,* 232–239.

Fetsch, R. J., & Hughes, R., Jr. (2002). *Evaluating family life web sites.* Consumer Series, No 10.253. Retrieved November 26, 2003, from http://www.ext.colostate.edu/pubs/consumer/10253.html

Fine, M. J. (1980). *Handbook on parent education.* New York: Academic Press.

Fine, M. J. (1989). *Second handbook on parent education: Contemporary perspectives.* New York: Academic Press.

Fine, M. J., & Lee, S. (2000). *Handbook of diversity in parent education: The changing face of parenting and parent education.* New York: Academic Press.

Fink, L. D. (2003). *Creating significant learning experiences.* San Francisco: Jossey-Bass.

Finkelhor, D. (2007). Prevention of sexual abuse through educational programs directed toward children. *Pediatrics, 120,* 640–645.

Finkelhor, D. (2009). The prevention of childhood sexual abuse. *The Future of Children, 19*(2), 169–193.

Fincham, F. D. (2000). The kiss of the porcupines: From attributing responsibility to forgiving. *Personal Relationships, 7,* 1–23.

Fincham, F. D., Stanley, S. M., & Beach, S. R. H. (2007). Transformative processes in marriage: An analysis of emerging trends. *Journal of Marriage and Family, 69,* 275–292.

First, J. A., & Way, W. L. (1995). Parent education outcomes: Insights into transformative learning. *Family Relations, 44,* 104–109.

Fiske, S. T., & Taylor, S. E. (1984). *Social cognition.* Reading, MA: Addison-Wesley.

Flay, B. R., & Petraitis, J. (1994). The theory of triadic influence: A new theory of health behavior with implications for preventive interventions. In G. S. Albrecht (Ed.), *Advances in medical sociology: Vol. IV. A reconsideration of models of health behavior change* (pp. 19–44). Greenwich, CT: JAI.

Fogg, B. J. (2002). *Stanford guidelines for Web credibility.* Retrieved from http://www.webcredibility.org/guidelines/index.html

Fogg, B. J., Soohoo, C., Danielson, D. R., Marable, L., Stanford, J., & Tauber, E. R. (2003, June). *How do users evaluate the credibility of Web sites? A study with over 2,500 participants.* Paper presented at the Designing for User Experiences Conference, San Francisco, CA.

Fowers, B. J. (2000). *Beyond the myth of marital happiness: How embracing the virtues of loyalty, generosity, justice, and courage can strengthen your relationship.* New York: John Wiley.

Fowers, B. J. (2001). The limits of a technical concept of a good marriage: Exploring the role of virtue in communication skills. *Journal of Marital and Family Therapy, 27,* 327–340.

Fox, S., Zickuhr, K., & Smith, A. (2009). *Twitter and status updating, fall 2009.* Washington, DC: Pew Internet & American Life Project. Retrieved December 2, 2009, from http://pewinternet.org/Reports/2009/17-Twitter-and-Status-Updating-Fall-2009.aspx

Freire, P. (1971). *Pedagogy of the oppressed.* New York: Herder & Herder.

Fry, R., Johnson, M. S., Melendez, P., & Morgan, R. (2003). *Parent project: Changing destructive adolescent behavior* (8th ed.). Rancho Cucamonga, CA: Parent Project, Inc.

Gardner, D. (2008). *The science of fear: Why we fear the things we shouldn't and put ourselves in greater danger.* New York: Dutton.

Gaston, S., & Daniels, P. (n.d.). *Guidelines: Writing for adults with limited reading skills.* Retrieved December 11, 2003, from http://www.cyfernet.org/research/writeadult.html

Gates, B., Newell, R., & Wray, J. (2001). Behavior modification and gentle teaching workshops: Management of children with learning disabilities exhibiting challenging behavior and implications for learning disability nursing. *Journal of Advanced Nursing, 34,* 86–95.

Gavin, L. E., Catalano, R. F., David-Ferdon, C., Gloppen, K. M., & Markham, C. M. (2010a). Positive youth development as a strategy to promote adolescent sexual and reproductive health. *Journal of Adolescent Health, 46*(35), S75–S91.

Gavin, L. E., Catalano, R. F., David-Ferdon, C., Gloppen, K. M., & Markham, C. M. (2010b). A review of positive youth development programs that promote adolescent sexual and reproductive health. *Journal of Adolescent Health, 46*(35), S1–S3.

Giblin, P. (1989). Effective utilization and evaluation of indigenous health care workers. *Public Health Reports, 104,* 361–367.

Giblin, P., Sprenkle, D. H., & Sheehan, R. (1985). Enrichment outcome research: A meta-analysis of premarital, marital, and family interventions. *Journal of Marital and Family Therapy, 11,* 257–271.

Gilliand, T. G., & Goddard, H. W. (2006). *Making a difference: Your guide to strengthening marriages and families.* Provo, UT: Family Life Education Institute.

Ginott, H. G. (1965). *Between parent and child.* New York: Macmillan.

Ginott, H. G. (1969). *Between parent and teenager.* New York: Macmillan.

Ginott, H. G., Ginott, A., & Goddard, H. W. (2003). *Between parent and child.* New York: Three Rivers Press.

Glenn, J. (with Taylor, N.). (1999). *John Glenn: A memoir.* New York: Bantam.

Gloppen, K. M., David-Ferdon, C., & Bates, J. (2010). Confidence as a predictor of sexual and reproductive health outcomes for youth. *Journal of Adolescent Health, 46*(35), S42–S58.

Goddard, H. W. (1994). *Something better than punishment.* Auburn: Alabama Cooperative Extension System.

Goddard, H. W. (1995). *The great self mystery.* Auburn: Alabama Cooperative Extension System.

Goddard, H. W. (1999). Haim Ginott. In C. A Smith (Ed.), *Encyclopedia of parenting theory and research* (pp. 202–204). Westport, CT: Greenwood.

Goddard, H. W., & Ginott, A. (2002). Haim Ginott. In N. J. Salkind (Ed.), *Child development* (pp. 167–168). New York: Macmillan Reference.

Goddard, H. W., Marshall, J. P., Olson, J. R., & Dennis, S. A. (2010). *Steps toward creating and validating an effective couples curriculum.* Unpublished manuscript.

Goddard, H. W., Myers-Walls, J. A., & Lee, T. R. (2004). Parenting: Have we arrived? Or do we continue the journey? *Family & Consumer Sciences Research Journal, 33,* 21–38.

Goddard, H. W., & Olsen, C.S (2004). Cooperative Extension initiatives in marriage and couples education. *Family Relations, 53,* 433 -439.

Goff, B. G., Goddard, H. W., Pointer, L., & Jackson, G. B. (2007). Measures of expressions of love. *Psychological Reports, 101,* 357–360.

Golembiewski, R. T., Billingsley, K., & Yeager, S. (1976). Measuring change and persistence in human affairs: Types of change generated by odd designs. *Journal of Applied Behavioral Science, 12,* 133–157.

Gossart, M. (2007). *There's no place like home . . . for sex education.* Eugene: Planned Parenthood of Southwestern Oregon. Retrieved April 23, 2010, from http://www.noplacelikehome.org/english.php

Gottman, J. (1997). *Raising an emotionally intelligent child.* New York: Simon & Schuster.

Gottman, J. (n.d.). *Gottman's marriage tips 101.* Retrieved January 5, 2010, from http://www.gottman.com/marriage/self_help/

Gottman, J. M (1994). *Why marriages succeed or fail.* New York: Fireside.

Gottman, J. M. (1999). *The marriage clinic.* New York: Norton.

Gottman, J. M., Coan, J., Carrere, S., & Swanson, C. (1998). Predicting marital happiness and stability from newlywed interactions. *Journal of Marriage and the Family, 60,* 5–22.

Gottman, J. M., & DeClaire, J. (2001). *The relationship cure: A 5-step guide to strengthening your marriage, family, and friendships.* New York: Three Rivers Press.

Gottman, J. M., & Gottman, J. S., (1999). The marriage survival kit: A research-based marital therapy. In R. Berger & M. T. Hannah (Eds.), *Preventive approaches in couples therapy* (pp. 304–330). Philadelphia: Brunner/Mazel.

Gottman, J. M., Ryan, K., Swanson, C., & Swanson, K. (2005). Proximal change experiments with couples: A methodology for empirically building a science of effective interventions of changing couples' interaction. *Journal of Family Communication, 5,* 163–190.

Gottman, J. M., & Silver, N. (1999). *The seven principles for making marriage work.* New York: Three Rivers Press.

Grant, T. R., Hawkins, A. J., & Dollahite, D. C. (2001). Web-based education and support for fathers: Remote but promising. In J. Fagan & A. J. Hawkins (Eds.), *Clinical and education interventions with fathers* (pp. 143–170). New York: Haworth.

Gray, B. (1989). *Collaborating.* San Francisco: Jossey-Bass.

Grieshop, J. I. (1987). Games: Powerful tools for learning. *Journal of Extension, 25*(1). Retrieved June 13, 2003, from http://www.joe.org/joe/1987spring/iw2 .html

Guerney, B., & Guerney, L. F. (1981). Family life education as intervention. *Family Relations, 30,* 591–598.

Guerney, B. G., Jr., & Maxson, P. (1990). Marital and family enrichment research: A decade review and look ahead. *Journal of Marriage and the Family, 52,* 1127–1135.

Guilamo-Ramos, V., & Bouris, A. (2009). Working with parents to promote healthy adolescent sexual development. *The Prevention Researcher, 16*(4), 7–11.

Guion, L., Broadwater, G., Chattaraj, S., Goddard, H. W., Lytle, S. S., Perkins, C., et al. (2003). *Strengthening programs to reach diverse audiences.* Gainesville: University of Florida Cooperative Extension Service.

Gunnings, R. (1968). *The technique of clear writing.* New York: McGraw-Hill.

Guttmacher Institute. (2010). *Sex and STI/HIV education.* Retrieved April 23, 2010, from www.guttmacher.org/statecenter/spibs/spib_SE.pdf

Haidt, J. (2003). Elevation and the positive psychology of morality. In C. M. Keyes & J. Haidt (Eds.), *Flourishing: Positive psychology and the life well-lived* (pp. 275–289). Washington, DC: American Psychological Association.

Haidt, J. (2006). *The happiness hypothesis: Finding modern truth in ancient wisdom.* New York: Basic Books.

Halford, W. K. (2004). The future of couple relationships education: Suggestions on how it can make a difference. *Family Relations, 53,* 559–566.

Halford, W. K., Markman, H. J., Kline, G. H., & Stanley, S. M. (2003). Best practices in couple relationship education. *Journal of Marital and Family Therapy, 29,* 385–406.

Halford, W. K., Markman, H. J., & Stanley, S. (2008). Strengthening couples' relationships with education: Social policy and public heath perspectives. *Journal of Family Psychology, 22,* 497–505.

Halford, W. K., Moore, E., Wilson, K. L., Farrugia, C., & Dyer, C. (2004). Benefits of flexible delivery relationship education: An evaluation of the couple CARE program. *Family Relations, 53,* 469–476.

Halford, K. W., Sanders, M. R., & Behrens, B. C. (2001). Can skills training prevent relationship problems in at-risk couples? Four-year effects of a behavioral relationship education program. *Journal of Family Psychology, 15,* 750–768.

Hanna, S. M., & Brown, J. H. (2004). *The practice of family therapy.* Belmont, CA: Brooks/Cole Thomson Learning.

Harm, M. J., & Thompson, P. J. (1997). Evaluating the effectiveness of parent education for incarcerated mothers. *Journal of Offender Rehabilitation, 24*(3/4), 135–152.

Harris, V. W. (2002). *Creative ways to teach marriage and family relations.* Logan, UT: EnVision Entertainment.

Hart, B., & Risley, T. R. (1995). *Meaningful differences in the everyday experience of young American children.* Baltimore: Brookes.

Harter, S. (1983). Developmental perspectives on the self-system. In E. M. Hetherington (Ed.) & P. H. Mussen (Series Ed.), *Handbook of child psychology: Vol. 4. Socialization, personality and social development* (pp. 275–385). New York: John Wiley.

Hawkins, A. J., & Blanchard, V. L. (2009, November). *Programmatic discriminators of marriage and relationship education program efficacy: A meta-analytic perspective*. Paper presented at the Association of Behavioral and Cognitive Therapies Conference, New York City, New York.

Hawkins, A. J., Blanchard, V. L., Baldwin, S. A., & Fawcett, E. B. (2008). Does marriage and relationship education work? A meta-analytic study. *Journal of Consulting and Clinical Psychology, 76,* 723–734.

Hawkins, A. J., Carroll, J. S., Doherty, W. J., & Willoughby, B. (2004). A comprehensive framework for marriage education. *Family Relations, 53,* 547–558.

Hawkins, A. J., Fowers, B. J., Carroll, J. S., & Yang, C. (2007). Conceptualizing and measuring marital virtues. In S. L. Hofferth & L. M. Casper (Eds.), *Handbook of measurement issues in family research* (pp. 67–83). Mahwah, NJ: Lawrence Erlbaum.

Hawkins, A. J., Wilson, R. F., Ooms, T., Nock, S. L., Malone-Colon, L., & Cohen, L. (2009). Recent government reforms related to marital formation, maintenance, and dissolution in the United States: A primer and critical review. *Journal of Couple & Relationship Therapy, 8,* 264–281.

Hawkins, J. D., Catalano, R. F., & Miller, J. Y. (1992). Risk and protective factors for alcohol and other drug problems in adolescence and early adulthood: Implications for substance abuse prevention. *Psychological Bulletin, 112,* 64–105.

Heath, H. (1998). *Choosing parenting curricula based on the interests, needs, and preferences of the parents who will use it*. Retrieved April 15, 2010, from http:// parenthood.library.wisc.edu/Heath/Heath.html

Heath, H., & Palm, G. (2006). Future challenges for parenting education and support. *Child Welfare, 85,* 885–895.

Heider, F. (1958). *The psychology of interpersonal relations*. New York: John Wiley.

Herman, J. L., Morris, L. L., & Fitz-Gibbon, C. T. (1987). *Evaluator's handbook*. Newbury Park, CA: Sage.

Herman, M. R., Dornbusch, S. F., Herron, M. C., & Herting, J. R. (1997). The influence of family regulation, connection, and psychological autonomy on six measures of adolescent functioning. *Journal of Adolescent Research, 12,* 34–67.

Higginbotham, B. J., & Skogrand, L. (2010). Relationship education with both married and unmarried stepcouples: An exploratory study. *Journal of Couple & Relationship Therapy, 9,* 133–148.

Hildreth, G. J., & Sugawara, A. I. (1993). Ethnicity and diversity in family life education. In M. E. Arcus, J. D. Schvaneveldt, & J. J. Moss (Eds.), *Handbook of family life education: Vol. 1. Foundations of family life education* (pp. 162–188). Newbury Park, CA: Sage.

Hobbs, C. R. (1972). *The power of teaching with new techniques*. Salt Lake City, UT: Deseret Book.

Hoff, T., Greene, L., & Davis, J. (2003). *National Survey of Adolescents and Young Adults: Sexual health knowledge, attitudes, and experiences*. Menlo Park, CA: Henry J. Kaiser Family Foundation.

Hoffman, M. L. (1983). Affective and cognitive processes in moral internalization. In E. T. Higgins, D. N. Ruble, & W. W. Hartup (Eds.), *Social cognition and social development* (pp. 236–274). Cambridge, UK: Cambridge University Press.

Hoffman, M. L. (2000). *Empathy and moral development: Implications for caring and justice*. Cambridge, UK: Cambridge University Press.

Holman, T. B., Carroll, J. S., Busby, D. M., & Klein, D. M. (2008). *Preparing, coupling, and marrying: Toward a unified theory of marriage development*. Unpublished manuscript.

Horrigan, J. (2009). *Home broadband adoption 2009*. Washington, DC: Pew Internet & American Life Project.

House, L. D., Bates, J., Markham, C. M., & Lesesne, C. (2010). Competence as a predictor of sexual and reproductive health outcomes for youth: A systematic review. *Journal of Adolescent Health, 46*(35), S7–S22.

House, L. D., Mueller, T., Reininger, B., Brown, K., & Markham, C. M. (2010). Character as a predictor of reproductive health outcomes for youth: A systematic review. *Journal of Adolescent Health, 46*(35), S59–S74.

Howard, G. S., & Daily, P. R. (1979). Response-shift bias: A source of contamination of self-report measures. *Journal of Applied Psychology, 64,* 144–150.

Howard, G. S., Ralph, K. M., Gulanick, N. A., Maxwell, S. E., Nance, D., & Gerber, S. L. (1979). Internal invalidity in pretest/posttest self-report evaluations and a reevaluation of retrospective pretests. *Applied Psychological Measurement, 3,* 1–23.

Howard, G. S., Schmeck, R. R., & Bray, J. H. (1979). Internal invalidity in studies employing self report instruments: A suggested remedy. *Journal of Education Measurement, 16*(2), 129–135.

Hughes, R., Jr. (1994). A framework for developing family life education programs. *Family Relations, 43,* 74–80.

Hughes, R., Jr. (1997). A guide to evaluating the quality of human development and family life web sites. Unpublished paper.

Hughes, R., Jr. (1999, Spring). Frequently asked questions about the use of information technology in family life education. *Ohio State University Extension: Human Development & Family Life Bulletin, 5,* 4–5.

Hughes, R., Jr. (2001). A process evaluation of a website for family life educators. *Family Relations, 50,* 164–170.

Hughes, R., Jr., Ebata, A. T., & Dollahite, D. C. (1999). Family life in the information age. *Family Relations, 48,* 5–6.

Human Resources Research Organization (HumRRO). (2001). *Market analysis of family life, parenting, and marriage education for the National Council on Family Relations*. Alexandria, VA: Author.

Iding, M., Crosby, M. E., & Speitel, T. (2002). Teachers and technology: Beliefs and practices. *International Journal of Instructional Media, 29*(2), 153–170.

Institute for American Values. (2005). *Why marriage matters: Twenty-six conclusions from the social sciences* (2nd ed.). New York: Author.

Institute for Mental Health Initiatives. (1991). *Anger management for parents: The RETHINK method*. Champaign, IL: Research Press.

Jackson, S. (1997). *Life among the savages*. New York: Penguin.

Jacobs, F. H. (1988). The five-tiered approach to evaluation: Context and implementation. In H. B. Weiss & F. H. Jacobs (Eds.), *Evaluating family programs* (pp. 37–68). Hawthorne, NY: Aldine de Gruyter.

Jacobson, N. S., & Christensen, A. (1996). *Acceptance and change in couple therapy: A therapist's guide to transforming relationships*. New York: Norton.

Jakubowski, S. F., Milne, E. P., Brunner, H., & Miller, R. B. (2004). A review of empirically supported marriage enrichment programs. *Family Relations, 53,* 528–536.

John, R. (1998). Native American families. In C. H. Mindel, R. W. Habenstein, & R. Wright Jr. (Eds.), *Ethnic families in America: Patterns and variations* (4th ed., pp. 382–421). New York: Prentice Hall.

Johnson, C. A., Stanley, S. A., Glenn, N. D., Amato, P. A., Nock, S. L., Markman, H. J., et al. (2002). *Marriage in Oklahoma: 2001 baseline statewide survey on marriage and divorce* (S02096 OKDHS). Oklahoma City: Oklahoma Department of Human Services.

Jordan, B., & Stackpole, N. (1995). *Audiovisual resources for family programming*. New York: Neal-Schuman.

Kaiser, A. P., & Hancock, T. B. (2003). Teaching parents new skills to support their young children's development. *Infants and Young Children, 16,* 9–21.

Katz, B. (1988). *How to market professional services*. New York: Nichols Publishing.

Kennedy, T., Smith, A., Wells, A. T., & Wellman, B. (2008). *Networked families*. Washington, DC: Pew Internet & American Life Project.

Kerpelman, J., Pittman, J., Adler-Baeder, F., Stringer, K., Eryigit, S., Cadely, H. S., et al. (2010). What adolescents bring to and learn from relationships education classes: Does social address matter? *Journal of Couple & Relationship Therapy, 9,* 95–112.

Kerr, M., & Stattin, H. (2000). What parents know, how they know it, and several forms of adolescent adjustment: Further support for a reinterpretation of monitoring. *Developmental Psychology, 36,* 1–15.

Kibel, B. M. (1999). *Success stories as hard data*. Boulder, CO: Perseus.

Kibel, B. M. (n.d.). *Success stories as hard data*. Retrieved from http://www.pire .org/resultsmapping/abridge.htm

Kirby, D. (2007). *Emerging answers 2007: Research findings on programs to reduce teen pregnancy and sexually transmitted diseases*. Washington, DC: National Campaign to Prevent Teen and Unplanned Pregnancy.

Kirby, D., & Miller, B. C. (2003). Pregnancy, adolescence. In T. P. Gullotta & M. Bloom (Eds.), *Encyclopedia of primary prevention and health promotion* (pp. 838–846). New York: Kluwer Academic/Plenum.

Klemer, R. H., & Smith, R. M. (1975). *Teaching about family relationships*. Minneapolis, MN: Burgess.

Knowles, M. S. (1998). *The adult learner* (5th ed.). Houston, TX: Gulf Publishing Co.

Kohler, P. M., Manhart, L. E., & Lafferty, W. E. (2008). Abstinence-only and comprehensive sex education and the initiation of sexual activity and teen pregnancy. *Journal of Adolescent Health, 42,* 344–351.

Kohn, A. (1994). The truth about self-esteem. *Phi Delta Kappan, 76*(4), 272–283.

Kotler, P., & Roberto, E. L. (1989). *Social marketing: Strategies for changing public behavior.* New York: Free Press.

Krysan, M., Moore, K. A., & Zill, N. (1990). *Identifying successful families: An overview of constructs and selected measures.* Washington, DC: Child Trends, Inc.

Kurtus, R. (2005). *Benjamin Franklin's thirteen virtues.* Retrieved April 20, 2010, from http://www.school-for-champions.com/character/franklin_virtues.htm

L'Abate, L. (1983). Prevention as a profession: Toward a new conceptual frame of reference. In D. R. Mace (Ed.), *Prevention in family services: Approaches to family therapy and counseling* (pp. 46–52). Beverly Hills, CA: Sage.

Lambert, N. M., & Dollahite, D. C. (2006). How religiosity helps couples prevent, resolve, and overcome marital conflict. *Family Relations, 55,* 439–449.

Lamborn, D. S., Mounts, S. N., Steinberg, L., & Dornbusch, M. S. (1991). Patterns of competence and adjustment among adolescents from authoritative, authoritarian, indulgent, and neglectful families. *Child Development, 62,* 1049–1065.

LaRocque, P. (2003). *The book on writing.* Oak Park, IL: Marion Street Press.

Larson, J. H. (1988). The marriage quiz: College students' beliefs in selected myths about marriage. *Family Relations, 37,* 3–11.

Larson, J. H. (2000). *Should we stay together?* San Francisco: Jossey-Bass.

Larson, J. H. (2004). Innovations in marriage education: Introduction and challenges. *Family Relations, 53,* 421–424.

Larson, J. H., & Halford, W. K. (In press). One size does not fit all: Customizing couple relationship education for unique couple needs. *Journal of Couple & Relationship Therapy.*

Leary, M. R. (2004). *The curse of the self: Self-awareness, egotism, and the quality of human life.* New York: Oxford University Press.

LeCroy, C. W., Carrol, P., Nelson-Becker, H., & Sturlaugson, P. (1989). An experimental evaluation of the caring days technique for marital enrichment. *Family Relations, 38,* 15–18.

Lee, T. R., Mancini, J. A., Miles, C. S., & Marek, L. I. (1996, June). *Making a difference: Community programs that last.* Paper presented at the Linking Families and Communities Conference, Louisville, KY.

Lengua, L. J., Roosa, M. W., Schupak-Neuberg, E., Michaels, M. L., Berg, C. N., & Weschler, L. F. (1992). Using focus groups to guide the development of a parenting program for difficult-to-reach, high-risk families. *Family Relations, 41,* 163–168.

Lenhart, A. (2009a). *Adults and social network websites.* Pew Internet & American Life Project, January 14, 2009. Retrieved December 2, 2009, from http://pewinternet.org/Reports/2009/Adults-and-Social-Network Websites.aspx

Lenhart, A. (2009b). *Teens and sexting: How and why minor teens are sending sexually suggestive nude or nearly nude images via text messaging.* Washington, DC: Pew Internet & American Life Project.

Lerner, R. M. (1991). Changing organism-contest relationships as the basis process of development: A developmental contextual perspective. *Developmental Psychology, 27,* 27–32.

Lerner, R. M. (1995). *America's youth in crisis: Challenges and options for programs and policies.* Thousand Oaks, CA: Sage.

Levant, R. F. (1987). The use of marketing techniques to facilitate acceptance of parent education programs: A case example. *Family Relations, 36,* 246–251.

Levin, J., Levin, S. R., & Waddoups, G. (1999). Multiplicity in learning and teaching: A framework for developing innovative online education. *Journal of Research on Computing in Education, 32*(2), 256.

Lewis-Rowley, M., Brasher, R. E., Moss, J. J., Duncan, S. F., & Stiles, R. J. (1993). The evolution of education for family life. In M. E. Arcus, J. D. Schvaneveldt, & J. J. Moss (Eds.), *Handbook of family life education* (Vol. 1, pp. 26–50). Newbury Park, CA: Sage.

Llewellyn, G., McConnell, D., Russo, D., Mayes, R., & Honey, A. (2002). Home-based programmes for parents with intellectual disabilities: Lessons from practice. *Journal of Applied Research in Intellectual Disabilities, 15,* 341–353.

Lowry, D., & Echols, E. (2000). *Flying your true colors for true success.* Riverside, CA: True Colors.

Lyles, A., Cohen, L., & Brown, M. (2009). *Transforming communities to prevent child sexual abuse and exploitation: A primary prevention approach.* Retrieved April 23, 2010, from www.preventioninstitute.org

Lyubomirsky, S. (2008). *The how of happiness: A scientific approach to getting the life you want.* New York: Penguin.

Maccoby, E. E. (2002). Parenting effects: Issues and controversies. In J. G. Borkowski, S. L. Ramey, & M. Bistol-Power (Eds.), *Parenting and the child's world* (pp. 35–46). Mahwah, NJ: Lawrence Erlbaum.

Maccoby, E. E., & Martin, J. A. (1983). Socialization in the context of the family: Parent child interaction. In E. M. Hetherington (Ed.), *Handbook of child psychology: Vol. 4. Socialization, personality, and social development* (4th ed., pp. 1–101). New York: John Wiley.

Mace, D. R. (1981). The long, long trail from information-giving to behavioral change. *Family Relations, 30,* 599–606.

Maddi, S. M. (1989). *Personality theories: A comparative analysis.* Chicago: Dorsey.

Maddux, J. E. (2002). Stopping the "madness": Positive psychology and the deconstruction of the illness ideology and the *DSM.* In C. R. Snyder & S. J. Lopez (Eds.), *Handbook of positive psychology* (pp. 13–25). New York: Oxford University Press.

Mahoney, A., Pargament, K. I., Jewell, T., Swank, A. B., Scott, E., Emery, E., et al. (1999). Marriage and the spiritual realm: The role of proximal and distal religious constructs in marital functioning. *Journal of Family Psychology, 13,* 321–338.

Maiorano, J. J., & Futris, T. G. (2005). Fit 2-B FATHERS: The effectiveness of extension programs with incarcerated fathers. *Journal of Extension, 43*(5). Retrieved from http://www.joe.org/joe/2005october/a7.php

Maldonado-Molina, M. M., Reyes, N. A., & Espinosa-Hernandez, G. (2006). Prevention research and Latino families: Resources for researchers and practitioners. *Family Relations, 55,* 403–414.

Markham, C. M., Lormand, D., Gloppen, K. M., Peskin, M. F., Flores, B., Low, B., et al. (2010). Connectedness as a predictor of sexual and reproductive health outcomes for youth. *Journal of Adolescent Health, 46*(35), S23–S41.

Markman, H. J., Stanley, S. M., & Blumberg, S. L (2001). *Fighting for your marriage.* San Francisco: Jossey-Bass.

Marshall, J. P., & Goddard, H. W. (2006). *The marriage garden.* Little Rock: The University of Arkansas Cooperative Extension Service.

Martino, S. C., Collins, R. L., Elliott, M. N., Strachman, A., Kanouse, D. E., & Berry, S. H. (2006). Exposure to degrading versus nondegrading music lyrics and sexual behavior among youth. *Pediatrics, 118*(2), e430–e441.

Marton, C. (2000). Evaluating the Women's Health Matters website. *CyberPsychology & Behavior, 3,* 747–760.

Maslow, A. H. (1970). *Motivation and personality.* New York: Harper & Row.

McAdoo, H. P. (1998). African-American families. In C. H. Mindel, R. W. Habenstein, & R. Wright Jr. (Eds.), *Ethnic families in America: Patterns and variations* (4th ed., pp. 361–381). New York: Prentice Hall.

McCall, R. B., & Green, B. L. (2004). Beyond the methodological gold standards of behavior research: Considerations for practice and policy. *Social Policy Report, 18,* 1–12.

McCullough, M. E., Rachal, K. C., Sandage, S. J., Worthington, E. L., Jr., Brown, S. W., & Hight, T. L. (1998). Interpersonal forgiving in close relationships: II. Theoretical elaboration and measurement. *Journal of Personality and Social Psychology, 75,* 1586–1603.

McDermott, D. (2001). Parenting and ethnicity. In M. J. Fine & S. W. Lee (Eds.), *Handbook of diversity in parent education* (pp. 73–96). San Diego: Academic Press.

McKeachie, W. J. (1999). *Teaching tips: Strategies, research, and theory for college and university teachers* (10th ed.). Boston: Houghton Mifflin.

McKenzie, B., & Bacon, B. (2002). Parent education after separation: Results from a multi-site study on best practices. *Canadian Journal of Community Mental Health, 4*(Suppl.), 73–88.

Mecca, A. M., Smelser, N. J., & Vasconcellos, J. (1989). *The social importance of self-esteem.* Berkeley: University of California Press.

Meek, J. (1992a). *How to build coalitions: Collaboration.* Ames: Iowa State Extension Service.

Meek, J. (1992b). *How to build coalitions: Turf issues.* Ames: Iowa State Extension Service.

Melaville, A. I., & Blank, M. J. (1991). *What it takes: Structuring interagency partnerships to connect children and families with comprehensive services.* Washington, DC: Education and Human Services Consortium.

Merrill, M. D. (1983). Component display theory. In C. M. Reigeluth (Ed.), *Instructional design theories and models* (pp. 279–333). Hillsdale, NJ: Lawrence Erlbaum.

Merrill, M. D. (1994). *Instructional design theory.* Englewood Cliffs, NJ: Educational Technology Publications.

Merrill, M. D. (2000). First principles of instruction. In *Second generation instructional design.* Retrieved from http://www.id2.usu.edu

Merrill, M. D. (2001). First principles of instruction. *Journal of Structural Learning and Intelligence Systems, 14,* 459–466.

Mezirow, J. (1995). Transformation theory of adult learning. In M. Welton (Ed.), *In defense of the lifeworld: Critical perspectives on adult learning* (pp. 39–70). Albany: State University of New York Press.

Miller, B. C. (2002). Family influences on adolescent sexual and contraceptive behavior. *Journal of Sex Research, 39*(1), 22–26.

Miller, B. C., Benson, B., & Galbraith, K. A. (2001). Family relationships and adolescent pregnancy risk: A research synthesis. *Developmental Review, 21*(1), 1–38.

Miller, S. D., Duncan, B. L., & Hubble, M. A. (1997). *Escape from Babel: Toward a unifying language for psychotherapy practice.* New York: Norton.

Mindel, C. H., Habenstein, R. W., & Wright, R., Jr. (1998). *Ethnic families in America: Patterns and variations.* Upper Saddle River, NJ: Prentice Hall.

Miner, F. D., Jr., & Barnhill, J. V. (2001). Dollars for answers. *Journal of Extension, 39*(6). Retrieved June 13, 2003, from http://www.joe.org/joe/2001december/iw6.html

Minnesota Council on Family Relations (MCFR). (2009). *Ethical thinking and practice for parent and family life educators.* Minneapolis: Minnesota Council on Family Relations.

Minuchin, S., & Fishman, H. C. (1981). *Family therapy techniques.* Cambridge, MA: Harvard University Press.

Mohr, B. J., & Watkins, J. M. (2002). *The essentials of appreciative inquiry: A roadmap for creating positive futures.* Waltham, MA: Pegasus Communications.

Morgan, D. L. (1996). Focus groups. *Annual Review of Sociology, 22,* 129–152.

Morgan, D. L., Krueger, R. A., & King, J. A. (Eds.). (1998). *Focus group kit.* Thousand Oaks, CA: Sage.

Morris, L. L., Fitz-Gibbon, C. T., & Freeman, M. E. (1987). *How to communicate evaluation findings* (2nd ed.). Newbury Park, CA: Sage.

Morris, S. N., Dollahite, D. C., & Hawkins, A. J. (1999). Virtual family life education: A qualitative study of father education on the World Wide Web. *Family Relations, 48,* 23–30.

MSNBC News. (2004). *NBC/People: National survey of young teens' sexual attitudes and behaviors.* Retrieved April 23, 2010, from http://msnbcmedia.msn.com/i/msnbc/Sections/TVNews/ Dateline%20NBC/NBCTeenTopline.pdf

Myers, D. G. (2000). *The American paradox: Spiritual hunger in an age of plenty.* New Haven, CT: Yale University Press.

Myers, I. B. (1981). *Introduction to type.* Palo Alto, CA: Consulting Psychologists Press.

Myers-Walls, J. A. (2000). Family diversity and family life education. In D. H. Demo, K. R. Allen, & M. A. Fine (Eds.), *Handbook of family diversity* (pp. 359–379). New York: Oxford University Press.

Myers-Walls, J. A. (2007). *Interpretation of "what are your parenting recommendations?"* Unpublished manuscript, Purdue University.

Na, J., & Chia, S. W. (2008). Impact of online resources on informal learners: Parents' perception of their parenting skills. *Computers and Education, 51,* 173–186.

The National Campaign to Prevent Teen Pregnancy. (2006a). *Science says: Characteristics of effective curriculum-based programs.* Retrieved April 23, 2010, from www.teenpregnancy.org

The National Campaign to Prevent Teen Pregnancy. (2006b). *Teen birth rates: How does the United States Compare?* Retrieved April 23, 2010, from www.thenationalcampaign.org/resources/pdf/TBR_International Comparison2006.pdf

The National Campaign to Prevent Teen and Unplanned Pregnancy. (2010, March). *Briefly . . . A summary of effective interventions.* Retrieved April 23, 2010, from www.TeenPregnancy.org

National Center for Health Statistics. (2009). *Births, marriages, divorces, and deaths: Provisional data for 2008* (National Vital Statistics Reports, Vol. 57, No. 19). Hyattsville, MD: Author.

National Council on Family Relations. (2009a). *Careers in family science.* Minneapolis, MN: Author.

National Council on Family Relations. (2009b). *Family life education content areas: Content and practice guidelines.* Retrieved April 21, 2010, from www.ncfr.org

National Fatherhood Initiative. (2005). *With this ring . . . A national survey on marriage in America.* Gaithersburg, MD: Author.

National Guidelines Task Force. (2004). *Guidelines for comprehensive sexuality education: Kindergarten–12th grade* (3rd ed.). Washington, DC: Sexuality Information and Education Council of the United States. Retrieved April 23, 2010, from www.siecus.org/_data/global/images/guidelines.pdf

National Parenting Education Network. (n.d.). Retrieved April 15, 2010, from http://npen.org/index.html

National Research Council. (1993). *Understanding child abuse and neglect.* Washington, DC: National Academy Press.

Nelson, P. T. (1986). Newsletters: An effective delivery mode for providing educational information and emotional support to single parent families? *Family Relations, 35,* 183–188.

NLM Gateway. (2004). All4You! A randomized trial of an HIV prevention intervention for youth in alternative schools. Retrieved April 23, 2010, from http://gateway.nlm.nih.gov/MeetingAbstracts/ ma?f=102282091.html

Norcross, J. C., Santrock, J. W., Campbell, L. F., Smith, T. P., Sommer, R., & Zuckerman, E. L. (2003). *Authoritative guide to self-help resources in mental health.* New York: Guilford.

O'Donnell, L., Wilson-Simmons, R., Dash, K., Jeanbaptiste, V., Myint-U, A., Moss, J., et al. (2007). Saving sex for later: Developing a parent-child communication intervention to delay sexual initiation among young adolescents. *Sex Education, 7*(2), 107–125.

Office of Juvenile Justice and Delinquency Prevention. (n.d.). *Model programs guide.* Retrieved April 15, 2010, from http://www2.dsgonline.com/mpq/

Olson, D. H., Stewart, K. L., & Wilson, L. R. (1990). Health and stress profile (HSP), revised. Minneapolis, MN: Profile of Health Systems.

Olson, J. R., Goddard, H. W., Solheim, C. A., & Sandt, L. (2004). Making a case for engaging adolescents in program decision-making. *Journal of Extension, 42*(6). Retrieved from http://www.joe.org/joe/2004december/rb4.php

O'Neill, B. (2003). How to create and use an interactive PowerPoint quiz game. *Journal of Extension, 41*(2). Retrieved June 13, 2003, from http://www.joe.org/joe/2003april/tt2.php

Ono, H., & Zavodny, M. (2003). Gender and the Internet. *Social Science Quarterly, 84*(1), 111.

Ooms, T., & Wilson, P. (2004). The challenges of offering relationship and marriage education to low-income populations. *Family Relations, 53,* 440–447.

Orgel, A. R. (1980). Haim Ginott's approach to parent education. In M. J. Fine (Ed.), *The handbook on parent education* (pp. 75–100). New York: Academic Press.

Oyserman, D., Mowbray, C., Meares, P., & Firminger, K. (2003). Parenting among mothers with a serious mental illness. *Annual progress in child psychiatry and child development: 2000–2001* (pp. 177–216). New York: Brunner-Routledge.

Palm, G. F. (2009). Professional ethics and practice. In D. J. Bredehoft & M. J. Walcheski (Eds.), *Family life education: Integrating theory and practice* (pp. 191–197). Minneapolis, MN: National Council on Family Relations.

Patterson, K., Grenny, J., McMillan, A., & Switzler, R. (2002). *Crucial conversations.* New York: McGraw-Hill.

Pawel, J. J. (2000). *The parent's toolshop: The universal blueprint for building a healthy family.* Springboro, OH: Ambris Publishing.

Peterson, G. W., & Hann, D. (1999). Socializing children and parents in families. In M. B. Sussman, S. K. Steinmetz, & G. W. Peterson (Eds.), *Handbook of marriage and the family* (2nd ed., pp. 327–370). New York: Plenum.

Peterson, G. W., & Steinmetz, S. K. (2002). *Pioneering paths in the study of families: The lives and careers of family scholars.* Philadelphia: Haworth.

Pfander, S., & Bradley-Johnson, S. (1990). Effects on an intervention program and its components on NICU infants. *Children's Health Care, 19,* 140–147.

Popenoe, D. (2001, May). *Marriage decline in America.* Testimony before the Subcommittee on Human Resources, Committee on Ways and Means, United States House of Representatives, Washington, DC.

Powell, J. (1974). *The secret of staying in love.* Allen, TX: Argus Communications.

Powell, L. H., & Cassidy, D. (2007). *Family life education: Working with families across the lifespan* (2nd ed.). Long Grove, IL: Waveland.

Price, D. W. (2000). Philosophy and the adult educator. *Adult Learning, 11,* 3–5.

Prochaska, J., & DiClemente, C. C. (1983). Stages and processes of self-change of smoking: Toward an integrative model of change. *Journal of Consulting and Clinical Psychology, 51,* 390–395.

Prochaska, J. O., Norcross, J. C., & DiClemente, C. C. (1994). *Changing for good.* New York: Avon Books.

Promising Practices Network. (2010). *Programs that work.* Retrieved April 23, 2010, from www.promisingpractices.net/programs_alpha.asp

Quick, S., & Lasueur, A., Jr. (2003). Take time to be slow and quiet. In *A world of possibilities.* Retrieved from http://www.ca.uky.edu/agcollege/fcs/areas/hdfr/articles/Media_Article_8.htm

Radey, M., & Randolph, K. A. (2009). Parenting sources: How do parents differ in their efforts to learn about parenting? *Family Relations, 58,* 536–548.

Rasmussen, W. D. (1989). *Taking the university to the people: Seventy-five years of cooperative extension.* Ames: Iowa State University Press.

Reid, M. J., Webster-Stratton, C., & Baydar, N. (2004). Halting the development of conduct problems in Head Start children: The effects of parent training. *Journal of Clinical Child and Adolescent Psychology, 33*(20), 279–291.

Reid, M. J., Webster-Stratton, C., & Beauchaine, T. P. (2001). Parent training in Head Start: A comparison of program response among African American, Asian American, Caucasian, and Hispanic mothers. *Prevention Science, 2*(4), 209–227.

Rhoades, G. K., Stanley, S. M., & Markman, H. J. (2009). Working with cohabitation in relationship education and therapy. *Journal of Couple & Relationship Therapy, 8,* 95–112.

Rico, G., & Volk, T. (1999). *Writing the natural way: Turning the task of writing into the joy of writing.* New York: Tarcher.

Ritter, S. H., & Gottfried, S. C. (2002). *Tomorrow's child: Benefiting from today's family-school community-business partnerships.* Greensboro, NC: The Regional Educational Laboratory at SERVE.

Roach, R. (2003). Digital divide rooted in home computer ownership. *Black Issues in Higher Education, 20,* 50.

Robinson, E. A. R. (1994). Implications of the pre/post/then design for evaluating social group work. *Research on Social Work Practice, 4,* 224–239.

Robinson, P. (Director). (1989). *Field of Dreams* [Motion picture]. United States: Universal Studios.

Rockwell, K., & Bennett, C. (2004). *Targeting outcomes of programs.* Retrieved from http://citnews.unl.edu/TOP/index.html

Rogers, E. (1983). *Diffusion of innovations* (3rd ed.). New York: Free Press.

Rogoff, B. (1990). *Apprenticeship in thinking.* New York: Oxford University Press.

Rothbaum, F., Martland, N., & Jannsen, J. B. (2008). Parents' reliance on the Web to find information about children and families: Socio-economic differences in use, skills and satisfaction. *Journal of Applied Developmental Psychology, 20,* 118–128.

Rutter, M. (1987). Psychosocial resilience and protective mechanisms. *American Journal of Orthopsychiatry, 53,* 316–331.

SafePlace: Domestice Violence and Sexual Assault Survival Center. (2002). *Kid&TeenSAFE: An abuse prevention program for youth with disabilities.* Harrisburg, PA: National Resource Center on Domestic Violence.

Sarkadi, A., & Bremberg, S. (2005). Socially unbiased parenting support on the Internet: A cross-sectional study of users of a large Swedish parenting website. *Child: Care, Health, & Development, 31,* 43–52.

Satter, E. (1995/1997). *Ellyn Satter's feeding with love and good sense* [Video and teacher's guide]. Madison, WI: Ellyn Satter Associates.

Satter, E. (1999). *Secrets of feeding a healthy family.* Madison, WI: Kelcy Press.

Saunders, J. A. (2005). Adolescent pregnancy prevention programs: Theoretical models for effective program development. *American Journal of Sexuality Education, 1*(1), 63–84.

Schaaf, K., & Hogue, T. (1990). *Preparing your community: A guide to community action planning in Oregon.* Salem: Positive Youth Development of Oregon.

Schaefer, E. S. (1965). Children's reports of parental behavior: An inventory. *Child Development, 36,* 413–424.

Schorr, L. (1988). *Within our reach: Breaking the cycle of disadvantage.* New York: Anchor.

Schorr, L. (1997). *Common purpose: Strengthening families and neighborhoods to rebuild America.* New York: Anchor.

Schumm, W., & Denton, W. (1979). Trends in premarital counseling. *Journal of Marital and Family Therapy, 5,* 23–32.

Schumm, W. R., & Silliman, B. (1997). Changes in premarital counseling as related to older cohorts of married couples. *Journal of Sex and Marital Therapy, 23,* 98–102.

Seligman, M. E. P. (1991). *Learned optimism.* New York: Knopf.

Seligman, M. E. P. (1993). *What you can change . . . and what you can't.* New York: Fawcett Columbine.

Seligman, M. E. P. (1995). *What you can change and what you can't: The complete guide to successful self-improvement.* New York: Ballantine.

Seligman, M. E. P. (1999). The president's address. *American Psychologist, 54*(8), 559–562.

Seligman, M. E. P. (2002). *Authentic happiness.* New York: Free Press.

Seligman, M. E. P., Reivich, K., Jaycox, L., & Gillham, J. (1995). *The optimistic child.* New York: Houghton Mifflin.

Shanklin, S. L., Brener, N., McManus, T., Kinchen, S., & Kann, L. (2007). *2005 Middle School Youth Risk Behavior Survey.* Atlanta, GA: U.S. Department of Health and Human Services, Centers for Disease Control and Prevention. Retrieved April 15, 2010, from http://www.cdc.gov/Healthy Youth /yrbs/middlesch0012005/pdf/YRBS_MS_05_fullreport.pdf

Shifflett, K., & Cummings, E. M. (1999). A program for educating parents about the effects of divorce and conflict on children: An initial evaluation. *Family Relations, 48,* 79–89.

Silberman, M. (1996). *Active learning: 101 strategies to teach any subject.* Boston: Allyn & Bacon.

Silver, H. F., Strong, R. W., & Perini, M. J. (2000). *So each may learn: Integrating learning styles and multiple intelligences.* Alexandria, VA: Association for Supervision and Curriculum Development.

Simpson, A. R. (1997). *The role of mass media in parenting education.* Boston: Center for Health Communication, Harvard School of Public Health.

Small, S. A. (1990). Some issues regarding the evaluation of family life education programs. *Family Relations, 39,* 132–135.

Small, S. A., Cooney, S. M., & O'Connor, C. (2009). Evidence-informed program improvement: Using principles of effectiveness to enhance the quality and impact of family-based prevention programs. *Family Relations, 58,* 1–13.

Small, S. A., & Hug, B. (1991). Research-based youth programming. *Journal of Extension, 29,* 27–29.

Small, S. A., & Memmo, M. (2004). Contemporary models of youth development and problem prevention: Toward an integration of terms, concepts, and models. *Family Relations, 53,* 3–11.

Smith, C. A. (1999). Family life pathfinders on the new electronic frontier. *Family Relations, 48,* 31–34.

Smith, C. A. (2004). *Raising courageous kids.* Notre Dame, IN: Sorin Books. Retrieved July 5, 2004, from http://www.ksu.edu/wwparent/programs/courage/Media%20 guide.pdf

Smith, C. A., Cudaback, D., Goddard, H. W., & Myers-Walls, J. A. (1994). *National extension parent education model.* Manhattan, KS: Kansas Cooperative Extension Service.

Smith, C., Perou, R., & Lesesne, C. (2002). Parent education. In M. H. Bornstein (Ed.), *Handbook of parenting: Vol. 4. Social conditions and applied parenting* (2nd ed., pp. 389–410). Mahwah, NJ: Lawrence Erlbaum.

Snyder, I. B., Duncan, S. F., & Larson, J. (2010). Assessing perceived marriage education needs and interests among Latinos in a select Western community. *Journal of Comparative Family Studies, 41,* 347–367.

Sprangers, M. (1989). Subject bias and the retrospective pretest in retrospect. *Bulletin of the Psychonomic Society, 27*(1), 11–14.

Stahmann, R., & Salts, C. (1993). Educating for marriage and intimate relationships. In M. E. Arcus, J. D. Schvaneveldt, & J. J. Moss (Eds.), *Handbook of family life education* (Vol. 2, pp. 33–61). Newbury Park, CA: Sage.

Stanley, S. M. (2001). Making a case for premarital education. *Family Relations, 50,* 272–280.

Stanley, S. M., Allen, E. S., Markman, H. J., Rhoades, G. K., & Prentice, D. (2010). Decreasing divorce in army couples: Results from a randomized clinical trial of the PREP for Strong Bonds program. *Journal of Couple & Relationship Therapy, 9,* 149–160.

Stanley, S. M., Amato, P. R., Johnson, C. A., & Markman, H. J. (2006). Premarital education, marital quality, and marital stability: Findings from a large, random household survey. *Journal of Family Psychology, 20,* 117–126.

Stanley, S. M., & Markman, H. J. (1992). Assessing commitment in personal relationships. *Journal of Marriage and the Family, 54,* 595–608.

Stanley, S. M., & Markman, H. J. (1997). *Marriage in the 90s: A nationwide random phone survey.* Denver, CO: PREP.

Stanley, S. M., Whitton, S. W., & Markman, H. J. (2004). Maybe I do: Interpersonal commitment and premarital or nonmarital cohabitation. *Journal of Family Issues, 25,* 496–519.

Steimle, B. M., & Duncan, S. F. (2004). Formative evaluation of a family life education website. *Family Relations, 53,* 367–376.

Steinberg, L. (1990). Autonomy, conflict, and harmony in the family context. In S. S. Feldman & G. R. Elliot (Eds.), *At the threshold: The developing adolescent* (pp. 255–276). Cambridge, MA: Harvard University Press.

Stolz, H. E., Henke, T. M., Brandon, D. J., & Sams, J. M. (in press). Professional preparation systems for parenting educators: Identification, perceived value, and demand for a national credential. *Journal of Extension.*

Stolz, H. E., Rector, M., & Cooke, B. (2009, March). *"Looking here and there . . .": Where do you find high quality parenting education materials and resources?* Paper presented at the Prevent Child Abuse Louisiana Annual Conference, Baton Rouge, LA.

Stolz, H. E., Vargas, L., Clifford, L. M., Gaedt, H. A., & Garcia, C. F. (2010). Evaluating "Parent Project": A multi-site inquiry. *Family Science Review, 15*(1), 1–12.

Stop It Now! (2008). *Prevent child sexual abuse: Facts about sexual abuse and how to prevent it.* Retrieved from http://www.stopitnow.com/sites/stopitnow.rivervalleywebhosting.com/files/webfm/green/Prevent_CSA.pdf

Strecher, V., & Rosenstock, I. (1997). The health belief model. In K. Glanz, F. M. Lewis, & B. Rimer (Eds.), *Health behavior and health education* (2nd ed., pp. 41–59). San Francisco: Jossey-Bass.

Strover, S. (2003). Remapping the digital divide. *Information Society, 19*(4), 275.

Stuart, R. (1980). *Helping couples change: A social learning approach to marital therapy.* New York: Guilford.

Suarez, Z. (1998). The Cuban-American family. In C. H. Mindel, R. W. Habenstein, & R. Wright Jr. (Eds.), *Ethnic families in America: Patterns and variations* (4th ed., pp. 172–198). New York: Prentice Hall.

Substance Abuse and Mental Health Services Administration (SAMHSA) Center for Substance Abuse Treatment (2006). *Treatment: Vol. 1. Understanding evidence-based practices for co-occurring disorders.* Retrieved April 15, 2010, from http://www.coce.samhsa.gov

Suchman, E. A. (1968). *Evaluative research: Principles and practice in public service and social action programs.* New York: Russell Sage Foundation.

Suellentrop, K. (2010). *What works 2010: Curriculum-based programs that help prevent teen pregnancy.* Washington, DC: The National Campaign to Prevent Teen and Unplanned Pregnancy. Retrieved April 15, 2010, from www.TeenPregnancy.org

Sullivan, K. T., & Bradbury, T. N. (1997). Are premarital prevention programs reaching couples at risk for marital dysfunction? *Journal of Consulting and Clinical Psychology, 65,* 24–30.

Tavris, C. (1989). *Anger: The misunderstood emotion.* New York: Simon & Schuster.

Taylor, E. (1997). Building upon the theoretical debate: A critical review of the empirical studies of Mezirow's transformative learning theory. *Adult Education Quarterly, 48*(1), 34–59.

Taylor, S. E., & Brown, J. D. (1999). Illusion and well-being: A social psychological perspective on mental health. In R. F. Baumeister (Ed.), *The self in social psychology* (pp. 43–66). Philadelphia: Psychology Press.

Terborg, J. R., Howard, G. S., & Maxwell S. E. (1980). Evaluating planned organizational change: A method for assessing alpha, beta, and gamma change. *Academy of Management Review, 5*(1), 109–121.

Thomas, J., & Arcus, M. (1992, November). *Teaching as storytelling: Personal narratives in family life education.* Paper presented at the Annual Meeting of the National Council on Family Relations, Orlando, FL.

Thomas, J., Schvaneveldt, J. D., & Young, M. H. (1993). Programs in family life education: Development, implementation, and evaluation. In M. E. Arcus, J. D. Schvaneveldt, & J. J. Moss (Eds.), *Handbook of family life education: Foundations of family life education* (Vol. 1, pp. 106–130). Newbury Park, CA: Sage.

Thompson, R. W., Grow, C. R., Ruma, P. R., Daly, D. L, & Burke, R. V. (1993). Evaluation of a practical parenting program with middle-and low-income families. *Families Relations, 42,* 21–25.

Thorndike, F. P. (2009). Commentary: Interest in Internet interventions—an infant sleep program as illustration. *Journal of Pediatric Psychology, 34,* 470–473.

Tilsen, J. (2007). We don't need no education: Parents are doing it for themselves. *Journal of Progressive Human Services, 18*(1), 71–87.

Tisdell, E. J., & Taylor, E. W. (2000). Adult education philosophy informs practice. *Adult Learning, 11,* 6–10.

Tortolero, S. R., Markham, C. M., Fleschler Peskin, M., Shegog, R., Addy, R. C., Escobar-Chaves, S. L., et al. (2010). It's your game: Keep it real: Delaying sexual behavior with an effective middle school program. *Journal of Adolescent Health, 46,* 169–179.

Twenge, J. (2006). *Generation me.* New York: Free Press.

U.S. Census Bureau. (2001). *Home computers and Internet use in the United States: August 2000* (No. P23–207). Washington, DC: Government Printing Office.

U.S. Census Bureau. (2009). *Internet use triples in decade, Census Bureau reports* (CB09–84). Washington, DC: Government Printing Office. Retrieved from http://www.census.gov/PressRelease/www/releases/archives/communication_industries/013849.html

U.S. Department of Education, National Center for Educational Statistics. (2003, October). *Computer and Internet use by children and adolescents in 2001* (No. NCES 2004–014). Washington, DC: Government Printing Office.

U.S. Government Accountability Office. (2008). *Abstinence education: Assessing the accuracy and effectiveness of federally funded programs* (GAO-08–664T). Retrieved April 23, 2010, from http://www.gao.gov/new.items/d08664t.pdf

Van Dijk, J., & Hacker, K. (2003). The digital divide as a complex and dynamic phenomenon. *Information Society, 19*(4), 315.

Vance, B. (1989). *Planning and conducting family cluster: Education for family wellness.* Newbury Park, CA: Sage.

Vincent, C. E. (1973). *Sexual and marital health.* New York: McGraw-Hill.

Waite, L. J., & Gallagher, M. (2000). *The case for marriage.* New York: Broadway.

Walker, S. K., & Greenhow, C. (2008, November). *What Facebook tells us about the future (and present) of parent and family education.* Paper presented at the annual meeting of the National Council on Family Relations, Little Rock, AR.

Wandersman, A., & Florin, P. (2003). Community interventions and effective prevention. *American Psychologist, 58,* 441–447.

Warnock, P. (1988). You don't have to be funny to use humor. *Journal of Extension, 26*(2). Retrieved June 13, 2003, from http://www.joe.org/joe/1988summer/f1.html

Weinreich, N. K. (1999). *Hands-on social marketing: A step-by-step guide.* Thousand Oaks, CA: Sage.

Weissbourd, B. (1994). The evolution of the family resource movement. In S. L. Kagan & B. Weissbourd (Eds.), *Putting families first: America's family support movement and the challenge of change* (pp. 28–47). San Francisco: Jossey-Bass.

Werner, E. E. (1990). Protective factors and individual resilience. In S. Meisel & J. Shonkoff (Eds.), *Handbook of early intervention* (pp. 97-116). Cambridge, England: Cambridge University Press.

Werner, E. E., & Smith, R. S. (1977). *Kauai's children come of age.* Honolulu: University of Hawaii Press.

Werner, E. E., & Smith, R. S. (1982). *Vulnerable but invincible: A longitudinal study of resilient children and youth.* New York: McGraw-Hill.

Werner, E. E., & Smith, R. S. (1992). *Overcoming the odds: High risk children from birth to adulthood.* Ithaca, NY: Cornell University Press.

Werner, E. E., & Smith, R. S. (2001). *Journeys from childhood to midlife: Risk, resilience, and recovery.* Ithaca, NY: Cornell University Press.

Whipple, E. E., & Wilson, S. R. (1996). Evaluation of a parent education and support program for families at risk of physical child abuse. *Families in Society, 77,* 227–239.

White, B. A., & Brockett, R. G. (1987). Putting philosophy into practice. *Journal of Extension, 25*(2). Retrieved October 15, 2001, from http://www.joe.org/joe/1987summer/a3.html

Whitehead, B. D., & Pearson, M. (2006). *Making a love connection: Teen relationships, pregnancy, and marriage.* Washington, DC: The National Campaign to Prevent Teen Pregnancy.

Whitton, S., Stanley, S., & Markman, H. (2002). Sacrifice in romantic relationships: An exploration of relevant research and theory. In A. L. Vangelisti, H. T. Reis, & M. A. Fitzpatrick (Eds.), *Stability and change in relationships* (pp. 156–182). New York: Cambridge University Press.

Williams, L. M., Riley, L. A., Risch, G. S., & Van Dyke, D. T. (1999). An empirical approach to designing marriage preparation programs. *Journal of Family Therapy, 27,* 271–283.

Wiley, A. R., & Ebata, A. (2004). Reaching American families: Making diversity real in family life education. *Family Relations, 53,* 273–281.

Wilson, T. D., & Linville, P. W. (1982). Improving academic performance of college freshmen: Attribution therapy revisited. *Journal of Personality and Social Psychology, 42,* 367–376.

Wirthlin Worldwide. (1999, September/October). *International survey on marriage and the family.* Reston, VA: Author.

Wirthlin Worldwide. (2000, August). *Americans rank strengthening families as highest priority.* Reston, VA: Author.

Woods, B. (1998). *Feedback on EDUFAIM: Montana's state strengthening project.* Unpublished manuscript.

Worthington, E. L., & Drinkard, D. T. (2000). Promoting reconciliation through psychoeducational and therapeutic interventions. *Journal of Marital and Family Therapy, 26,* 93–101.

Yarber, W. L. (1994). Past, present, and future perspectives on sexuality education. In J. C. Drolet & K. Clark (Eds.), *The sexuality education challenge: Promoting health sexuality in young people* (pp. 3–28). Santa Cruz, CA: ETR Associates.

YouthNet Partners in Reproductive Health and HIV Prevention. (2000). Parental involvement. Retrieved April 3, 2010, from www.FHI.org/en/Youth/YouthNet/ProgramsAreas/SexEducation/ parents.htm

Zaidman-Zait, A., & Jamieson, J. R. (2007). Providing Web-based support for families of infants and young children with established disabilities. *Infants & Young Children, 20,* 11–25.

AUTHOR INDEX

SUBJECT INDEX

Note: In page references, *f* indicates figures and *t* indicates tables.

ABOUT THE AUTHORS

Stephen F. Duncan is Professor in the School of Family Life at Brigham Young University. He received a master's degree in Family Sciences (Family Life Education emphasis) from Brigham Young University and a Ph.D. in Family Studies from Purdue University. He has authored or coauthored numerous outreach publications for lay audiences and professionals; written hundreds of articles for newspaper columns; been interviewed numerous times for television, radio, and magazine outlets; and directed nationally recognized outreach family life education programs. He served as an Extension Family Life Specialist at Auburn University in Alabama for 5 years and held a similar position at Montana State University for over 7 years. At BYU, he teaches undergraduate and graduate courses in family life education, conducts research geared to improve the practice of family life education, and directs outreach projects for the school. He was content director for *Real Families, Real Answers,* a Rocky Mountain Emmy Award–nominated documentary series appearing on public television channels nationwide. He has certification as a Family Life Educator.

Dr. Duncan has actively contributed to the scholarship of family life education, authoring numerous articles on outreach programs and evaluation, many of which have appeared in leading family life education/outreach outlets. He serves or has served on several editorial boards, including *Marriage and Families;* the *Children, Youth and Families Education and Research Network* (CYFERNet); *Journal of Couple and Relationship Therapy;* and *Family Relations*, widely recognized as the world's leading applied family research/practitioner journal. Steve and his wife, Barbara, are parents of five children.

H. Wallace (Wally) Goddard is Professor of Family Life with the University of Arkansas Cooperative Extension Service. He is well known nationally for his TV program, *Guiding Children Successfully*, as well as a multitude of creative programs: The Great Self Mystery, The Personal Journey, Managing Stress, The Marriage Garden, The Parenting Journey, Principles of Parenting, and See the World Through My Eyes—which has won several national awards.

In the professional world of family life educators, Dr. Goddard may be best known for his work on influential models. He was a member of the team that developed the National Extension Parent Education Model (NEPEM), which defines the critical content areas of parent education. He was also involved in the development of NEPEM's companion document, *The National Extension Parenting Educators' Framework*, which defines the essential elements of professional development. In addition to work in the parenting arena, he is also a member of the team that created the National Extension Relationship and Marriage Education Model (NERMEM).

Wally has participated in many book projects, including the revision of the classic *Between Parent and Child*. He provided content expertise to Stephen R. Covey when he wrote *The 7 Habits of Highly Effective Families*. He and his colleague, James Marshall, have written *The Marriage Garden*. He has also written *Soft-Spoken Parenting* and various books for general, professional, and Christian audiences.

Of course, family life education is more than academic for Wally. He and his wife, Nancy, have raised three children, cared for 20 foster children, and are looking after a growing number of grandchildren.

●●●●●

Susan Calahan is an Associate Professor of Health Education in the Department of School Health Education at Southern Connecticut State University, where she teaches both graduate and undergraduate courses. She received her B.S. degree in Secondary Education from Eastern Oregon University, an M.S. in Health Education from Brigham Young University, and a Ph.D. in Health Education from Southern Illinois University at Carbondale. Dr. Calahan has conducted and published research related to adolescent health behaviors, sexuality, and the media, as well as curriculum development and evaluation. She also has worked internationally studying health behaviors of adolescents in Ukraine. She has been an educator for 24 years and is a former junior and senior high school teacher and also has worked in the field of occupational health.

Steven A. Dennis is a faculty member at Brigham Young University–Idaho in the Department of Home and Family. He received graduate training in both instructional technology (M.S., 1992) and family science (Ph.D., 1995) from Utah State University. Prior to joining the faculty at BYU–Idaho, Dr. Dennis worked as a Family Life Specialist for the University of Arkansas Cooperative Extension Service and a faculty member of the School of Human Environmental Science at the University of Arkansas, Fayetteville. He also worked as a project director at the Center for Persons with Disabilities at Utah State University.

Aaron T. Ebata is an Associate Professor of Social Development in the Department of Human and Community Development at the University of Illinois at Urbana–Champaign, where he also holds an appointment as an Extension Specialist with the University of Illinois Extension. He received his B.S. degrees in Biology and Psychology from the University of Hawaii and completed his M.S. and Ph.D. degrees in Human Development and Family Studies at Penn State. Dr. Ebata came to Illinois in 1990 after completing a research fellowship in the Department of Psychiatry and Behavioral Sciences at Stanford University. A former elementary and preschool teacher, Dr. Ebata has conducted applied research on how children and families cope with stress and now develops outreach programs for parents and conducts training for professionals who work with children. He has developed a number of online programs for parents and professionals. He is married and the father of two sons.

Tonya Fischio is a public relations professional who has worked in the field for 15 years. After receiving her communications degree from Brigham Young University, she worked in the New York office of Edelman Public Relations, at Nu Skin International in Utah, and at the Family Studies Center at Brigham Young University. At the Family Studies Center, she used both the local and national media to share family research findings and university-sponsored family-related programs with target audiences. Currently, she manages the external relations for the J. Reuben Clark Law School. Throughout her career, she has held positions in internal communications, international relations, crisis management, and media relations.

Alan J. Hawkins is Professor of Family Life at Brigham Young University in Provo, Utah. He earned a Masters of Organizational Behavior from BYU in 1984 and Ph.D. in Human Development and Family Studies at The Pennsylvania State University in 1990. He has been teaching and conducting research and outreach at BYU since then. Professor Hawkins's current scholarship and outreach has focused on educational and policy interventions to help couples form and sustain healthy marriages and prevent divorce. He has published widely on this topic in leading journals. In 2003–2004, he was a visiting scholar with the Office of Planning, Research, and Evaluation, Administration for Children and Families, U.S. Department of Health and Human Services, working on the federal healthy marriage initiative. He was the Research Director of the National Healthy Marriage Resource Center from 2004–2006. He serves as Chair of the Utah Healthy Marriage Initiative. He is a member of the National Advisory Committee for the National Center for Families and Marriage Research and the National Center for African American Marriages and Families at Hampton University.

Charles A. Smith is Professor and Extension Parent Educator in the School of Family Studies and Human Services at Kansas State University. He holds a B.S. in Psychology from the University of Dayton and both an M.S. and Ph.D. in Child Development from Purdue University. He has worked extensively with young children as director of the Child Development Center at Texas Tech University, as a preschool teacher, and as a play therapist in a children's hospital. *Raising Courageous Kids: Eight Steps to Practical Heroism* (2004) is the most recent of his five books. His websites, The WonderWise Parent (http://www.ksu.edu/wwparent/) and Raising Courageous Kids (www.raisingcourageouskids.com), provide additional information about his programs.

Heidi E. Stolz is Associate Professor in the Department of Child and Family Studies at the University of Tennessee, where she also serves as the Co-Director of the Center for Parenting. She received her B.A. in Economics from Whitman College; B.Ed. in Secondary Education from the University of Puget Sound; M.A. in Human Development from Washington State University; and Ph.D. in Marriage, Family, and Human Development from Brigham Young University. Dr. Stolz conducts basic research on mothering, fathering, and parenting, as well as program evaluations of parent training programs. She is a board member of the National Parenting Education Network (NPEN).